PROCESSES AND PHENOMENA

OF SOCIAL CHANGE

PROCESSES AND PHENOMENA OF SOCIAL CHANGE

Gerald Zaltman

Northwestern University

and

MARK A. CHESLER
JAMES S. COLEMAN
ALAN E. GUSKIN
HERBERT C. KELMAN
CHARLES A. KIESLER
PHILIP KOTLER
NAN LIN
JOHN C. MALONEY
DENTON E. MORRISON
BEECHAM ROBINSON

EVERETT M. ROGERS
EUGENE P. SCHONFELD
J. JOSEPH SPEIDEL
J. TIMOTHY SPREHE
LINDLEY J. STILES
HENRY TEUNE
DONALD P. WARWICK
GOODWIN WATSON
BRUCE H. WESTLEY

ROBERT E. KRIEGER PUBLISHING COMPANY
HUNTINGTON, NEW YORK
1978

Original Edition 1973
Reprint Edition 1978

Printed and Published by
ROBERT E. KRIEGER PUBLISHING CO., INC.
645 NEW YORK AVENUE
HUNTINGTON, NEW YORK 11743

Printed in the United States of America

Library of Congress Cataloging in Publication Data

Zaltman, Gerald.
    Processes and phenomena of social change.

    Reprint of the edition published by Wiley, New York.
    Bibliography: p.
    Includes index.
    1. Social change—Addresses, essays, lectures.   2. Diffusion of innovations—Addresses, essays, lectures.
I. Title.
[HM101.Z285 1978]   301.24   78-8950
ISBN 0-88275-725-3

To Jeffrey and Lindsay

ACKNOWLEDGMENTS

There is an invisible co-editor to this volume to whom the first acknowledgment must be given. Richard Schwartz, Dean of the School of Law, State University of New York at Buffalo, made very important contributions during the early development of this book. His name does not appear on the cover only because he objects so strongly to taking credit for joint work unless he contributes an equal amount of time, something his other responsibilities would not permit.

This book would not exist without the labors of the contributors. I would like to express my appreciation first to those who were reasonably on schedule with their papers and second to those others who tolerated so well my incessant prodding. It might be added at this point that although all papers were prepared explicitly for this book, three papers (those by Watson, Kotler, and Morrison) appear here as they did in the July 1971 issue of *The American Behavioral Scientist*. I would like to express my thanks to those several individuals too numerous to mention here who reviewed the manuscripts. Finally, and still valued highly, is the general support provided by the Graduate School of Management, Northwestern University.

Evanston, Illinois
September 1972

GERALD ZALTMAN

vii

CONTENTS

PROCESSES AND PHENOMENA

OF SOCIAL CHANGE

INTRODUCTION

Themes Characteristic of Contemporary Social Change

The study of social change has never been of any greater importance than it is today. It is difficult to think of an area of society that is untouched by the processes of social change. The general magnitude of change and rapidity with which it is occurring may be without precedent in human history. Although some of the changes taking place today may in some future historical prespective be viewed as rivaling, say, the French revolution, most contemporary social changes considered individually do not seem to approach that order of magnitude. When considered collectively, however, today's changes may indeed be the most dramatic anyone has yet witnessed or participated in. What is particularly noteworthy is that the secondary consequences of change are having impacts on social life which in some cases match the immediate impact of the initial change. These second-order consequences may be dysfunctional and may conflict with one another even when their first-order consequences do not. This has been noted most recently by Rogers and Shoemaker (1971) and Bauer (1969). In general, however, it must be concluded that although there is considerable concern with change, insufficient attention has been given to the individual and social factors that precede change and are its products as well (Campbell and Converse, 1972).

Contemporary social change is creating many strains and much frustration for both the scientists who study it and the people who are its objects. For example, it is Lerner's (1971) hypothesis which appears to bear up well in empirical tests (Winham, 1970), that developing nations want what developed nations already have but do not possess the means to obtain it. The numerator of the want : get ratio is increasing at a much faster rate than the denominator. This is producing considerable frustration and anger among large numbers of the world's population. As Lerner (1971) observes, when 7P of the United States population is able to

1

produce vastly more foodstuffs than can be consumed by the total nation while 70P of the population of India is engaged in agriculture and yet is unable to prevent large scale malnutrition or starvation, there is something wrong in human society.

There is another considerable gap between that which is scientifically and technologically available to provide desired standards of living and that which the prevailing social-psychological conditions permit. This is a source of consternation to professional change agents. Rivlin (1971), Smigel (1971), and others, point out that we have made much progress in identifying and measuring social problems and social change. This is borne out by the current strides being made in the area of social indicators (Moore and Sheldon, 1968; U.S. Department of Health, Education and Welfare, 1969). Yet we are comparatively ignorant about knowing how to produce more effective social services. Solutions, partial ones at least, to such problems as malnutrition and population growth are already visible as a result of recent advances in science and technology. Yet we are still unable to mobilize resources adequately and address these problems effectively. However, we do not mean to strike too pessimistic an outlook. Social science *is* making headway in what has been called "people technology," and a quick glance at the literature of the last few years shows that the social sciences have gained new strength through increased knowledge of individual and social behavior. Consider the optimistic note suggested by the titles of the following recent works on social change: *Inducing Change in Developing Communities* (Hyman et al.), *The Planning of Change* (Bennis et al., 1969), *Intervention Theory and Methods* (Argyris, 1970), *Planning for Innovation* (Havelock, 1971), *Systematic Thinking for Social Action* (Rivlin, 1971), *Social Control and Social Change* (Scott and Scott, 1971), *Behavioral Intervention in Human Problems* (Richard, 1971), *Social Intervention* (Hornstein et al., 1971), *Introducing Social Change* (Arensberg and Niehoff, 1971), *Motivating Economic Achievement* (McClelland and Winter, 1971), and *Creating Social Change* (Zaltman et al., 1972). These and other authors take the positivistic view that although the social sciences may still be in their infancy compared to other sciences, we already know enough to intervene in social problems and bring about change with some success. Increasingly, for example, social scientists are thinking in terms of social change strategies and tactics. Table 1 presents a typology of change strategies from the current literature. These strategies reflect or are the product of an increasing confidence that people eventually will control and shape the forces in the social environment that affect them.

Moreover, the area of evaluative research is becoming more sophisticated methodologically and is receiving increased attention by social scientists (Hyman and Wright, 1967; Fairweather, 1967; Suchman, 1967; Campbell, 1969; Caro, 1971; Rivlin, 1971; Rossi and Williams, 1972; Guttentag and Struening, in press). Although there are sizable problems associated with evaluative research in social change, these problems can be surmounted and some very imaginative thinking is going on in this area (e.g., Campbell, 1969). As evaluative research improves and provides corrective feedback, our capacity for effective planned intervention at both micro and macro levels will show corresponding improvement.

Knowledge about unplanned change is of course essential to our understanding of planned change and in a special way the reverse is true in that planned change, implicitly at least, represents a test of theories of unplanned change. Theories of unplanned social change abound in the literature. A number of these theories, some micro, some middle-range, and some macro, can be found in Zollschan and Hirsch (1964), Barringer et al., (1965), Smelser (1968), Heine (1971), Rogers (1969), Appelbaum (1970), Hagen (1962), Barnett (1953), and King and McGinnies (1972).

It is not our intention to review these here. Whether one should pursue grand theories of social change such as those put forth by Smelser, Parsons, and others, or middle-range theories such as pursued by Rogers is dependent on the function the theory is intended to serve. It would seem that the more action oriented the scientist is, the more attractive and fruitful he will find middle-range and micro theories. A greater understanding of social change is required at all levels of discourse than now exists for us to adequately understand both planned and unplanned change. Much more work still remains to obtain a fuller understanding of the strategies, tactics, and general management of social change (Berelson, 1969; Zaltman et al., 1972). Going hand-in-hand with this and perhaps preceding it is a need for a greater comprehension of the more macro social processes at work in both planned and unplanned change.

By looking at both micro and macro patterns of social change and focusing more attention on bridging the gap between them, we move one step further toward achieving a normative consensus on what the means and ends of social change processes are and should be. Such a consensus is necessary for social change to proceed with a minimal (or optimal) amount of conflict. In effect, resistance and conflict may be better understood and better coped with through the creation of common understandings concerning the micro and macro processes of social change in society.

Given the very fundamental changes occurring in the structure and functioning of contemporary society, it is not surprising that value systems and ethical norms are also in a state of flux. Values and ethics shape our understanding of problems and the solutions we attempt; they even

Table 1 Typology of Change Strategies

Coercive strategies (*a*)	Nonmutual goal setting and one-sided deliberativeness
Normative strategies (*a*)	Compliance achieved through the issuance of directives based on values internalized as proper and legitimate
Utilitarian strategies (*a*)	Control over the allocation of resources serving as rewards and punishments
Empirical-rational strategies (*b*)	Provision of rational justification for action
Normative-reeducative strategies (*b*)	Change of attitudes, values, skills and significant relationships
Power-coercive strategies (*b*)	Application of moral, economic, and political resources to achieve change
Power strategies (*c*)	Use and/or threat of force
Persuasi•e strategies (*c*)	Bias in the structuring and presentation of a message; use of reasoning, urging, inducement based on rational and/or emotional appeals
Reeducative strategies (*c*)	Communication of fact and relearning through affective and cognitive change
Individual change strategies (*d*)	Use of change among individuals as a means toward social or organizational change

(*a*) Garth N. Jones, *Planned Organizational Change,* New York: Praeger, 1969.
(*b*) Robert Chin and Kenneth Benne, "General Strategies for Effective Changes in Human Systems. In W. G. Bennis, K. D. Benne, and R. Chin (eds.), *The Planning of Change,* New York: Holt, Rinehart & Winston, 1969.
(*c*) Gerald Zaltman, Philip Kotler, and Ira Kaufman, *Creating Social Change,* New York: Holt, Rinehart & Winston, 1972.

determine whether one will be motivated to intervene in a problem situation. In addition, even though values influence the course and character of social change, social change influences values and ethics in nonreinforcing ways. Accordingly, it is very important that this sensitive, even volatile issue of ethics and values be confronted and the issues defined (Kelman, 1968; Commission on Population Growth, 1971).

The Present Volume

A number of themes have been expressed in the preceding paragraphs: change is a very major characteristic of contemporary social life; wants of

Table 1 (Continued)

Data-based strategies (*d*)	Collecting and presenting data to initiate problem-solving activity and to provide a basis in which to root decision
Organizational development (*d*)	Creating a supportive climate or culture for organizational change
Violence and coercive strategies (*d*)	Actions designed to inflict personal injury or property damage
Nonviolence and direct action strategies (*d*)	Attempts to change attitudes and/or behavior
Manipulation (*e*)	A deliberate act of changing either the structure of the alternatives in the environment or personal qualities affecting choice without the knowledge of the person involved
Persuasion (*e*)	Interpersonal influence in which one person tries to change the attitude or behavior of another by means of argument, reasoning, or, in certain cases, structured listening
Facilitation (*e*)	Increase the ease with which an individual or group can implement their choice or satisfy their desires

(*d*) Harvey A. Hornstein et al., *Social Intervention: A Behavioral Science Approach*, New York: Free Press, 1971.
(*e*) Donald Warwick, "Ethical Issues in Social Intervention," working paper, 1972, York University.

all sorts are very high yet in much of the world there is a great gap between the level of wants and the extent to which wants are satisfied; progress is being made in social problem diagnosis and measurement; social scientists are becoming more positive and action oriented in their views and approaches to these problems; learning about both planned and unplanned change is important, and knowledge gained in the one context furthers knowledge in the other context; evaluative research is reaching a point where experimentation and corrective feedback is possible; ethical and value systems are changing profoundly; and it is necessary to consider social change both at the macro level and the micro level but perhaps with greater emphasis on the micro level.

Given these observations, the editor decided that a volume on social change at this point in time should cover a wide range of perspectives, especially considering the number of other books devoted exclusively to particular themes.

The main advantage of this approach is that it provides the reader with a greater sense of the breadth of social change issues. The quality of the papers are such that readers are offered considerable depth of exploration in each of the issue areas covered. This book is very contemporary—it is about our times—and it goes a step beyond what already exists in the literature. Put somewhat differently, what is distinctive about the approach of this volume to the process of social change is that it does not purport to explain change primarily in terms of one particular idea or theme. It does not, for instance, try to explain change in terms of personality dynamics in the manner of Lewis Namier, David McClelland, or Patrick Heine, or (in his earlier works) Harold Lasswell or Everett Hagen. Nor does the book seek to explain change directly with the grand transformation of societies in the tradition of Comte, Marx, Weber, and Karl Polanyi. Rather, the chapters in this book look within a given society at the processes of interaction between individuals and groups which tend to produce changes in social structures and the way social systems function.

The chapters in this volume are especially relevant for planned change and to this extent are user oriented. The chapters have more immediate surface interest for change agents be they directors of national development programs or family planning advisors located in rural clinics. But the theorist will also find considerable fuel for his interests and the papers will surely hone his insights into social change.

Although the reader of this volume, as with any other volume, may find something missing which is of importance to him, the authors of the papers in this book have done an exemplary job in carrying out their assignments and the reader will be both excited and challenged by the ideas presented.

A common theme of the essays in this volume is a concern with the mechanics of social change. Chapters deal with such topics as resistance to change, the use of incentives in social change, attitude change, the dimensions of innovation, change processes in education. At the same time they are not exclusively concerned with processes; many also address change in specific social contexts such as education, public policy, and population. Substantive issues such as value and ethical questions, problem diagnosis, and the evaluation of social change are also covered. Theories of social change, too, are not neglected and various types of theories are presented in a number of the chapters.

The book is divided into five parts. Part One contains a variety of perspectives on social change. Parts Two and Three are concerned with the more basic elements of the social change process looking first at those elements most closely tied to individuals (Part Two) and those elements that are most prevalent at the social level (Part Three). Part Four takes a sectoral approach and looks at social change as it relates to different sectors of society. Finally, Part Five examines some of the social issues involved in social change.

PART ONE

GENERAL PERSPECTIVES
ON SOCIAL CHANGE

In Part One we are concerned with theoretical outlooks on the social change process. All three chapters have theory relevant discussions. One chapter is concerned with theories of planned change; another chapter discusses theories of unplanned change and presents specific theoretical propositions for testing. The three chapters all contain elements of micro and macro analysis of social change and to some extent all three bridge the gap between micro and macro analysis as do many chapters in subsequent parts of this book. The "bridging" task is such an important one in social change that the first chapter in Part One is explicitly devoted to this task.

There are two types of theory of social change: those placing their roots in the social structure—the macro level of life—as the starting point for change, and those placing their roots in the individual—the micro level of life—as the starting point for change. In fact, individuals are affected by social structures and institutions, and social structures and institutions are influenced by the values, beliefs, and actions of individuals; the individual and social structure are interactive in the change process. This is the major theme of Kelman and Warwick in their chapter "Bridging Micro and Macro Approaches to Social Change: A Social Psychological Perspective." It is their position that concepts common to social psychology provide needed insight into the ongoing interactive process between the individual and social structure in social change. It is therefore not surprising that many of the topics touched upon in this chapter constitute the main subject matter of most chapters in this book. Their treatment of the induction of new behavior is followed up in more detail in Rogers' chapter on the role of incentives in family planning; the discussion of resistance to change is pursued in depth (in Part Two) by Watson, who also follows the individual versus social structure dichot-

omy of Coleman while recognizing as does Coleman that such a dichotomy is primarily one of convenience and not a mutually exclusive classification scheme. Later in the book the discussion of evaluative research
and methodology is a central focus of Kiesler's chapter; the discussion of
aspiration, satisfaction, and modernization is more fully developed by
Morrison's paper; the treatment of attitude change is elaborated on in
greater detail by Maloney and Schoenfeld; the general topic of social
structure is the key focus of the second Rogers' chapter; and so forth.

In the first essay Kelman and Warwick make clear the folly of pursuing either a micro or macro approach to the exclusion of the other. The
one theme that is repeated frequently and convincingly is that macro and
micro approaches to the study of social change must be bridged; each orientation must listen to and maintain some interaction with the other.

It should be noted that this chapter gives prominence to and
touches upon a large variety of micro and macro analytic concepts without treating specific contexts. To be sure, some contexts such as national
development are introduced but generally the concepts are topic free;
they are not illustrated by examples consistently taken from one context.
Herein lies a major challenge to the reader whose interests are more context bound than process bound: What are the most important micro and
macro phenomena that interact with each other in the context of interest,
for example, technology transfer or health maintenance? Given these interactive phenomena, *how* do they interact? At one level of analysis, one
can explain employee resistance to innovation in organizations as a result
of the interaction between organizational structure and employee attitudes. At a more specific level of analysis where context is introduced we
may find that the *nature* of the interaction is different. What constitutes
a relevant attitude and a relevant feature of an organizational structure
in a health organization is not necessarily identical to what one would isolate as a relevant attitude and structural feature in a small electronics
firm. Since different attitudes and structures may be involved, different
kinds and forms of interaction may occur in the two situations. Thus the
reader is challenged to operationalize in the context(s) of his concern the
many variables and processes mentioned by Kelman and Warwick. Precisely because differences are likely to be found in different contexts, at
least at some levels of analysis, the reader who is interested in basic processes such as attitude change, the development and satisfaction of aspirations, or the evolution of communication structures should find challenging the task of determining when—under what conditions—and
how—through what set of mechanics—particular processes function differentially. In other words, the context-oriented reader is challenged to
learn how the ideas in this chapter manifest themselves in his area of con-

cern while the process-oriented reader is challenged to look for patterns that would provide more powerful explanations of the (differential) functioning of the process of his concern.

There are many theories of social change put forth which have gained such general labels as evolutionary, functional, atomistic, holistic. Most of these suffer shortcomings by virtue of their being unrealistically oriented toward a macro approach or, conversely, a micro approach, by being too context bound in some instances or too narrow within the philosophical scope of their assumptions or giving insufficient recognition to competing theories or integration with alternative but compatible schools of thought. Perhaps what is needed now is not another theory but rather a statement about some of the basic sources of conflict among social change theories and a decision as to whether the conflict is necessary; that is, are the different approaches absolutely in conflict or can particular situations require more than one approach? Perhaps, as the first chapter in this book suggests, there are interactions between social conditions and individual traits discussed by different existing theories or change. These interactions suggest that portions of apparently conflicting theories might well be brought together.

The chapter by James Coleman, "Conflicting Theories of Social Change," examines conflicting theories of planned social change. This is an especially important chapter, first, because of the general paucity of theories of planned or directed change, and second, because it addresses itself in its examples to particularly relevant contemporary social problems and demonstrates conflicting assumptions held by various groups in society about desirable ways of bringing about change. Coleman distinguishes between theories that have their starting point in social conditions in which individuals find themselves and theories that start with changes in the individual. Among the former are theories that choose a predominantly legal approach versus those that emphasize the use of economic constraints and incentives. The individual-based theories divide on the issue of individualism versus collectivism. The reader will find this paper especially intriguing. It is suggested to the reader that as he reflects upon the Coleman chapter he consider different social problems and ask three questions for each problem: What is the optimal emphasis that should be placed upon the individual versus social condition approach? Within each approach, which of the two alternative strategies— or what relative balance between the two—should be pursued? What specific strategies and tactics are available after answering the two preceding questions? These are the basic questions which Coleman is challenging the reader to consider.

Coleman concludes that some synthesis between theories located in the individual and in the social structures is needed if we are to provide a satisfactory account of the change process. He adds the interesting possibility that planned change in our society may have been ineffective precisely because no institution exists which satisfactorily brings together social and individual considerations. If so, one of the products of a study of change processes might well be a truer perception of the loci of change and a consequent ability and willingness to design institutions that can generate and manage change. Clearly this task is one of the most important and challenging facing social scientists today.

One of the central concerns in the study of change is the reciprocal relationship between social structure and social change. Numerous scholars have confronted with modest success such questions as how particular social structures are affected by particular kinds and forms of social change. Similarly, other scholars have been concerned with the reverse, the influence of existing social structures on the nature of social change taking place within the particular social system. The chapter by Everett Rogers, "Social Structure and Social Change," addresses in a single effort the issue of reciprocal causation. Moreover, this paper examines social change originating both at the "top" and "bottom" of a social system and offers several testable and falsifiable middle-range theoretical propositions about social structure and social change. Rogers' propositions have a potentially wide range of applicability in that they are abstracted from a variety of social contexts.

The reader should be challenged in several ways by this chapter. One challenge lies in the testing of each proposition against data provided by one's own experience with social change. The reader is also encouraged to face the difficult task of setting up a study design which would constitute a proper test of each proposition. An equally challenging task is to establish a structure of relations among the several propositions in an effort to provide a tentative theory of interaction between social structure and social change. One especially provocative thought is the notion of the positive role played by conflict and crisis. Although this is not a new idea, it is understudied given its potential significance. The reader is urged to develop his own thoughts along these lines.

The Rogers chapter discusses change at the macro level and falls primarily within the domain of those treatments of change Coleman specifies as taking the social structure as the starting point for initiating change. The discussion does not, however, fall neatly into either the legal change or economic change categories. However, Rogers is mindful of the role of individuals in initiating social change. This is evident in his treatment of "bottom-up" change.

Herbert C. Kelman

Department of Psychology and Social Relations
Harvard University

Donald P. Warwick

Department of Sociology and Anthropology
York University

BRIDGING MICRO AND MACRO APPROACHES TO SOCIAL CHANGE: A SOCIAL-PSYCHOLOGICAL PERSPECTIVE [1]

Static processes usually can be studied adequately at a single level of analysis. By contrast, the study of change at a given level of analysis —whether it be individual or institutional—often requires the introduction of variables at a different level, which can provide some degree of analytic and explanatory leverage. Thus significant changes in the attitudes, values, or action orientations of individuals can best be understood in terms of the sociocultural context in which they occur. Similarly, changes in societal and institutional patterns can be clarified by exploration of the psychological and social-interaction processes that determine, mediate, and accompany them.

The study of social change therefore calls not only for models at both macro and micro levels of analysis, but also for conceptual and methodological approaches to bridging these two levels—to bringing each to bear upon the other. One relevant perspective for such bridging efforts—the one taken in the present chapter—is provided by social psychology. Social psychology is essentially a linkage discipline, concerned with the relationship between variables at two levels of analysis: the psychological and the sociological. From a psychological point of view, it explores the societal sources of action and interaction among individuals;

13

from a sociological point of view, it explores the micro processes that underlie societal functioning. This linkage character of social psychology makes it particularly useful in the study of change, both individual and social.

We shall briefly outline the nature of the methodological and substantive contributions that social psychology can make to the study of social change. Then we shall proceed to examine, from a social-psychological perspective, several issues in social change that bring micro and macro processes into direct relation with one another.

The Contributions of Social Psychology

Social psychology is concerned with the intersection between individual behavior and the functioning of social systems. Thus, for example, one set of questions that is distinctly social-psychological involves the relationship between a society's sociocultural institutions and the belief and value systems of its individual members—the way in which these beliefs and values are shaped by the society and the specific socialization processes that mediate their adoption. Conversely, a social psychologist might investigate the relationship between individual needs or perceptions and the properties of social systems—the way in which personality or value orientations dominant in a society shape its basic institutions and the specific interaction processes that define its political and economic life. At more micro levels, the social psychologist might examine the processes of social influence through which a group or organization induces acceptance of its norms and behavioral conformity to them among its members or the processes of communication and authority through which leaders formulate and execute organizational decisions. All of these examples refer to the relationship between societal or organizational inputs and individual outcomes or between individual inputs and societal or organizational outcomes, and to the interaction processes that mediate between such inputs and outcomes.

Methodological Contributions. Although some social psychologists are strongly identified with the use of a particular methodological tool (such as the laboratory experiment or the sample survey), the field as a whole is characterized by a considerable degree of methodological eclecticism and diversity. The data used in social-psychological work have ranged all the way from those derived from personality tests and intensive interviews to those derived from the content analysis of literary and political documents and the development of social indicators based on aggregated population statistics. At one end of the continuum, there are studies based almost entirely on the use of personality data, such as LeVine's (1966) study of achievement motivation and achievement values in the three major ethnic groups in Nigeria. On the other end of the continuum, there are studies designed to explore social-psychological hypotheses by relating various macro level indices (based, for example, on political events and aggregate data) to each other. A good example here are the studies of political stability as a function of social frustration and modernity, carried out by the Feierabends and their associates (see, for example, Feierabend and Feierabend, 1966). The well-known research by McClelland (1961) on the relationship between achievement motivation in individuals and the rate of economic development in their society is probably the best illustration of efforts to bring personality data and aggregate data together in the same investigation.

It is likely that social-psychological research, particularly in the areas of social change and development, will increasingly make use of social indicators and of data derived from historical documents. The bulk of social-psychological research, however, is based on data derived from direct observations of and interactions with individuals acting in a social context. The three major sources of such data are laboratory or field experiments, sample surveys, and participant observation. These three procedures are most naturally and distinctively suited to the study of social-psychological problems in that they permit detailed exploration of psychological and interactional processes that can be linked to societal inputs and outcomes. Furthermore, these three procedures are well suited to the study of change, both individual and social.

Experimental studies are, by their very nature, oriented to the study of change. The experimenter manipulates one or more independent variables and observes the effects of such variation on one or more dependent variables. Thus he can assess the causal relationships between a particular intervention and a particular outcome; in other words, he can specify whether and to what extent the introduction of one or another condition produces an anticipated change. In a typical experiment on persuasive communication, for example, it is possible to determine whether a given communication produces change in the listeners' behavior and attitudes (when compared to a no-communication control group), and whether this change is greater if the communication comes from, let us say, a high-prestige source as compared to a low-prestige source.

Social-psychological experiments have generally focused on individual change. It is possible, however, to adapt experimental procedures to the study of social change, particularly with the use of field experiments. Field experiments have been relatively rare, because of the practical difficulties that they entail, but their potential usefulness is considerable. For example, a particular social innovation or educational program may be introduced in one form in community A, in another form in community B, and not at all in community C, and the resultant changes—not only in the behavior and attitudes of individuals, but also in certain social indicators (such as productivity or birth rate)—can then be observed. There are also various extensions of the laboratory experiment that may prove useful in the study of social change, such as games and simulation exercises designed to reproduce, in a laboratory setting, some of the crucial features of national or international systems (cf. Gamson, 1969; Guetzkow et al., 1963).

The sample survey can contribute to the study of social change both by documenting change over time and by illuminating the micro processes of social change. By conducting surveys before and after the introduction of some major innovation, or at regular intervals over a period of major change or change efforts in a society, one can trace the amount and nature of change as manifested on a psychological level. Changes assessed through survey research—changes in the opinions, orientations, and commitments of a population—may in themselves be part of the goal toward which change efforts are directed. Furthermore, survey data may provide useful indicators of the success or difficulties of the institutional changes that are taking place. The state of public opinion in a nation or a community, as it fluctuates with changing events and experiences, is itself a measure—though, to be sure, a very partial one—of the health of political and economic institutions. Survey data may be useful in this context not only by serving as indicators of the mood of the population as a whole but, even more important, by revealing the distribution of reactions over the various segments of the population. It thus becomes possible to assess which groups are satisfied and which are dissatisfied by the course of the changes that are taking place, and which are open and which resistant to the new developments. Finally, survey research may contribute to the assessment of social change more specifically by helping to pinpoint those features of a change program that are successful and that the population finds satisfactory and congenial, as against those features that are unsuccessful and unsatisfactory and generate resistance.

Insofar as interviews are intensive and carefully constructed and allow for detailed probing into the views of the respondents, they may provide insights into the processes of social change as experienced by the participants. They may help us understand the sources of openness and resistance to change, the positive and negative pressures to which various population segments are subjected as a consequence of change efforts, the ways in which individuals relate themselves to these efforts, and the effects that they have upon them. In short, survey research can give us a detailed picture of the psychological and interactional processes—at least as perceived by the individual—through which change is adopted or rejected. Moreover, survey research can inform us not only about changes that have already taken place but also about changes that will or could or perhaps should take place. Thus a well-designed interview can help us predict how a population is likely to react to policies that are about to be introduced; it can help us explore reactions to various hypothetical alternatives that have not yet been seriously considered; and it can help us specify the kinds of policies that would meet the preferences and aspirations of a population.

The method of participant observation has been used extensively, particularly by anthropologists and sociologists, in the study of small societies, communities, organizations, and social movements. Typically, it has been applied to efforts to delineate stable cultural patterns and patterns of social interaction. However, it can be equally useful in the study of change. An investigator may, for example, come to live in a community in which important changes are introduced. Within the limits set by his status as an outsider and as an acknowledged social scientist, he could participate in the ongoing activities of the community and observe the processes of change and resistance to change at first hand. His observations could be supplemented by personal interviews with selected members of the community.

The procedures of participant observation lack the control over the independent variables provided by experimental procedures and the control over the representativeness of respondents provided by the sample survey. Thus participant observation studies generally do not permit us to establish causal relationships and to isolate the variables responsible for the change, nor do they provide a systematic basis for specifying the population to which findings can be generalized. On the other hand, they provide an unusually good opportunity to obtain rich, varied, and detailed data on the processes of change, at the time and place at whch these are unfolding. Participant observation gives the investigator greater access to the phenomena of change when they are happening. He can observe how individuals and institutions react when changes are introduced, and what kind of interpersonal and organizational processes are set into motion by the introduction of such changes. In short, the participant observer has the advantage of being embedded in a real-life situation where he can observe the ongoing processes of change in a total sociocultural context.

The various approaches to data collection that we have discussed are by no means mutually exclusive. They ought not to be viewed as competing alternatives but as complementary methods, each of which has special advantages and disadvantages. Social-psychological research on social change requires inputs of all of these types, each of which can make a unique contribution to filling out a larger picture. Usually, a given piece of research relies on one or another of the methodological approaches and sources of data that we have discussed. It is also possible, however, for the same research project to combine these different approaches. This is particularly true for two types of applied social-psychological research that are highly relevant to the study of social change: evaluation research and action research.

Evaluation research is concerned with assessing the effectiveness of a particular program in producing the changes that it was designed to produce. If an educational or informational program is being evaluated, one would try to assess what changes in attitudes and behavior it has brought about and, in the long run, in what ways it has affected the lives of the participants in the program. If an economic or political innovation is being evaluated, one would want to examine not only the resultant behavior and attitude changes in the individuals concerned, but also changes in various social indicators such as income level or level of political participation. In addition to establishing the occurrence and amount of change on various dimensions, evaluation research is concerned with identifying factors that facilitate and inhibit the occurrence of change.

Clearly, evaluation research can profitably combine the various methodological approaches and sources of data that we have outlined. It should ideally follow an experimental design, at least in the sense of having an experimental condition in which the change program is introduced and a control condition in which before- and after-measures are obtained from a comparable community or group without the introduction of the experimental program. Wherever feasible, it would of course be instructive to have different versions of an experimental program that can then be compared to each other and to the control condition. Survey techniques can be used to assess the changes in attitudes and behavior that the program has produced. Usually this would involve interviews with the same individuals at different points in time—before the introduction of the program, in the course of the program itself, after the program is completed, and at some later point to permit the assessment of longer-range effects. Ideally, interview data would be supplemented by data showing what institutional changes have actually occurred in the communities or organizations concerned, and what concrete effects these have had on the lives of their members (e.g., in terms of their educational, occupational, economic, or political status). Finally, the techniques of participant observation can be used in evaluation research in order to gain a more detailed insight into the factors that facilitated and impeded the occurrence of change. (See Kelman and Ezekiel, 1970, for an example of an evaluation study using a combination of experimental, interview, and observational procedures.)

Action research refers to an enterprise in which social research and an action program are directly linked to one another. The investigator works with a group, organization, or community that is concerned with improving its functioning or has decided to introduce a program of change. The research is governed by the requirements of the action program and is integrally related to that program. The community self-survey, which represents one of the earliest efforts to implement an action research philosophy, involves community members directly in the planning and execution of the research itself. Action research projects may differ in the extent to which the responsibility for research design and execution is in the hands of the participants, and in the extent to which the research is an actual component of the action program or a parallel activity. In any event, the research grows out of the needs of the group or community studied and is designed to facilitate the social change desired by that group or community. As in evaluation research (which may in fact constitute a form or component of action research), a combination of experimental, survey, and observational methods is often appropriate to the questions to which action research addresses itself.

Substantive Contributions. The empirical and conceptual work that has been and is being carried out in social psychology can provide a variety of substantive inputs to the study of social change and to the formulation of policies in this area. We have already noted that social psychology is particularly well suited to the analysis of change because of its position at the intersection of individual and social-system levels of analysis. More specifically, we would propose that social-psychological concepts and data —in conjunction with those derived from the other social science disciplines—can be useful in analyzing the processes, the contents, and the phasing of social change.

The contributions of social psychology to the analysis of *processes of social change* are in the study of changes in individual attitudes and behavior and of the distribution of such changes across a population. Processes of attitude and behavior change have been a primary focus for social-psychological research. Such research has concerned itself with the conditions that are conducive to change, the sources of resistance to change, and the ways of overcoming resistance, particularly in the context of persuasive communications and group influences. Another relevent area of concern has been the nature of change: What conditions are

conducive to changes of different types—changes at the level of overt behavior versus those at the level of private belief, superficial changes versus
those integrated into the person's value system, ephemeral changes versus
lasting ones? The relation between attitudes and actions in both directions has also been explored. On the one hand, questions have been
raised about the extent to which attitudes actually predict overt behavior; on the other hand, research has demonstrated that change in action
is often the most effective way of inducing change in attitude.

The study of such micro processes of change is relevant to the
broader issues of social change in several ways. First, any program of
planned change involves the introduction of specific innovations that
have to be accepted by the population, if the program is to be successful
—for example, new methods of farming, contraception, health care, or
community organization. Thus the processes underlying resistance to or
acceptance of such specific interventions in a community have direct implications for the long-run possibilities of social change. Second, it is
usually important—if change is to be sustained and if there is to be a
continuing readiness for further change—that certain changes in the underlying beliefs and attitudes of the population accompany the changes
in practices and in institutional arrangements. This is not to say, by any
means, that attitude change must precede behavioral or institutional
change. It is often true, as has already been suggested, that changes at the
behavioral or institutional level create the conditions most conducive to
attitude change. Whatever the sequence, however, psychological dispositions play an important role in the process of social change, and the conditions that facilitate or impede change on these psychological dimensions are therefore of more than casual interest. Third, certain changes in
attitudes and in broader values and personality orientations may in
themselves be among the goals of social change, so that analysis of the
processes by which such changes come about is *ipso facto* relevant to the
larger societal processes. In this connection, it is not only the processes of
influence directed to specific issues, policies, or practices that are of concern, but also the processes of influence that occur in the course of childhood and adult socialization. Childhood socialization is the source of
most of the basic values and orientations that guide the person's relationship to society and its institutions; adult socialization, for example, in the
occupational domain, affects the quality of the person's enactment of his
social roles. The processes of socialization thus have a direct bearing on
the nature of the personal dispositions that are likely to predominate
among members of a society or among incumbents of a particular role.

The relevance of a social-psychological analysis to a delineation of
the *contents of social change* is implicit in what we have already said
about the processes of change. By "contents of social change" we refer to

both the spontaneous and the planned outcomes of a change effort—that is, the conditions that emerge as the process of social change is set into motion and the conditions that must be deliberately fostered if the goals of social change are to be achieved. The latter conditions depend on the particular goals that a society has set for itself and therefore cannot simply be stated in terms of generally applicable scientific propositions. The spontaneous and planned outcomes of a change effort include not only new cultural patterns and institutional arrangements but also new psychological dispositions. It is in the specification of these psychological dispositions and their antecedents that social-psychological research can make its contribution.

The question for social-psychological analysis is usually phrased in these terms: What kinds of psychological dispositions are conducive to and congruent with the development of a modern growth economy and an effective political state? The assumption behind such a question is that psychological dispositions do indeed play a role in social change, and that it therefore may be useful to take them into account in the planning of change. We share this assumption, although we do not believe that any given set of such dispositions is a precondition for developmental change, either in the sense that it must precede institutional changes or in the sense that it represents the *only* pattern of dispositions compatible with "modernity." Rather, we hold that certain psychological dispositions are likely to *facilitate* economic and political development, without constituting either necessary or sufficient conditions for it. Among the dispositions that have been considered by social psychologists in relation to development are various general personality characteristics, including certain cognitive, motivational, and interpersonal orientations, and the sense of personal efficacy. In addition, there are certain more specific ideological orientations—such as conceptions of the national political system or commitments to ethnic identity—that may have a bearing on the course of economic and political development.

There have been a number of theoretical and empirical efforts to link such personality and ideological dispositions to indicators of economic growth and political effectiveness. To the extent that they are found to facilitate these development goals, they may well be included among the contents of planned social change; thus deliberate interventions may be designed to foster these particular psychological dispositions such as the attempts by McClelland and his colleagues to provide individual training in achievement motivation (see McClelland and Winter, 1969). In this connection, we want to stress that such interventions do not follow automatically from the empirical findings but represent a value choice. Though a society may be committed to economic growth and political effectiveness, and though certain psychological dispositions may be found conducive to these goals, they may be rejected because of inconsistency with the society's conception of the "ideal man." We shall return to this issue in Part Five, "Ethical Issues in Social Intervention."

The third problem area social-psychological concepts and data may contribute to is the *phasing of social change*. We assume that social change is not a smooth, progressive process, in which each step facilitates the next steps and in which the difficulties automatically diminish as the process continues. Rather, we see the possibility that changes in one area, though in themselves considered desirable, may create dislocations in other areas with serious consequences, at least in the short run. For example, changes in the traditional bases of power in a community may reduce group cohesiveness and social control and thus perhaps lead to increased delinquency and crime. Extension of educational opportunities may create a new class of young people who are unable to find jobs commensurate with their level of education (cf. McQueen, 1968).

These phasing problems clearly have social-psychological components. For example, a social-psychological analysis can help to explain the relationship between changes in traditional power structure and social cohesion by focusing on the psychic strain and the possible breakdown in interpersonal relationships that may result from the abandonment of traditional patterns. The impact of changes in capacities that outstrip opportunities and, more generally, the potentially disruptive effects that rapid educational and economic advancement may bring about can be analyzed in terms of such social-psychological concepts as level of aspiration, relative deprivation, and comparative and normative reference groups.

There is no reason to assume that the effect of change in one area on changes in other areas is always negative. Often such changes are mutually reinforcing of one another. A social-psychological analysis can help to identify the conditions under which phasing effects are likely to be positive and those under which they are likely to be negative. Moreover, it can help in designing planned change efforts that reduce the likelihood of boomerang effects, such as syncretic institutional arrangements in which traditional values are mobilized in the service of development, and educational efforts that are geared to the opportunity systems present in the society.

Micro Processes Mediating Social Change

We have sketched some of the ways in which an analysis of micro processes of change may be relevant to the problems of change at the institutional and societal level. Social-psychological concepts and findings on which such an analysis can draw derive mainly from three major sources of research: (1) studies of social influence and attitude change, mostly in the form of laboratory experiments, that focus on determinants of change in situations of persuasive communication or of small group interaction; (2) studies of socialization of children and of adults, the latter focusing particularly on socialization into occupational roles, assimilation of immigrants in a new society, and socialization in total institutions; and (3) studies of planned change, typically in the context of laboratory ("sensitivity") training, action research, or organizational development.

One of the great pioneers in the social-psychological study of change, particularly through the use of the group as vehicle and target of change, was Kurt Lewin. He spoke of change as involving three steps: unfreezing, moving, and freezing of group standards (Lewin, 1951, pp. 228–229). Schein has elaborated on these stages, using the terms *unfreezing, changing,* and *refreezing* to designate them (see Bennis, Schein, Berlew, and Steele, 1964, pp. 357–392; or Schein, 1969). Unfreezing refers, essentially, to the processes involved in overcoming resistances to change, that is, in counteracting those personal and social factors that help to stabilize existing behaviors and beliefs. Changing refers more specifically to the processes whereby new behavior is induced, that is, whereby the individual is led to adopt new patterns of action, belief, and attitude. Refreezing refers to the ways in which these new patterns become integrated into cognitive and social structures and thus, to a degree, stabilized.

We shall take these three stages as our organizing framework and discuss, in order, some relevant issues relating to each. We shall not, however, attempt to keep them completely apart, since there is considerable overlap between them and since change does not always follow the logical sequence that the distinction might imply. In discussing the three stages, we shall focus on changes in relatively discrete behavioral domains, that is, changes in specific practices and their associated beliefs and attitudes. These are the kinds of changes that are required if planned change in a society is to be accepted and sustained. We shall then briefly address ourselves to changes in more general underlying dispositions—personality characteristics, social values, and broad orientations to interpersonal relations and social institutions—which are often seen as ends or means of social change efforts. That brief discussion will be concerned, essentially, with the micro processes of socialization.

Much of the discussion in this section has a manipulative ring. It suggests steps that a change agent might take if he is to overcome resistances to change, to induce new behavior patterns, and to facilitate the integration of these new patterns. Such deliberate efforts to produce change raise a host of thorny ethical problems: What values—and whose values—is the change effort designed to serve? What are the implications of the particular induction techniques used by the change agent for the freedom and self-determination of the target population? What are the intended and unintended consequences of the change effort? For the moment, we merely note these issues as crucial to any responsible discussion of planned (or, for that matter, unplanned) change. We shall address ourselves more fully to some of these issues in Part Five, "Ethical Issues in Social Intervention."

Overcoming Resistance to Change. For change to occur, the individual has to abandon or at least modify old action patterns, beliefs, and attitudes. Typically, however, the existing patterns are resistant to change and are not readily given up. To the outside observer, it may often appear evident that the existing patterns are irrational in the face of new information or in the context of the person's own goals. But to the person himself the supposed irrationality of his existing behavior may not be as readily apparent, since the behavior may benefit from various kinds of support that strengthen the person's motivation and ability to maintain this behavior in the face of contradictory evidence. One can distinguish between informational, motivational, and social supports for existing patterns.

The inherent functioning of beliefs and attitudes creates a *supporting informational environment* for those beliefs and attitudes. A person's attitudes perform a selective function with respect to the kinds of information to which he will be exposed. This is most obvious in the case of interpersonal attitudes, as Newcomb (1947) proposed in his concept of autistic hostility: When A starts out with a negative attitude toward B, he will tend to avoid communication with B and thus deprive himself of the opportunity to gain new information that might alter his attitude; thus a hostile attitude tends to build upon itself. A similar mechanism might operate with attitudes toward various policies or practices. For example, a person with a negative attitude toward birth control is more likely to join groups, to have contact with individuals, and to expose himself to mass media communications that convey information antagonistic to birth control than to those conveying favorable information.

Even when the individual is exposed to information that goes counter to his attitudes, this information may not have much impact on him because of the operation of processes of selective perception and memory. People are more likely to notice and retain information that conforms to their expectations and that can be fitted readily into their cognitive structures. We are not implying here that misperception and distorted memory are necessarily motivated by a desire to keep one's attitudes intact. Rather, the very functioning of attitudes as a way of organizing new information increases the likelihood that supporting information will be received and contradictory information will be screened out.

Finally, attitudes also affect the way in which the person behaves toward the object of his attitude and thus may help to create a reality that confirms them. In other words, they may constitute self-fulfilling prophecies. For example, if a manager distrusts his subordinates' ability to make decisions and act responsibly, he is likely to act toward them in a way that discourages initiative and responsibility. Thus he would help to create a reality that confirms his attitude and to inhibit the manifestation of disconfirming behavior.

Thus far we have tried to show that the very functioning of attitudes —the way they affect the person's exposure to new information, his perception and memory, and his action toward the attitude object—tends to build and maintain informational support for the attitude and thus leads to resistance to change. In addition, resistance to change is further reinforced by *motivational supports* for the existing attitude or belief. A number of writers identified with a functional approach to attitudes (see especially Smith, Bruner, and White, 1956; and Katz, 1960) have distinguished different needs that attitudes may serve in an individual's personality. Another way of putting it is to say that a person's attitude toward a given object develops out of his interaction with that object in a particular motivational context, that is, while he is engaged in some attempt to cope with or adjust to the environment as it impinges on the achievement of his own goals. Drawing on the distinctions made by Katz and by Smith et al., we can identify five types of coping processes out of which attitudes may emerge: (1) efforts to manipulate aspects of the external environment to facilitate goal achievement; (2) efforts to come to grips with inner conflicts that cannot be resolved in direct or conscious ways; (3) efforts to find meaning and order in the environment; (4) efforts to enhance one's self-esteem and to actualize one's self-concept; (5) efforts to relate one's self to important others in the environment, particularly groups in which one holds or aspires to hold membership.

Insofar as an attitude is linked to one or more of these coping processes, the person will be motivated to maintain it. The attitude becomes part of a behavioral system with functional significance for the person— part of a pattern of instrumental relationships, or a strategy for resolving inner conflicts, or a meaning structure, or an approach to actualizing his identity, or a framework for relating to social groups. If the system continues to provide for effective coping, the person will be motivated to maintain it and to maintain the attitudes embedded within it. He would thus be motivated to avoid new information that might threaten the existing balance. In short, the motivational base of an attitude both gives it added strength and inhibits its reconsideration, thus serving to increase resistance to change.

A third and highly important source of reinforcement for existing behavior is the *social support* that it receives. The stability of a person's beliefs, of his values, and of his very self-concept is highly dependent on social support—on the extent to which they are shared and confirmed by significant others in the person's daily environment. Social support is closely linked to the informational and motivational supports that we have already discussed. A person depends on others to confirm his own perceptions of reality and evaluations of events. Usually he shares the attitudes and values of others in his immediate surroundings and thus his own views are constantly being reinforced. On matters of controversy, the individual (by virtue of the mechanism of selective exposure mentioned earlier) tends to surround himself with others who agree with him and to join groups and organizations that support his point of view. Motivationally, social support of one's attitudes is an indicator that his relations to others are in good order, and he will be reluctant to deviate from attitudes that receive such support. Furthermore, when a person agrees with the views of his group, he can expect acceptance and direct rewards (in terms of status and other perquisites); once he deviates, he can expect rejection and other forms of negative response. For all of these reasons, therefore, behavior that is supported by a person's group is highly resistant to change. As long as his behavior receives such support, the person is unlikely to sense a need for change and, moreover, insofar as change threatens the possible loss of social support, he is inclined to avoid it.

The three sources of resistance that we have discussed so far are based on the meaning that the particular behavior has for the individual in his interactions with his environment. There is one other source of resistance of a more general type, based not so much on the degree to which the existing behavior is supported but on a generalized reluctance to accept influence from others (or from certain others). The strength and generality of this tendency differs as a function of personality factors and, very probably, also as a function of cultural factors, but the existence of some such tendency is a rather frequently observed pehnomenon. One recent theoretical formulation centers around the threat to independence or freedom as a central motivation, which often leads to resistance to influence (Brehm, 1966). The need for personal autonomy, the desire for self-determination, and the pride in independent action are all manifestations of such a tendency. Insofar as this tendency is aroused in an influence situation and influence is seen as a threat to autonomy we would expect resistances to change to arise.

Such resistances are especially likely to arise when the influencing agent is an outsider—a representative of a different country, a different culture, or a different class. In such a case, the need for personal autonomy is augmented by a concern with the self-determination of one's group. This source of resistance becomes particularly relevant in development programs, in which the change agents are often outsiders to the target community such as representatives of international agencies, foreign aid organizations, or the urban elites and central bureaucracies of one's own country. There is always the danger that such interventions will be resented because they are seen as an imposition of foreign values and as carrying the implication that the outside culture is somehow superior to the target culture. A number of studies of foreign students have shown that the experience of national status deprivation has a strong inhibiting effect on cross-national contacts (cf. Lambert and Bressler, 1956; Morris, 1960), which may make for maximal resistance to change. Such sensitivities are particularly likely to arise in situations in which outsiders have come to help a community and thus are providing concrete evidence, from the aid-recipient's point of view, of his own inferior status (Kelman, 1962a).

In view of these various sources of resistance, it is clear that a crucial step in the induction of change involves the unfreezing of existing patterns—the overcoming of resistances—so that the person will be open to the adoption of new patterns. Two broad categories of procedures can be distinguished in this connection. One involves challenging or undermining the supports for existing patterns of behavior and attitude, thus forcing the individual to reexamine them. The other involves minimizing the arousal of anxiety or somehow reassuring the individual that change would not threaten the existing supports for his behavior as much as he fears it would. In other words, the first type of procedure is designed to overcome resistance by creating a situation in which support for the existing pattern of behavior no longer holds and in which the person recognizes that it no longer holds; thus *continuing* the existing behavior would be tantamount to losing support. The second type of procedure is designed to overcome resistance by creating a situation in which the person recognizes that changing the existing pattern will not deprive him of the support that he now enjoys.

The first strategy for overcoming resistance, in its most extreme form, involves a deprivation of support—particularly of social support—for the individual's beliefs, attitudes, values, and self-concept. This strategy is exemplified by the techniques of "brainwashing" or "thought reform" (Schein, 1964) and by the processes of mortification and stripping of identity to which inmates of total institutions are subjected (Goffman, 1961). In such situations the stability of the person's identity is undermined and he becomes open to new beliefs and attitudes in his search for a new identity. When this stripping process takes place as a result of personal choice and in relation to a personal value system—for example, as part of socialization into a religious order that the person has voluntarily selected—then it is quite likely that the deprivation of supports for the existing identity will lead to the development of a stable new identity. When the stripping is coercive, however, as in the brainwashing situation, it is unlikely that the new beliefs and attitudes will be fully integrated. The imposed and discontinuous character of the stripping process is likely to deprive the person of both the personal and social anchors around which new beliefs can be built, anchors that can aid in the process of refreezing.

In the context of social change, this extreme kind of unfreezing may occur when an individual totally separates himself from a traditional milieu and moves into a large urban area. As a result, he may be deprived of the social supports to which he is accustomed and find himself in an impersonal, unresponsive environment that repeatedly disconfirms his earlier self-concept. Such radical changes in life circumstances may be effective in unfreezing earlier patterns and overcoming resistance to change. However, unless there is some continuity of earlier supports, the possibility of establishing stable new patterns is likely to be reduced, a point we shall return to later.

A less extreme form of the "challenge" strategy involves confrontation of the individual with discrepant information, which raises questions about the extent to which his current pattern of action, belief, and attitude is indeed conducive to the achievement of his own goals and to the maintenance of social support (cf. Kelman and Baron, 1968a). One can distinguish between three major types of discrepant information that may have an unfreezing effect: the individual may be confronted with the information that his attitudes or expectations are out of keeping (1) with evidence about reality, (2) with his own actions, or (3) with the attitudes or expectations of significant others. The mere existence of such discrepancies, of course, is not enough; they must force themselves upon the person's attention. Only clear disconfirmation of a clear expectation would have an unfreezing effect and set a process of reexamination into motion. Techniques of persuasion and of planned change are generally designed to create situations in which the confrontation of such discrepancies cannot easily be avoided.

The second general type of strategy to overcome resistance to change is designed to avoid or counteract the threatening implications of change. Resistance can be minimized by somehow reducing the salience of the source of resistance—by diverting the person's attention from the major supports for his existing behavior or belief. Thus the change agent may use "side attacks," focusing on minor or subsidiary issues that do not arouse full-blown resistance; he may use a gradual, step-by-step approach, so that the full import of the change will be less apparent; he may create a context for the influence situation that removes it from the reference group in which the existing behavior is anchored (cf. Janis and Smith, 1965, for a discussion of some of these mechanisms). The question arises, of course, whether changes that are induced by avoiding the threatening implication of the change will be sustained once these implications become apparent. We would assume that such mechanisms are likely to induce sustained changes insofar as they constitute a first step, designed primarily to set a process of change into motion. They may be effective in bringing the individual into a new psychological situation in which more direct approaches to the overcoming of resistance can be utilized.

Another form of the second type of strategy, which is more directly conducive to sustained change, involves reassuring the individual that changing his behavior will not have the threatening consequences that he fears. Most effective, in this connection, would be the demonstration that the new behavior is not disapproved by the person's relevant reference groups, that it is at least acceptable or at best positively valued. One of the reasons for the effectiveness of the group decision procedure (Lewin, 1951; Coch and French, 1948; Bennett, 1955) is that it creates a new group standard and informs the individual of the existence of a new consensus, thus reducing the anxiety about the possible loss of social support that changed behavior might otherwise bring in its wake. Generally, when the group serves as the target of change, there is a built-in reassurance that change will not lead to a loss of social support. Group members may, of course, reinforce each other in resistance to change, but if there is an inclination toward change among them, the group setting will have a reassuring and legitimizing effect. The very source of resistance thus becomes converted into a vehicle for change.

A reassurance-type strategy is particularly important in those situations in which the change agent is an outsider, as discussed earlier. To overcome resistance, it is necessary for the change agent to make very clear his respect for the cultural integrity of the target community and to communicate in some concrete ways that the acceptance of change is not tantamount to loss of autonomy or deprivation of status. This can be accomplished to the extent to which status-enhancing features are deliberately built into the change program itself and into extraprogram relationships; for example, programs may increase skills and thus directly reduce the dependence of members of the community, or change agents may afford community members opportunities to reciprocate the help that they are receiving (Kelman, 1962a).

The different procedures for overcoming resistance that we have been discussing are by no means mutually exclusive. In most programs of planned change, a combination of them is employed to encourage an unfreezing of existing behavior. For example, the laboratory training procedure, which is most often used to induce changes in interpersonal sensitivity and group behavior, can also be used to induce changes in organizational functioning or in the management of intergroup conflict (cf. Kelman, 1972). The geographical isolation of the laboratory deprives the individual of many of the social supports to which he is accustomed, thus increasing his openness to new behavioral possibilities and his reliance on the immediate group as his source of support. At the same time, the isolation reduces the salience of the individual's usual groups and hence increases his freedom to experiment with new behavior. Of course, the well-known "reentry" problem arises here: Will the individual be able to sustain the new behavior once he returns to his usual environment and his reference groups are brought back into salience?

The setting of the laboratory, the definition of the task, the playfulness of the atmosphere, and the trust that develops among participants all help to loosen up old behavior. They facilitate the adoption of new patterns with minimal fear of adverse consequences. The encouragement that is often (though not always) obtained from other group members provides concrete reassurance that new patterns—at least in the immediate setting—do not spell a loss of social support. Finally, the interactions in the laboratory are designed to provide challenges to existing patterns of behavior by confronting each member with discrepancies between his own attitudes or expectations and information about external realities, or about his own actions, or about the attitudes and expectations of other group members. The here-and-now interactions in the group provide the raw material for such confrontations, very much in the way that "corrective emotional experiences" do in psychotherapy (cf. Kelman, 1963).

Induction of New Behavior: Processes of Social Influence. Once the old behavior has become unfrozen, there is no assurance that the individual will actually adopt the new behavior and that, ultimately, this new behavior will be refrozen or integrated. In fact, certain ways of overcoming resistance to change may decrease the likelihood that genuine movement will occur or that changes that do occur will be stabilized and integrated.

We have already indicated that the three stages in the change process cannot really be separated and do not represent a strictly temporal sequence. Nevertheless, one can inquire into the ways in which new behavior is induced, once resistances have been overcome, keeping in mind that the overcoming of resistances and the induction of the new behavior may in fact be part of the same process.

We can speak of induction in any situation in which an influencing agent makes some new behavior, attitude, or belief available to another person or a group. Induction does not imply that the influencing agent is necessarily engaged in a deliberate influence attempt: induction occurs, for example, even if the influencing agent is merely serving as a model for the influencee. The crucial point is that there is some specifiable bit of behavior that the agent is in some fashion offering to the target person. The question is, under what conditions will that person adopt the offered behavior? We will distinguish three classes of variables that determine the probability of positive social influence, that is, the probability that the induced behavior will be adopted:

1. *The perceived importance of the induction.* Only to the extent that the person sees the induction as relevant to the achievement of one or more important goals does he expose himself to communications from the influencing agent. The perceived importance of the induction may depend on the way in which the influence situation is defined. Thus an individual is more likely to expose himself to induction if the situation is clearly defined as one in which his personal welfare or the welfare of his community is at stake. The perceived importance of the induction is also affected by the nature of the appeal that is used. For example, communications on matters of public health or population problems may vary in the degree to which they use a fear appeal. Although a strong fear appeal creates strong motivations, a moderate appeal may in fact be more effective in producing change, since too high a level of fear may encourage avoidance behavior (Janis, 1967). In short, the importance of the induction depends on the nature and strength of the motivations that have been activated in the situation (which are themselves a function of both personality and situational variables) and on the perceived relevance of the induction to these motivations.

2. *The perceived power of the influencing agent.* Power can be defined as the extent to which the influencing agent is in a position to affect (by enhancing or hampering) the achievement of the influencee's goals. The agent's power may have different sources. It may rest on his control over specific resources, or on his attractiveness, or on his expertness and trustworthiness. When the influencing agent is a group or

speaks for a group, the importance to the influencee of membership—
actual or aspired—in this group will determine its power over him. The
perceived power of the influencing agent affects a person's degree of positive orientation toward him, that is, his inclination to accept induced behavior from him.

3. *The prepotency of the induced behavior.* Though the individual
may be motivated to accept induction and positively oriented toward the
influencing agent, the probability that he will adopt the specific behavior
being induced depends on the extent to which that behavior has become
prepotent, relative to the various other response alternatives that might
be available. That is, the induced behavior must somehow emerge clearly
as uniquely relevant in the context of the motivations that have been
aroused. The induced behavior must become prepotent both at the point
of perception and at the point of action: the precise nature of the behavior must be clear and clearly distinguished from other alternatives, and
the performance of this behavior must be facilitated.

So far we have spoken of factors that determine the adoption of induced behavior without specifying the nature of the changes that might
be produced. The nature of change, however, is of crucial importance to
the study of social change. It is of considerable moment whether a given
change is superficial or integrated, ephemeral or lasting, restricted to a
narrow range of situations or highly generalized. It would be valuable to
know what conditions are conducive to one type of change as compared
to another. A number of social psychologists have concerned themselves
with this problem and have proposed various distinctions between qualitatively different types of social influence or attitude change.

We shall briefly summarize one relevant scheme that distinguishes
three processes of social influence, each of which is characterized by a distinctive set of antecedent conditions and a distinctive set of consequences.
The three processes are called compliance, identification, and internalization (Kelman, 1961).[2] *Compliance* is said to occur when an individual
accepts influence from another person or a group in order to attain a favorable reaction from the other, that is, to gain a specific reward or avoid
a specific punishment controlled by the other, or to gain approval or
avoid disapproval from him. *Identification* is said to occur when an individual accepts influence from another person or a group in order to establish or maintain a satisfying self-defining relationship to the other. In
contrast to compliance, identification is not primarily concerned with
producing a particular effect in the other; rather, accepting influence
through identification is a way of establishing and maintaining a desired
relationship to the other, as well as the self-definition that is anchored in

this relationship. By accepting influence, the person is able to see himself as similar to the other or as enacting a role reciprocal to that of the other. Finally, *internalization* is said to occur when an individual accepts influence in order to maintain the congruence of his actions and beliefs with his value system. Here it is the content of the induced behavior and its relation to the person's value system that are intrinsically satisfying.

Each of the processes is determined by the three sets of variables described above—the importance of the induction, the power of the influencing agent, and the prepotency of the induced behavior—and for each, the magnitude of these determinants may vary over the entire range. The processes differ, however, in terms of the *qualitative* form that these determinants take. That is, they differ in terms of (1) the *basis* for the importance of the induction: the nature of the predominant motivational orientation that is activated in the influence situation; (2) the *source* of the influencing agent's power: the particular characteristics that enable him to affect the person's goal achievement; and (3) the *manner* of achieving prepotency of the induced behavior: the particular induction techniques that are used (deliberately or otherwise) to make the desired behavior stand out in preference to other alternatives. Thus compliance is likely to result if the individual's primary concern in the influence situation is with the social effect of his behavior, if the influencing agent's power is based largely on his means-control (i.e., his ability to supply or withhold material or psychological resources on which the person's goal achievement depends), and if the induction techniques are designed to limit the individual's choice behavior. Identification is likely to result if the individual is primarily concerned, in this situation, with the social anchorage of his behavior, if the influencing agent's power is based largely on his attractiveness (i.e., his possession of qualities that make a continued relationship to him particularly desirable), and if the induction techniques serve to delineate the requirements of the role relationship in which the person's self-definition is anchored (e.g., if they delineate the expectations of a relevant reference group). Internalization is likely to result if the individual's primary concern in the influence situation is with the value congruence of his behavior, if the influencing agent's power is based largely on his credibility (i.e., his expertness and trustworthiness), and if the induction techniques are designed to reorganize the person's means-ends framework, his conception of the paths toward maximization of his values.

As far as consequences are concerned, the basic assumption of this scheme is that the changes produced by each of the three processes tend to be of a different nature. The crucial difference is in the conditions under which the newly acquired behavior is likely to manifest itself.

Compliance-based behavior will tend to manifest itself only under conditions of direct or indirect surveillance by the influencing agent. Identification-based behavior does not depend on observability by the influencing agent, but it does depend on the salience of the person's relationship to the agent. That is, the behavior is likely to manifest itself only in situations that are in some way associated with the individual or group from whom the behavior was originally adopted. Thus whether or not the behavior is manifested will depend on the role that the individual takes at any given moment in time. Though surveillance is irrelevant, identification-based behavior is designed to meet the other's expectations for the person's own role performance and therefore remains tied to the external source and highly dependent on social support. It tends to be isolated from the rest of the individual's value system, to remain encapsulated. In contrast, internalized behavior depends neither on surveillance nor on salience, but tends to manifest itself whenever the values on which it is based are relevant to the issue at hand. Behavior adopted through internalization is in some way, rational or otherwise, integrated with the individual's existing values. It becomes part of a personal system, as distinguished from a system of social role expectations. It becomes relatively independent of the original source and, because of the resulting interplay with other parts of the person's value system, it tends to be more idiosyncratic, more flexible, and more complex.

Research using this scheme demonstrates the kinds of relationships that can be explored with the use of social-psychological concepts. In one experimental study, the source of the influencing agent's power was varied and attitudes were then assessed under different sets of conditions. As predicted by the scheme, changes induced by an agent whose power was based on means-control manifested themselves only under conditions of surveillance, changes produced by an agent whose power was based on attractiveness manifested themselves under conditions of surveillance or salience, and changes induced by an agent whose power was based on credibility manifested themselves regardless of surveillance or salience (Kelman, 1958). In a study of changes resulting from a T-group experience, Cooper (1969) found systematic links between the way in which the trainer was perceived and the kind of change (identification or internalization) that he induced: ". . . when the trainer is seen as attractive participants identify with him and become more like him in attitude and behavior; when the trainer is seen as self-congruent participants change in ways that foster their own congruence" (p. 528).

In sum, social-psychological research suggests various possibilities of linking the nature of individual changes that occur in the context of a social change program—including the generality, the flexibility, the degree of independence, and the degree of integration of the new behavior—to such factors as the setting in which influence occurs and the type of concern that it sets into motion; the relationship of the target population to the influencing agent; and the nature of the induction techniques used. Planned change efforts can take such relationships into account in designing change programs geared to a particular set of goals.

Integration of New Behavior and the Relationship Between Attitude and Action. The discussion of different processes of influence leads us directly to the question of "refreezing"—the way in which the new behavior becomes integrated into personal and interpersonal systems (see Bennis, Schein, Berlew, and Steele, 1964, pp. 386–389). The assumption is that the new behavior can gain continuity and stability only to the extent that new supports have been built around it. The term freezing or refreezing is somewhat misleading because it implies a fixity and lack of openness to further modification that is not essential to this integration process. The new behavior can become established, in the sense of representing something more than a temporary situational change, without becoming totally inflexible.

The process of internalization, discussed in the preceding section, implies by definition that the new behavior has become integrated into a personal system. To the extent that internalization has taken place, the new behavior becomes part of the person's value system and is likely to manifest itself whenever it is relevant to the issue. This does not mean that internalized behavior will always manifest itself; it may well be contravened by situational factors. It certainly does not mean that it is unchangeable; in fact, it is likely to be relatively flexible, since it is adapted to the requirements of a personal system, and it is open to adjustments and to complete revision as new value-relevant information develops. Internalized behavior gains stability, however, by being embedded in a personal structure and thus benefiting from the support of other cognitive and evaluative components of that structure.

A second and at least equally important condition for stability is the extent to which the new behavior is integrated into the structure of a person's social relationships. New attitudes and beliefs will be maintained if the person finds himself in a supportive social environment—if he interacts closely with others who share and confirm his views. Social support is important to the stability of new attitudes even when these have been internalized. In principle, internalized attitudes are independent of social support, but in the absence of social support an internalized attitude is less likely to be translated into action and therefore more likely to become eroded. Furthermore, although an internalized attitude is normally self-sustaining, a person's ability to sustain it under the pressure of challenging information is greatly aided by the opportunity to interact and compare notes with others who share his values.

The availability of a supportive social environment is, at least in part, a direct consequence of the nature of the change that has taken place. To a considerable extent, a person creates his own social environment by selecting the people with whom he interacts and the groups that he joins. An excellent illustration of the role of social support in maintaining changes and of the way in which support is generated comes from a follow-up study, after 25 years, of Bennington College students (Newcomb, Koenig, Flacks, and Warwick, 1967). In his original study of Bennington College, Newcomb (1943) found that many of the students had changed in the direction of more liberal attitudes. The follow-up study indicated that for most of these women their new "self-image was important enough to have influenced certain aspects of the environments that they later created for themselves, including husbands, friends, and coworkers in public or community activities. If so, the attitudes that they developed in the college environment were maintained, not *in vacuo,* but by way of supporting environments that were initially congenial to those attitudes and later supportive of them" (p. 225). It should be noted that the likelihood that a person will build a supporting environment for himself is at least as great when he has changed at the level of identification as it is when he has changed at the internalized level. To the extent that identification is accompanied by entry into supportive groups and establishment of supportive interpersonal associations, it may lead to lasting and at least socially integrated changes. They differ from internalized changes, however, in that they are far more directly dependent on the continuity of the supportive relationships (unless, of course, they gradually become integrated into the person's value system and thus increasingly independent of external support).

Thus far, we have been assuming that integrated change implies a change in attitude—at the level of internalization or at least at the level of identification. This raises a question that often comes up in discussions of social change: Does the achievement of sustained changes in practices (e.g., in the adoption of new farming methods, or public health measures, or birth control procedures, or decision-making patterns) presuppose prior changes in attitude? In other words, is it necessary to change attitudes *before* there can be changes—or at least integrated changes—in behavior? This question parallels the question about the relationship between changes in personality dispositions and changes in institutional patterns, which we shall take up in a later section, and both of these questions are aspects of the problem of the phasing of social change. In our view, integrated changes in practices do indeed imply accompanying changes in attitude, but we see no reason to believe that attitude change must come *first* in the sequence.

On the negative side, it must be noted that attitude change does not necessarily lead to expected changes in action. The lack of one-to-one correspondence between attitudes and actions has often been noted (cf. the recent review by Wicker, 1969). This does not mean that attitudes are irrelevant to action, but simply that they are not the only determinant of action. A mother, for example, may have become convinced that certain new patterns of child-rearing would be preferable to traditional practices in her society. Whether this change in attitude will be accompanied by changes in her actual child-rearing behavior will depend on the other changes that have taken place in her: Has she acquired the necessary skills that the new behavior calls for? Has she been encouraged to experiment with new procedures or has the change effort been confined to verbalizations? Furthermore, and most important, whether the new attitudes will eventuate in action depends on the situational forces that operate in the action situation. For example, if child-rearing takes place largely in the context of an extended family, there may be strong social pressures in favor of more traditional practices, which might outcompete the forces produced by the new attitude. In short, even genuine changes in attitude may not be a sufficient basis for producing changes in practices.

This possibility suggests that it might be more effective to begin a change effort at the level of concrete practices and their situational supports, and to leave attitude change—on which the ultimate stability of the new patterns of behavior may depend—to a later stage. It is very often true that the change in action itself creates the ideal conditions for attitude change. Insofar as this proposition holds, the question of the sequence of change has to be reformulated, since it suggests a circular, interacting process, in which changes in specific practices create the conditions for attitude change and these, in turn, support the integration (or refreezing) of the new practices.

The notion that changes in action may lead to changes in attitude became a central preoccupation for social psychologists with the advent of the theory of cognitive dissonance (Festinger, 1957; Brehm and Cohen, 1962). According to this theory, when a person engages in action that is discrepant from his attitudes, he experiences dissonance—a state of tension resulting from confrontation with two inconsistent cognitions. The stronger the dissonance, the greater the tendency to reduce it; one way of reducing dissonance is to change one's attitudes by bringing them into line with the originally discrepant action. This theory has led to a number of interesting and sometimes unexpected predictions. We are inclined to assume, however, that the theory is perhaps not as general as is sometimes implied. Whether or not discrepant action results in efforts at dissonance reduction, and what modes of dissonance reduction are likely to be utilized, would depend, in our view, on the specific motivational implications that the discrepant action has for the individual (cf. Kelman and Baron, 1968a, 1968b). Thus discrepant action is particularly likely to lead to a reexamination of attitudes if the individual engages in the action at a high level of involvement, so that his self-evaluation is at stake, and if the present action implies a commitment to continued action in the future, so that it carries long-run implications. If, for example, the action consists of the adoption of a new role, such as that of union steward or foreman in a factory (cf. Lieberman, 1956), it will almost surely lead the person to reconsider his attitudes, since he has made a long-term commitment to a highly invoving set of role behaviors.

There are various reasons why engagement in action may lead to attitude change, aside from the general motivation to reduce dissonance or the more specific motivations that action-attitude discrepancies may bring into play (cf. Kelman, 1962b). For one thing, the way in which we act toward an object is an important source of information about the object itself. For example, when a man associates on an equal basis with members of a minority group, this fact becomes part of his definition of these group members and enters into his evaluation of them (i.e., he will tend to see them as people worthy of his association).

Most important, action exposes a person to new experiences, which may serve as the basis for new attitudes. As a result of an action, a person may acquire new information about the attitude object that in the past was inaccessible to him. For example, the finding that white women moving into an interracial housing project become more favorable toward their black neighbors (Deutsch and Collins, 1965) can be accounted for partly by the fact that interracial housing provided them an opportunity to interact with black women on an equal-status basis and thus to acquire more direct information about them. When a person takes action, furthermore, he may receive various kinds of social support for it, which would increase his commitment and help persuade him that the practice he has adopted is legitimate and reflects a wider consensus than he had formerly assumed. Again, this would tend to strengthen attitudes that favor the action. A person might also find himself in a position where others treat him as a proponent of a particular point of view and force him to defend it, and this again would encourage a reassessment and lead to a strengthening of attitudes supportive of his action. When the action consists of the adoption of a new role, as in the Lieberman (1956) study cited previously, the requirements of the role itself will inevitably lead the person to new experiences and further choices that are likely to force a reexamination of his attitudes. Finally, when the action is officially sponsored and involves large numbers in the community, then the very fact that it is taking place tends to legitimize it and thus lend social and attitudinal support to it.

In sum, there are many reasons for proposing that one of the most effective ways of producing attitude change is to induce specific actions even though supportive attitudes for these have not yet been built. Under the proper circumstances, action-taking will create the conditions for attitude change and hence for the integration and stabilization of new patterns of practice. This is by no means a universal outcome, and it does presuppose that the action takes place under a special set of conditions, but it does suggest clearly that full-blown attitude change *prior* to the adoption of new practices is neither a necessary nor a sufficient condition for social change.

Processes of Socialization. Thus far we have been discussing changes in patterns of action, belief, and attitude relating to the adoption of a specific innovation and the achievement of a specific institutional change. We now turn briefly to the microprocesses of change in the course of socialization, which have an impact on the general orientations, values, and personality dispositions that may facilitate or impede the process of social change in a society and the functioning of the new economic and political institutions that this process calls for.

Socialization may be defined as the process by which individuals acquire the knowledge, motives, feelings, skills, and other characteristics expected in the groups of which they are or seek to become members. It is a process that begins at birth and continues through life, but it is more in evidence at some times than at others. The greatest impact occurs when the individual confronts new or sharply different expectations as a group member, for example, when he moves from childhood to adolescence, marries, or takes his first job.

An analysis of socialization processes can help to illuminate two basic questions confronting students of social change: (1) How does the socialization occurring within the present structure of a society affect the possibility for future development? (2) What kinds of deliberately staged socialization efforts, including educational programs, are necessary to accomplish the goals of planned change? Most of the existing research has focused on the first question, asking how experiences in the family, in religious systems, and in other social institutions affect personality characteristics thought to be related to developmental change. The well-known studies by Weber (1930), McClelland (1961), Pye (1962), and Hagen

(1962) fall into this tradition. Research on the socializing effects of planned social interventions, on the other hand, has been relatively rare. The most commonly explored laboratory of planned change has been the Russian Revolution, with its deliberate efforts to organize societal institutions around the production of values such as collective responsibility and cooperative work, as well as commitment to the new political system. Bronfenbrenner (1962) examined the effects of the Soviet educationsl system on these values and concluded that it has been a major vehicle for inculcating them. Similarly, Inkeles (1955) showed that Russian parents responded to changes in the political system by adjusting their child-rearing practices to produce attitudes and values appropriate to the new regime. Research on other revolutionary societies, especially China and Cuba, is now under way and should provide important insights into the dynamics of planned development and social intervention.

The implications of the socialization process are so vast that they touch, directly or indirectly, almost any substantive problem in the area of social change. Here we shall pose three questions that seem to suggest promising areas for future research.

1. How does childhood socialization affect adult economic behavior, including innovation and entrepreneurship as well as attitudes toward spending and saving? This is an old question, but one that has still not been satisfactorily answered for even a single society. Systematic cross-cultural research on socialization might help to explain, for example, why some minority groups, such as the Levantines in West Africa and the Chinese in Southeast Asia, show a disproportionately high rate of economic entrepreneurship. In his study of economic development in Pakistan, Gustav Papanek (1967) found that two-thirds of the private industrial investment owned by Muslims was controlled by a very small group of individuals and communities. Further research by Hanna Papanek (1970) makes a very strong case for the influence of economically related cultural norms in one of these communities, the Memons. These and other studies underscore the need for a complex theoretical model of socialization which takes account of varying social-structural and cultural conditions as well as of the specific patterns of influence found in the groups under study.

2. What is the relationship between bureaucratic or other organizational socialization and political effectiveness? In any country or even in smaller political units one might profitably consider three subquestions: What are the prevailing norms in organizations involved in public administration? How do these affect the employees? How are these effects related to political effectiveness? For example, Pye's (1962) analysis of the

Burmese administrative service suggests that its organizational culture under the British placed heavy emphasis on adherence to bureaucratic procedures and formally prescribed channels of communication. Pye claims that this pattern of socialization, reinforced by the normal rewards of a career system, imparted an overly strong faith among the Burmese in the power of procedure and ritual—an attitude that proved detrimental after independence. In view of the importance of large-scale organizations in the development efforts of most countries, similar analyses of bureaucratic socialization are very much in order.

3. What is the effect of seemingly inconsistent or incompatible patterns of socialization on the individual involved as well as on the society at large? This question is related to our later discussion of phasing of social change and its implications, especially for the political system. Here we would suggest that it is important to examine the specific ways in which individuals and social groups handle the strains produced by competing norms. Hanna Papanek's research on the Memon industrialists suggest that one response to divergent pressures from "modern" and traditional norms may be compartmentalization. That is, an industrialist may be modern in his business role and traditional in other areas of his life, including the observance of religious norms. At the moment we know very little about general patterns of coping with inconsistent socialization.

Personal Dispositions as Contents of Social Change

Our brief discussion of socialization leads us directly to the social-psychological aspects of the contents of social change—of the spontaneous and planned outcomes of change programs. These outcomes include certain psychological dispositions that may have a bearing on future social change and on the effective functioning of the political and economic institutions to which change efforts are directed. Thus research on the general orientations, values, and personality characteristics that may facilitate or hamper the process of development and the achievement of such development goals as economic growth, political effectiveness, and individual welfare is of potential relevance to the planning and evaluation of change efforts. Before turning to a discussion of some of the specific psychological dispositions that may play a role in social change and development, we shall address ourselves briefly to the general issue of whether such dispositions play any role in these processes at all.

For years there has been a running controversy among students of development on the importance of personality in social change. On the

one hand, proponents of a "structural" or "institutionalist" viewpoint
have argued that personality dispositions per se deserve little specific attention. The critical conditions in development, they hold, lie not in the
minds of men, but in the social, economic, and political environment. In
their view, if the environment is improved, either by providing positive
incentives for change (such as new investment opportunities) or by root-
ing out laggard institutions (such as antiquated land tenure systems),
enough individuals will step forth to produce development, whatever the
persoality traits of the masses. In the opposing camp are those who feel
that the most direct and expeditious route to development is through
modification of the attitudes, values, beliefs, motives, and behavior of individuals. This view is perhaps best represented in the efforts of David
McClelland and his colleagues to increase entrepreneurship through individual training in achievement motivation (cf. McClelland and Winter,
1969).

Perhaps the major contribution of the social psychologist to this debate is to point out that the distinctions on which it is based are over-
drawn. For example, although it is true that individuals are profoundly
affected by structures and institutions, it is also true that institutions are
firmly rooted in the values and beliefs of individuals. Moreover, it is clear
that in some programs of planned change the relationship between individuals and institutions in the change process is interactive. That is, a
cycle is begun in which a slight change in the environment produces a
slight change in individuals, which sets the stage for a further change in
the environment, and so on.

An interesting example of this interaction between individuals and
institutions is seen in the Peruvian village of Huayopampa (Whyte and
Williams, 1968). Over the past 15 years this community has transformed
its economy from cattle, corn, potatoes, and other traditional crops to the
more lucrative production of fruit trees. A significant feature of these
trees is that they require a lag of five to seven years before yielding a
crop—an unusually long delay by local standards. Careful scrutiny of
this changeover shows that both institutional and personality factors
played a vital role. The institutional components (broadly defined as
changes in the environment) included a new road to facilitate the transportation of a perishable product to the nearest market, loans to cover
the initial investment, and technical aids such as fertilizers, insecticides,
and spray pumps. But these seemingly would have had little impact without parallel shifts in the attitudes, values, and beliefs of the villagers. Especially important was an extension of their time perspectives to permit
acceptance of a seven-year lag between planting and payoff. Other pivotal
changes seem to have been an increase in the residents' trust for each

other, a shared feeling of confidence in the community's ability to complete the project, and a heightened belief that the resulting profits would be distributed equitably.

One of the clearest lessons of this study is that changes in personality and environmental opportunity affect each other. The chain of influence leading to the adoption of fruit trees might be interpreted as follows.[3] Some decades ago the villagers perceived a need for a new service, such as a road to communal farmlands. Previous success with cooperative community projects contributed to the initial perception of a need and also left a residue of organizational skills supporting the conviction that the task could be accomplished. The completion of the road had a twofold effect: first, it led to a modest increase in the agricultural opportunities open to the villagers (an "institutional" change); and second, it further strengthened their belief in the possibility of effecting change, their mutual trust, and their sense of self-confidence and efficacy. This favorable cycle continued as the positive outcome of one manageable project predisposed the villagers to perceive new needs and to choose other projects that were challenging, useful, and within their capacities. In this way a spiral of success was initiated, which gradually created a favorable climate for larger economic changes. In the later stages, the attitudes in the community, especially trust of each other and of outsiders, paved the way to contact with governmental agencies and facilitated the acceptance of innovations suggested by extension agents. The final shift to fruit production was thus the result of two types of accumulated infrastructure: the institutional-environmental infrastructure resulting from the completion of numerous small projects; and the social-psychological infrastructure consisting of knowledge and organizational skills, the readiness to perceive new opportunities, and individual self-confidence and similar traits, all of which encouraged the villagers to respond to the opportunity presented by fruit-growing.

The illustration of the process of social change in the village of Huayopampa suggests a variety of personality characteristics deserving of serious consideration in discussions of national development. We shall examine several of these—cognitive, motivational, and interpersonal orientations, and the sense of personal efficacy—for illustrative purposes, and then turn briefly to a consideration of more specific ideological orientations that may have a bearing on the course of economic and political development.

Our view of the relationship of various personality characteristics to social change is based on the assumption that certain personal dispositions prevalent within a society or a subgroup of that society may facilitate, and others may impede, the development process. We do not assume, however, that "underdevelopment" in a given society can be accounted for by the characterological deficiencies of its population, or that it can be overcome by somehow removing these deficiencies. A population seemingly incapable of development may show a great deal of movement once the opportunity structures in the society have changed. Conversely, changes in cognitive, motivational, and interpersonal orientations that are favorable to development may not in fact promote development, unless they are accompanied by changes in opportunity structures.

Cognitive Orientations. Cognition refers to the thought life of the individual, the ways in which he perceives and stores information and uses it in forming concepts, reasoning, solving problems, and making decisions.

One aspect of a person's cognitive orientation that seems closely bound to the possibility of economic and political development is his *time perspective*. We hypothesize that the possibility of developmental change is enhanced by two kinds of time perspectives. The first consists of a time span that extends into the future rather than being confined to either the present or the past. Persons who cannot transcend present concerns, or who are dominated by the legacy of the past, will be reluctant to try new ways of thinking and acting—both important components of development. It is interesting to note that almost every political system, whatever its ideological orientation, seems anxious to inculcate a future orientation, in its members. This does not mean that all aspects of the traditional past must be given up, or that one must have his thoughts constantly fixated on the future. Rather, the essential quality seems to be an ability to relate one's present condition to long-range goals. The second favorable condition is a positive but not excessively optimistic evaluation of what the future will bring. A stable disposition to be pessimistic may encourage the exclusive enjoyment of present satisfactions, whereas exaggerated optimism may lead to foolhardy economic speculation or immersion of the self in millenarian movements.

Another relevant aspect of cognition, whose significance we sometimes miss in our oversophistication about personality theory, is simply the possession of specific knowledge and information. There is considerable evidence that access to information plays a vital role in many areas of development, ranging from entrepreneurship to population control programs. For example, Gustav Papanek's (1967) study of industrial development in Pakistan underscores the importance of information about the economy in the emergence of entrepreneurship. His findings show that industrial entrepreneurs came disproportionately from groups with a background in trade, especially importing. One of the major factors explaining this tendency is differential knowledge and information about market opportunities. "Traders were directly exposed to the incentives for industrial activity because they knew more about the opportunity in industry and were more accustomed to taking economic risks. Traders had the ability to act in response to both push and pull because they possessed liquid capital and some relevant knowledge" (p. 45). Two reasons can be cited for the superior knowledge possessed by merchants and traders: (1) their own internal operating records provide a more accurate picture of changes in market demand, especially in areas where public information is scarce; and (2) experience in importing permits greater access to information about how products should be designed and about production technology, especially through contacts with overseas suppliers. Similar examples could be cited showing the vital role of information in centralized economies.

Motivational Orientations. The concept of motivation refers to the dynamic forces in human behavior—why people think, feel, and act the way they do. More specifically, it is used to explain why individuals act at all (activation), why they choose some alternatives over others (direction), why they differ in the vigor with which they pursue their goals (energy), and why they continue to think, feel, or act in certain ways over time (persistence).

Motivation has both stable and situational aspects. The stable component can be called a *motivational dispostion*—the stored expectation of pleasant or unpleasant reactions associated with a given class of events, such as food, wealth, power, risk-taking, or authoritarian dependence. Each individual develops a characteristic hierarchy of motivational dispositions—the classes of events that provide the greatest satisfaction across a variety of situations. Thus, in the study of social change, the first question confronting the investigator concerns the major stable dispositions operative in a given society at a given time, and their ranking within and across individuals. It is clear that although there is some constancy across cultures in the classes of events providing satisfaction, there are also wide differences in the hierarchy of dispositions.

Within any given situation, the dispositions that seek expression can be described as *aroused motives.* The chances that a person will be motivated to take entrepreneurial risks, for example, thus depend on two interacting factors: the overall strength of his disposition to derive satisfaction from either risk-taking or the wealth that it may produce; and the situational cues at work in activating this disposition. In general, the weaker the underlying disposition, the stronger the cues needed to activate it.

In the case of any given motivational disposition, such as a desire for wealth, we may further distinguish between two standards commonly used by individuals in setting levels of aspiration for their own satisfaction (March and Simon, 1958). The first is that of *optimizing*, or seeking the maximum amount possible. The second is *satisficing*, or gaining enough satisfaction to maintain oneself at a certain level, but no more. As March and Simon point out: "To optimize requires processes several orders of magnitude more complex than those required to satisfice. An example is the difference between searching a haystack to find the sharpest needle in it and searching the haystack to find a needle sharp enough to sew with" (pp. 140–141).

The utility of this distinciton in the study of development is again illustrated in Papanek's (1967) study of industrial entrepreneurship in Pakistan. From the evidence presented one might conclude that the behavior of the entrepreneurs fell somewhere between the extremes of optimizing and satisficing. On the one hand, they could not be called chronic optimizers since the possibility of moving from trade to industry did not occur to them until they began to be pushed out of their businesses by declining profits. Once this pressure was felt, however, they were more willing to take economic risks than, for example, the established landlords, who seemed content with satisficing. "The strong economic disincentives which operated against the traders did not exist for the elite, who were doing well and had no strong incentive to take risks or accept the lower status involved in becoming traders or industrialists. Landlords did not earn the high returns of industrialists, but their traditional occupation had prestige and provided a steady income" (p. 43).

No discussion of motivation and development would be complete without some mention of David McClelland's important work, *The Achieving Society* (1961). This study traces its theoretical origins to Weber's theory of the Protestant ethic, and its empirical base to the author's innovative efforts to devise quantitative measures of human motives. McClelland's central thesis is that the relationship between the Calvinistic ethic and the spirit of capitalism is mediated by the achievement motive (*n*Ach). As he puts it: "a society with a generally high level of *n* Achievement will produce more energetic entrepreneurs who, in turn, produce more rapid economic development" (p. 205). The first task in his research was to demonstrate that achievement motivation is correlated with economic growth at the aggregate level. This was done by relating the level of *n*Ach reflected in children's stories to an indicator of economic growth. The next challenge was to trace the origins of achievement motivation in individuals. His major conclusion was that the conditions most favorable to the emergence of this motive include parental pressures toward achievement and independence between the ages of six and ten, and the *absence* of father dominance, overindulgence, and very early achievement demands.

Numerous criticisms have been made of both the theory and research reported in *The Achieving Society,* but these are beyond the scope of this chapter. Here we will note only that there are ambiguities in the meaning of "achievement motivation" itself, and inconsistencies and difficulties of interpretation in the results. Whatever its weaknesses, however, McClelland's study offers a useful model for others who wish to carry out concrete, specific, and meaningful reserarch on the role of motivation in development. One of its outstanding strengths lies in the attempt to combine various methodologies and levels of analysis (aggregate and individual) in a single, comprehensive study.

Other specific motives that may have either facilitative or inhibiting effects on economic development have been identified, but none has been explored as extensively as the achievement motive. Thus Pareek (1968) has proposed that "extension motivation"—which he defines as "a need to extend the self or the ego and to relate to a larger group and its goals" (p. 119)—may contribute positively to economic development, whereas "dependence motivation" may have a negative effect. Iacono (1968) proposes that a strong affiliative orientation, which he and his collaborators found to be characteristic of Southern Italian society, tends to inhibit technological innovation. In his view, innovation is not ruled out in an affiliative society, but requires a unique set of conditions if it is to meet with acceptance.

Interpersonal Attitudes. Over time individuals develop stable attitudes toward others, which may influence their behavior in both the economic and political spheres. Two sets of attitudes closely tied to the possibility of economic growth and political effectiveness are interpersonal trust and authority orientations.

Both economic growth and political effectiveness require that individuals in the same society share a minimal level of trust—that they be able to get along with each other. Adam Smith argued that the division of labor—a major contributor to increased economic productivity— is limited only by the size of the market. His point is only partly true, for the division of labor is also limited by the disposition of people to cooperate (Powelson, 1969). Thus the major contribution of the economist to the study of development is to show the importance of optimal combinations of the factors of production: land, labor, and capital. The social psychologist would add his voice by pointing out that these optimal combinations presume cooperation, confidence, and trust among the owners.

If groups such as politicians, landowners, businessmen, farmers, and workers do not trust each other and do not have open lines of communication, some of the ideal combinations may be ruled out. For example, when owners of capital feel that labor makes unrealistic demands (a feeling not uncommon in Latin America), they may place a disproportionate amount of their capital in labor-saving machines, relying on technology rather than labor, even though from a theoretical "optimizing" standpoint this practice may be inadvisable (cf. Powelson, 1969).

A lack of trust may also pose serious problems for the political development of a country, especially by undermining the capacity to form effective organizations. As Huntington (1968) points out, "mutual distrust and truncated loyalties mean little organization. In terms of observable behavior, the crucial distinction between a politically developed society and an underdeveloped one is the number, size, and effectiveness of its organizations" (p. 31). This observation, particularly its reference to effectiveness, seems to hold true whatever the ideological orientation of the society. Mistrust also creates obstacles to the development of effective industrial organizations by erecting barriers between foremen and workers, one work group and another, or individuals in the same unit.

A pervasive climate of mistrust in a society can set the stage for the development of organized intergroup conflicts that lead to socioeconomic paralysis. In rural Peru, for example, rivalries between villages, especially over communal land, consume a high proportion of the resources that might otherwise be available for economic improvement. Whyte and Williams (1968) suggest three harmful side-effects of these conflicts: (1) large amounts of money must be spent to support local lawyers representing the villages, and eventually to support litigation in Lima; (2) the heightened climate of suspicion generated by the disputes makes it difficult for neighboring villages to cooperate on projects of mutual interest and benefit, such as roads passing through common land; and (3) heavy reliance on lawyers and representatives in Lima increases the psychological dependence of villagers on outsiders to deal with their problems, thereby reducing their own sense of competence and initiative.

A second set of interpersonal attitudes that are highly relevant to development are attitudes to authority. In every society individuals take part in relationships involving differential power between themselves and others, beginning with parent-child interactions and continuing through life. These experiences impart an enduring attitude toward authority, encompassing one's role as both superior and subordinate. Social psychologists have been especially interested in the constellation of attitudes known as the "authoritarian personality," which consists of a tendency to conform uncritically to the standards and commands of perceived authorities, and to expect such conformity from others when one occupies a position of authority (cf. Adorno, Frenkel-Brunswik, Levinson, and Sanford, 1950).

Everett Hagen (1962) has placed great emphasis on the role of authoritarian attitudes in the process of development and, more generally, social change: "One must conclude that the hierarchical structure of authority and power in traditional societies has been so stable because the simple folk as well as the elite accepted it. The simple folk must feel satisfaction in depending for decisions and direction on individuals above them, in submitting their wills to authority; and, conversely, they must feel uneasy about making judgments or coping with problems on their own initiative" (pp. 71–72). Hagen concludes that authoritarian attitudes breed a fear of using one's own initiative, thereby suffocating incipient tendencies to creativity in the economic or political order.

Attitudes toward authority may interact with interpersonal trust in determining reactions to different leadership styles which, in turn, may have significant implications for both economic and political development. Social-psychological studies in the United States have suggested that, in general, an employee-oriented or participatory style of supervision in a work organization is more conducive to its overall effectiveness —its ability to reach its goals—than more close, autocratic, or production-oriented methods (cf. Katz and Kahn, 1966; Likert, 1961). It is difficult to know, however, to what extent these findings can be generalized to other countries, in which underlying attitudes toward authority may be differently distributed. A recent study suggests that the assumed positive effects of a democratic-participative style of leadership may not be universal (Williams, Whyte, and Green, 1966). Results from a sample of Peruvian white-collar workers indicate that the effectiveness of various styles of supervision, as measured by worker satisfaction, depends on the values of the employees themselves. Workers showing a low level of interpersonal trust preferred supervisors strong on technical and administrative skills, but not necessarily on "human relations" ability. The results for the "high trust" group, on the other hand, were very close to those seen among American workers. Pye's study (1962) of authority relationships in the Burmese civil service also underscores the critical role of confidence and trust for effective governmental administration.

Personal Efficacy. Perhaps one of the most critical personality characteristics related to social change is a sense of personal efficacy; also known as subjective competence, fate control, or environmental mastery. An individual possesses this quality when he knows and feels that he is an origin of action, an agent and a cause who can control events and shape his own destiny. Personal efficacy, like several other traits considered in this discussion, can be viewed as both an end and a means in the development process. From a humanistic standpoint one could argue that the task of raising the citizen's level of environmental control—both perceived and actual—should be a cardinal goal of development. Thus efficacy could be used as one yardstick for measuring the success of various development projects, including those in education, culture, and science. At the same time we would hypothesize that this quality plays an important instrumental role in promoting economic growth and political effectiveness. In economies placing heavy reliance on the private sector, for example, efficacy seems vital to the development of entrepreneurship. The entrepreneur is likely to be a person with a sufficient sense of mastery to permit risk-taking and with a conviction that success in economic affairs is not the result of luck, astrological rules, or the fates, but in large measure the fruit of one's own efforts.

A sense of efficacy seems to arise as the person receives positive feedback from his engagements with the physical and social environment. Initial success heightens his feeling of control and encourages him to move on to more difficult feats. The case of the village of Huayopampa cited earlier illustrated this process of adding incremental gains in both individual and community efficacy. M. Brewster Smith (1968) provides a more detailed statement on the route to efficacy:

> The person is attracted to moderate challenges that have an intermediate probability of success. By setting his goals realistically at a level somewhat higher than that of his previous performance, he reaps the maximum cumulative gain in sensed efficacy from his successes. This is, in effect, an active, coping orientation high in initiative, not a passive or defensive one characterized by very low goals (which can yield little sense of efficacy when attained) or unrealistically high ones (the main virtue of which is the readiness with which non-attainment can be explained away and "failure" neutralized) (p. 282).

Personal efficacy may be considered the most appropriate criterion for evaluating the success of education in developing countries. This is, in essence, the position adopted by such critics of the educational system as Ivan Illich and Julius Nyerere. They have taken issue with the implicit criteria by which the success of schools is now assessed in many developing countries—their effectiveness in preparing individuals to enter the labor market, and the proportion of students finishing one level of school who continue to the next—and have instead advocated others, akin to the concept of efficacy. Illich (1969) has been especially sharp in his criticisms of the impact of school on the student's self-conception. He writes:

The higher the dose of schooling an individual has received, the more depressing his experience of withdrawal. The seventh-grade dropout feels his inferiority much more acutely than the dropout from the third grade. The schools of the Third World administer their opium with much more effect than the churches of other epochs. As the mind of a society is progressively schooled, step by step its individuals lose their sense that it might be possible to live without being inferior to others. As the majority shifts from the land into the city, the hereditary inferiority of the peon is replaced by the inferiority of the school dropout who is held personally responsible for his failure (p. 22).

Illich's impression that the educational system often has the effect of reducing rather than increasing the sense of personal efficacy can and ought to be subjected to empirical test.

Julius Nyerere (1968) argues further that primary education (in Tanzania) has been misguided in its emphasis on preparing students to pass the competitive examinations that will permit them to enter secondary school. Such a policy, he holds, makes little sense in a society in which only 13 % of the students will find a place in secondary school. Thus Tanzania is now experimenting with a program of Education for Self-Reliance whose aims come close to what we have described as efficacy. Nyerere describes these aims in the following terms:

However much agriculture a young person learns, he will not find a book which will give him all the answers to all the detailed problems he will come across on his own farm. He will have to learn the basic principles of modern knowledge in agriculture and then adapt them to solve his own problems. Similarly, the free citizens of Tanzania will have to judge social issues for themselves; there neither is, nor will be, a political "holy book" which purports to give all the answers to all the social, political, and economic problems which will face our country in the future (p. 421).

Another area in which personal efficacy can be taken as a goal and developed in varying degrees is the teaching of literacy. The Brazilian educator Paulo Freire (1971) has criticized traditional methods of literacy instruction for reinforcing attitudes of helplessness and dependence in the individual by treating him as a vessel into whom knowledge is poured. His own approach, which he calls a process of *conscientização,* aims at producing not only an ability to read, but also personal qualities approximating what we have called efficacy. In his view, one of the major handicaps among illiterates is a magical world-view in which their own action has little relevance, coupled with a sense of fatalism and passivity. To break out of this pattern, he claims, people must become convinced not only that they can read, but that they can be origins of action and agents of change. Thus his own approach to literacy instruction, which has been tried with success in several parts of Latin America, makes the training experience a critical, active process. In the first stage he studies the context in which illiterates live to uncover common problems as well as words reflecting them. His emphasis is on personal, local problems, so that the lists of words he develops are different for each area. In the second stage he chooses 16 to 20 words that include the basic sounds in the language, that enable the student to move from the simpler sounds and letters to the more complex, and that are highly relevant to the local political, cultural, and social reality. Through this process Freire attempts both to produce literacy and to bring about a change of attitudes on the part of the participants, including an accurate assessment of their locus in the society and a will to shape their own destinies.

Ideological Orientations. Some of the dimensions that we have been discussing—such as interpersonal trust, attitudes toward authority, and personal efficacy—may be used to describe a person's relationship to the various basic institutions of his society. For example, to describe the relationship of an individual to the political system, we would want to assess the degree to which he places trust in political institutions, he accepts the legitimacy of political authorities, and he feels efficacious in affecting the political process (three dimensions, incidentally, that are closely interrelated). An individual's position on these dimensions is affected by his general personality orientations: his level of interpersonal trust, his attitudes toward authority, and his sense of personal efficacy are likely to generalize to his interactions with the political system. His position on these dimensions, however, is also affected by his orientations toward the political system as such—that is, by the conception of the political system that he has acquired as a member of his society or of a certain segment of the society. We are speaking here of ideological orientations, which are specific in the sense that they refer to particular institutions rather than the whole array of social relationships but general in the sense that they represent a pervasive framework of attitudes and beliefs concerning an institution rather than an opinion about a given set of policies or leaders.

The ability of political authorities to promote social change and to maintain satisfactory levels of economic growth and political effectiveness is greatly influenced by the orientations toward the central institutions held within the population and its various segments. In the long run, central authorities cannot achieve development goals unless they are widely perceived as legitimate and trustworthy, and unless this perception is shared by the diverse class, occupational, ethnic, regional, and other groupings that make up the society. Thus part of the contents of a development program—as both an end and a means—is the promotion of ideological orientations, among all segments of the population, that would insure support for the central political authorities and be conducive to their perceived legitimacy. Social-psychological analyses of political ideology, of ways in which individuals orient themselves to the political system and the sources of their orientations, may provide some relevant inputs.

At the social-psychological level, the legitimacy of a political system is reflected in the sense of loyalty that its members have toward it. Perceived legitimacy implies that the individual member is in some fashion personally involved in the system, that he feels attached to it and is integrated into its operations. We can distinguish two sources of loyalty or attachment to the nation-state: sentimental attachment and instrumental attachment (Kelman, 1969).

An individual is sentimentally attached to the national system to the extent that he sees it as representing him—as being a reflection and extension of himself; he is loyal because he views it as the embodiment of a people in which his personal identity is anchored. An individual is instrumentally attached to the national system to the extent that he views it as an effective vehicle for achieving his own ends and those of other system members; he is loyal because it provides the orgainization for a smoothly running society in which individuals can participate to their mutual benefit and have some assurance that their needs and interests will be met. Both types of attachment may be channeled in three different ways, roughly corresponding to the processes of internalization, identification, and compliance discussed in an earlier section:

1. The individual may share some of the basic values on which the system is established—either the cultural values defining the national identity, or the social values reflected in the society's institutions, or both.

2. He may participate personally in system roles significant for his self-definition—through emotional involvement in the role of national as such with its associated symbols, and/or through functional involvement in various social roles that are mediated by the national system.

3. He may accept the rules or norms of the system, if set by duly constituted authorities, as automatically and self-evidently binding—because he perceives the state as a sacred object in its own right and/or respects law and order as an end in itself.

Development is likely to be facilitated to the extent that both sentimental and instrumental attachments to the central system are strong. and widespread. Within limits, these two types of attachment can substitute for one another. By appealing to the common national identity of the population, political leaders may be able to mobilize support even though they may not be adequately meeting the needs and interests of the majority of the population. Similarly, if instrumental attachments are strong, because the society is functioning effectively and equitably, the system can maintain its legitimacy even though it does not adequately reflect the ethnic-cultural identity of the entire population.

Furthermore, the two types of attachment can have a mutually reinforcing and facilitating effect on one another. If a population perceives the system as being genuinely representative and reflective of its identity, it is inclined to extend to political leaders the kind of trust that they need in order to push for economic development and to organize the society in a way that will in fact meet. the needs and interests of the population. Similarly, a well-functioning society, which provides meaningful roles for its citizens, is likely to develop a set of common values and traditions and a sense of unity that are tantamount to a national identity, even if the population was originally diverse in its ethnic and cultural composition. In fact, such a sense of national identity (which need not displace the original ethnic-cultural identities of the component groups, but can exist alongside them) is most likely to emerge, in our view, out of an effective national system that meets the needs and interests of the entire population, rather than out of deliberate attempts by central political authorities to create it directly (cf. Kelman, 1971).

Social-Psychological Factors in the Phasing of Social Change

An adequate model of social change, either from a theoretical or applied standpoint, must take account of the "systems effects" of one type of change on others. Too often, particularly in the literature on development, social change has been viewed as a unilinear process of evolution, sometimes speeded by human intervention, leading simultaneously to several desired outcomes, such as economic growth, political effectiveness, and personal efficacy. Some writers have built this assumption of unilinearity into their very definition of modernization. It is now clear that social change must be viewed as a multifaceted process, which may run in many directions at once, some of which may be considered "development" and others "antidevelopment." Huntington (1968), for example, has suggested that economic growth and social modernization (education, literacy) are a major source of strain on the political system. He writes: "Not only does social and economic modernization produce political instability, but the degree of instability is related to the rate of modernization. The historical evidence with respect to the West is overwhelming on this point" (p. 45).

An important task for social-scientific analysis, therefore, is to identify the conditions under which change in one area—though in itself desirable—may create dislocations in other areas that have socially undesirable consequences and that may even impede the development process itself. The social-psychological concepts of strain and aspiration may be useful in such an analysis.

Psychic Strain. Students of development have been concerned with the extent to which anxiety, fear, mental disorder, and other signs of psychic strain are produced by the change process, and with the effect that consistently high levels of strain may, in turn, have on economic and political development.

The question of the effects of development on strain is most often raised in the context of urbanization. The notion has long existed in the West, and is shared by many social scientists, that the city is the major source of social disorganization, personal alienation, mental illness, and anxiety. Many studies on the effects of rural-urban migration in developing countries have expected to find psychic strain as a consequence of urban living and, not surprisingly, many have obtained results supporting their hypothesis.

Although urbanization may indeed produce anxiety and mental disorder, we feel that the nature of the causal relationship is far from clear. A recent study by Inkeles and Smith (1968), for instance, found no consistent differences in psychological adjustment, measured by psychosomatic symptoms, between men who moved to the city and those like them who remained in the villages. Other research suggests that there may be stages of adaptation to the city, ranging from early insulation, through a painful time of crisis, to a later stage of seemingly comfortable adjustment.

In view of these ambiguities, it is essential that future social-psychological studies of the impact of urbanization, as well as of social change in general, begin with clear definitions, both conceptual and operational, of anxiety and other forms of strain. A sharp distinction should be drawn, for example, between such minor symptoms of strain as reports of uneasiness in the city, and more drastic forms such as schizophrenic breakdown. Moreover, research in this area should be designed to allow for the measurement of *positive* effects of development on "mental health," such as a greater sense of self-confidence, feelings of liberation from restrictive kinship obligations, and the like. Finally, studies aimed at producing generalizations about the differences between urban and rural areas should include representative samples from the rural areas, and not simply assume that the strains observed in the urban sample do not arise in the villages.

The effect of psychic strain, in turn, on the development process also requires further analysis. Although there is evidence that high levels of anxiety, fear, and other forms of strain may work against development, it does not follow that all forms of strain will have this effect or that development is most likely where strain is minimal. Sometimes, in fact, strain may contribute indirectly to national development. A moderate level of anxiety, for example, may serve as a motivational substratum for creativity and innovation in many spheres—business, government, and art. The classic statement of this positive side of strain is found in *The Protestant Ethic and the Spirit of Capitalism* (Weber, 1930).

Level of Aspiration. In many cases the latent or unanticipated effects of change arise from the fact that modifications of the existing order in one area, such as education, bring about shifts in attitudes and aspirations that carry over to other areas. The utility of a social-psychological approach to the sequence of change can be illustrated with a few simple concepts suggested by research on levels of aspiration. We begin with the assumption that satisfaction is the ratio of achievement to aspiration, whereas frustration is the reverse. Following March and Simon (1958, p. 18), let us further assume that: (1) the less satisfied the individual, the more he will search for new ways of meeting his needs; (2) the greater the search, the higher the level of aspiration; and (3) given constant levels of achievement, the higher the level of aspiration, the lower the satisfaction and the greater the frustration. When applied to the problem of national development, these concepts suggest some interesting relationships between socioeconomic and political change:

1. *Economic growth decreases satisfaction and increases search.* Economic growth is typically accompanied by other types of social change, including a challenge to traditional authority, as well as shifts in residence, occupation, education, and experience (e.g., through increased use of transistor radios). The first effect is often a negative one—a breaking away from the old without a parallel commitment to the new. Karl Deutsch (1961) describes this effect as *social mobilization,* "the process in which major clusters of old social, economic, and psychological commitments are eroded and broken and people become available for new patterns of socialization and behavior" (p. 494). The psychic vacuum that results may lead to lower satisfaction and a search for new kinds of group membership and new sources of psychological security.

2. *Increased search coupled with "modernizing" stimuli produces higher levels of aspiration.* Social mobilization, we migh hypothesize, increases the individual's perceptual readiness for new experiences, identifi-

cations, and products. At the same time, higher levels of education, increased contact with the mass media, and often residence in or near a cosmopolitan center expose him to new options related to his search. These conditions may produce a sharp rise in the individual's aspirations for himself and particularly for his children. A pattern of rising aspirations for one's children is strongly suggested by a study carried out in Peru by the Centro de Investigaciones Sociales por Muestro (1966). The results of a sample survey of the city of Arequipa showed that the educational aspirations of heads of households for their oldest sons rose with the head's own educational level. Thus among those with no formal education only 35% hoped that their children would reach college; for those with primary school training the figure rose to 57%; and among those who had completed secondary school it was 96%. The novelty and glamor of the new stimuli, as well as the instability created by mobilization, may lead to an "elation effect" through which aspirations in many spheres (consumer goods, education, political participation) reach totally unrealistic proportions.

3. *The society's capacity to satisfy the aspirations tends to rise at a slower rate than the aspirations themselves.* In the early stages of economic development political leaders promise and the citizens come to expect an unreasonably high level of output. Growth rates of 6 to 7% annually, although acceptable by ordinary standards, fall far short of satisfying the rising desires. Similarly, the unequal distribution of the early gains of growth within the society may lead some groups (such as the industrial entrepreneurs in Pakistan) to improve their positions at a faster rate than others. Social-psychological research on social comparison processes suggests that people often use the achievements of significant and visible others (who constitute relevant reference groups) in setting their own aspirations and evaluating their own success. Thus *absolute* gains may be accompanied by a sense of *relative* deprivation. As a result, even though economic growth in its early stages may raise the income level and standard of living of the poor, their frustrations may show a net increase if the gap between them and the rich has widened.

4. *The resulting imbalances may create new forms of psychic strain placing severe pressure on the political system.* Several specific sources of strain may be cited. The first lies in the economic area, caused by the fact that aspirations for productivity outrun achievement. To make matters worse, just as economic aspirations begin to rise, especially for the middle classes, the government is often forced to clamp restrictions on consumption (e.g., on purchases of luxury goods). This policy may help the masses but increase the frustration of the elite. A second source of strain stems from status incongruities. The older elite, for example, has been accus-

tomed to set its aspirations on the basis of its past position in the social order but finds itself moving downward in the new order. Strain may also increase among the new university elite as they find that their education (a source of aspirations) is far above their occupational prestige (achievement). Third, in some nations, strain may be generated by the efforts of entire groups, such as clans, castes, and tribes, to seek collective mobility. Such groups may try to raise their aspirations for power and participation in the political sphere, only to find that others are doing the same. Finally, when traditional forms of authority break down and are not replaced by intermediary groups standing between the individual and the state, the aspirations for direct popular political participation may also rise dramatically and exceed the potential provided by the system. To predict the effects of these strains and pressures on the political system, one would have to assess its flexibility and adaptability. A system that systematically excludes that participation of many groups, such as the narrowly based military dictatorship of Batista in Cuba, may be forced to give way in the face of rising pressures. Systems with greater flexibility may be able to respond to the pressures noted without cracking.

Facilitative Sequences. In citing examples of negative phasing effects, in which changes in one area have detrimental consequences and inhibit changes in other areas, we do not mean to imply that this is a necessary or even common sequence of events. We have already indicated that there are many occasions when a change sets a positive cycle into motion and the occurrence of change at one level facilitates changes at another level. Our earlier discussions of the interactive effects between action change and attitude change, and between institutional changes and personality changes, have suggested some of the processes that may promote facilitative sequences. The crucial problem for social-scientific research is to specify the precise nature of these processes and the conditions that set them into motion. A social-psychological analysis, with its emphasis on the microprocesses of social change and their effects on the individual, may be particularly helpful in this connection. It suggests, for example, the importance of some continuity of values if radical unfreezing is to be followed by integrative refreezing, of maintaining a balance between increases in aspirations and the expansion of opportunity systems, and of assuring that the adoption of specific new practices and the introduction of new institutional arrangements occur in a context that permits experiences of success, heightened self-esteem, cognitive reorganization, and social support.

Notes

1. This chapter is based on a working paper prepared for the UNESCO Symposium on the Role of Social Sciences in Development, held in Paris during the summer of 1970.

2. The following discussion draws on an earlier summary in Kelman (1963).

3. This interpretation is not contained in the report on Huayopampa by Whyte and Williams, but seems consistent with their observations.

James S. Coleman

Department of Social Relations
Johns Hopkins University

CONFLICTING THEORIES
OF SOCIAL CHANGE [1]

Recently I set out to study as a sociologist a problem that confronts each of us as members of American society: the problem of how blacks in America can come to gain the power over their conditions of existence comparable to that of other Americans. This task led me directly into the study of theories of social change with an additional constraint that appears to be quite fruitful indeed. This constraint is the limitation to theories of directed or intentional change. This limitation allows one to hold constant the direction or goal of change, and thus to compare the different paths to that goal specified by different theories.

Moreover, in the various intentional theories of change that are being implemented throughout the world today, there is general agreement upon the goal. Whether it is change for whole societies, as in Africa, or change for a minority within society, such as blacks in the United States, the general direction of intended change is the same. In its most general terms, it may be described as an increase in control over the conditions of existence or, alternatively, an expansion of resources. This includes an increase in material wealth, but it is not limited to wealth. More fundamentally, it implies the holding of a greater set of resources, either individually or collectively, making possible a wider range of choice. This narrowing of the problem of social change provides an enormous simplification for theories of change, because it imposes a single dimension on the various factors in change, just as the idea of an economic "good" imposes such a simplification in economic theory. Having more of any good, whatever its nature, is a better state than having less. Such theories of directed change, then, differ from general theories of so-

61

cial change in imposing an evaluation upon any element in the system—
an evaluation derived from its contribution to the ultimate goal.

When one examines theories of social change with this orientation,
several sharp differences appear between theories upon which various actions toward change are based. What makes this difference particularly
interesting is that different groups of intellectuals tend to hold one or another theory, dictated by the factors they have some control over or
knowledge about. One theory may be labeled the "lawyer's theory"; a second, the "economist's theory"; a third, the "psychologist's theory"; and a
fourth, the "revolutionary's theory." I will try to describe each of these.

The major distinction between theories of change, which divides
them into two broad classes, is between theories that start with changes
in the social *conditions* in which individuals find themselves versus those
that start with changes in *individuals*.[2] This distinction is one that per-
vades nearly all action programs designed to produce change. One approach is based on the premise that if only the material conditions in
which a group or a society finds itself are changed, then the group or the
society will itself go ahead to expand its resources. An opposing approach
is based on the premise that if only the individuals themselves are
changed, then they will move toward an expansion of resources. This distinction is particularly important because it mirrors a difference in current beliefs about change that divides the black movement in the United
States, as well as a difference that divides different beliefs about change
in developing countries. It is of additional interest because it does not reflect a general radical-conservative split: the most conservative and the
most radical are found in the same camp.

Changes in Social Conditions

Legal Changes. The theories that place the starting point of change
in social conditions can be conveniently divided into two: those that take
legal change as the starting point, and those that take an increase in economic resources as the starting point. An example of the former kind of
argument in a context far removed from current issues is a thesis put
forth by Berle and Means (1932) and by John R. Commons (1924) to account for the growth of corporate industry in the United States in the
late nineteenth and early twentieth centuries. The argument goes somewhat as follows: In a publicly owned business firm, there is a conflict of
interest between the managers, who are interested in the total amount of
profit and in the reinvestment of this profit for expansion, and the stockholder-owners, who are interested in the rate of return on investment.

In the United States, incorporation is done not by the federal government but by individual states. Thus the states, interested in having firms incorporate within them, competed for firms by allowing attractive terms of incorporation. Since the managers in most publicly owned firms had control over the place of incorporation, they chose to incorporate in those states that gave them most freedom from owners; Delaware is one example. This freedom from stockholder-owners (exhibited, for example, in majority voting rules in place of unanimity, the introduction of proxy votes, and more power for the board of directors in issuing new stock) gave the managers power that they used toward reinvestment of profits, attraction of new capital, and general expansion. According to this argument, then, the rapid growth of corporate industry was made possible by the laws of incorporation, which themselves were shaped by the existence of competition between the states, in turn determined by the Constitution, which gives residual powers to the states. The general thesis on which this argument rests is found in one strategy of change for blacks in America, and one strategy for developing countries. It is a thesis generally held by lawyers who see the courts as a principal mechanism for change. The general thesis is that if legal changes are made, the desired social change will follow. Examples are the Supreme Court ruling on school desegregation and antidiscrimination laws in employment, housing, and public accommodation. Thirty years ago, this thesis motivated the National Labor Relations Act, which gave organized labor more legal rights in negotiations with management. Examples in developing countries include the argument that a certain form of government or a certain type of constitution will bring about development.

Obviously, as these examples indicate, this thesis is neither completely correct nor completely false. Ten years after the Supreme court decision outlawing legal segregation in school systems, only about 1% of blacks in the 11 states of the deep South were attending school with whites. And although there are now rulings by some state education departments in the North requiring school districts to create racially balanced schools, the few tentative efforts in those directions have met with such resistance by whites that the rulings have not been enforced. On the other hand, when the U.S. Army introduced a policy of integrated units, the policy was quickly implemented. Similarly, the public accommodations section of the Civil Rights Act of 1964 led very quickly to opening of places of public accommodation to blacks. Or after the Labor Relations Act, the strength of unions, and thus the power of organized labor to gain wage increases, grew greatly. Yet in the less industrialized South, it grew much more slowly. Thus the evidence appears quite contradictory.

The opponents of this strategy and theory of social change have two principal arguments: first, that legal changes themselves seldom occur unless the distribution of effective power in society has itself changed, and thus is only a reflection of "real" social changes; and second, that the legal change will have effects only when there is "real power" to implement it. When it occurs without this "real power" to back it up, it is ineffective. An example sometimes used is the constitutions of unions, which ordinarily impose all the legal machinery for democracy in union government. But because the social structure of unions cannot sustain stable political opposition, these forms do not result in democratic government, but in a strong and entrenched bureaucracy. (See Lipset et al., 1956).

The obvious question becomes, under what conditions will a change in the law bring about social change? Under what conditions is this thesis a correct one? Some of the foregoing examples suggest general principles; I will mention several of these, as a way of indicating the kind of conditions that could make this theory of change a useful one.

One obvious condition under which legal changes are effective may be found when those who must implement the change are in a direct line of authority below those who are responsible for the change. In the military, officers responsible for effecting the change to integrated army units merely implemented the order; but in school integration, local control of schools meant that no such direct line of authority existed from federal to local authority.

A second principle is exemplified by the effectiveness of the National Labor Relations Act in increasing the real power of unions. In this case, there were in many industries, particularly in the North, organized agents, in the form of unions, already in existence to make use of the new formal power they possessed. The general principle this suggests is that change will occur when there are individuals or organizations already prepared to make use of the formal authority created by the legal change.

A third general principle is suggested by the success of the public accommodations section of the Civil Rights Act. Before the Act, there was the curious anomaly that *associations* of restaurant owners in many localities favored such a law, but no *individual* owner would desegregate. The condition was one that might be termed innovator loss: if one owner admitted blacks, he stood to lose his white customers because of the free mobility of customers, whereas if all did so, no one stood to lose. The general principle, then, is that when a situation of innovator loss exists, a legal change can be expected to be quickly effective.

These three principles suggest how one might go about making this "legal change" theory of directed social change more useful; but the intent here is not to develop such theory but rather to contrast the different positions. Thus we continue to the second thesis, the economist's theory of social change.

Addition of Economic Resources. The second general thesis that takes changes in social conditions as the starting point in change is one that depends on economic resources. The major deficit of the society or the subgroup is seen to be a deficit of economic resources. In the case of a change in a whole economy; such capital is required as resources for increasing the rate of investment, which in naive economic arguments directly increases the rate of economic growth. This thesis has been implicitly or explicitly the basis for much of the economic aid in recent years from developed to developing countries. It was the basis as well for the Marshall plan that preceded such aid and constituted a kind of model for it.

In the case of individuals within societies, the thesis is that the poor cannot pull themselves out of their condition because of a severe lack of economic resources. It is the basis for those strategies for overcoming poverty which depend on income supplements or on consumer goods subsidies, as in housing and food, and in free services, such as health, child care, education, and retraining.

It is clear, both in the case of foreign aid and in the case of welfare to the poor within a country, that two aims are ordinarily intermixed. The first is that the aid be self-liquidating, that it change a society or a household from a state of low resources and dependence to a state of high resources and economic independence. The second aim is merely that of maintaining some level of living—in the case of India, preventing starvation; in the case of welfare to the poor within a society, to maintain a minimal standard of living. It is obviously only the first of these aims that is relevant here: the use of economic resources in the form of foreign aid or income supplements to pull a nation or a household out of self-perpetuating poverty, so that the aid is self-liquidating.

The evidence for this economic-investment theory of directed change is mixed. In Europe under the Marshall Plan, in Puerto Rico, and in Mexico, the inputs of external capital appear to have been quite important in facilitating economic growth. In Egypt, India, and Ghana, to name only three, the inputs seem to have had little effect. Nor has private investment had much apparent effect on the economies of the banana republics and the oil shiekdoms. More generally, the economic aid to developing countries in Asia, Africa, and Latin America seems to have had little effect on economic growth, and some economists (see Bauer, 1966) argue that it has had the effect of suppressing economic growth in many of these countries.

For the poor within a country, the evidence on this provision-of-economic-resources thesis is mixed as well. Although research results are scarce, there are some: provision of public housing to replace dilapidated housing, at least as practiced in the United States, appears to have little effect on the family's functioning, on the basis of several careful studies. There is also evidence to suggest that income supplements in the form of aid for dependent children creates a disincentive for economic productivity and for family stability. At the same time, educational subsidies under the GI Bill of Rights appear to have had important effects in increasing the productivity of recipients.

As some of these examples suggest, the naive theory as I have described it may be defective principally because of its lack of attention to the conditions and kind of economic aid. The success of foreign aid in the developed countries of Europe and its lack of success in developing countries suggest that such aid is effective when it restores a previously productive economy. In such a circumstance all the *other* factors for development are presumably present; the lack of growth in truly undeveloped economies suggests that these "other factors" are indeed essential.

There is an interesting parallel within societies, provided by an intensive study of 86 families of working-class children in England who after the abolition of fees for grammar schools in 1944, passed the 11 + examination and went all the way through the sixth form and passed A-level examinations (making University entrance possible) (Jackson and Marsden, 1962). The investigators found to their surprise that 34 of these families were what they termed "sunken middle class," which had in the preceding generation been middle class on at least one parent's side. More generally, the broader statistical evidence indicates that the abolition of fees in 1944 brought about little if any increase in the proportion of working-class students continuing through A-level examinations.

In the United States, the free city colleges in New York City have been important in increasing the productivity of Jews from Eastern Europe. They have been much less important in increasing the productivity of Catholics from Ireland and blacks from the South.

Why this difference? Why was the Marshall Plan valuable for Europe while much more extensive aid has been of little value for undeveloped countries? Why was it that the 1944 Education Act which made grammar schools free in England was of so little value to those who most needed this aid, and appears to have aided most a temporarily sunken middle class? Why has New York City's system of free higher education been such an important element in change for working-class Jews from Eastern Europe, but so much less valuable for Irish immigrants and for blacks?

In all these cases, there appears to be a strong interaction between some pre-existing condition in the society or the subgroup and the usefulness of economic resources. The paradoxical point is that those societies or those subgroups for which the added economic resources appear most valuable are exactly the ones that would have progressed farthest without this added resource. The relationship is so strong that one observer has suggested, with regard to foreign aid, that if a country has not developed capital internally, it is not likely to be aided by the addition of external economic resources. Whether or not such a pessimistic view is warranted, there is less optimism than existed 10 years ago among most observers about the benefits of external aid programs in bringing economic development to undeveloped countries, and in the benefits of economic subsidies to the chronically poor in leading them out of a cycle of poverty.

Certainly other kinds of conditions are important as well: if aid for dependent children creates a disincentive to enter the labor market and to maintain stable families, there are other types of income supplements that do not. If naive foreign economic aid leads to creation of inefficient heavy industry to bolster national pride, more careful investment need not.

Merely from the examples I have given, one general condition for the effectiveness of economic aid could be conceived, in its simplest terms, as a two-factor theory of productivity: The society or the household has a given "productive potential," and the external resources provide the opportunity for realizing that potential. Economic aid can supply the second factor but not the first; thus it will promote productivity when the first factor is already present but the second is missing. But this is only the merest beginning in making the economic-investment theory a useful theory of directed social change. The aim of this chapter is not theory-development but theory-confrontation, so we turn now to the second broad class of theories, in which directed social change depends upon changes in individuals.

Changes in Individuals

There are strange bedfellows in the camp of theorists for whom directed social change depends on individual change. This camp includes the sociologists Max Weber and Everett Hagen, the psychologist David McClelland, the philosopher Jean-Paul Sartre, and the revolutionaries, Lenin, Mao Tse-Tung, and Frantz Fanon. As this heterogeneous collection of writers suggests, there is at some point a parting of the ways; but what is important initially is the major point of similarity. This point is the focus on change of individuals. For all these men, change is predicated upon change in the personalities or beliefs of individuals. For Weber, the value placed on individual effort and thrift, as embodied in the protestant ethic, is paramount. For Hagen and McClelland, it is a similar value, the need for achievement. For Sartre, Lenin, Mao, and Fanon, it is similar, the release from a psychology of passivity, the release from traditional custom, the breaking away from ascribed authority.

For these various theorists the source of the personality change arises at different points. For Weber, the personality change that preceded the rise of capitalism lay in the ideals and values embodied in the new religious belief of Protestantism. For Hagen and McClelland, the development of a "need for achievement" lies principally in socialization practices in the family—but it is reinforced by the school, and by other elements in the family. McClelland has, for example, subjected businessmen from India to a training program designed to increase the need for achievement, and then measured the subsequent productivity of their businesses. For the revolutionary theorists, the essential belief in one's power arises, as indicated earlier, not in early socialization but through action itself, in the revolutionary act which transforms the personality.

Beyond this psychological core, two sets of theorists divide sharply on the question of individualism and collectivism. This divergence is sharp indeed, for the very element that one set of theorists sees as necessary for change the other sees as an impediment to change.

The Individualists. The theory of industrialization that is compatible with Weber's ideas of the protestant ethic includes as a part of it a strong norm and practice of individualism. This value is part of the protestant ethic itself, and Weber notes it when he describes the conflicts between Methodist and non-Methodist workers in early English factories, when the Methodist workers refused to be bound by work norms which limited production. In India, the strength of the extended family, destroying the individual's willingness to be geographically mobile, is sometimes cited as an impediment to industrialization. Numerous anthropologists note the power of the collectivity (family, clan, tribe) in preventing the individual from adopting new ways, and often they present this collectivity strength as the major obstacle to economic development and social change. Much of applied anthropology is research in the adoption of innovation in the face of such community norms, the study of how such norms can be overcome to produce change.

Among the individualist theorists, then, it is the combination of high value placed on effort, achievement, and frugality in consumption, with a high value placed on individual freedom from the constraints of a collectivity, which brings about change. This combination of achievement orientation and individualism allows each member of society to pursue to the fullest his interests, unimpeded by extended family or by communal ties. He is free to move to follow occupational opportunities; and his need for achievement leads him to do so. The need for achievement creates human capital; and the freedom from social constraints allows this capital to be employed where it is most productive. The change of society as a whole, then, is seen as the aggregate of the individual change—first an internal activation of individuals, and then a freedom from social constraint which allows them to take full advantage of opportunity.

The Revolutionary Theorists. The psychological change that forms part of the thesis of the revolutionary theorists has a different origin from that of the individualists. The change is wrought by the revolutionary action itself, which brings a goal and the hope of achieving the goal. The theory has some affinity with certain social-psychological theories that emphasize the effect of action in changing beliefs. For it is the action itself which brings the change, according to this thesis. The changed personalities and beliefs are then seen, as in the individualist theories, to constitute human capital, which can be transformed into economic productivity and social change. However, the mechanism of transformation is precisely the opposite of that of the individualists.

Where the individualist theory depends on the freedom of the individual from social constraints, the revolutionary theories depend on total commitment of the individual to the revolutionary movement. A total submersion of the individual will to the collectivity is essential to this theory of social change, so that the collectivity becomes the single-minded instrument of change. Through this principle, the social change comes about not as an aggregate of the changes wrought by transformed personalities, but by the collective force of the revolutionary group. This principle implies the abdication of any right to hold diverse views, either about goals or about means, and the consequent transformation of the revolutionary group into a single force that can be directed at the enemy. It is perhaps best expressed in the writings of Lenin, Mao Tse-Tung, and Fanon, but it is an essential element of all the revolutionary theorists.

It is useful to note that this half of the revolutionary theories is logically independent of the first half. Theories of social change have been based on the collective strength of a community, quite apart from the personal effects of revolutionary action. The collective strength of a community that is manifested in a marketing cooperative, or in a general strike, is an indication of the importance of this mechanism for change.

One way of looking at the similarities and differences of the individualist and revolutionary theories of social change or approaches to change is to say that they both depend on the disciplined effort of individuals as the essential resource that produces change. For the first, the market system, with its possibilities of individual mobility through individual effort, acts as the mechanism to induce this self-discipline and effort. The second depends on collective identity, and the existence of a collective enemy to overcome, as the source of self-discipline and effort. This second approach to change tends to arise when the market system has broken down for an identifiable group, thus providing the basis for such collective identity. It appears as well to have an inherent instability, because of the special conditions necessary to maintain the collective identity.[3]

It is true that these two theories have often been applied to different situations of social change. The protestant ethic or individual achievement theories have been more often applied to social change within social structures that have been most open, most characterized by a division of labor, least characterized by a fixed hierarchical order in society. The collective force theories have more often been applied to social structures closer to a fixed hierarchical order. Nevertheless, there are large areas of overlap: the collective force thesis has been applied to systems with an advanced division of labor, though its notable successes have been in the hierarchically organized peasant societies. Similarly, the individual-achievement thesis has been applied to the whole range of social systems, though its greatest successes have been in the least hierarchically organized, most open societies.

This partial consistency of theories and social structures does not, however, carry one very far. It implies that the theories discussed earlier, those concerning the social conditions in which individuals find themselves, are relevant to the question of which of these mechanisms is most effective for change. Yet it does so without specifying these conditions. It goes no farther than to suggest that the more open is the legal structure and the more opportunities provided by the economic resources, the more conducive is the structure to the individualist mechanisms. Yet in a concrete situation, the matter is not clear. For example, with regard to the present situation of blacks in the United States, is the social structure appropriate to the individualist or the revolutionary theories? For immigrant groups not racially different from the majority, the openness of the social structure has meant that initial social deficits were overcome through individualist mechanisms. For the black in America, the answer is not so clear. Certainly a major split between civil rights groups is based on a disagreement about the answer to this question.

Similar questions can be raised about Latin America. Is the social structure such that the individualist theory can hold (assuming that such personality transformation can take place without revolutionary action), or such that the revolutionary theory can hold (assuming that, in fact, the revolutionary action would produce the necessary personality transformations)?

Yet even to raise such questions implies the acceptance of a too simple view of social change. For the very examination of these four theories of directed social change shows the extremely fragmentary character of any one of them. As a consequence, it becomes important to ask how some more adequate orientation to directed social change might be achieved. Before doing this, however, there is one peculiar omission in all these theories that should be examined in some detail. This is the role of formal education.

If education were to have appeared anywhere in these theories, its most natural place would appear to be in the individualist theories; but it is quite clear that the changes in individuals described by these theorists are not intellectual, nor changes of skill, but rather changes in motivation and personality. In the large-scale societal changes described by Max Weber and those described by David McClelland, schools played no part, nor did the existence of any other institutions designed to transmit knowledge or skills. Yet much current discussion about social change, either change in developing countries or change in the position of blacks in American society, focuses on the educational system as the institution that can bring about change.

In order to somehow bring the role of educational institutions into the framework of the present discussion, it is necessary to separate the kinds of things that schools do teach or could teach. Ordinarily, these are seen to consist of two attributes: knowledge and skill. However, the focus of the individualist theorists of social change suggests another as well: changes in personality and motivation, the development of a need for achievement, a strong goal-orientation.

It appears that the first two of these attributes, knowledge and skill, which are the traditional products of education, have a closer affinity to the theories that depend on the addition of economic resources. This knowledge and skill is, although an attribute of the individual himself, a condition under which he, as an active agent, must work. It is, of course, a more intrinsic part of him than the tools or the authority system which are also part of the conditions in which he finds himself. Nevertheless, there is a clear substitutability between many of these purely economic resources and his knowledge or skills. His tools and capital equipment are the same *kind* of resource as are his skills or his knowledge: they are part of the equipment he employs to gain his ends. Furthermore, both can be obtained through economic investments: either in capital equip-ment or in training institutions which provide knowledge and skills. Schools are the most obvious of such training institutions, but others exist in industrial training programs, apprenticeship programs, and else-where.

But the other attributes, the motivation and personality characteris-tics themselves, are a different kind of entity altogether. These attributes are the elements that make the individual an active agent, that lead him to use the equipment, knowledge, and skill he has toward specific goals. They constitute the motive-power which, according to the last two sets of theorists discussed previously, are the essential sources of social change.

Yet it is not schools where these attributes are ordinarily seen to be created. It is, for the individualist theorists, either in family socialization patterns or in religious beliefs (which themselves operate in part through such socialization). For the revolutionary theorists, it is in the revolution-ary action that these attributes are created. But for neither is it the edu-cational institutions. This may be explained partly by the fact that none of these theorists has studied social change in societies where formal edu-cational institutions were widespread. But I believe the principal reason lies in the fact that educational institutions are not designed to bring about such changes. Their role has been and is principally that of pro-viding the equipment for change—knowledge and skills—which the in-dividuals may employ.

In short, it appears that the very institutions in society that are de-signed to change individuals have little effect on those very attributes of individuals that many theorists feel are most important for change. Their role instead has been to provide better equipment with which to work—minds or hands that are more able to accomplish a task—not to create motivated actors who will employ this equipment most productively.

The very absence of such institutions in society, together with the ex-tremely variable ability of the family to provide socialization which cre-ates such personalities, suggests that modern societies may be very poorly designed for change. It suggests that an institution is missing in modern society, an institution that would bring about these important changes in individuals, making them active, goal-oriented agents. Such a gap in the institutional structure of society was less evident when most of the eco-nomic and socialization activities in society were the province of the fam-ily. But as the family has relinquished these activities to the community or the society, no agency has developed to supplement (and later sup-plant) this important family function. I think the knowledge about so-cialization and about personality change and motivational change exists to do so; but certainly the schools are not designed for this purpose, nor is any other institution.

Beyond this extended query about the role of educational institutions in social change, the question arises of what a more adequate theory of social change might look like. I will do no more than suggest a few points, since my aim here is not to construct such a theory.

The first point that is clear is that change depends on an interaction between the conditions described in the lawyers' and economists' theories, and the personalities described in the psychologists' and revolutionaries' theories. Change appears in some fashion to be a product of these two kinds of elements, operating in a number of institutional arenas.

One can distinguish, as a consequence, two matters that are ordinarily not distinguished in theories of directed change: the general model of change, on the one hand, and the elements which, in a given society or subgroup, are deficient. When such a distinction is made, it may well be that the same general theory of change can lead to the lawyers', or the economists', or the psychologists', or the revolutionaries' *prescriptions* for change in a given case—depending on what elements are deficient in that case.

In developing the general model of change, it appears useful to think of a set of resources held at any point in time by a society or a subgroup in society, and a set of transformation processes by which these resources create further resources. One can conceive of the institutions of a society as arenas within which these transformation processes take place, creating a given set of output resources from a set of input resources. The courts are one such arena, the economic system is another set of arenas, the government decision-making bodies are another, schools another, religious institutions another, families another, and so on.

If one begins to look at directed social change in this way, I suggest that portions of the four theories I've described will find a place; and I suggest that it then provides a tool by which one can examine the appropriate strategies for change in a society. For if there is to be a more abundant set of output resources—which is the direction of change toward which all these theories aim—then with such a framework it becomes possible to locate deficiencies in input resources that may be externally supplied or, alternatively, inefficiencies in the transformation processes in particular arenas of action, which again may be externally modified. Finally, it appears that despite the extreme conflict among the current theories of directed change, it might be possible to construct from their components a theory of directed change that would be adequate for the problems of change with which societies are faced—and that prescriptions for social change would begin to stem less from ideological or professional preconceptions and more from a theory of change itself.

Notes

1. See James S. Coleman, *Resources for Social Change: Race in the United States* (New York: John Wiley, 1971), for an elaboration and application of the ideas presented in this paper.

2. Carried to its logical conclusion, this distinction, as any, would break down, for any theory of directed social change must, to be complete and other than self-contradictory, have its starting point as knowledge itself. For its very construction implies that this change in knowledge will come to change the behavior of persons whose actions will bring about change. For this reason, a theory that locates the starting point for change as changes in individuals is especially incomplete. Such a theory has left out the step by which such changes are induced, a step that may be especially difficult in a pluralistic authority system. Nevertheless, if such a theory were held by persons in high positions of government, resulting policies would be different than if different theories were held.

3. A very reasonable interpretation of the activities of the Red Guards in China is the attempt by Mao Tse-Tung to re-create the collective identity which was earlier created by the revolution itself.

Everett M. Rogers

Department of Communication
Michigan State University

SOCIAL STRUCTURE AND
SOCIAL CHANGE [1]

The purpose of this chapter is to explore the way in which the social structure of a system affects the nature of social change, and how, in turn, change affects structure. Our work is synthetic, using examples from such varied fields as the diffusion of innovations, organizational communication, national development programs, and social movements. The minor theme of this chapter is that social scientific research on these topics has a number of implicit biases, inherent in what is studied, and what is ingored, how it is investigated, and for whose benefit. Identification of such biases may lead to a more socially relevant social science, and one with wider intellectual perspectives.

This chapter contains a series of generalizations dealing with social structure and social change. These propositions are in the middle range [2] between strict empiricism and general theory. Although we have induced these generalizations from research findings and observations, they are only partway to the abstracted general level of theoretical statements about social change which is an eventual goal of social science. Our propositions are not limited in their applicability to such specific behaviors as the diffusion of innovations, social movements, and the like, but deal with change and structure in a more general sense. Our eventual goal in middle-range analysis is the development of an integrated, interrelated series of concepts that are linked in a set of general theories.

What is Social Change?

We define *social change* as the process by which alteration occurs in the structure and function of a social system.[3] Change is seen as a process, not as a state. Because of its process nature, social change is without beginning or end, continuous, and flowing through time. For analytical purposes, we often dissect social change as if the process could be temporarily and heuristically stopped, and we follow this convenience in our present inquiry.

Communication is the process by which messages are transferred from a source to a receiver. The main elements in any human communication process are source, channel, message, and receiver,[4] which are combined with an intent to bring about certain desired effects of communication. These effects are changes in human behavior; they are social changes if they occur in the structure or function of a social system. Thus communication flows are inherent in social change, although the two concepts of communication and change are not synonymous.

At the heart of all social change is an *innovation,* defined as an idea, practice, or object perceived as new by an individual. As far as human behavior is concerned, it matters little whether a new idea is objectively new, measured by the lapse in months or years since its discovery or first use. An individual's reaction to an innovation is determined by his perception of its newness, which affects his feelings of its riskiness, his desire for further information about it, and his judgment whether to adopt or reject it.

Diffusion is the process by which innovations spread to members of a social system. As such, diffusion is a type of communication in which the messages are new. Central elements in the diffusion of new ideas are the *innovation* which is communicated through certain *channels* over *time* among the members of a *social system* (Rogers with Shoemaker, 1971).

Early research on the diffusion of innovations was conducted by sociologists in the 1940s on the spread of agricultural innovations (such as hybrid seed corn) in the Midwestern United States. By the early 1960s, a synthetic paradigm of diffusion was formulated which has since been called the "classical diffusion model." [5] It specified:

1. The stages in the innovation-decision process, and the relative importance of various communication channels at each stage.

2. The perceived characteristics of innovations which affect their rate of adoption.

3. The behavior and characteristics of relatively earlier and later adopters.

4. The role of opinion leaders in diffusing innovations.

5. Factors in the relative success of change agents.

Social Structure and Diffusion

Diffusion does not occur in a vacuum; the actors involved in the spread of an innovation are members of a social system. A *social system* is a collectivity of units engaged in joint problem solving with respect to a common goal. To the extent that the units in a system are differentiated from each other, structure exists in the system. Such differentiation may be on the basis of social status, power, or other variables. The arrangement of statuses or positions in a system, such as in hierarchical levels, is one aspect of social structure. Most formal organizations have well-developed social structures, but even an informal group usually has differential degrees of participation and power.

Whereas diffusion scholars have generally emphasized the importance of the system in which that process occurs, other communication researchers and theorists have generally ignored the structural influences and determinants of communication effects. Perusal of communication research literature, at least prior to the mid-1960s, would almost lead one to assume that social structure did not affect human communication. For example, communication theorists who postulated the S-M-C-R and similar models did not accord much importance to the nature of the social relationships of source and receiver, or to point out that both had to be members of a common system. Perhaps this shortcoming arose because early communication scientists sprang mainly from psychological backgrounds and emphasized intraindividual aspects of human communication in their choice of concepts, units of analysis, and paradigms. Only when communication science attracted individuals with theoretical orientations in social sciences that featured structural variables [6] did systemic and structural aspects of communication gain their due. The belated convergence in the 1960s of sociologists studying diffusion with social psychologists analyzing persuasion and mass communication, led to the current intellectual focus on structure and change in communication research. As Katz (1960) pointed out: "It is unthinkable to study diffusion without some knowledge of the social structures in which potential adopters are located as it is to study blood circulation without adequate knowledge of veins and arteries."

A system's social structure affects the diffusion of innovations, and vice versa. We specify this interrelationship in the propositions that follow.

Proposition 1. Social structure acts to impede or to facilitate the rate of diffusion and adoption of new ideas through system effects. The norms, social statuses, hierarchy, and so on, of a social system influence the behavior of individual members of that system. *System effects* are the influences of the system's social structure on the behavior of the system's members.[7]

Although system effects have been fully recognized in diffusion research only in recent years, several investigations point out their importance. Van den Ban (1960) studied the system effects of modern and traditional norms[8] (in Wisconsin townships) on farmers' innovativeness. The township norms were an even stronger influence on farmers' decisions to adopt new ideas than were such individual characteristics as the farmers' education and wealth. A farmer with high education and wealth, residing in a township with traditional norms, was less likely to adopt innovations than a farmer with low education and wealth living in a system with modern norms.

A somewhat parallel investigation in 26 Filipino villages by Qadir (1966) showed that in modern systems, even individuals lacking much education, mass media exposure, or modern attitudes acted in an innovative manner. Companion investigations in India (Saxena, 1968) and in Nigeria (Davis, 1968) disclosed that system (village) variables explained a portion of the variance in individual (peasant) innovativeness that was not also explained by individual variables like literacy, mass media exposure, and the like.

These inquiries, and others like them, show that such structural aspects of a system as its norms have an important influence on changes in individual behavior. This is not a particularly surprising conclusion: If a rat doesn't like a maze, he cannot do much about it. So one strategy for speeding the rate of diffusion is to restructure the social system.

We see one illustration of this approach in most family planning campaigns in developing countries. Before the 1960s, there was a strong desire for relatively large-sized families of four or five children, a value vestige from the days prior to the demographic transition. Before the successful introduction of family planning methods like the IUD, the pill, or sterilization, a small-family norm must be created. Otherwise, fertile couples become knowledgeable about contraceptive ideas but remain opposed to their use. Hence massive investments are frequently made in communication campaigns in developing nations to preach the advantages of a family of two or three children. Once this small-family norm is developed (i.e., once the existing norms on fertility have been restructured), the way is cleared for the widespread adoption of family-planning ideas. And when norms on family size are not altered before promoting specific family planning methods, a "KAP-gap" often ensues, in which there is a high level of knowledge of such methods, but low levels of practice.

For example, in India today, national surveys show that about 75 to 80% of the fertile couples know about contraceptive methods, but only 12 to 15% have adopted them. The small-family norm is not yet widely accepted because such an alteration in the social structure of Indian society is intertwined with such other norms as the role of children in caring for parents in old age and the importance of a son in his father's funeral ceremony. But until the relevant aspect of the structure (the small-family norm) is adopted, the widespread diffusion and adoption of family planning techniques will not be successful.

In studying a social problem like poverty, social scientists have often ignored structural variables: "We have studied poverty as an individual symptom rather than as a societal phenomenon" (Copp, 1970). Thus researchers and policy makers in the United States assumed that the purpose of War on Poverty programs was "to change people in the lowest ranks, rather than to change the basic mechanics of the ranking system." Possible solutions to the poverty problem consist not of eliminating or moving up those individuals who are at the bottom of the stratification system, but of changing the stratification system. "Only very recently have some students of the poor come to see that it is the social structure, not the poor as individuals, that needs change. It is incomplete, for instance, to say that the poor lack knowledge when the system does not make information available to them" (Dervin, 1971, p. xiii).

Economists, as well as sociologists, have oversimplified the problem of poverty; for instance, they have almost completely neglected the structural factors that determine the nature of income distribution in the U.S. economy, as Copp (1970), Michelson (1970), Piore (1970), and Schultz (1970) pointed out. Of course, it is seemingly much easier to alter individual poverty behavior than to change societal mechanisms for income distribution, the structural bases for information flows, and the nature of the stratification system. But such individual change is largely futile, and may only lead to heightened frustration of those who are encouraged to struggle against the social structure.

A further example of the restructuring approach to diffusion and change is provided by *bürolandschaft,* a movement begun in Germany and Sweden, and now introduced in the United States as "office landscaping." The physical structure of an office, school, or factory (walls, corridors, and floors) reflects its organizational structure, which acts to chan-nel its communication flows and hence its patterns of change. Over a period of time, an organization's physical structure acts to stabilize its so-cial structure, and to prevent appropriate change.

So the office landscaping approach does away with most physical structures in an office; all desks are arranged (ideally) on a large, flat plane, separated only by small planters, low file cabinets, and the like. Communication flow audits are run from time to time to suggest rear-rangements in the organizational structure, which are easily effected by moving desks and other office furniture. The central assumption of the *bürolandschaft* approach is that (usually) physical structure→social struc-ture→communication behavior in an organization. By keeping the physical structure more flexible, communication behavior→social structure→physical structure.

Proposition 2. Diffusion can change the social structure of a social sys-tem. Some new ideas are restructuring innovations in that they change the structure of the social system itself. Illustrations are the initiation of a marketing research department in a business firm or the decentralization of authority in an organization, or the addition of student representation on a university council. Such restructuring may affect the rate of future innovation diffusion within the system, since the structure also affects dif-fusion (Proposition 1).

Those of greatest power and status in a system, the "power elite," serve as gatekeepers [9] in controlling the flow of innovations into a system from external sources. Such elites naturally tend to favor functioning in-novations, which do not threaten to disturb the status quo of the system's social structure, rather than restructuring innovations. An illustration is provided by the oligarchic leaders of Latin American nations who pro-mote technological innovations in agriculture and industry but oppose restructuring innovations in land reform and in overhauling the tax sys-tem. Often, however, the ostensibly functioning innovations have a re-structuring effect on the system. For instance, chemical fertilizer has been imported into Colombia to raise crop production. One long-range effect is increased labor efficiency in agriculture, rural migration to urban slums, and a shift in political power to more liberal parties, and of reli-gious affiliation to Protestant sects. None of these second-generation con-sequences were anticipated by the power elites of Colombia, who are gen-erally political conservatives and devout Roman Catholics.

So while Proposition 2 is most appropriate for restructuring innovations, it may also characterize many functioning innovations that are actually restructuring in the long range.[10] We next summarize our discussion about elites and the two types of innovations.

Proposition 3. *Power elites act as gatekeepers to prevent restructuring innovations from entering a social system, while favoring functioning innovations that do not immediately threaten to change the system's structure.*

Social structure and change are interrelated in yet another way: Structure acts to determine the nature of an innovation's consequences. The functioning innovations that power elites allow to enter a system are channeled within the system so that their consequences accrue disproportionately to certain individuals. A recent example is the so-called Green Revolution in India, Pakistan, and other Asian countries. The Green Revolution is the sudden, dramatic increase in grain yields brought about by the adoption of improved crop varieties, chemical fertilizers, pesticides, and mechanization. When the new "miracle" wheat seeds from Mexico were introduced in India and Pakistan, the limited supplies were given to large, progressive farmers. Hence the spectacular consequences of the Green Revolution were mostly reaped by already rich agricultural elites (Rogers et al., 1970).

The structure determined the innovation's consequences in yet another way. The landowners want the full benefits from increased yields, so they squeeze tenants to become sharecroppers and pressure them to become landless workers. "Farm mechanization is as irreversible as the Green Revolution which fathered it" (Ladejinsky, 1970); the net result is an estimated 35 to 40 million landless laborers, who will migrate in search of already scarce nonfarm employment.

The Green Revolution's unequal consequences have created widespread frustration among peasants in India, leading to violence in some areas. "According to the [Indian] Ministry of Foreign Affairs, in the first nine months of [1969], 346 incidents of forcible occupation of land (totalling 100,000 to 300,000 acres) with many murdered and injured have taken place in West Bengal alone" (Ladejinsky, 1970). The government of India seems deeply disturbed by the land seizure movement and may be thus motivated to deal directly with one of its main causes, the unequal consequences of the Green Revolution. In fact, a Small Farmers Development Agency was created in 1970 to aid the peasant with credit and technical advice.

It is not the new technology per se that is the main source of rising discontent. The improved seeds and fertilizer *could* provide higher yields on small farms as well as large acreages. What the high-yielding varieties have done is bring to the forefront the inherent inequalities in the rural institutional structure. The Green Revolution's "unfair" consequences stem from the elitist selectivity of credit availability, from the homophilous tendencies of change agents to contact clients much like themselves,[11] and from the concentration of land and power in few hands. From these illustrations, and other data,[12] we draw Proposition 4.

Proposition 4. *A system's social structure helps determine the nature and distribution of an innovation's consequences.*

Bottom-up Change

Most past research on social change studied a particular type of change —that promoted or at least favored by power elites in a system. The process of top-down change is quite different from that occurring for bottom-up change. And our understanding of bottom-up change is not aided much by most past investigations, which dealt only with elite-initiated change. Perhaps one partial exception is work on the social psychology of social movements, which has seldom received much financial sponsorship, perhaps because of the spontaneous nature of the movements, and, of necessity, of the research on them. We shall draw on this research on social movements in the present section when we discuss bottom-up change.

Social science is itself part of the process of social life that it studies. So the social structure affects social science also. The choice of research topics, for instance, is directly affected by the availability of funds. And one could hardly expect the research topics for which sponsorship exists to be identical to those topics that are not considered worthwhile by sponsors. Because social science research sponsors predominantly tend to represent government, large businesses, and others in elitist positions, we understand much more about top-down than we do about bottom-up change.[13] It is simply more valuable for elites to understand top-down change.

For example, most of the past research on the diffusion of innovations has concentrated on marginal innovations that do not seriously challenge the power structure of the systems investigated. Further, most such research has been limited in that it deals with optional innovation-decisions by individuals, rather than with collective or authority innovation-decisions (in which the system's structure plays a more important role). Hence the uses to which diffusion research has been put tend to help maintain existing structures, rather than leading to real transformations of such structures.

As a result, the elites have usually been studied as the *sources* of innovations, rather than as the *targets* of change. The respondents in most social science investigations represent the "common man," who is studied for the benefit of those in power. They are the planners and leaders of most programs of planned change; the poor are the audience. "Most of the talking has usually been done by the upper level; the people of the lower [class] sit by quietly, even sullenly, often without listening" (Gans, 1962; p. 2).

Proposition 5. *Top-down change in a system, which is initiated by the power elites, is more likely to succeed than is bottom-up change.*[14] The power structure of a system is a force toward the success of top-down change, whereas it works against bottom-up change.

Another basic reason for Generalization 5 is that bottom-up change usually involves a greater degree of conflict, in that restructuring change poses a threat to authority. Most social sciences seem to have implicitly assumed that a state of nonconflict is prefereable to one of conflict. For example, economists prefer models of "balanced growth," anthropologists criticize change programs that disturb the existing structure, sociologists concentrate on studies of top-down change, and political scientists imply that political conflict is inherently undesirable and disruptive. Only in recent years have the implicit orientations of these social sciences shifted so as to acknowledge that, in many circumstances, conflict *may* be functional, especially if the actors manage it in certain ways.[15] In fact, any change probably involves at least some degree of conflict; in an extreme form, such conflict may be so great as to destroy the equilibrium of the system.

Proposition 6. *Bottom-up change involves a greater degree of conflict than top-down change.* Most systems are structured so as to expect change to be initiated by the elites. When, instead, such change is initiated by nonelites, the nature of power is threatened and conflict frequently ensues.

For instance, most organizations are designed for stability, not for change. Most principles of management and administration implicitly assume that the role of an executive is mainly that of managing stability. Standardized procedures are established to ensure equal treatment of employees and the public. But once such standards are routinized, they are difficult to alter, even when the organization's external environment has changed, necessitating an appropriate change in the system's structure. In fact, there is usually a lag between the environmental change and the corresponding response by the organization. One reason is because the organization's power centers are so far removed from direct contact with the operational level, which deals with the environment.[16]

An illustration is provided by government agencies in many developing nations. Ministries were typically established by former colonial rulers in order to facilitate law and order. Such a stability operation, however, is inconsistent with another, stronger demand upon such organizations: To become change agencies, seeking to effect changes in the public's behavior in agriculture, family planning, health, and so forth. The organizational structure that was created in the colonial era is not very satisfactory today for a development agency. Under these circumstances, how does change ever occur in a social system, especially from the bottom? One important way is through *crisis*, a situation that is perceived to be so threatening that the future of the system is at stake.[17] When a crisis occurs, the previous social structure is considered at least partially inadequate by the participants, and so they are particularly open to consider major changes in the existing structure.

Proposition 7. *Bottom-up change is more likely to be successful at times of perceived crises in a system.*

It is just such perceived crises that spark the initiation of most social movements. The crisis may be an economic depression, a political or military setback, a competitor's breakthrough, or a status threat. *Social movements* are collectivities of individuals seeking to effect bottom-up change. In the early stages of a movement, it is usually headed by a charismatic leader. But as the movement is successful in accomplishing its original goals (of protesting against the existing social order), the movement usually must become an organization. Its original spontaneity of structure is replaced by formalization, bureaucratization, and an orientation to long-run survival. Indicators of this institutionalization are when the movement is named, selects titled officers, develops a treasury, hires salaried employees, and obtains the use of physical facilities. Although social movements are initiated as a protest against the establishment, a successful movement usually becomes part of a new establishment. Thus an antistructure force for change may become structured and represent the target for a future social movement.

A perceived crisis is not the only important prerequisite for bottom-up change; so is the presence of a charismatic leader.[18] In fact, the leader may "create" the crisis, as Gandhi seems to have occasionally done in British India (Erickson, 1969). The influence of the charismatic leader's personality is so great that it partially overcomes the inertia of the system's structure.

Proposition 8. *Bottom-up change is more likely to be successful when a social movement is headed by a charismatic leader.* In fact, without a charismatic leader, most social movements may die early or else not even be launched. The strong force of a charismatic personality may enable the attempt at bottom-up change to overcome the inertia of the social structure.

Once bottom-up change is successful, and the social movement becomes an organization, the charismatic leader becomes potentially dangerous surplus baggage. During the process of institutionalization of the social movement, the need for a charismatic leader decreases and the demand for a more bureaucratic leader arises. In other words, the social structure of the system again becomes more functional for the system than is the charismatic leader's personality. And so a routinization of charisma occurs; either the charismatic leader becomes more bureaucratic in his style, or he is replaced by a new, more administratively adept executive. So the appropriateness of a charismatic leader fades with the success of his efforts for change.

Proposition 9. *The role of the charismatic leader in a social movement decreases as the movement becomes institutionalized into a more highly structured organization.* This generalization implies that, for a system to have permanence, it must have at least a certain degree of structure. But such structure tends to stabilize the organization in its former nature, and to impede appropriate change. Thus we return full circle to Proposition 1.

Summary

In this chapter, we explored some of the interrelationships between social structure and social change. We drew examples and evidence from social science research on the diffusion of ideas, social movements, and several other related fields to support nine middle-range propositions:

1. Social structure acts to impede or to facilitate the rate of diffusion and adoption of new ideas through system effects.
2. Diffusion can change the social structure of a social system.
3. Power elites act as gatekeepers to prevent restructuring innovations from entering a social system, while favoring functioning innovations that do not immediately threaten to change the system's structure.
4. A system's social structure helps determine the nature and distribution of an innovation's consequences.

5. Top-down change in a system, which is initiated by the power elites, is more likely to succeed than is bottom-up change.

6. Bottom-up change involves a greater degree of conflict than top-down change.

7. Bottom-up change is more likely to be successful at times of perceived crisis in a system.

8. Bottom-up change is more likely to be successful when a social movement is headed by a charismatic leader.

9. The role of the charismatic leader in a social movement decreases as the movement becomes institutionalized into a more highly structured organization.

Notes

1. This chapter is a revision of Rogers (1971).

2. We take our notion of middle-range analysis from Merton (1957, p. 9), who called attention to the need for bridging the gap between the grand theorists and raw empiricists with "theories of the middle range," and who postulated relationships which are testable and which deal only with a rather limited and specific type of behavior.

3. This definition of social change, and certain notions in the present section, are based on Rogers with Svenning (1969, pp. 3–8) and Rogers and Shoemaker (1971).

4. These elements are included in Berlo's (1960) S-M-C-R model of human communication.

5. The details of this classical diffusion model are described by Rogers (1962).

6. Sociologists have probably been more interested than any other social scientists in structural variables: "Sociologists . . . have been far more concerned with structures than with processes . . ." (Lauer, 1971).

7. Systems effects have also been synonymously referred to as compositional effects, contextual effects, and structural effects by various authors.

8. *Norms* are the established behavior patterns for the members of a social system. They define a range of tolerable behavior and serve as a guide for the system's members.

9. *Gatekeepers* are the individuals who control the flow of messages in a channel. An example is the boss's secretary, who determines which memos from his subordinates reach him.

10. General evidence for the long-range restructuring consequences of short-range functioning innovations is provided by Nie et al. (1969a; 1969b), who utilize the Almond-Verba five-nation data to show that changes in economic development (i.e., functioning innovations) lead to such changes in social structure as an enlarged middle class, increased organizational complexity, and wider political participation.

11. *Homophily* is the degree to which two or more individuals who interact are alike in social status, attitudes, and the like. *Heterophily* is communication between two or more individuals who are dissimilar. Most communication flows occur between individuals who are homophilous; thus we see again that structure affects (and channels) communication (Rogers and Bhowmik, 1971). One of the most distinctive aspects of the diffusion of innovations is that the source and the receiver are usually quite heterophilous. A university graduate change agent, for instance, is much more technically competent than his peasant clients. This heterophily gap often leads to ineffective communication; the two do not speak the same language or share similar meanings for the message-symbols that are employed.

12. These are summarized by Rogers with Shoemaker (1971) in their Chapter 11.

13. Further, and for some of the same reasons, social scientists have, at least until fairly recent times, been much more interested in stability than in change: "A considerable amount of sociological thinking has viewed change as in some sense a violation of the normal" (Lauer, 1971).

14. To the extent that this proposition is true, we see another reason why scientists concentrate on top-down change; it is simply much more frequent than bottom-up change. Applied anthropologists, perhaps more than other social scientists, have investigated attempts to change peasants, many of which are unsuccessful. However, even these case studies of change that failed are analyzed more for the benefit of the elite sources than for that of the peasant receivers. Social science has relatively little to say to the nonelite receiver who wants to know how to resist change.

15. In a parallel sense, diffusion scientists have begun to question their implicit assumption of the inherent goodness of all change, especially in very recent years (Rogers and Shoemaker, 1971).

16. Those at the top of an organization live in a "cocoon of abstraction" without much unfiltered contact with the operational level, says Gardner (1963).

17. The role of crisis in initiating organization change is discussed by Greiner (1970).

18. A *charismatic leader* is one who exerts his influence by a special gift, a particular ability to appeal to the emotions of his followers.

PART TWO

BASIC ELEMENTS IN THE
CHANGE PROCESS: A MICRO VIEW

The papers in this part have in common a very micro view of social change. Lin and Zaltman examine in detail the change object which is at the core of social change, Watson considers various forces that work against adoption of the change object, and Rogers considers a very specific idea for overcoming resistance. Morrison presents a psychological theory concerning the motivation of groups for embracing the change object and implicitly suggests another tactic for overcoming resistance to change, the induction of feelings of relative deprivation with regard to the change object. These chapters are somewhat more micro oriented than the others in this book, but like the others, they retain some macro perspectives.

At the core of social change lies a present condition that did not characterize a social system at any prior time. The condition may involve more or less of something previously present or may involve something totally unique. This something or condition—the innovation—is responsible for the alteration in the structure and/or functioning of a social system which allows us to pronounce an instance of social change as having occurred. An innovation is any idea, practice, or material artifact perceived to be new by the relevant unit of adoption. The various dimensions of innovations are the concern of the chapter by Nan Lin and Gerald Zaltman, "Dimensions of Innovations." Lin and Zaltman provide a comprehensive view of the process of change but then concentrate on that aspect which seems to them most important, innovations. Unlike some writers on the subject, they examine innovations not so much to determine what kinds of conditions and people produce the innovation, but rather to locate those dimensions that seem likely to affect their acceptance. For example, they cite research showing that the tendency to adopt innovation relates to communicability of the innovation, its compatibility with other practices, its publicness, and the reversibility of its effects. None of these could be known without some knowledge of both the innovation and the group that perceived it as a new item for possible adoption. Of particular interest is their reference to the consequences of certain innovations for the group's readiness to accept subsequent innovations. The paper concludes with a discussion of important theoretical considerations and a number of empirical questions affecting social action. The reader is urged to address himself to some of these questions.

It is understandable that most studies of change, particularly planned change, focus on forces and processes serving to further change. The intervention literature, for example, is oriented this way—planners prefer to emphasize the successes rather than their failures, the diffusion tradition tends to highlight successful rather than unsuccessful innovations, and we find in the general literature not theories of social resistance or status quo maintenance but theories of social change. Perhaps our value orientations toward success and change are a partial cause of these general orientations. None of this would be curious if it were not for the fact that in any social sector most efforts to induce change fail. Yet it is important to study failure. We study instances where change does come about in hope of learning formulas that can be employed to produce change later on. It is similarly valuable to study instances of unsuccessful change efforts in order to learn what not to do. Goodwin Watson, in his chapter "Resistance to Change," identifies many sources of resistance to which the change agent should be sensitive. Watson divides his discussion into two basic parts: he first focuses on forces of resistance as they operate within the individual personality and then looks at those forces rooted in the social system. He recognizes the artificialness of this separation. Watson writes, "In reality, the forces of the social system operate within the individuals and those attributed to separate personalities combine to constitute systemic forces. The two work as one." Here again, then, is an acknowledgment of the necessity of looking at both micro and macro phenomena jointly when studying a given problem, in this case resistance to change. Watson concludes his chapter with serveral very useful propositions about reducing resistance. In these concise propositions he sketches the manner in which he would intertwine individual and social factors.

In a later chapter Charles Kiesler stresses the need for true experiments to evaluate research involving social change programs as a means of providing policy guidelines. A chapter by Alan Guskin and Mark Chesler in effect urges that we be sensitive to and explicit about partisan values held by researchers, which color the character of their problem diagnosis and research. This is a particularly important message for scholars engaged in evaluative social research.

It is difficult to find a context of research where the messages of these two chapters is more appropriate than in the context of family planning. Everett Rogers, in his chapter "Effects of Incentives on the Diffusion of Innovation: The Case of Family Planning in Asia," notes that "No other field of behavioral research has utilized field experiments so extensively to formulate and test alternative public policies for social change as has family planning." Within the family planning area there is probably no issue more controversial—and hence no more deserving of careful evaluation and open acknowledgment of partisan diagnosis—than the issue of incentives. Generally speaking, incentives are payments of cash or kind that are given to an individual or group to encourage some overt behavioral change. Rogers discusses different types of incentives and their consequences. He presents five significant generalizations about the effects of incentives and calls for an integrated series of well-designed true field experiments to test various types of incentives. Throughout the paper indications are given of undesirable consequences that may stem from the use of incentives. This dictates caution in social experimentation and supports Rogers' argument for careful evaluation.

There is one very intriguing finding which shows dramatically how change directed at individuals can accumulate and manifest itself in the form of significant changes in social structure. It was observed that one effect of incentives is a reversal of who adopts first in a social situation. In nonincentive-motivated change programs there is a tendency for the elite to be more innovative and thus become still more of an elite (through a process described in this chapter), whereas in incentive-motivated change programs the nonelite tend to be most innovative and to that extent may become somewhat less disadvantaged relative to the elite, with a corresponding change in the social structure. Rogers is properly cautious in presenting these ideas and is wary about generalizing to other contexts. Still, the reader will find it difficult not to conjecture beyond this context; the implications of Rogers' findings for the ethics and strategies of diffusion are profound.

Without really labeling it as such, Morrison, in his chapter "Some Notes Toward Theory on Relative Deprivation, Social Movements, and Social Change," develops a social-psychological theory of social movements and social change and presents what could be the psychological mechanism of some of the general change processes discussed by Rogers in his chapter on social structure. In this regard, the reader is directed to Morrison's treatment of the structural conditions for the emergence of social movements. This describes some of the possible dynamics involved in "bottom-up" change. In general, Morrison concerns himself with the interelationship between aspiration toward goals and the probability of blockage in attainment of the desired goal. In cases where limited resources must be utilized for the achievement of group objectives frustration is an increasing function of the pervasiveness and intensity of aspiration. Thus to explain change, one must know not only about the aspiration level of individuals or about the resources available in the environment, but the coordination, over time, of these two elements in relation to each other.

Consider for a moment Morrison's summary statement that "social movements create social change, but they are also created by social changes that take away opportunities or create expectations faster than opportunities for reaching the expectations are created, resulting in relative deprivation." The reader might ask himself—with regard to a given social problem—which particular strategy or particular blend of strategies represented by the different theories of planned change discussed in the chapter by Coleman he would choose to better match opportunities and expectations. The problem may be seen as one of resource allocation. It is also an intriguing strategy question as to whether or when it would be an appropriate strategy to dampen expectations as opposed to creating new opportunities. This becomes a relevant question when resources are relatively fixed or immobile or scarce. As Westley indicated in his essay, some societies alter the want/get ratio by stimulating the want while others adjust the ratio to a satisfactory level by decreasing aspirations to "get."

Nan Lin

Department of Sociology
State University of New York at Albany

Gerald Zaltman

Graduate School of Management
Northwestern University

DIMENSIONS OF INNOVATIONS

The current tempo of social change in most areas of the world is unparalleled in history. In many societies this change is taking place exponentially and it is well at the outset of this paper to define social change and mention some of its elements. A good working definition of social change is provided by Rogers (1969, p. 3): social change is "the process by which alteration occurs in the structure and function of a social system. . . . The structure of a social system is provided by the various individual and group statuses of which it is composed. The functioning element within this structure of status is a role, or the actual behavior of the individual in a given status."

However, even this definition becomes vague as the structure and function or process of a social system are further defined. As Parsons (1961) points out, the structure consists of units and patterned relations (reciprocal interactions) among units; the process is of two types: (1) those that maintain the stability of a system both internally and in its exchange with the environment; and (2) those that alter the structure and the more elementary processes to lead the system to a new and different state. Cancian (1960) continues to specify that change may occur either within the system or of the system. A change within the system occurs when the system, in effect, undergoes differential processes that affect the structural units and patterns but do not affect the basic goals or needs of

93

the system. A change of a system, according to Cancian, occurs when the basic goals and needs of the system undergo change.

There are many other commentaries on social change. In Figure 1 we have attempted to outline or distill some of the more salient dimensions of the social change process as discussed by Rogers, Parsons, Cancian, Barnett, Hagen, and other scholars concerned with social change. The paradigm, necessarily oversimplified as presented here, states that there exists a set of wants which together with some impetus or stimulus provides an incentive to innovate. This incentive triggers creative cognitive processes (so called because the thinking mechanism acts upon new data) in which for the first time there is an interaction between the attributes of the innovation itself and certain attributes of the unit of adoption, such as size, personality, or social structure. The process of innovation is the next element. It involves a process of empathy or identification. At this point the individual imagines himself to be using the innovation; he projects himself psychologically into a situation in which he has adopted the innovation and assesses the probable experience. Depending on the nature of innovation is a process of persuasion. If, as a result of the innovative process, the individual decides to commit himself to the innovation on a more or less permanent basis, then adoption is said to occur.

The adoption of an innovation by an individual or other relevant unit of adoption such as family (Grambois, 1964), city (Crain, 1966), or state (Walker, 1969), represents one-half of the dynamic core of social change. It is the fruition of a decision-making process often influenced by deliberate plans or strategies made by others (change agents), affected by personality and creative ability, basic wants, and so forth. The diffusion process is the other half of the dynamic core of social change. It is a phenomenon that emerges (Blau, 1964), from the adoption of an innovation by potential adopter units and is usually a partial result of interaction among these units. Thus it is something more than the simple summation of many individual adoption decisions. It involves the additional and emergent phenomenon of patterned interaction among adopter and potential adopter units. Often the result of the adoption and diffusion processes is a change in the structure and/or function of the relevant social system. Depending on the nature of the original impetus to change, the resulting social change may be called immanent social change (when such change results from voluntary behavior) (Rogers and Shoemaker, 1971) or contact social change (when such change results from some organized effort).

The basic dynamic core of social change, the adoption and diffusion processes, evolves around an innovation. It can be argued (e.g., Barnett, 1953) that the innovation is the basis of all personality, social, and cul-

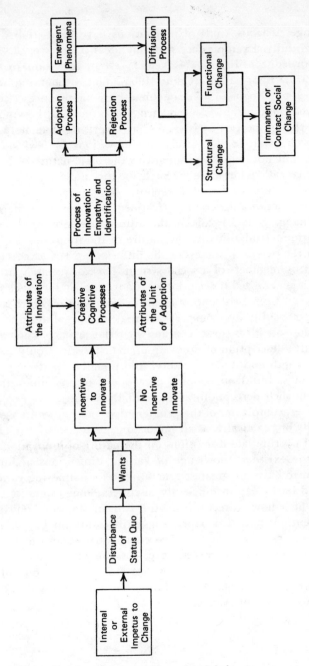

Figure 1. Summary paradigm of social change.

tural change. Various kinds of innovations have been studied carefully and thoughtfully. Examples are scientific ideas (Garvey et al., 1970), scientific knowledge utilization (Havelock, 1969), television in education (Evans, 1970), fluoridation (Crain, 1966), family planning techniques (Berelson, 1967; Bogue, 1967), and new farming practices (Lionberger, 1960). Given the central and permanent importance of the innovation in the social change process, it is somewhat surprising that more attention has not been given to the nature of innovations. A few authors have given some but not extensive thought to the basic nature of innovations and all have called for more research on this topic (Rogers and Shoemaker, 1971; Fliegel and Kivlin, 1966b).

This neglect of a generalized treatment of innovation characteristics in social change generally and in the diffusion research tradition specifically is curious. Undoubtedly, the nature of the innovations contributes directly to the extent of success of the diffusion, or the acceptance of the innovation by members of a social system. Lack of research attention focusing on a generalized description of innovation characteristics seems to have stemmed from two conceptual problems, both of which are significant and not readily overcome. First, the definition of an innovation includes almost all ideas, practices, and material artifacts known to man; an exhaustive description of innovation characteristics would create a list of infinite length and dimensionality. Additionally, the description of innovations must build on people's perceptions of any innovations. The variations of such perceptions are potentially almost infinite.

However, complexity of the problem does not reduce its significance, theoretically or practically, as an important research concern. This paper is intended to stimulate discussions on the nature of innovations by summarizing the existing knowledge of various dimensions of innovations that appear to have the greatest generality in encompassing various innovations and have been insufficiently discussed. Some topics for suggested research which flows directly from the current state of knowledge will also be mentioned in this paper, suggesting additional general dimensions of innovations, raising two theoretical issues about the nature of innovations in light of the preceding discussions and methodological advances, and discussing the relevance of research on innovation characteristics to social action programs. We will begin with a discussion of the definition of innovations.

The Innovation

The term "innovation" is usually found in one of three different contexts. In one context it is used synonymously with invention: it refers to a creative process whereby two or more existing concepts or entities are combined in some novel way to produce a configuration not previously known by the person involved. A person performing this type of activity is usually said to be innovative.

Innovation is also used to describe the process whereby an existing innovation becomes a part of an adopter's cognitive state and behavioral repertoire. This is a process of adoption and internalization (Lin et al., 1966; Reynolds and Zaltman, 1972). In the first case the individual can be innovative without adopting, whereas in the second case he can be innovative without being inventive. It is acknowledged, however, that one could argue that the adoption or internalization of an innovation might be viewed as an inventive activity since two previously unconnected constructs, the individual and the innovation, are combined in some novel way.

The third use of the term is to describe that idea, practice, or material artifact which has been invented or which is regarded as novel independently of its adoption or nonadoption. Note that the emphasis here is on description, whereas invention and adoption involve processes. This chapter focuses on the third notion presented, that is, on the description of relevant attributes and dimensions of innovations with little or no regard for inventive and adoption processes. The latter considerations are dealt with elsewhere in this book.

Barnett (1953) views an innovation broadly by emphasizing objectively measurable qualitative differences. According to Barnett, an innovation is "any thought, behavior or thing that is new because it is qualitatively different from existing forms." He goes on to emphasize the distinction between thought, behavior, and thing. "Strictly speaking, every innovation is an idea, or a constellation of ideas; but some innovations by their nature must remain mental organizations only, whereas others may be given overt and tangible expression" (p. 7).

Similarly, Hagen (1962, p. 87) has commented that there is no such thing as innovation in the abstract. It is always in some specific field, involving some specific materials or concepts, or some relationships to other persons. He defines an innovation as an organization of reality into relationships embodying new mental or aesthetic concepts with the new relationships being an improvement over the old.

The Federal Trade Commission has emphasized Barnett's definition in an advisory opinion in stating that a consumer or industrial product can be called "new" only when it is "either entirely new or has been changed in a functionally significant and substantial respect" (Federal Trade Commission, 1967). Others have defined as innovations only those ideas, products, or services that have not yet secured more than 10% acceptance within the relevant social system (Bell, 1963). Robertson (1971) has suggested that the critical factor in defining an item as an innovation should be its effect upon established patterns of consumption or behavior. He suggests three possible patterns of effect. An innovation which has little disruptive impact on behavior patterns is called a *continuous innovation;* fluoride toothpaste is an example. In this case the item constitutes only slight alteration of a current practice or product. Next are *dynamically continuous innovations,* such as electric toothbrushes, which have a moderate impact on behavior patterns. Finally there are *discontinuous innovations,* which involve the establishment of new behavior patterns. This generally entails the creation of previously unknown items. The preventive tooth decay pill may be an example of this type of innovation.

In this chapter we shall consider as an innovation *any idea, practice, or material artifact perceived to be new by the relevant unit of adoption.* The adopter unit may vary from a single individual to a city (Crain, 1966) or state legislature (Walker, 1969). This position is very similar to the stance taken by Rogers and Shoemaker (1971): "An innovation is an idea, practice, or object perceived as new by the individual. It matters little, as far as human behavior is concerned, whether or not an idea is 'objectively' new as measured by the lapse of time since its first use or discovery. . . . If the idea seems new and different to the individual, it is an innovation." Our definition differs from Rogers' primarily in allowing for the possibility that the unit of adoption may be larger than an individual. This in turn allows the possibility that not all members of a multimember unit of adoption may perceive the item as an innovation. The value of a definition emphasizing what the individual perceives is that it applies equally well to static and dynamic populations. For example, Bennet (1969) has recently distinguished between *innovativeness* (how soon a member of an original group adopts the item or innovation after its initial appearance) and *precocity* (the speed of acceptance of an item by an individual after his entry into a group in which an innovation already exists and may have been widely accepted). Other definitions do not apply very well in dynamic populations where precocity is an important factor.

One caveat to be added here concerning the use of the perception of the unit of adoption as a criterion for defining innovativeness is that perception varies according to the physiological state of the individual and according to the different contextual situations the adopter unit may be in. Perception may also vary over time according to the adoption process stage. For example, when a person has only limited knowledge of an item he may not perceive it as an innovation. As further information is accumulated and attitudes toward the object are formed or changed, the individual may develop a new perception in which the object is cast as an innovation. The reverse may also take place. An item initially perceived as new may over the course of the decision-making process lose its character of being significantly different. This can occur for at least two reasons. Upon closer inspection the potential adopter may conclude that the item is not so new after all. Additionally, as the decision process becomes protracted and the innovation gains acceptance and becomes a part of the social milieu, the individual through sheer familiarity with the item may cease to perceive it as new.

To sum up the discussion thus far, the important characteristic of an innovation is that instead of being an external object, it is the perception of a person or a social system which decides its newness. Thus a practice may be an innovation for one person or one system but not for another. The process by which an innovation is spread through communication channels to members of a social system over time is called *diffusion*. Similarly, certain innovations to be accepted by systems can spread across systems over time. When an innovation is diffused and adopted (either symbolically or behaviorally) by a sufficient number of the relevant units in a social system so as to register an impact (becoming an integrated part of the normative patterns in the system), it is said that a social change has occurred for the system under discussion.

Dimensions of Innovations: Existing Knowledge of Innovation Characteristics

There are many dimensions of innovations which are made implicit or explicit in literature. There are also several relevant dimensions that have received little if any attention. In this section various dimensions of innovations are presented and their importance noted. Although this list is extensive, it is not exhaustive. Furthermore, all attributes do not pertain to all possible innovations. Some characteristics are uniquely associated with particular innovations, whereas other characteristics are irrelevant. Indeed, as we shall note later, an important task for future research is to determine under what kinds of situations particular innovation attributes are likely to become salient.

We first discuss attributes of innovations that have been widely discussed in the literature (Rogers and Shoemaker, 1971; Fliegel and Kivlin, 1966). Table 1 presents a list of such discussions. The particular dimensions selected here are those that seem to have relevance for a wide array of innovations found in different contexts. It is important to add one caveat: Much of the existing "knowledge" rests more on discussion and speculation rather than on concrete evidence.

Table 1   Characteristics of Innovations Discussed in the Literature

Innovation Characteristics	*Source of Reporting*
Relative advantage; communicability; complexity, divisibility; compatibility	Rogers, 1962
Congruence	Brandner and Keal, 1964
Symbolic and functional compatibility	Thio, 1971; White, 1969; Klonglan and Coward, 1970
Slack innovation	
Continuous, dynamically continuous, and discontinuous innovations	Robertson, 1969
Original versus adapted innovations; product, component, process	Myers and Marquis, 1969
Terminality	Lin, 1970
Competitive versus noncompetitive	Allvine, 1968
Cost, regularity of reward, clarity of results, social approval, pervasiveness, mechanical attraction	Kivlin and Fliegel, 1968
Structural radicalness	
Publicness versus privateness	Olson, 1971
Alteration, perturbation, restructuring, value orientation	Chin, 1963
Absolute (new to organization and environment) versus relative innovation (new only to organization, not to environment)	Miller, 1971

Cost is one of the most obvious dimensions. One type of cost is *financial* in nature. This can be divided into initial cost and continuing cost. Initial financial cost, in a study by Fliegel and Kivlin, was found to have a positive partial correlation of +.43 with the adoption rate when controlling for 14 other attributes. Continuing cost and the adoption rate had a fourteenth-order partial correlation of −.24. One explanation is that there is a cost-quality relationship which states that the more expensive an innovation is, the higher its perceived quality. This would seem to apply primarily to durable industrial and consumer goods which are purchased infrequently and are supposed to have a long life. Thus the perceived extra cost of a particular durable good innovation is in a psychological sense and in an accounting sense prorated over a long period of time, which makes the incremental cost appear small.

Social cost is another form of expense. Fliegel and others (1968) found that social cost was an important factor in explaining the rate of adoption in a developing country ($r = +.46$, eleventh-order partial correlation), whereas it was not important in the United States (r between $+.13$ and $-.10$, eleventh-order partial correlation). Social cost may come in the form of ridicule, ostracism, or even exclusion or explusion from some relevant reference group. Social position within a group influences the degree to which such a cost may occur and how serious the individual may perceive this cost (Homans, 1961). The marginal member of a group may have little to lose by innovating and therefore even in the presence of considerable disapproval he may proceed to adopt an innovation. There is always the possibility that the decision might prove to be a wise one and he may gain stature as a consequence. A high-status member of a group may also adopt, again, even in the presence of potential or actual ridicule. The high-status person can do so because he will generally have an inventory of good will or social credit upon which he may draw and will suffer little if the innovation does not succeed.

A second dimension concerns the *returns to the investment*. This is of special significance among individuals who have little tolerance for situations where a deferral of gratification is necessary. This deferral of gratification varies according to culture and within cultures according to class, education, and income, achievement motivation, and cosmopolitanism. The more modern a society is (measured in part by the variables just cited), the more likely it is to allocate resources to projects with longer payoff periods. Furthermore, individuals having lower levels of education, achievement motivation, and income are less likely to adopt innovations having no immediate and substantial rewards (Rogers, 1969).

The *efficiency* of an innovation in terms of (1) time saving and (2) the avoidance of discomfort is also a potentially important factor. In fact, one of the most basic wants acting as a stimulus for change are relief and avoidance wants (Barnett, 1953), which represent the desire for nonexistent or not presently possessed means or goals and seem to appear in both industrial and consumer marketing contexts. Time-saving attributes appear to be important in labor-intensive industries, for example, in adoption decisions of moderately small but technically advanced adopters (Fliegel et al., 1968). The time factor and avoidance of discomfort factor are also important dimensions for innovations dealing with household operation and maintenance.

The *risk and uncertainty* associated with innovations is also an important factor, and we shall elaborate somewhat more extensively here than with other traits. The relevance of perceived risk varies across social sectors. For some, the consequence of a wrongly (out-of-fashion, poor quality, etc.) chosen wardrobe is much less severe than that of selecting the wrong physician or even that of a physician prescribing an inappropriate drug.

Becker (1970), in a study of public health officers, focused on attributes of innovations which emphasize or involve political risk. Among the attributes he considers important are the opportunity for opposition inherent in the proposed innovation and the risk it involves vis-à-vis the officials' reputation or position.

A situation where risk and uncertainty could be expected to be an important factor, but is not, is the choice of a physician (Feldman, 1966). There is evidence that people choose their physicians rather casually, and only rarely leave through dissatisfaction. What apparently happens is that people are drawn to believe that they are using the "right" doctor, while the objective situation plays only a minor role in their evaluation. The notion that standards of certification make almost all doctors highly capable, intertwined with the lack of ability to judge quality of treatment, leads to the casual, noncompetitive selection of physicians.

The communicability of an innovation exerts considerable influence on whether or not it is accepted. First, the ease and effectiveness with which the results of the innovation can be disseminated to others constitutes a major force in the diffusion process (Rogers, 1962). Linked with this is the clarity of results of an innovation. Often innovations are introduced into dynamic situations involving the operation of several factors, where there are no effective controls over those other factors. It then becomes difficult to ascribe or attribute to the innovation any changes that may occur after the innovation has been introduced. There is clearly a need for much more work on research techniques in such instances, although some recent advances have already been made (Campbell, 1969; Sonquest, 1967). There may also be obstacles (system-imposed or otherwise) to communications about innovations. Industry codes of ethics, for example, allow only wine and beer to be advertised through the broadcast media, shutting this channel off to new high-alcoholic-content beverages.

Other obstacles for innovation communication are cultural in nature. In some societies, for example, there are norms or customs against husbands and wives discussing family planning matters despite an eagerness on the part of both parties to implement the family planning concept (Stycos, 1955). This represents a breakdown in the interpersonal communications processes which, as we have noted, are often essential for the effective diffusion of innovations, at least in rural areas where the mass media have their lowest penetration. Thus processes of communication innate to the innovation (particularly the interaction of the mass media and interpersonal communications) are important.

Compatibility concerns the similarity of the innovation to an existing product which it may eventually supplement, complement, or replace (Rogers, 1962). This assumes that an innovation is perceived in a particular context and the perceived relationship between the innovation and other elements in that context influence the adoption and diffusion of the innovation. The *pervasiveness* or degree to which an innovation relates to and requires changes or adjustments on the part of other elements in the social situation influences the speed of adoption (Menzel, 1960; Linton, 1936; Barnett, 1953). The greater the pervasiveness of an innovation, the slower will be its acceptance.

The concept of compatibility as a salient attribute of innovations has been most thoroughly reviewed by Thio (1971), who traces its treatment from first use at a cultural level of analysis, to a social level, and most recently at socio-psychological level of analysis where attention has been given to its "goodness of fit" with such adopter characteristics as personality, emotional attitude, value orientation, previous innovative experience (Brandner and Keal, 1964), beliefs (Yeracaris, 1961), and education and income level (Graham, 1954). The notion of compatability is particularly tied to the psychosocial-cultural world of the potential adopter and, perhaps more than any other innovation attribute, must be considered in conjunction with that psychosocial world. Elaborating further, Thio adds two other (in addition to the cultural, social, and social psychological dimensions) types of adopter-innovation compatibility. Symbolic compatibility refers to the subjective perception of the potential adopter, that is, what the adopter-to-be sees in the innovation. Functional compatibility concerns what is functionally required of the potential adopter in order to make use of the innovation.

Brandner and Keal (1964) tested and found supporting evidence for the proposition that persons having an opportunity to evaluate an innovation (hybrid sorghums) as congruent with a previously favorably evaluated practice (hybrid corn) will accept the innovation more quickly than persons not having this opportunity. However, the more interesting finding was that where congruence was a factor it was so important that it seemed to supersede the significance of factors such as age, education, mobility, economic importance, and other factors normally associated with speed of adoption.

The *complexity* of the innovation clearly has a bearing on its acceptance. Generally, the more complex an innovation is in terms of its operation, the less rapid its acceptance will be. Complexity may become manifest on two levels: (1) the innovation may contain complex ideas; (2) the implementation of the innovation may be complex. We might hypothesize that an innovation that is easy to use but whose essential idea is complex is more likely to be adopted than an innovation that is difficult to use but whose essential idea or concept is readily understood.

The *perceived relative advantage* the innovation has over other al-

ternatives including current practice is important. Those things the innovation does that other alternatives do not do are its critical attributes.
The larger the number of critical attributes and the greater their magnitude, the more likely it is that the innovation will be adopted. The *visibility* or salience of the relative advantage is important. Obvious innovations are more likely to be adopted than are obscure innovations. This
suggests still another factor: The more amenable to *demonstration* the innovation is, the more visible its advantages will be and thus the more
likely it is to be adopted. Demonstration may be viewed in two ways.
First there is "use demonstration" or method demonstration, which consists of showing how the innovation is employed. Second there is "result
demonstration," intended to show the benefits of adopting a particular
innovation. Ideally it is desirable to be able to conduct both forms of
demonstration. Practically speaking, however, this is not often feasible,
especially when the innovation is an idea having no physical manifestation.

Perceived relative advantage has been considered by some (Knight,
1967) to be perceived radicalness. Little new is added to our knowledge
when only discussing performance radicalness, that is, the amount of
change in output that results from one innovation when compared with
other alternatives. However, another dimension of innovation radicalness
often overlooked (and suggested by Knight, 1967) is *structural radicalness*. Structural radicalness occurs when the unique qualities of an innovation bring about alterations in such basic structural elements as communication, authority, and reward systems.

Caution is suggested by one study of several characteristics of
innovations (divisibility, communicability, relative advantage, compatibility, complexity) introduced by Rogers (1962) and later presented to a
panel of educators who were asked to rate each of six widespread educational innovations by applying the five characteristics to the six innovations (Carlson, 1968). The result was little agreement among panel members in their ratings.[1] This suggests caution in utilizing the various
innovation characteristics indiscriminately in different contexts. Moreover, Ostlund (1969) found that product perception factors had greater
power in predicting innovativeness for the six new products he studied
than did all of several predispositional variables, including such frequently used concepts as venturesomeness, cosmopolitanism, and social integration, and demographic and socioeconomic variables including education, age, income, and occupational status. The product perception
factors studied and their relative order of (decreasing) importance were:
relative advantage, compatability, perceived risk, divisibility, complexity, and communicability.

The relevance of a particular attribute may depend upon the perspective from which it is viewed. A manufacturer may define the relevant aspects of an innovation in a way totally dissimilar to the consumer's description. The manufacturer may view a new product as a major labor-saving device and develop his promotional strategy accordingly. Consumers, however, may not perceive the time saved as significant and thus reject the new product; or they may adopt it for other reasons such as the desire for social approval, ease of operation, or low cost.

Myers and Marquis (1969, pp. 19–29), in a study of factors underlying industrial innovations in selected firms, identified a wide range of innovation characteristics. Their first approach was to classify innovations according to origin: Did it originate within the firm or did the firm adopt it? This relates to our earlier discussion of inventive and adoption processes. They found 77% of the innovations studied were originated within the firm. This particular classification factor—point of origin—is important, for it suggests a significant theoretical issue. The salient characteristics of an innovation as seen by the originator need not coincide with those perceived by an adopter or potential adopter. Furthermore, the characteristics of an innovation which are considered important before adoption may yield in perceived importance to other factors once the adoption is made and some time has passed. Thus the salient characteristics of innovation may vary according to whose vantage point it is being perceived from and may also vary over time within the viewpoint of any particular observer. Moreover, beyond the adopter-nonadopter dichotomy, the innovation may be viewed differently by different ideal-type categories, suggesting that it might be equally profitable to categorize individuals or multimember units of adoption on the basis of their perceptions of innovations as opposed to or as well as the time they require before adopting. Certainly in terms of planning social change it would be more fruitful to group individuals according to their perceptions of the innovation in question.

Meyers and Marquis also distinguished between new and modified items; a modified item was one that the firm was already producing but now changed. Modifications fell into five meaningful categories: improved aesthetics, increased utility, increased durability, increased efficiency of performance, and lowered production costs. Approximately two-thirds of the innovations studied were new items. "Almost one-half of the adopted innovations were modifications, compared with less than one-third of the original innovations" (Myers and Marquis, 1969, p. 20). The authors further distinguish between product, component, and process innovations.

New Concepts of Innovation Characteristics

Contributions concerning the characteristics of innovations so far have
come mainly from studies of agricultural, health, and educational innovations. Recent interests in the study of innovations in other areas such as
family planning, consumer products, political participation, and scientific
communication have unveiled other dimensions of innovations. We will
attempt to specify some of these new dimensions that seem to stimulate
both theoretical and practical interests.

Terminality is an important but relatively unstudied dimension of
many innovations. A terminal represents a specific point in time beyond
which the adoption of an innovation becomes less rewarding, useless, or
even impossible. Many innovations have intrinsic terminals. Mass immunization programs in rural areas of the underdeveloped world are an example. For many—if not most—of this population acceptance of inocula-
tions is an innovation. When an immunization program is launched—when
medical team visits rural communities and uses jet-gun injectors for mass
immunization—the adoption of the immunization or perhaps more accurately the implementation of the decision to use the service can occur only
while the team is in the community.

Many innovations have perceived terminals. Women's fashions have
almost annual terminals—last year's miniskirt when adopted this year
may indicate loss of the "value" ("in-fashion") of the innovation. There
may also be terminality in terms of adoption costs. Some innovations are
introduced free or at a reduced charge for a limited period when they
first become available. This is true of many consumer goods and services.
Participation in mass movements, an innovation for many individuals,
may also be terminal in nature. Either one did or did not join the March
on Washington in opposition to the Vietnam War. Terminality indeed
represents a pervasive perception held of many innovations.

Another consideration about terminality of innovations concerns the
frequency and spacing of terminals. In agriculture a new seed either is
tried during one planting season or must wait another year or half year
before the opportunity again develops to use the new seed. Similarly, a
new legislative bill must be acted upon during this session of the legislature or held until the next session (Walker, 1969). In some instances if it
is acted upon and rejected, it may require a longer minimum period determined by law before it can come up for adoption again. Some innovations have one or few terminals, whereas others have many. When an innovation has several terminals, but the spacing involves long periods of

time, it may be perceived as having one or few terminals. There is also a tendency on the part of innovation sources to promote adoption by presenting one or few terminal images of the innovation. The number and spacing of terminals may therefore affect the diffusion process drastically.

The degree to which and the ease with which the status quo ante can be reinstated is another factor having a positive relationship with the adoption of an innovation. This characteristic can be termed *reversibility*. Some evidence shows that when a number of alternative innovations are available, the more reversible ones are more likely to be adopted earlier (Taylor, 1970). The use of birth control pills can readily be stopped, frequently with no significant change in conditions as they existed before the use of the birth control pills. A vasectomy, a form of male sterilization, can also be reversed but requires a simple medical operation which is not certain to restore fertility. *Divisibility*, a dimension found in the existing literature, is related to reversibility. Divisibility concerns the ability to try or to implement the innovation on a limited basis. The more limited that basis is—the smaller the amount of resources committed—the more easily the preinnovation status quo can be reinstated.

Related to reversibility and divisibility is the degree of *commitment* required for successful use of the innovation. However, this dimension, in contrast to reversibility and divisibility, involves considerations of attitudinal and behavioral acceptance. Either of these two factors may precede the other. The most favorable condition for adoption and diffusion occurs when at least a partial behavioral change can precede attitudinal change. First, once a partial commitment has been made it is more likely to be followed by full commitment than if no prior partial commitment were obtained (Freedman and Frazer, 1968). Second, there is evidence even under conditions of involuntary behavioral change attitudes will soon become consistent with actual behavior. Furthermore, although it is desirable for the behavioral change to be voluntary, it need not be in order to gain acceptance.

Another attribute of innovations which has been little studied as an attribute per se concerns the *impact* of an innovation *upon interpersonal relationships* among adopters or between adopters and nonadopters. Certainly many studies have focused on the impact and consequences of an innovation upon individuals and groups of various characteristics. But the potentiality of innovations for having various consequences has received little attention. For example, innovations may vary along a disruptive-integrative continuum. Related to this is the consideration of whether the innovation is more relevant to the socio-emotional (internal) functioning of a group than to its task and goal (external) function, or

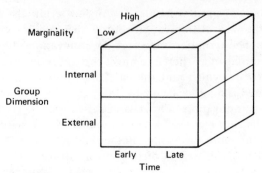

Figure 2.   Related dimensions of innovations.

vice versa. Is the innovation one whose adoption makes an individual a more (or less) marginal group member? This question touches upon the joint issues of the role played by time in defining innovations and the question of adopter categories. There are a number of possibilities here, as represented in Figure 2. Although the dimensions in Figure 2 are dichotomous, it is possible that initial nonadoption by an individual may reinforce or strengthen his relative integration in a group, but as the innovation gains acceptance by others within a group the nonadopter becomes increasingly marginal (at least with respect to the innovation in question) while the reverse process occurs for the earliest adopters.

Earlier discussion focused on the perception of individuals. It is appropriate here to ask about the multimember adopter unit. Relatively little work has been done concerning the perceptual processes of informal and formal groups as single entities. Consequently, little is known about group perceptions of innovations. They may or may not parallel the dimensions and attributes considered earlier with regard to individuals. Groups are something more than the summation of many individual attributes, and it is in this "something more," in the emergent phenomena that are by-products of interpersonal interactions, that properties of innovation unique to multimember adopter units are to be found.

Publicness versus privateness is still another dimension and trait of an innovation (Olson, 1971). A public good is one which, if available to one party in a social system, is more or less automatically and simultaneously available to all members of the social system. Fluoridation of a community water system is a public good. Those opposing the concept must accept it. This suggests a related dimension concerning the *size of the decision-making body* required to act on public goods. Can only one person make the decision? Does it require the consent of a simple majority or a smaller or larger number?

A related characteristic focuses on the *number of "gatekeepers"* involved between the introduction of an innovation into a social system and the actual adoption of the innovation by the system or its members. Some innovations require going through a large number of the legitimating channels before it can be adopted effectively, whereas others do not.

Related to number of gatekeepers is the *number of nodes* in the social system through which an innovation passes. An example of this is the dissemination of scientific ideas, which constitutes a special instance or case of the diffusion of innovations. The extension of certified knowledge is the major goal of science and the one most affecting its social structure. In fact, the reward structure in science virtually ensures continuous innovation (Cole and Cole, 1967). Extending knowledge involves doing something new, novel, or different compared to the existing state of the art. The contribution that is new, novel, or different constitutes the innovation and is what the most important rewards in science serve to bring about. In science the innovation passes through a number of nodes (Garvey et al., 1970): preliminary reports of findings (oral and/or written) to local colloquia; delivery at national meetings and exchange with attendants; the completion of the manuscript and circulation of preprints; submission of manuscript to journal; reviewing and refereeing process; journal publication; reprints; citations and integrative reviews.

Susceptibility to successive modifications constitutes still another innovation characteristic. In science, for example, most knowledge is cumulative. Each discovery inspires the potentiality of further discoveries and, in most cases, new theories and hypotheses generate revisions in the existing body of knowledge. The refinement, elaboration, and modification of scientific theories and findings are evidence of the acceptance of the original or essential idea.

Another characteristic concerns the *gateway capacity* of the innovation. In addition to the intrinsic value derived from the adoption of an innovation, value may accrue to the extent that the *adoption of an innovation may open avenues to the adoption of other innovations.* It could well be that the increased opportunity for the adoption of other innovations is the intrinsic value of the initial facilitating innovation. The adoption of radio has been demonstrated to be a frequent precursor of the adoption of other modern innovations. The rationale is that increased exposure to the mass media (as a result of radio ownership) establishes a more cosmopolitan outlook, which is conducive to adopting new ideas, practices, and things (Lerner, 1958). Thus the adoption of some innovations serve as gateways to other innovations.

In cases where large-scale social change is desired it is useful to think in terms of *gateway innovations.* What constellation of gateway innovations is most likely to bring that change about? Even small changes in the social structure may have a dramatic impact in the long run by setting the stage for large-scale innovations. After a certain threshold of accumulated adoptions of gateway innovations has been reached, a sudden takeoff may occur.

Finally, *ego-involvement,* the extent to which a person's beliefs and values are affected by an innovation, should also influence a person's decision to adopt the innovation. Social psychologists (Sherif and Cantril, 1947) have long observed that when a person is very much *ego-involved* in an issue, it becomes difficult to persuade him to accept a message opposing his own on the issue. On the other hand, if the persuasive message is also in the same direction as the person's attitude about the issue, the probability of his accepting the message is greatly increased. These contrast and assimilation effects may apply to the extent of a person's willingness to adopt an innovation. It may be hypothesized that as a person becomes more ego-involved in the type of innovation under consideration, the likelihood of his adopting the innovation will increase as the innovation is viewed closer to his own position.

One more point is to be made here. Many attributes commonly associated with innovations are not necessarily related to their being perceived as new. Examples of such attributes are divisibility, communicability, and terminality. This is not to say, of course, that such factors do not affect the behavior of adopter units toward an innovation. Rather, we must distinguish between factors that are likely to be the components of the newness being perceived, on the one hand, and factors associated with an innovation which function to retard or facilitate its adoption, on the other hand. In addition, there are variables that represent the antecedents of perceived newness. One example is the recency with which the potential unit of adoption has been exposed to the innovation. Often (but by no means always) this is related to the period of time an item has been in existence. Only those attributes constituting newness are necessary and sufficient conditions for an idea, practice, or thing to qualify as an innovation. Antecedent variables are necessary but not sufficient, whereas factors, variables, or attributes whose only impact is to influence

Table 2   Innovation-Related Attributes

Antecedent Attributes	Newness Attributes	Facilitator or Inhibitor Attributes
Necessary but not sufficient	Necessary and sufficient	Neither necessary nor sufficient

rate of adoption are neither necessary nor sufficient to qualify an item as an innovation. Two caveats must be noted. First, the three categories of attributes shown in Table 2 are not mutually exclusive. A given attribute in a given instance could conceivably qualify as an antecedent, newness, and facilitative attribute. Second, the classification of a particular attribute could fall into any one category depending upon (1) the context in which the innovation is introduced, (2) the inherent character of the innovation, and (3) the perceptual processes of the potential adopter.

Theoretical Considerations

In this chapter, we have tried to specify various dimensions of innovations. Some were familiar dimensions in need of further research and some were new dimensions in the sense of not having been treated in the literature to any significant degree, if at all. Of ultimate concern, of course, is the construction of viable theoretical statements about the relationship between the dimensions of innovations and their rate of acceptance and dissemination. Such statements will provide an essential part of the foundation of a theory of the adoption and diffusion of innovations. The definition of various dimensions and needed research on them is the first step toward a theory of adoption and diffusion processes. It is also the first step toward a subtheory of this relationship between characteristics of innovations and the adoption rates. Many other factors will have to be taken into account, such as the nature of communication channels, the social environment, and the potential adopters' personal, social, economic, and cultural characteristics.

Even for the simple relationship propositions under discussion, we are still far from making a viable statement. A viable sociological theory, according to Homans (1964), needs three ingredients: concepts, propositions, and contingency (Falsifiability). We have singled out a number of dimensions of one concept—the nature of innovations—and have stated a number of propositions throughout the discussion. What is needed as a next step involves the falsification process. Falsification, or verification, should focus on two areas, the dimensionality of innovations and the relationship between dimensionality and adoption rate.

Falsification of the Dimensionality of Innovations. An important step would be an empirical verification of the dimensionality of innovations. At this time, we may assume that there exists a limited set of innovation dimensions, independent of one another, which specify the universe of innovations. Such an assumption was utilized and verified to

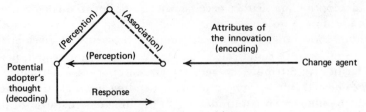

Figure 3.   Perception as a mediational process.

many scholars' satisfaction for the dimensions of meaning existing in verbal forms (Osgood et al., 1957).

Both Barnett (1953) and Hagen (1963) suggest that perception is a key process affecting the interpretation of an innovation. Although we cannot go into the complex and numerous psychosocial and physiological determinants of perception, we can present an overall view of the role of perception as a mediational process between the source of an innovation, for example, a professional change agent, and the potential adopter (Figure 3). The change agent presents an innovation as a set of "cues" or "signs" associated with the innovation. The potential adopter perceives these particular cues as well as the larger and more general abstract concept of the innovation and through a decoding process assembles a meaningful interpretation of the innovation. This ultimate interpretation of the meaning may or may not coincide with the intended meaning of the change agent.

It has been suggested (Osgood et al., 1962, p. 248) that there are three basic dimensions of verbal meaning: activity, evaluation, and potency. Perhaps, then, these three factors can be used to classify by semantic differential techniques the basic perceived attributes of innovations. This is common practice by marketers in the preparation of promotional programs for new products. A different issue is raised here. We are not now concerned with the activity, evaluative, and potency dimensions of the innovation viewed as a gestalt, although this is important. Rather, our concern is whether such basic underlying attributes of innovations as communicability, gatewayability, terminality, compatibility, and complexity can be classified according to the three dimensions. This seems to be an empirical question that apparently has not been investigated. Underlying attributes refer here to characteristics of innovations which customarily affect their rate of adoption.

The situation posited here is diagrammed in Figure 4. The psychosocial and physiological state of the individual is influenced by his perceptual process, which are influenced by the psychosocial and physio-

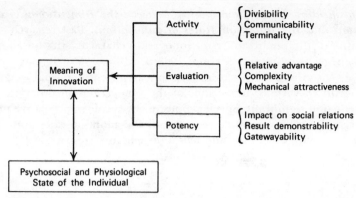

Figure 4.   Dimensions of meaning.

logical state. Thus a situation of reciprocal or mutual causation is present. The impact of the various potentially relevant attributes of innovations is felt through one or more of three basic dimensions of meaning—activity, evaluation, and potency. Thus terminality (now versus later) may relate most closely with activity, complexity and mechanical attractiveness (easy versus hard) with evaluation, and structural radicalness (weak social system impact versus strong impact) with potency.

Another potentially useful way of classifying the basic underlying dimensions of innovation may be found in the creative process. The manner in which people identify with or project themselves into an innovative situation may be subject to categorization with each potential adopter category consistently emphasizing different dimensions such as activity, evaluation, and potency. Although the physical attributes of a material innovation may provide certain limits as to what is or can be perceived, their perception is also influenced by the cultural, social, and psychosocial qualities influencing the perceiver. An innovation having a direct physical manifestation is more subject to standardization and hence may be most readily classified according to potential adopter perceptions. Ideas and practices would be more difficult to investigate along these lines.

As we strive to determine the various dimensions of innovations, a systematic research effort should be made to test the structure of hypothetically independent dimensions of innovations. The empirical evidence of the existence of such a structure may provide the needed basis to ascertain the theoretical significance of the concept.

Falsification of the Relationship between the Dimensionality of Innovations and the Adoption Rates of Innovations. Past research shows instability of the predictability of innovation characteristics on adoption rates (Fliegel, Kivlin, and Sekhon, 1968; Carlson, 1965). It may well be the case that different types of innovations require differential weights to be assigned to various dimensions of the innovations in order to make the prediction significant. Specifications of the typology of relative predictive strength of innovation dimensions for the adoption rates of different innovations will constitute another indispensable step toward a viable theory about the nature of innovations.

Some Unanswered Empirical Questions Affecting Social Action

An understanding of the salient aspects of innovations as perceived by the unit of adoption is essential for success in programs of planned social change. This essay has presented some of the dimensions of innovations most likely to be perceived as relevant by adopter units. Strategies and tactics of planned intervention must consider explicitly the nature of innovations. To the extent that attributes of innovations can be manipulated, they are important to the change agent as entry points into the social change process. Thus two steps are involved. The first is to determine current or most probable perceptions of the innovation. The next step is, where necessary, to alter the attributes of the innovation thereby or the perception of them. In doing so, the change agent is controlling the most fundamental element in the social change process, the social change object itself.

In instances where perceived attributes of the innovation can be altered, the manipulation of the innovation becomes a strategy or tactic. However, in many instances the attributes of innovations are fixed and the process of planned intervention must develop or adjust strategies accordingly. Unfortunately, we do not yet have a schema telling us where, when, or for whom particular attributes are likely to be fixed or variable. Perhaps this is the next step beyond this paper. Another need is to spell out the possible relationships between the attributes of innovations and the kinds of strategies and tactics available for use. We have excellent inventories of strategies and tactics peculiar to social change but little information on their interaction with the nature of the innovation itself (Hyman et al., 1967).

Interaction among the attributes of innovations also needs further exploration. Some studies (e.g., see Fliegel and Kivlin, 1966b) have presented high-order partial correlations between time of adoption and innovation characteristics but offer little discussion on the intercorrelations among attributes and still less discussion in describing any social or psychological mechanisms that would bring two or more attributes together.

In conclusion, we mention briefly that there are many more implications that may stem from relating the characteristics of the innovation to other concepts. Our research experiences point to the significance of uncovering the relationships between the nature of the innovation and (1) the form of adoption, (2) the size and kind of unit of adoption required for effective use, (3) the length of time of the adoption process, and (4) the dynamics of the decision-making process.

Notes

1. Chin (1963) has characterized education innovations as involving substitution (e.g., one textbook for another), alteration (e.g., a minor change such as lengthening the school day by a few minutes), perturbation (e.g., moving a class to a mobile classroom), restructuring (e.g., adopting team teaching), and value orientation (e.g., replacing the teacher by self-administered simulation games).

Goodwin Watson

Associate Director
Union for Experimenting Colleges
Antioch College

RESISTANCE TO CHANGE

The acceleration of technological change in all industrialized countries had led to growing recognition of, and concern to remedy, institutional lag. While speed of travel and power of destruction are multiplied by factors of ten or one hundred, family life, schools, communities, and nations tend to operate in traditional ways. Resistance to change is not uniform. Although electric lights, telephones, automobiles, and television had to overcome some fear and suspicion at first, they quickly "caught on." New developments in the behavioral sciences, with implications for child care, schooling, business, race relations, and international affairs, have been less welcome.

All forces that contribute to stability in personality or in social systems can be perceived as resisting change. From the standpoint of an ambitious and energetic change agent, these energies are seen as obstructions. From a broader and more inclusive perspective, the tendencies to achieve, preserve, and return to equilibrium are most salutary. They permit the duration of character, intelligent action, institutions, civilization, and culture. Klein (1967) has called this "the defender role."

Resistance to change has sometimes been misinterpreted as simple inertia in human nature. It is said that people are "in a rut," or "set in their ways." Actually, almost everyone is eager for some kind of change in his life and situation. He would like better health, more money, and more freedom to satisfy his desires. Excitement is more attractive than a humdrum existence. If people and organizations do not change, it must be because the natural drives toward innovation are being stifled or held in check by countervailing forces.

117

Lewin's (1951) concept of apparently static systems as in "quasi-stationary equilibrium" has directed attention to the importance of reducing resistance if change is to be accomplished with minimal stress. The more usual strategies of increasing pressures by persuasion and dissuasion raise tensions within the system. If the opposite strategy—that of neutralizing or transforming resistance—is adopted, the forces for change already present in the system-in-situation will suffice to produce movement. For example, administrators may try by exhortation to get teachers to pay more attention to individual differences among pupils. Or they may analyze the factors that now prevent such attention (e.g., large classes, single textbooks, standard tests) and by removing these pressures release a very natural tendency for teachers to adapt to the different individual pupils.

Change may evolve from within a social system or come by adoption or adaptation from outside it. Most studies of change—for example, in farming methods—have focused on the adoption of new devices, techniques, or methods. Anthropologists have followed the diffusion of artifacts from one culture to its neighbors. Frequently there is some adaptation of the item to its new setting. Mechanical devices like tractors or moving pictures are usually accepted with little local modification. But the history of religious contacts shows more often a blend between the old beliefs and the new movement. Resistance has been particularly apparent in the case of reform movements struggling to win acceptance.

During the life of a typical innovation or change-enterprise, perceived resistance moves through a cycle: In the *early stage,* when only a few pioneer thinkers take the reform seriously, resistance appears massive and undifferentiated. "Everyone" knows better: "no one in his right mind" could advocate the change. Proponents are labeled crackpots and visionaries. In the *second stage,* when the movement for change has begun to grow, the forces pro and con become identifiable. The opposition can be defined by its position in the social system, and its power can be appraised. Direct conflict and a showdown mark the *third stage,* as resistance becomes mobilized to crush the upstart proposal. Enthusiastic supporters of a new idea have frequently underestimated the strength of their opponents. Those who see a favored change as good and needed find it hard to believe the lengths to which opposition will go to squelch that innovation. This third stage is likely to mean life or death to the proposed reform. Survival is seen as depending on building up power to overcome the enemy. Actually, as Lewin's force-field analysis indicates, an easier and more stable victory can be won by lowering the potency of the opposing forces.

The *fourth stage,* after the decisive battles, finds supporters of the change in power. The persisting resistance is, at this stage, seen as a stubborn, hidebound, cantankerous nuisance. For a time, the danger of a counterswing of the pendulum remains real. Any conspicuous failure of the reform may mobilize latent opposition which, joined with the manifest reactionaries, could prove sufficient to shift the balance of power. Strategy in this fourth stage demands wisdom in dealing not only with the overt opponents but with the still dissonant elements within the majority which appears, on the whole, to have accepted the innovation. Many teachers of a "new math" today may be less than wholehearted about its value. In a *fifth stage*, the old adversaries are as few, and as alienated, as were the advocates in the first stage. The strategic situation is now that new change-enterprises are appearing and the one-time fighters for the old innovation (e.g., junior high schools) are being seen as resisters of the emerging change (Edwards, 1927).

At each stage of the innovation, from its inception to its defense as status quo, wise strategy requires perceptive analysis of the nature of the resistance. For purposes of this study, we shall focus first on the forces of resistance as they operate within the individual personality. Then we shall inventory the forces most easily identified in the social system. This is, of course, an arbitrary separation, utilized to facilitate the recognition of factors. In reality, the forces of the social system operate within the individuals and those attributed to separate personalities combine to constitute systemic forces. The two work as one.

Resistance in Personality

Homeostasis. Some of the stabilizing forces within organisms have been described by Cannon (1932) as "homeostasis." The human body has built-in regulatory mechanisms for keeping fairly constant such physiological states as temperature or blood sugar. Exercise increases pulse rate, but "resistance" to this change presently brings the heartbeat back to normal. Appetites rise and are satisfied, and the organism returns to its steady state. Raup (1925) generalized the reversion to *complacency* as the most basic characteristic of the psychological as well as the physiological behavior of man.

The conception of organisms as naturally complacent unless disturbed by intrusive stimuli has had to be modified in recent years because of contradictory evidence showing a hunger for stimulation. Years ago, W. I. Thomas proposed the "desire for new experience" as one of the four most basic wishes underlying human behavior (Thomas and Znaniecki, 1918–1920). Observers of rats, dogs, and chimpanzees have

noted an "exploratory motive" strong enough to counterbalance fear of
the unknown (Hebb, 1958, p. 171). Experiments with perceptual isolation of human subjects showed that lying quietly awake in a comfortable
bed, free from disturbing stimuli, soon became intolerable. People need
to interact with a changing environment (Lilly, 1956).

Frequently, educational changes prove temporary. For a time, after
sensitivity training, a school principal may be more open and receptive to
suggestions from teachers. But with time, the forces that made her behave
as she did before training return her to her more brusque and arbitrary
manner.

Habit. Most learning theory has included the assumption that unless
the situation changes noticeably, organisms will continue to respond in
their accustomed way. At least one psychologist (Stephens, 1965) has argued that the *repetition* of a response—often used as a criterion for having "learned" it—offers no conceptual problem. The model resembles a
machine which, unless something significant is altered, will continue to operate in a fixed fashion. There should be no need for repeated exercise or
for a satisfying effect to "stamp in" the learned response: once the circuit
is connected it should operate until rearranged. Once a habit is established, its operation often becomes satisfying to the organism. Gordon
Allport (1937) has introduced the term "functional autonomy" to refer to
the fact that activities first undertaken as a means to some culminating
satisfaction often become intrinsically gratifying. The man accustomed
after dinner to his chair, pipe, and newspaper may resist any change in
the details of his routine. The term "busman's holiday" reflects the fact
that men sometimes enjoy continuing in free time an activity that has
been part of their required work. The concept of functional autonomy is
probably too inclusive. Not all activities that are frequently repeated take
on the character of drives. We have no wholly correct basis for predicting which habits will show most intrinsic resistance to change.

Sometimes a new educational practice (e.g., a changed form of teacher's class record book or report card) arouses much resistance. After it has
been established, perhaps with some persuasion and coercion, it becomes
as resistant to change as was its predecessor. The familiar is preferred.

Children commonly feel that it is not just a mistake but actually
wrong to vary a habitual routine. The familiar is not only preferred but
sanctified. To tell a well-known story in other words and phrases may
arouse the same distress in a child that a modern translation of the Bible
arouses in an adult brought up on the King James version.

To be "good" means to conform to the customary; to deviate means
to be "bad."

Primacy. The way in which the organism first successfully copes with a situation sets an unusually persistent pattern. Early speech habits may be recognized despite much effort in later life to change. A child who has several times heard a story told in certain words is likely to be annoyed if the key phrases are not repeated exactly when the story is retold. Part of the joy in familiar music is the accord between established expectations and the flow of melody and harmony. Dreams of adults are often located in the settings of childhood. Even in senility, the recent experiences fade first, and the earliest associations persist longest. All later concepts perforce build on some of the earliest generalizations.

It is often observed that teachers, despite in-service courses and supervisory efforts, continue to teach in much the same way they themselves were taught. Lippitt has found that it is more nearly correct to say that they continue to teach in about the same way as they themselves taught during their first years as a teacher. Both interpretations illustrate the factor of primacy.

Selective Perception and Retention. Once an attitude has been set up, a person responds to other suggestions within the framework of his established outlook. Situations may be perceived as reenforcing the original attitude when they actually are dissonant. Thus in one famous experiment a common stereotype associating Negroes with carrying razors led observers of a cartoon to think they had seen the razor in the hand of the Negro rather than the white man (Allport and Postman, 1945). Experiments with materials designed to bring about changes in attitude revealed that subjects did not hear clearly or remember well communications with which they disagreed (Watson and Hartmann, 1939; Levine and Murphy, 1943). It is a common observation that people usually prefer news sources, whether in print or broadcast, with which they are already in agreement (Klapper, 1960). By reading or listening to what accords with their present views, by misunderstanding communications which, if correctly received, would not be consonant with preestablished attitudes, and by conveniently forgetting any learning which would lead to uncongenial conclusions, subjects successfully resist the possible impact of new evidence upon their earlier views. There are relatively few instances in which old prejudices have been changed by better information or persuasive arguments.

The process of innovation is usually set in motion by a perception that customary behavior is not bringing desired results. Selective perception may prevent one from seeing that the old pattern is failing. His ego defenses let him believe in continuing success.

Dependence. All human beings begin life dependent on adults, who incorporate ways of behaving that were established before the newcomer arrived. Parents sustain life in the helpless infant and provide major satisfactions. The inevitable outcome is conservative. Children tend to incorporate (imitate, introject) the values, attitudes, and beliefs of those who care for them.

All teachers were once beginners in the lower grades. At that time their teachers loomed large and influential, whether friendly or hostile. The little pupil has to conform. His later adoption of the kind of teaching he then experienced is as natural as his acceptance of a particular alphabet and number system.

There may later, in adolescence, be outbursts of rebellion and moves toward independent thought. But the typical adult still agrees far more than he disagrees with his parents on such basic items as language, religion, politics, child-rearing, and what a school should do.

Illusion of Impotence. An emotional carry-over from childhood dependence echoes in the feeling of adults—even quite competent individuals—that they are the helpless victims of circumstances beyond their control. A New Yorker may curse the crowded subway, the highway traffic, or the regimented school system but feel that it would be quixotic to assume that he could possibly do anything to change the situation. It is up to "them"—some vague authorities. "They" ought to do this or that—it is not in my sphere of influence.

Feeling trapped and helpless, the average citizen fails to exert the influence he might have to gain goals of change in local or national policy. In the big corporation or university, a single individual is likely to believe that his only possible contribution will be to do his own limited job properly. The big changes that he may feel are needed seem hopelessly beyond his reach.

Enmeshed in the system, many participants fail to use the leeway for improvement which they have. It is said that after a sheep has been tethered to a stake for a time, he will not venture beyond the circumference of his customary circle, even though the rope be no longer tied. Teachers seem frequently to assume—without testing the limits—that they would not be allowed to innovate as they might wish to.

Superego. Freud (1922) conceived one of the basic personality functions as engaged in the enforcement of the moral standards acquired in childhood from authoritative adults. From the first "No! No!" said to the baby, on through all the socializing efforts of parents, a code of controls is internalized. When the Oedipus complex is resolved, the child sets standards for himself corresponding to his image of the perfect and omni-potent parent. Any violation of these demanding rules is punished with a severity whose energy is derived from the attachment to parents as this operated in the Oedipal period, age three to five.

Here, then, in the superego, is a powerful agent serving tradition. The repressive constraints that operate—partly unconsciously—do not derive from the realities of life in the present or the preceding genera-tion. The superego of the child corresponds to the superego of the par-ent, not to that parent's rational conclusions based on experience. Each mother and father passes on a heritage of taboos which he, in his child-hood, acquired from ages past. An individual needs considerable ego-strength to become able to cope realistically with changing life situations in disregard of the unrealistic, perfectionistic demands of his superego ac-quired in childhood.

A characteristic of superego control is that it is enforced by a threat of vague terror. All the irrationality of the id—all the demons—may be let loose if a taboo were to be violated. Social changes are sometimes viewed as likely to result in such "utter chaos." If this control were relaxed—if children were reared permissively, if the races were inte-grated, if sex relations before marriage were acceptable, if war making were abandoned—the consequences are imagined to be appalling beyond description.

There is reason to believe that people who choose occupations in which they try to inculcate higher standards in others (clergymen, teach-ers, law-enforcers) are persons with extra strong superego components. They take pride in making severe demands on themselves and on others. They bitterly resist any change which they conceive to be a relaxation of the firmest discipline and the highest expectations of perfection in perfor-mance. The influx of less able students into secondary schools and col-leges has created almost intolerable conflict in teachers who still require achievement at levels few can attain.

Self-Distrust. As a consequence of childhood dependence and the stern authority of the tradition-oriented voice of the superego, children quickly learn to distrust their own impulses. Each says, in effect, "What I would really want is bad! I should not want it!"

John Dewey, in *Human Nature and Conduct* (1922), saw the possi-bility of human betterment by liberating the creative impulses of youth: "The young are not as yet subject to the full impact of established cus-toms. Their life of impulsive activity is vivid, flexible, experimenting, cu-rious." What Dewey did not say is that within each young person there are powerful forces condemning and repressing any impulses that do not correspond to the established routines, standards, and institutions of society as it is and has been. The Puritan view that the enjoyable is evil gets a firm hold on children. Every clash between their desires and what adults expect of them adds an increment to each child's self-rejection: "They must be right; I must be naughty to have such terrible feelings." Thus guilt is mobilized to prevent action for change. Men conclude that they are not worthy of any better life. To be "good" is to accept the status quo ante. Agitators and rebels speak with the voice of the evil serpent and should not be heeded.

The author, during the depth of the economic depression, found that most of a sample of unemployed men did not lay the blame for their predicament on faulty social mechanisms. Rather, they internalized the responsibility. They said, "I ought to have stayed on in school," or, "It was my fault that I lost the job; I shouldn't have said what I did!," or, "I should have waited to get married and have a family." Only about one in five wanted to change the economic system; the majority blamed themselves only (Watson, 1941).

Innumerable pupils, parents, teachers, and administrators have felt impulses to alter school procedures. Most of them have been stifled by a feeling suggested by the expression: "Who am I to suggest changes in what the wisdom of the past has established?"

Insecurity and Regression. A further obstacle to effective participation in social change is the tendency to seek security in the past. The golden age of childhood is a Paradise Lost. When life grows difficult and frustrating, individuals think with nostalgia about the happy days of the past.

The irony is that this frustration-regression sequence enters life at just the time when change would be most constructive. When old ways no longer produce the desired outcome, the sensible recourse would be to experiment with new approaches. But individuals are likely at such a time to cling even more desperately to the old, unproductive behavior patterns. They are dissatisfied with the situation; but the prospect of change arouses even more anxiety, so they seek somehow to find a road back to the old and (as they now see it) more peaceful way of life.

Demands for change in school organization and practice become acute as a result of such social changes as automation, rapid travel to other lands, or racial desegregation. The reaction of insecure teachers, administrators, and parents is, too often, to try to hold fast to the familiar or even to return to some tried-and-true fundamentals that typify the schools of the past. A candidate for State Superintendent of Schools in California based his successful campaign in the mid-1960s on return to the old-fashioned. The fact that California had been changing more rapidly in population, occupations, and so on, than had any other state was one factor in the appeal of this program of action.

Deprived and / or Anxious. The individual who lives near the minimum level of subsistence must pour all available energy into efforts to survive. He has no spare attention to direct toward innovation. The fairly affluent person can take a playful interest in trying out something new; the impoverished individual cannot take the risk. There is, of course, the case of desperation which may arise in the extremity where one has nothing to lose by any change. There is a popular myth that expects the poor to lead in revolution; history shows that most leaders of revolutionary movements have come from more favored classes.

Anxiety may arise also from concerns other than economic survival. Some individuals live in an almost constant state of apprehension. They do not trust this kind of world and are particularly threatened by changes.

Most social change involves some redistribution of power. Persons not pathologically anxious or economically insecure may resent any change which they perceive as reducing the scope of their control, influence, or prestige.

Other Personality Factors. Studies show younger persons generally are more ready for change than are those who, with age, have acquired property, skills, or prestige within the older order of things. More cosmopolitan individuals, who have a wider variety of contacts and experiences, are usually more open-minded about change; those more isolated and provincial resist because they have little basis for imagining a new way of working or living.

Some individuals find their security in avoiding notice. They resist being exposed. Perhaps they expect that they can conceal their limitations by melting into the crowd. They resist changes that might bring attention upon them.

There are other quirks of the neurotic personality that may undergird powerful resistance to change in particular areas. There is a curious component of white opposition to desegregation of races which arises from sexual fears; for example, "Would you want your sister to marry one?" (Watson, 1966, pp. 402–409). We cannot here explore all such hidden personal dynamics, but we turn now to resistances arising from social systems.

Resistance to Change in Social Systems

Conformity to Norms. Norms in social systems correspond to habits in individuals. They are customary and expected ways of behaving. Members of the organization demand of themselves and of other members conformity to the institutional norms. This is the behavior described by Whyte in *The Organization Man* (1956). It includes time schedules, modes of dress, forms of address to colleagues, superiors, and subordinates, indications of company loyalty, personal ambition to rise, appropriate consumption, and forms of approved participation in recreation and community life. Teachers, even more than businessmen, have been expected to exemplify certain proper behaviors.

Norms make it possible for members of a system to work together. Each knows what he may expect in the other. The abnormal or anomic is disruptive.

Since norms are shared by many participants, they cannot easily change. Above all, the usual individual cannot change them. He can get himself rejected for deviant behavior, but the norm will persist. A laboratory experiment (Merei, 1949) showed that even a child with strong leadership qualities was required, nevertheless, to conform to the established play norms of a small group of kindergarten children. An excellent teacher, who declined to submit the prescribed advance lesson plans for each week, did not alter the norm; he was fired.

When one person deviates noticeably from the group norm, a sequence of events may be expected. The group will direct an increasing amount of communication toward him, trying to alter his attitude. If this fails, one after another will abandon him as hopeless. Communication to him will decrease. He may be ignored or excluded. He no longer belongs (Festinger and Thibaut, 1951).

The famous experiments by Lewin (1952) on altering norms of eating during the war indicated that changes are better introduced by group decision than by expecting individuals to pioneer a practice not being used by their associates.

The evidence indicates that if norms are to be altered, change will have to occur throughout the entire operating system. The sad fate of experimental schools and colleges (Miles, 1964) indicates the power of the larger system to impose its norms even on units that have been set apart, for a time, to operate by different standards and expectations.

Systemic and Cultural Coherence. The gestalt principle that parts take on characteristics because of their relationship within the whole implies that it is difficult to change one part without affecting others. Innovations helpful in one area may have side effects which are destructive in related regions. For example, a technical change which increased the efficiency of pieceworkers in a factory enabled them to earn more than supervisors were being paid, so the new technique had to be abandoned. Electronic data processing in another company altered the size and relative responsibilities of related departments, generating considerable resentment (Mann and Neff, 1951). Studying change in a city YMCA, Dimock and Sorenson (1955) concluded:

> No part of institutional change is an "island unto itself": changes in program call for changes in every other part of the institution . . . and advance in one sector cannot proceed far ahead of change in other sectors. For example, program groups cannot be changed without officer training . . . which in turn depends upon staff reeducation. Similarly, changes in staff goals and ways of working are dependent upon administrative procedures, policies, and budgets which in turn require changes in Boards and Committees.

A parallel statement for school systems might indicate that a change in teacher-pupil relationships is likely to have repercussions on teacher-principal interaction, on parent-principal contacts, on pressure groups operating on the superintendent, on board-member chances for reelection, and perhaps on the relationship of the local system to state or federal agencies. Any estimate of resistance which considers only the persons primarily and centrally concerned will be inadequate; the repercussions elsewhere may be even more influential in the survival of the innovation.

Our school systems are probably less cohesive and integrated than most business organizations. A teacher has more autonomy than a salesclerk or middle-manager. Considerable change can take place within one classroom and have relatively minor effects on what other teachers are doing. Yet, in the long run, the deviate is likely to be brought into line by his peer group, his supervisors, the pupils, or their parents. Coercive conformity is felt even more in business and government agencies.

The Sacrosanct. Anthropologists have observed that, within any culture, some activities are easily changed, whereas others are highly resistant to innovation. Generally the technology is receptive to new ideas and procedures. The greatest resistance concerns matters connected with what is held to be sacred. Some women can become managers of businesses or presidents of colleges in our male-dominated society, but they find it almost impossible to become priests, rabbis, bishops, or ministers in a conservative denomination. Translations of Scriptures into the vernacular have met strong disapproval. The ritual reading of some verses from the

Bible or the recitation of a prayer is held onto with far more fervor than is spent on retention of school texts or equipment. Traditional ceremonies are likely to persist despite doubts as to their educational impact. The closer any reform comes to touching some of the taboos or rituals in the community, the more likely it is to be resisted. Introduction of improved technology in underdeveloped countries runs into formidable obstacles if it seems to impinge on religious superstitions, beliefs, or practices (Spicer, 1952).

Cultures resist almost as stubbornly alterations that enter the realm of morals and ethics. Even when few live by the traditional code, it must still be defended as "ideal" (Linton, 1945). A well-recognized illustration is the expectation of sexual continence between puberty and marriage. Kinsey may find very few youths who practice it, but schools, churches, and courts must operate as if the prescription were unquestionable.

There is a clear connection between the operation of the superego in individuals and the taboos persisting in the culture. Both uphold impossibly high standards and react punitively to recognized infractions of the excessive demands.

Rejection of "Outsiders." Most change comes into institutions from "outside." Griffiths, studying change in school systems, concluded, "The major impetus for change in organizations is from outside" (in Miles, 1964, p. 431).

Few psychological traits are as universal as are suspicion and hostility toward outsiders. Kohler (1922) observed this kind of behavior among his chimpanzees on the island of Tenerifa many years ago. Wood (1934) explored, across different cultures, the mixture of curiosity and antagonism toward foreigners. A typical attack on any new proposal is that it does not fit our local conditions. Struggles to improve labor and race relations have commonly been discounted as inspired by "outside agitators" or "atheistic Communists." Research, development, and engineering units are familiar with the way in which a new project is hampered if it is seen as NIH (not invented here). Argyris (1952) outlined common defenses against "outsiders."

The history of experimental demonstration schools is that they were often observed but seldom replicated: "This is fine, but it wouldn't work in our system." Differences in class of children, financial support, equipment, and tradition helped to rationalize the resistance. The genius of agricultural agents a century ago led them away from model farms run by state colleges and toward demonstration projects within the local neighborhood. Farmers would accept what was being done within their county, although they would not import new practices from far away.

A major problem in introducing social change is to secure enough local initiative and participation so the enterprise will not be vulnerable as a foreign importation.

*Hierarchy.*The more stratified the power structure in an organization, the easier it can be changed from the top down but the harder it is for grass-roots change to occur.

A similar obstacle to change is the dependence of an organization on some kind of outside or remote control. All the personnel of a community agency may favor a change which cannot be realized because of opposition from outside political agencies such as the mayor's office, the state legislature, or the state department administrators.

Affluence and Leeway. The most common resistance to educational improvements that would cost money comes from organized or unorganized taxpayers. Mort (1941) found that desirable school innovations were most likely to be adopted by communities with high financial resources. Poverty has been—at least until the recent antipoverty programs—a block to educational experimentation. Watson (1946) found that YMCA's located in communities with a high volume of retail sales per capita were more likely to adopt recommended new practices.

Similar studies in business have shown that organizations which are large (Carrole, 1967) and affluent (Mansfield, 1963; Richland, 1965; McClelland, 1968; Havelock, 1969) have more leeway to introduce innovation. In prosperous times, more funds are available for research, for retraining personnel, and for experimental programs. During financial stringency, these are all cut back.

The situation is rather like that with individuals described earlier. Prosperity permits change; poverty restricts the resources available for imaginative improvements; but when the situation is desperate and collapse is imminent there may be a moment of readiness for any radical change.

A corollary is that organizations in which there have already been many changes are more likely to accept new proposals than are organizations that have previously been slow to change. This is partly a matter of an organizational climate which favors or opposes change (Bright, 1964; Dykens et al., 1964; Sapolsky, 1967).

Restricted Communication. An organizational climate of free communication, mutual trust, and supportive interpersonal relations facilitates innovation. Organizations in which workers distrust supervisors and officials are jealous of one another have massive impediments to change.

(The supporting studies are too numerous to list here. Outstanding examples are McGregor, 1960; Argyris, 1962; Likert, 1961; Schein and Bennis, 1965; Glaser and Taylor 1969). A corollary is that organizations which, because of pervasive suspicion, live by written job definitions and rule books are likely to be resistant to innovations. They find it difficult to become self-renewing (Gardner, 1969).

Nature of the Innovation. Proposed innovations can be adopted more easily if they are simple to understand and to operate. They will be resisted increasingly as they are increasingly complex, hard to grasp, and require new skills.

Changes that can be introduced piecemeal are more easily accepted than are those which require sudden, large-scale alterations.

Changes that cannot easily be retracted or reversed must overcome more resistance than those easily withdrawn if unsatisfactory.

Changes based on concepts, theories, or values incompatible with those of the organization or the individuals involved are likely to meet insuperable resistance.

Reducing Resistance: A Summary

Our observations on sources of resistance within persons and within institutions can be summarized in some concise principles. These are not absolute laws but are based on generalizations that are usually true and likely to be pertinent. The recommendations are here reorganized to answer three questions: Who brings the change? What kind of change succeeds? How is it best done—by what procedures and in what climate?

Who brings the change?

1. Persons involved, teachers, board members, and community leaders should feel that the project is their own—not one devised and operated by outsiders.

2. The project should have wholehearted support from top officials of the system.

What kind of change?

3. Participants should see the change as reducing rather than increasing their present burdens.

4. The project should accord with values and ideals that have long been acknowledged by participants.

5. The program should offer the kind of *new* experience that interests participants.

6. Participants should not feel that their autonomy and their security are threatened.

Procedure in instituting change.

7. Participants should join in diagnostic efforts so they can agree on the basic problem and feel its importance.

8. The project should be adopted by consensual group decision.

9. Proponents should be able to empathize with opponents, to recognize valid objections, and to take steps to relieve unnecessary fears.

10. Innovations are likely to be misunderstood and misinterpreted, so provision should be made for feedback of perceptions of the project and for further clarification as needed.

11. Participants should experience acceptance, support trust, and confidence in their relations with one another.

12. The project should be open to revision and reconsideration if experience indicates that changes may be desirable.

Climate for change.

13. Readiness for change gradually becomes a characteristic of certain individuals, groups, organizations, and civilizations. They no longer look nostalgically at a Golden Age in the past but anticipate their Utopia in days to come. The spontaneity of youth is cherished and innovations are protected until they have had a chance to establish their worth. The ideal is more and more seen as possible.

Everett M. Rogers

Department of Communication
Michigan State University

EFFECTS OF INCENTIVES ON THE DIFFUSION OF INNOVATIONS: THE CASE OF FAMILY PLANNING IN ASIA [1]

Critics and skeptics . . . often view incentive-payment systems as Machiavellian mixtures of bribery and coercion, particularly if they are to be applied with sophisticated popularization techniques to an unsophisticated, tradition-oriented peasant population.

Lenni W. Kangas, 1970

National programs have found that the profit motive is a useful way to support the family planning motive.

Bernard Berelson, 1969, p. 355

The purpose of this chapter is to synthesize what is known about the effect of incentives on the diffusion of innovations. In the "classical model of diffusion," [2] based heavily on the diffusion of agricultural ideas, little attention was given to the role of incentives and it was thought they were generally ineffective in speeding rates of diffusion. More recent research, beginning in the mid-1960s, on family planning incentives in Asia, indicates that incentives can have a considerable effect, but that they also lead to a number of undesired consequences.

We shall present a brief review of the history of incentives and their current status in the field of family planning, develop a classification of

133

different types of incentives, and propose five generalizations about their effects. These generalizations are propositions that are supported by research findings and experiences of family programs, but that need further evidence before they can be considered definitive.

Incentives are direct or indirect payments of cash or in kind that are given to an individual, couple, or group, in order to encourage some overt behavioral change.[3] Such change usually entails the adoption of an innovation, such as a new product, a family planning method, or an agricultural practice. We define an *innovation* as an idea perceived as new by an individual (Rogers with Shoemaker, 1971, p. 19). Thus incentives are one technique of directed or planned social change.

A theme of this essay is the potential value of field experiments as a way to test policies about change. Probably no other field of behavioral science has utilized field experimental research as extensively as has family planning in Asia, and this is one reason why we deal primarily with family planning in this chapter. Certainly no other field of behavioral research has utilized field experiments as extensively to formulate and test alternative public policies for social change as has family planning.

Background

Incentives have been widely used for years in business as a reward system for salesmen. Such commission plans claim the following advantages: (1) they maximize sales effort by directly rewarding its success; (2) selling expenses are roughly proportional to sales volume; (3) flexible direction of the salesmen's efforts is provided if different commissions are offered on different products; and (4) ambitious, self-motivated individuals are attracted to the salesman position (Kotler, 1947, pp. 516–529). However, company control over salesmen may be less with a commission system than with a straight salary; for example, it may be difficult to encourage commissioned salesmen to engage in nonsales activities like customer follow-up and sales reporting. There has been little or no attempt to date to apply the lessons learned from analyses of salesmen's incentives to the diffusion of agricultural or family planning innovations.

In the United States, Sweden, the Netherlands, and a number of developing nations, government agencies have offered incentives or subsidies to farmers in order to encourage the adoption of farm innovations. For instance, the U. S. Soil Conservation Service, since the 1930s, provided cash payments to farmers to encourage the adoption of various conservation practices. In general, farmers tended to adopt only conservation methods like tiling and the application of lime, which were consistent with their values on increasing crop production, and to avoid such subsidized innovations as terracing and dam-building, which were perceived as contrary to this value, even though they prevent soil erosion. Thus it was concluded by the Soil Conservation Service that incentives could not change strongly held beliefs. Further, many farmers seemed to adopt the conservation practice in order to earn the incentive, rather than to realize the benefit of the innovation itself, leading to discontinuance of the conservation method once the subsidy was stopped. In the face of such difficulties, most nations have dropped their strategy of paying agricultural incentives.

Family planning programs in Asia began with strictly a voluntary approach to fertile couples: Information about family planning was made available, as were contraceptive services, usually through government health clinics. However, the number of families adopting was discouragingly low, and in the mid-1950s various national officials began to turn to incentives in hopes they would speed the rate of diffusion. Crucial policy decisions, such as how large the incentive payments should be, when, how, and to whom they should be paid, and the form they should best take, were made on the basis of intuition and conjecture (and occasionally experience). Little thought was given in the early days of family planning incentives to the use of experimental studies to empirically derive alternative incentive policies, or even to evaluation research on existing policies.

Since Enke (1960a, 1960b, 1960c, 1961a, 1961b, 1962, 1966) proposed that incentive payments for birth prevention would lead to considerable economic returns in developing countries, a variety of incentive schemes has been set forth and debated (e.g., Krueger and Sjaasted, 1962; Chandrasehar, 1960; Demeny, 1961; Simon, 1968, 1969; Spengler, 1969; Ridker, 1969, 1971; Kangas, 1970). However, most of these proposals have consisted of hypothetical analysis without supporting data.

In the field, there has been a tendency to underplay the role of incentives. Thus in several nations in which incentives have been introduced, they have not attained the status of an openly recognized program policy. India has had the most intensive experience with incentives and has been the site of the most research on their effects. About 22 % of the total family planning budget in India's 1969–1974 Five-Year Plan is designated for incentives. Yet many family planning officials in India act as if incentives do not exist. Thus incentives are officially referred to as "compensation for loss of earnings" due to adoption of the IUD or sterilization. Freedman (1969) noted:

> Promoters [who are paid a "finder's fee" or diffuser incentive] have an important role in the program for vasectomies. They do not have any official status in most states. No records are kept on them, no significant checkup is done

on their work. . . . The opportunities for corruption, abuse, waste, and eventual serious repercussions on the public image of, and respect for, the program are too obvious to require elaboration.

Perhaps one reason for the low official status of incentives can be found in the motivation for introducing them. In many instances, incentives are initiated so a program may compete for clients with a nearby program (that offers incentives). This reason for introducing incentives is demonstrated in the case of the earliest incentive programs.

The first large-scale family planning incentive scheme was begun in 1956 by the government of Madras State (now called Tamil Nadu) in South India. Thirty rupees (about U.S. $6.67 at the then existing rate of exchange, and $4.00 since a currency devaluation in 1966) were paid to a man or woman who adopted sterilization. Starting in 1959, 10 rupees were paid to a canvasser (known as a motivator, field worker, or promoter) who motivated an individual to come to the clinic for the operation. Thus, even at the early stages of the incentive program in India, two types of incentives were recognized: (1) *adopter incentives,* paid to the adopter to motivate his adoption, and (2) *diffuser incentives,* paid to the canvasser to speed the rate of diffusion of the innovation.

Vacillations in incentive policies in Tamil Nadu State occurred from 1956 to 1971 as the state government modified its incentive scheme because of criticism, the availability of funds, and evidence of the incentives' results. These alterations in diffuser incentive policies provide us with data on the effects of incentives that could hardly be improved upon if the purpose had been experimental (Repetto, 1969). The diffuser incentive (10 rupees in 1972) was discontinued (April 1963), partially reinstated (September 1964), fully reinstated (1964), paid only to government-registered canvassers (1966), paid only to government employees (1969–1970), and paid to anyone who motivated an adopter (1970–1972). Finally, an additional diffuser incentive of 10 rupees has been paid, since 1960, as a "group incentive" to the village *panchayat* (council) in which the adopter lives in order to encourage local leaders to recruit adopters.

The Tamil Nadu vasectomy program spurted ahead of other Indian state programs in rates of adoption. In 1965–1966, Tamil Nadu paid the highest sterilization diffuser incentive (only 5 of 15 other states paid 2 or 3 rupees, and the rest had no canvasser fee) and adopter incentive (5 states had none). Tamil Nadu had 3.42 sterilizations per thousand populations, whereas the other 15 states averaged about 1.00. Some states were forced to pay incentives because otherwise some of their residents traveled to a neighboring state to adopt a family planning method and to obtain the accompanying incentive that was paid. Evidence of considerable movement into Tamil Nadu from adjoining states is provided by Repetto (1969). The central government in New Delhi began to reimburse states for partial costs of incentives and by 1969–1970 agreed to provide the entire cost of adopter incentives for IUD (11 rupees), vasectomy (up to 30 rupees), and tubectomy (up to 40 rupees), plus diffuser incentives.[4]

Concurrently, a country-to-country diffusion of incentive policies occurred. In 1966–1967 a family planning official in a Pakistan district bordering India realized that many of his potential clients were illegally traveling across the frontier to obtain vasectomies (and the accompanying adopter incentives). Some of them were recruited by Indian canvassers, Bengalis who were ethnically similar to the East Pakistanis. The Pakistan district official was forced to begin an incentive scheme, which had encouraging results, and consequently spread to other districts in East Pakistan, and then to West Pakistan. Today several other nations in Asia and Africa (in addition to India and Pakistan) have either adopter or diffuser incentives, or both.

For over a decade there was no empirical investigation of the effects of incentives. Recently, however, two useful studies have been completed in Tamil Nadu State. Fortunately for our present purposes, the results of these studies, viewed in concert, provide insights about the diffusion effects of family planning incentives. In one investigation, Repetto (1969) compiled data from a sample of about 30 vasectomy canvassers to describe how such canvassers encourage adoption. Repetto also used aggregate data over time in an economic analysis of the effects of incentives.

The second main study from which we shall draw was carried out by Srinivasan and Kachirayan (1968), who interviewed 297 vasectomy adopters in rural areas of Tamil Nadu State. These respondents had vasectomies between 1965 and 1967, a period during which the adopter incentive of 30 rupees and the diffuser incentive of 10 rupees to canvassers, and 10 rupees to *panchayats,* were paid.

In this chapter we shall also summarize results from a study of the effects of diffuser incentives initiated in Indonesia in 1970–1971 (Rogers, 1971b).

Before considering these studies on the effects of incentives, we present a categorization of types of incentives.

Types of Incentives

A variety of incentives are paid by family planning programs, and many other possibilities have been proposed. We list here several different criteria by which incentives can be classified.

1. *Adopter versus diffuser incentives.* As previously pointed out, incentives can be paid either directly to an adopter, or to a canvasser to encourage him to persuade an adopter.

2. *Individual versus group incentives.* Payments can be made to individual adopters or canvassers, or to groups to which they belong (as in the case of the *panchayat* incentives in India). Kangas (1970) points out that: "All of the incentives used thus far in the vast majority of programs are given to individuals—acceptors or providers." However, a number of programs have policies that provide group incentives, although they are not defined as such. For instance, the allocation of the national family planning budget in India to states can be considered a group incentive. This allocation was on the basis of total population until 1970 (e.g., the salary of a nurse-midwife was paid to each state per 10,000 population); in 1970 the allocation formula was changed to reward the past relative success of the state's family planning program.

3. *Positive versus negative incentives.* Although all these incentives are positive (in that they reward a desired behavior change), it is also possible to penalize an individual by imposing an unwanted penalty or by withdrawing some desiderata for not adopting an innovation. For instance, the Uttar Pradesh State government in India uses a family planning disincentive: Any government employee who gives birth to a fourth (or further) child is not eligible to receive maternity leave and must pay all hospital and delivery costs, amounting to about 100 to 200 rupees (U.S. $13.33 to $26.67). Similarly, the government of Ghana decided in 1969 to grant maternity leaves and to pay child allowances and traveling expenses only for an employee's first three children. Similar policies are followed in Indonesia's state-owned textile factories.

4. *Monetary versus nonmonetary incentives.* Although we have described only financial payments, incentives may also take the form of some commodity or object desired by the recipient. For example, in Andhra Pradesh State a *sari* with red triangles (the symbol of family planning in India) was awarded to each tubectomy adopter in 1969, and each vasectomy adopter received a similarly decorated *lungi* (male garment).

5. *Immediate versus delayed incentives.* Most of these incentives are immediate, in that payment is made at the time of adoption, but delayed incentives may have advantages under certain conditions. In the United Arab Republic, the government pays an adopter incentive for an IUD insertion at the time of the clinic follow-up, when it can be ascertained that the device is still in place; hence discontinuance is less likely. Certain incentives can be awarded only on a delayed basis; examples are a guarantee of priority in government employment or educational enrollment for the children of a couple who adopt a contraceptive. Similarly, a retire-

ment bond is offered to the female workers on tea plantations in South India for nonpregnancy, to partially compensate them for the loss of old-age security provided by children (Ridker, 1969, 1971).

6. *Graduated versus nongraduated incentives.* It might be argued that an incentive of 30 rupees is not equal in value to all adopters; a landless agricultural laborer with a monthly income of 50 rupees will perceive the incentive quite differently from someone with an income of 400 rupees. Further, if the purpose of family planning incentives is to motivate adoption, there is no reason why the payments need be identical for each adopter or for each canvasser. A graduated diffuser incentive is used in Taiwan, where family planning field workers receive a higher incentive payment for motivating adoption among women under 30 years of age than for those over 30, and they receive 10 times as much credit for an IUD adoption as for a pill adoption. An illustration of a graduated incentive for adopters is provided by one Indian factory that offers acceptors 75 rupees for sterilization after three children, and 25 rupees after five or more children (International Planned Parenthood Federation, n.d., p. 11). This sliding system of payments is designed to reward births-prevented rather than simply the adoption of a contraceptive.

7. *Contraception versus births-prevented incentives.* The purpose of securing the adoption of contraceptives is to prevent births. Incentives can be classified by whether they encourage the prevention of births directly or only indirectly by rewarding adoption. The Indian retirement bond, mentioned previously, is a births-prevented incentive in that the bond is withheld if the tea estate worker gives birth to a fourth child. Almost all the incentives currently used in developing countries are contraception incentives, although births-prevented incentives would be more demographically effective.

Further classification of incentives that could be postulated include whether the payment is made by a government or a private source, and whether the incentive is large or small. However, the main purpose of the present taxonomy is to illustrate some important criteria by which incentives can be classified so that these attributes can be combined to form an incentive policy that maximizes certain desired aspects.

To illustrate our classifications, consider the field-worker incentive program that was begun on an experimental basis in Sialkot District, West Pakistan, in 1970 (Ahmad, 1971). This program, since broadened to other districts in Pakistan, provides a bonus for field workers on the basis of their success in preventing births. Each team, consisting of a male and a female field worker, is assigned to recruit acceptors from about 1200 fertile client couples. At the end of each year, the field workers are paid an incentive bonus based on the number of eligible couples who did not become pregnant during the year. The Pakistan field worker incentive system, classified by our criteria, is (1) diffuser not adopter; (2) individual not group; (3) positive rather than negative; (4) monetary; (5) delayed (until the end of the year); (6) graduated (in that some field workers are paid larger bonuses than others); and (7) on a births-prevented basis.

Generalizations about the Incentives on Diffusion

On the basis of experience with incentive schemes and the research completed on them, we suggest five generalizations about the role of incentives in diffusing family planning innovations.

Generalization I. Adopter incentives increase the rate of adoption of an innovation. Family planning policy makers who offer adopter incentives implicity assume this point, and the limited evidence available indicates that it is probably justified. Repetto's (1968, 1969) studies of the Tamil Nadu vasectomy program confirm our generalization.

Additional evidence for Generalization I comes from a comparison of adoption rates of sterilization between: (1) 3988 married workers in four factories in the Tata industrial group in India, which has offered an adopter incentive of 200 rupees (about U.S. $27) since September 1967; and (2) 3872 married workers in five factories, of similar size and located nearby, three of which offer no incentive and two of which offer less than 25 rupees (Research and Marketing Services, 1970). All workers are also eligible to receive the government incentive of 10 to 20 rupees in the states in which the factories are located.

Figure 1 shows that the relatively high adopter incentives were associated with higher rates of adoption of sterilization in each of five six-month periods, although the differences due to the large incentive were not spectacular, averaging about 3% (while adoption ranged from almost zero to about 9% over 2.5 years). This difference in adoption rates appears to be due solely to an adopter incentive.

Further evidence for Generalization I comes from analysis of the Ernakulam District vasectomy campaigns. When a "large" adopter incentive (in cash and in kind) of 86 rupees (U.S. $11.70) was paid in the first Ernakulam vasectomy campaign in India in 1970, 15,000 vasectomies were obtained in one month, and, in 1971, 63,000 more vasectomies were obtained in one month with a 114 rupee incentive. However, this effect was due in part to such other factors as the sound management of the campaign (Krishnakumar, 1971). The effects of the higher incentive are not

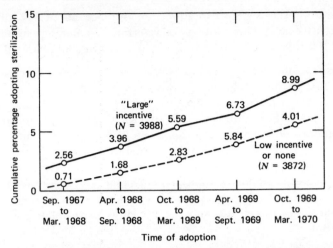

Figure 1. Vasectomy adoption levels among factory workers, by level of incentives. India, 1967–1970. (*Source:* Research and Marketing Services, 1970, p. 27.)

only suggested by the great number of adopters but also by the fact that about 60% of the adopters in the second campaign came from outside of Ernakulam District, presumably attracted mainly by the higher incentives. Many of the other campaign strategies that were used, like the organization of local committees to motivate adopters, did not extend outside of Ernakulam District (Rogers, 1972).

Generalization II. Adopter incentives lead to adoption of an innovation by different individuals than those who would otherwise adopt. Usually adopters of an innovation have higher socioeconomic status than nonadopters.[5] However, analysis of the Research and Marketing Services (1970, pp. 30–31) data shows that the adopter incentive described previously was most effective in leading to higher adoption rates among those factory workers with *lower* incomes, for whom an incentive of 200 rupees corresponded to several months' pay. At the higher levels of monthly income (above 500 rupees), the incentive had little effects. Similarly, the incentives had greater effects (there were more adoptions) on workers with less education, with three or more children, with at least one son, and with a husband who was over 35 years of age. The workers who adopted because of the incentive tended to have *lower* socioeconomic status and larger families. Perhaps adopter incentives especially encourage lower-status clients to adopt; for instance, about 75% of the 30,-000 incentive-motivated adopters of vasectomy in Bombay in 1967–1968 earned 100 rupees (U.S. $13.33) or less per month (Pohlman, 1971, p. 4).

Perhaps one very important effect of incentives is a reversal of who adopts first in an audience; incentives seem to encourage the poorest, rather than the richest, to be most innovative. If this reversal of the point at which the diffusion process starts in a social system is found in further investigations of incentives, the implications for the ethics and strategies of diffusion are profound. Studies of nonincentive-motivated diffusion have found that the relatively most elite clients in a system have the highest degree of contact with agents of change, and as a result these elite clients adopt first (Rogers et al., 1970). Hence most change programs make the elites more elite and the nonelites more relatively disadvantaged. But this vicious circle of eliteness→change agent contact→innovativeness→greater eliteness seems to be broken when incentives are paid.[6] We do not yet know—and we should determine—whether this reversal of where diffusion starts in a system is due more to adopter incentives or to diffuser incentives, and whether the reversal is more likely with relatively smaller incentives. The reversal may be characteristic of family planning but not other types of innovations, or it may even be limited to vasectomy, as a family planning method that may appeal particularly to low-status individuals.

Generalization III. Although adopter incentives increase the quantity of adoptions of an innovation, the quality of such decisions to adopt may be relatively low, leading to limitations in the intended consequences of adoption. If individuals adopt an innovation partly in order to obtain an incentive, there is relatively little motivation to continue using the innovation (if it can be discontinued). The incentive may also attract adopters of the innovation who cannot obtain its officially intended advantages or consequences (e.g., adoption by a couple beyond their fertile years will not prevent births). For these reasons, a births-prevented incentive is more likely to guarantee continued adoption and intended consequences than is a contraception incentive.

Srinivasan and Kachirayan (1968) found that of their 297 vasectomized respondents, 43% stated that money was their "sole motivating factor" for adoption; 41% reported a combination of monetary and family size limitation reasons; 4 % reported being "compelled to adopt" by the canvasser; and 5% adopted to obtain promised medical and monetary help without really possessing information about the vasectomy that they had. By contrast, 86% of vasectomy adopters in East Pakistan (where an adopter incentive of 20 rupees, or U.S. $4.00, was paid) said they wanted permanent protection from an unwanted child but had been precipitated to adoption by the incentive (Family Planning Division, Government of Pakistan, 1969, p. 15). At least in this instance, the adopter incentive seems to have acted as a "cue-to-action" (Hochbaum, 1958; Rosenstock, 1966) in triggering a decision.

According to Srinivasan and Kachirayan (1968), only 63.3% of the adoptions among their respondents could result in preventing births; age and marital status of the other adopters made contraception unnecessary: "A good proportion who underwent vasectomy were either sterile or subfertile at the time." Further, only 38% of the adopters met the legal requirements of sterilization (of being married, with two or more children, and a wife in the fertile age range).

In a 1957 follow-up survey of 265 vasectomized men in Delhi, 10% were not married and 50% did not have their wives' consent, which was officially required (Kapoor and Chandhoke, 1968).

On the basis of such evidence, Repetto (1969) estimated that in Tamil Nadu State about 25% of all wives' signatures were forgeries, and that in about 50% of all vasectomy cases, some aspect of official policy was violated (either relating to number of children, age, or the wife's permission).

Thus the picture that emerges of the incentive-motivated vasectomy adopter is of an individual who is likely to adopt for the "wrong" (in the eyes of family planning policy makers) reasons, and, in many cases, whose adoption may not lead to the desired consequences of births-prevented. This relatively low quality of vasectomy adoptions seems mostly caused by the payment of adopter (and diffuser) incentives.

Many researchers and program officials have largely ignored the "quality" dimension of adoption in the past. It is sometimes assumed that all adoptions are equal in reaching the goal of most family planning programs, preventing births. Recently, we have recognized two dimensions of quality: (1) continuation rates (quality-over-time), and (2) whether desired consequences are attained (indicated by whether those adopting a family planning method could actually prevent births).

Generalization IV. *Diffuser incentives increase the rate of adoption of an innovation by encouraging interpersonal communication about the innovation with peers.* A promoter of an innovation who has adopted an innovation, who is similar to the potential adopter in socioeconomic status, life style, and attitudes, and who is a trusted friend is the greatest motivation force for adoption of family planning ideas. Thus diffuser incentives increase the degree to which the results of an innovation are effectively communicated to others (Rogers and Shoemaker, 1971).

Repetto (1969) found that the vasectomy canvassers in India shared many characteristics with the adopters, who were poor, illiterate, low-caste, employed as agricultural laborers or urban manual workers, least knowledgeable about family planning methods, and least accessible through the conventional promotional approaches. The canvassers' identification, as evidenced by dress and life style, is "not with the lower civil service but with the common man" (Repetto, 1969, p. 9). There are pressures from canvassers in India for guaranteed wages, uniforms, badges, and other marks of status, perhaps suggesting a desire to shift their identification to being more like government family planning employees. Such a shift would of course widen the perceived gap between canvassers and potential acceptors, and probably decrease the effectiveness of the canvassers. All the canvassers that Repetto studied had been vasectomized themselves. A crucial point in the adopter's decision process occurred when the canvasser showed his operation scar, as evidence that the sterilization was physically insignificant, and that the canvasser knew what he was advocating to the potential adopter. The canvassers ranged over a 100-mile radius in searching for adoptors and worked a six- or seven-day week, at a task publicly viewed as having very low prestige.

Repetto (1969, p. 9) states: "Despite a structure of social workers and health educators, virtually all operations . . . are promoted by canvassers." [7] In short, professional government family planning field workers could not accomplish the results obtained by the cavassers.

Empirical evidence to support the relative importance of vasectomy canvassers in speeding diffusion can be found in the experiences of the Tamil Nadu sterilization campaign, as reported by Srinivasan and Kachirayan (1968). This campaign incorporated the use of nonprofessional aides (who are on the same status level as their poorer clients) and the use of both diffuser and adopter incentives.

1. Of the Tamil Nadu vasectomy adopters, 48% reported that canvassers were their most important source of information about vasectomy.

2. Of these respondents, 4% reported being "compelled to adopt" by a canvasser. Although this figure is comparatively low, it is still noteworthy because alternative reasons for adoption are more socially acceptable.

3. Respondents contacted by canvassers passed through the decision process more quickly than vasectomy adopters contacted by family planning staff. [8]

4. In April 1963, after four years' experience with a diffuser incentive for vasectomy (and seven years' experience with an adopter incentive), the Tamil Nadu government discontinued the diffuser incentive on the assumption that by then a sufficient number of people were informed of the innovation and therefore its diffusion would continue without the incentive payments. However, the rate of vasectomy adoption dropped so alarmingly that within six months the state government reinstated the diffuser incentive.[9]

Repetto's (1969) statistical analysis of the Tamil Nadu State vasectomy campaign concludes that "the canvasser program has had a substantial impact," which he estimates conservatively to be about 75,000 additional adoptions per year, or more than 25% of the total in 1966. The value of the 900,000 expected births-prevented over the following five years, in terms of labor and consumption, is U.S. $70,000,000. Repetto's analysis of the campaign indicates that the diffuser incentive was more important in effecting the rate of adoption than was the adopter incentive, but this conclusion may be a function of the relative size of the two types of incentives or of other idiosyncratic factors.

In Greater Bombay, incentives were first paid to adopters and canvassers in July 1967. The number of vasectomy adoptions per month jumped from 200 to 7000 within six months.

All this evidence has dealt with diffuser incentives for vasectomy, and hence the conclusions drawn may be limited to that method. However, a recent study of the effects of diffuser incentives for IUD and pills is provided by a recent quasi-experiment in Indonesia (Rogers, 1971b). No incentives were paid in Indonesia from 1968, when the national family planning program was initiated, until Fall 1970, when 100 rupiah (about U.S. $0.27) were paid to the individual recruiting each IUD or pill adopter. About six months later, the amount of the diffuser incentive was increased to 200 rupiah. What effects did the smaller and the larger incentives have?

Rogers (1971b) generally concluded that both of these diffuser incentives had a very major effect in increasing adoption rates. For example, data on incentives' effects for the province of Bali are shown in Figure 2. The smaller of the two incentives leads to a 174% increase in adoption rates; the initiation of the larger incentive led to a further increase of 62%. During the 20-month period of study (January 1970 to August 1971), the rate of adoption of IUD and pills was increasing somewhat due to factors other than incentives, and this increase is unfortunately included as a residual along with the incentives' effects. But this residual is quite small, probably representing not more than 5 to 10% of the in-

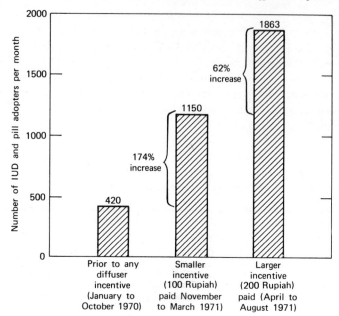

Figure 2.   Initiation of a smaller and a larger diffuser incentive in Indonesia lead to an increase in rates of adoption of IUD and pills. (*Source:* Rogers, (1971b.)

crease in the number of adopters.[10] Thus there is little doubt that the diffuser incentives, which were paid without a concurrent adopter incentive, led to an immediate and direct increase in rates of adoption of family planning methods in Indonesia.

Perkin (1970) found that the highest rate of family planning clinic visits (to adopt the IUD or pills) by Ghanian women occurred during weeks when an adopter and a diffuser incentive (of free powdered milk) were offered. Further, the lowest cost per adopter was secured when both types of incentives were available, although a reanalysis of his data shows that the adopter incentive was more important than the diffuser incentive in reducing cost. The cost per adopter (of clinic services for family planning) averaged $9.85 without either adopter or diffuser incentives, $5.74 with an adopter incentive only, and $4.47 with an adopter and a diffuser incentive.

Generalization V. Although diffuser incentives increase the rate of adoption of an innovation, the quality of the decision to adopt may be rela-

tively low, leading to undesired consequences. There is an obvious parallel here to Generalization III, about adopter incentives and the quality of adopter decisions, and much of the evidence cited in that discussion is applicable here. The most clear-cut support of Generalization V is provided by Srinivasan and Kachirayan (1968), who found that "The proportion of malpractices . . . appears to be much less among those informed [about vasectomy] by the village officials or health staff than among those informed by canvassers, or other vasectomized persons." Respondents contacted by canvassers, when compared to those motivated by official family planning staff, were more likely (1) to have undergone sterilization without their wife's consent; (2) to be motivated primarily by the incentive, rather than by a desire to limit family size; and (3) to hold an unfavorable attitude toward vasectomy even after adoption. These points suggest a high degree of coercion by the canvassers. On all three counts, sterilizations motivated by canvassers were of lower quality.[11]

A dissatisfied customer who adopted because of pressure from a canvasser is the worst kind of interpersonal advertisement for an innovation.

Abuse of diffuser incentives is common in India. Repetto (1969) estimates that such malpractice occurs in 50% of the vasectomy cases, most of it due to the diffuser rather than the adopter incentives. Kapoor and Chandhoke (1968) found that 15% of the vasectomy adopters received considerably less than the full adopter incentive of 30 rupees; 2% got less than half of it. The canvassers were cheating the adopter out of part of the adopter incentive.

Possible solutions to the quality problem associated with diffuser incentives may lie (1) in a thorough control system, which provides better enforcement of incentive policies; (2) in a communication campaign to convey accurate information about the family planning innovation to the intended audience (so as to decrease reliance on canvassers for educating clients); and (3) in alteration of incentive policies so they will be more easily enforceable (e.g., allowing a man with one child to adopt vasectomy). Incentive systems designed to increase rates of adoption are also incentives to cheat the incentive system; prevention of malpractice involves a redesign of the incentive system or the creation of a control system to prevent cheating.

Previously, we showed that initiation of the 100 rupiah and the 200 rupiah diffuser incentives in Indonesia led to an increased rate of adoption of IUD and pills. But there also seem to have been undesirable consequences: The payment of diffuser incentives acts as a strong reward system for the sole goal of achieving new acceptors, at the risk of discouraging proper follow-up of previous adopters. This lack of follow-up activities by the field staff contributes to a mushrooming discontinu-ance rate, caused in part by rumors about side-effects of IUD and pills (Rogers, 1971b). The incentive reward system in Indonesia encouraged adoption at the expense of follow-up (which was not rewarded). Only about 5 to 10% of IUD and pill adopters are followed-up; the result is to encourage negative rumors, which in turn leads to spiraling discontinu-ance rates, and a plateau in the rates of adoption.[12]

Experiments for Testing Policy Alternatives

The field experiments on family planning incentives in Asia are not only valuable for the understandings they provide directly about changing fer-tility behavior (a type of behavior that is tied to particularly strongly held beliefs), but also because those studies are illustrative of what Camp-bell (forthcoming) terms the "experimenting society." Such a system is one which "will vigorously try out proposed solutions to recurrent prob-lems, which will make hard-headed and multi-dimensional evaluations of the outcomes, and which will move on to try other alternatives when evaluation shows one reform to have been ineffective or harmful." Unfor-tunately, Campbell concluded that we do not have such a society today. Not only are most reforms adopted as though they were certain to be suc-cessful (Campbell, 1969), but social scientists generally lack the method-ological tools for conducting field experiments that are scientifically cor-rect, politically feasible, and ethically acceptable.

However, numerous types of experimental designs, especially versions of "quasi-experiments," [13] have been suggested recently by Camp-bell (1968, pp. 259–263) to remedy the methodological lacunae. Other reasons for optimism are several important experimental tests of new public policies. One is the series of field experiments on negative income taxes for low-income people in New Jersey, Pennsylvania, Iowa, North Carolina, Indiana, Washington, and Colorado. These studies were begun in 1968 in order to understand the effect of a guaranteed minimum in-come on motivation to work, migration, children's health and school per-formance, and attitudes toward self and others. The field experiments were planned by the Institute for Research on Poverty at the University of Wisconsin and were sponsored by the U.S. Office of Economic Oppor-tunity, the U.S. Department of Health, Education and Welfare, and the Ford Foundation. Some of the early results, plus certain of the method-ological lessons, are now available (Bawden, 1970; Orcutt and Orcutt, 1968; Watts, 1969). The significance of the research results, whatever they turn out to be, is overshadowed by the fact that the federal government was willing to experimentally evaluate a proposed reform before enacting it as law. This is a step, although only one, toward Campbell's (forthcoming) notion of the experimenting society.

The various quasi-experiments on family planning incentives in Asia reviewed in this chapter, and a series of experiments planned for the future (Rogers, 1972), also constitute an important lesson in the formulation of policy alternatives through experimentation. As we have shown in this chapter, the payment of family planning incentives began in one state in India in 1956, spread throughout India, and then spread to eight other nations. In this early era of family planning incentives, no attention was given to behavioral research in evaluating the incentives' effects or in testing alternative incentive policies. Only after more than a decade of the large-scale payment of incentives were they subjected to even the first research attention.

The first studies were mostly post hoc evaluations of incentive programs, utilizing survey research methods. Typical of the several studies in this first generation of incentives research was the Repetto (1969) investigation of incentive-motivated vasectomy canvassers in India. Much can be learned about designing improved policy alternatives from survey research on exemplary programs, as the Repetto study illustrates. Unfortunately, however, survey research is necessarily bound to studying the relative effectiveness of *existing* policy, policy that is aleady implemented on a large scale. Thus survey research is severely limited in its ability to break outside the bounds of current practice.

Exploration of innovative policies was facilitated in the second generation of incentives research by the use of quasi-experimental designs. In such investigations, a new incentive policy is tried on an experimental basis, and its results are compared with previous practice. Examples of such second generation quasi-experiments, previously mentioned in this chapter, are:

1. The Tata factory workers experiment in India, which tested the effects of a relatively large incentive on the adoption of sterilization (Research and Marketing Services, 1970).

2. The South India tea estates experiment, which tests the effect of a births-prevented incentive, paid as a retirement bond to tea pickers (Ridker, 1969, 1971).

3. The Taiwan educational bond study, which evaluates the consequences of a births-prevented incentive paid for nonbirths (Finnigan, 1972).

These studies are all quasi-experiments, rather than "true" experiments. For instance, in the India factory workers study the researchers could not manipulate the treatments (incentives), and there were no true control groups because the workers and the factories were not randomly assigned to treatment and control groups. Hence the degree to which the research design removes the effect of extraneous variables is low.

Another quasi-experiment mentioned previously is the tea estates retirement bond scheme, now under way in South India on three tea estates with about 600 workers (Ridker, 1969, 1971). Although this investigation advances the understanding of incentive effects, it was impossible to select randomly the three companies involved, and so one cannot be certain that all extraneous variables were removed. A comparison of the fertility rates of the tea-pickers receiving the incentives with the fertility rates of employees of other companies will not tell us the effects of the incentives alone. The experimental companies may employ workers who are older, better educated, or different in other ways from the "control" workers, and these variables will affect their birth rates as well as the incentives.

The main limitation of quasi-experiments, in comparison with "true" experiments, is the difficulty in drawing solid conclusions about the treatment effects. Further, the quasi-experiment usually cannot break as far outside of the bounds of current practice. The treatments are often only a minor modification of existing policy. True experiments, however, offer a way to test new approaches to incentive policies.

But radically different treatments are almost impossible to "sell" to government officials. Almost none of the 15 or 20 delayed, births-prevented incentive schemes (which probably have the greatest promise of demographic effectiveness) proposed since Enke's (1961a) have been approved by any government. For example, the tea estates experiment, when it was originally proposed by Ridker to the government of India, was rejected (although it was later accepted by the tea companies).[14] The Taiwan educational bond is being tested experimentally, with research sponsorship by the Population Council, and with the full knowledge (even if not the enthusiastic support) of the Taiwan government (Finnigan, 1972). Perhaps the India tea estates and the Taiwan project will help usher in a next era of testing incentive policies.

A third generation of incentives experiments is currently being planned for several Asian countries, to be conducted (1) on a multinational, comparative basis, so that the results will synergistically constitute something more than a series of unrelated studies, and (2) with designs that more closely approach true experiments, in that control groups are included, as well as the random assignment of treatments to subjects, so that more precise conclusions about treatment effects can be drawn (Rogers, 1972).

Clearly the main questions needing answers in these forthcoming experiments are: *What is the ideal combination of incentive policies (e.g., births-prevented versus contraception, delayed versus immediate) to optimize (1) the rate of adoption of a family planning innovation, and (2) desired declines in fertility rates; (3) at a maximum efficiency?* The answers can only be found through an integrated series of well-designed and well-conducted field experiments in which various incentives are tested.

Such future studies should design incentive programs that maximize the "quantity" aspects of their effects and minimize the low "quality" consequences of incentives. Our conclusion, based on the present synthesis, is that higher quantity *and* quality effects of incentives are possible, although they are far from being reached by present incentive programs. If improved incentive schemes can be designed, based on behavioral science, we may be able to solve society's population problem without recourse to more coercive measures that might violate or destroy individual values of independence and freedom. Then, indeed, we will have taken an important step toward an experimenting society.

Notes

1.   The present chapter is a revision of Everett M. Rogers (1971), "Incentives in the Diffusion of Family Planning Innovations," *Studies in Family Planning, 2* (12): 241–248. It is based on a chapter in the author's forthcoming book, *Communication Strategies for Family Planning.* The observations and data reported here were gathered while the author was investigating family planning communication behavior (1) in India, Pakistan, and Indonesia on a Ford Foundation travel-study grant in 1970–1971, and (2) in India, Taiwan, and Indonesia as a Population Council consultant in 1971–1972.

2.   The so-called classical diffusion model was described by Rogers (1962), although it was not then referred to by that name.

3.   This definition is based on Pohlman (1971, p. 5). Our definition is purposefully narrow in that it does not include the wide range of advantages and disadvantages of an innovation that affects an individual's innovation-decision, and the subjectively defined rewards and punishments that affect such a decision. For instance, in the case of family planning we do not include the prestige of having another child, the cost of raising an additional child, and the potential returns from labor that he might contribute. These forms of "incentives" are very important in decisions about family planning methods, of course, but in this chapter we follow the narrower meaning because we intend to synthesize past research on incentives that are paid by national family planning agencies.

4.   Starting in 1971, the Indian government enriched the adopter incentive for vasectomy to 100 rupees in 25 selected districts, on the basis of the spectacu-

lar results from the Ernakulam vasectomy campaign in July 1971, described later in this chapter and by Krishnakumar (1971).

5. For extensive evidence on this point, see Rogers with Shoemaker (1971), who review the results of several hundred research studies.

6. Perhaps because the payment of diffuser incentives creates a corps of low-status canvassers who contact potential adopters who are similar in socioeconomic status. The usual professional change agent contacts relatively more elite clients, who are similar, or homophilous, to him. Thus both professional and nonprofessional change agents tend to communicate homophilously with clients like themselves (Rogers and Bhowmik, 1971).

7. Although several important changes in diffuser incentive payments have occurred in Tamil Nadu State since Repetto's data were gathered in 1966, the present author observed in 1970–1971 that Repetto's conclusions about the overwhelming importance of canvassers in motivating vasectomy adopters were still correct for that state, and probably for most other Indian states.

8. In a somewhat parallel case, Perkin (1970) found that an adopter incentive in Ghana shortened the time lag between knowledge and decision to adopt an innovation.

9. Repetto (1969) and Srinivasan and Kachirayan (1969) give details on this government vacillation in incentive policies.

10. We estimate the size of this residual from inspection of the month-by-month total number of adopters in Bali, compared to similar data for selected family planning clinics on Java that did not initiate incentive payments until a later time, and thus constitute a kind of control group.

11. Although this quality difference might be due to the health staff's clients being more favorable to vasectomy before the operation than were the canvassers' clients (Pohlman, 1971, p. 73).

12. Such plateau effects have occurred in country after country in Asia for such family planning methods as IUD, pills, and vasectomy. Effective follow-up of previous adopters is one of the most important approaches to fighting negative rumors about side-effects, and thus to preventing the plateaus in rates of adoption.

13. A quasi-experiment is not a "true" experiment in that (1) no true control groups are included in the design, and (2) the investigators do not have control over the treatments so they cannot be randomly assigned to subjects. For these reasons, one cannot fully control an extraneous variable that may affect the treatment effects. For detail on the nature and the shortcomings of quasi-experiments, see Campbell and Stanley (1966, p. 34), Campbell (1968), and Campbell (1969).

14. Although the government of India had approved of the partial support of the tea estates project by the U.S. Agency for International Development, and after the incentive plan had been in operation for six months the government of India granted $150,000 (U.S.) to the project to extend greatly its scope.

Denton E. Morrison

Department of Sociology
Michigan State University

SOME NOTES TOWARD THEORY
ON RELATIVE DEPRIVATION,
SOCIAL MOVEMENTS, AND SOCIAL CHANGE [1]

It is now commonplace to use relative deprivation explicitly or implicitly as a central variable in the explanation of social movements, and thus also to explain the processes of social change that are engendered by social movements.[2] The basic notion is that feelings of deprivation, of discontent over one's situation, depend on what one *wants* to have, that is, deprivation in relation to desired points of reference, often "reference groups," rather than on how little one has. In turn, social movements are thought to emerge and flourish when groups of persons experience relative deprivation. Indeed, much evidence supports this view. For instance, it is clear that persons who have experienced steady and abject poverty are not as likely as others to be involved in movements of protest and change, particularly others who have experienced some improvements in their situation and who assumedly want those improvements to continue (Pinard, 1967).

However, much of the evidence relevant to the connection of relative deprivation and social movements is *indirect* evidence (see, e.g., Grindstaff, 1968). It is clear evidence *against* absolute deprivation but not definitive evidence *for* relative deprivation since data on the feeling-states of individuals are usually not offered. Often, in those cases where data on individual attitudes are offered, both data and theory on the processes by which individuals acquire feelings of relative deprivation, and on the way in which relative deprivation is related to the beliefs and attitudes about social change that characterize participants in social movements, are lacking. Further, accounts that attempt to explain social movements by rela-

153

tive deprivation often contain little evidence, theory, or even speculation on the structural conditions that give rise to relative deprivation.

Some recent work has made progress toward alleviating these shortcomings (Geschwender, 1968; Runciman, 1966; Gurr, 1970). This paper attempts to offer some further theoretical considerations on the notion of relative deprivation as it applies to social movements, building on a framework developed as a result of previous research on a contemporary farmers' bargaining movement, the National Farmers' Organization (NFO) (Morrison and Steeves, 1967). In particular, attention is given to beliefs about social structure that develop from relative deprivation in social movement participants, and the structural conditions that are likely to generate such beliefs. Also, I will discuss some notions that relate coercive and goal-displacement tendencies in social movements. The paper, however, is intended to be speculative, heuristic, and preliminary rather than definitive.

The notion of a social movement used in this paper (and implicitly in most accounts that involve relative deprivation as a crucial explanatory variable) is that of primarily a *power-oriented* movement: a deliberate, voluntary effort to organize individuals to act in concert to achieve group influence to make or block changes. In power-oriented movements, in contrast with participation-oriented movements (like the Pentecostal movement), group actions are not in and of themselves viewed as primary sources of the benefits or gratifications desired by individual participants (see Killian, 1964, pp. 448–452). Rather, coordinated group actions are thought to be the necessary means to obtain from some elements in the larger social context the changes desired by the participants, as in the labor movement and the civil rights movement.

A further specification is that this analysis applies particularly to power movements in relatively open, democratic societies that stress individual mobility, though many of the notions have broader application. In addition, the analysis probably applies more to what Smelser (1963) has termed "norm-oriented" movements (changes *within* the system that involve the means to more basic values) than to "value-oriented" movements (basic goal changes *of* a system), though broader relevance is implied.

Relative Deprivation and Social Movements

The basic notion of relative deprivation outlined above needs elaboration in two important ways before the sense in which the discontent that arises from relative deprivation is suitably described: the desires involved must become (1) legitimate expectations that are (2) perceived as blocked.

In relative deprivation theory a person not only desires a given goal, but he also feels that he has a *right* to obtain that goal, that he *deserves* it, at least under certain conditions. These conditions will here generically be termed his "investments." The investments that give rise to feelings that a goal is legitimately expected can be either ascribed or achieved statuses or roles, or the actions that constitute the means by which statuses and roles are achieved. Naturally, before a goal can be legitimately expected we must presuppose contacts of the kind and intensity that establish the awareness, the desirability, and the possibility of certain goal-states. The general process by which desires become legitimate expectations involves, beyond this, learning that certain investments *are* generally rewarded by certain outcomes, so that it becomes expected that such investments *should* be so rewarded. Such learning is probably most poignant when actual behavioral reinforcement is involved, for example, experiencing promotion and income increases as a result of certain investments in energy, effort, education, and seniority. But we also know that expectations can be formed and legitimized by identification with persons and groups whose investments are perceived as similar to and thus no more deserving of certain awards than one's own but whose actual returns are greater. Thus one comes legitimately to expect returns equivalent to persons in such "reference groups." [3]

Relative deprivation also involves the notion that a negative discrepancy between what one legitimately expects and what one has will generate discontent only to the extent that there is a high perceived probability that the discrepancy will not be reduced, that is, a high probability of blockage. This in fact is the social-psychological definition of "deprivation." If one expects something and thinks he will get it, he does not feel "deprived" of it.

An expectation, however, always has a time dimension—the belief that a goal will be reached within a certain time, or approached at a certain rate. Thus to have a legitimate expectation and at the same time have a high perceived probability of blockage requires, in general, that the perception of blockage probability must increase rather suddenly. This is because there is an interactive relationship, a relationship of a mutual feedback, adjustment, and learning between the development of a legitimate expectation (i.e., the translation of a desire into a legitimate expectation) and the subjective as well as the objective probability that the expectation will be fulfilled. Where the probability that a given desire will not be fulfilled has been high over a period of time and remains high, the desire does not develop into a legitimate expectation. Thus le-

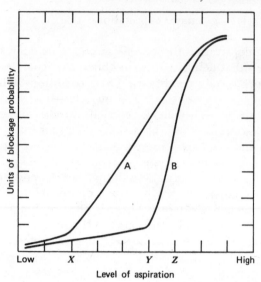

Figure 1.   Hypothetical relationship of aspiration level and probability of blockage.

gitimate expectations tend over time to be for those desires that have a relatively low probability of blockage, that is, where the opportunities for realizing such desires have been relatively good; increases in blockage probability must involve a declining ratio of opportunities in relation to desires. Since actual levels of blockage probability are unknown, blockage probability is perceived to be high to the extent that increases in blockage probability exceed increases in aspiration ("aspiration" is the absolute magnitude of the desire).[4]

These notions can be illustrated by Figure 1, where the hypothetical curves represent differing opportunity structures for reaching aspirations of varying magnitudes. Although it is accurate to interpret the vertical axis as representing the *level* of blockage probability, the specific interpretation here, in keeping with the foregoing rationale, is that it represents units of blockage probability. It is assumed, then, in Figure 1 that all social systems provide some region where the curve is relatively flat and low, that is, where increasing aspirations bring relatively small increases in the probability of blockage. Where relatively large increases in aspiration bring relatively small increases in the probability of blockage, the flat, low portion of the curve is a lengthy one, as in curve B.

One way in which sudden increases in blockage can come about in terms of Figure 1 is the situation in which, for a certain constant level of aspiration, opportunities decline because the opportunity curve itself suddenly changes in a way that restricts opportunities, for instance, curve B changes to curve A for aspiration Y. In a previous context I have termed this phenomenon "decremental deprivation" (Morrison and Steeves, 1967). Examples are situations in which a depression or recession takes opportunities away from persons, or where social, institutional or legal changes take opportunities away as in the confiscating of lands from elites in developing countries, or, perhaps, the situation of small businessmen in the United States in recent years. Such situations are those that are typically involved in movements to block changes or to bring about changes that will restore a former condition, that is, rightist or reactionary movements.

The opposite, "aspirational deprivation," occurs when the magnitude of aspiration increases to a much greater extent than opportunities for realizing the increased aspiration. This can involve an increase in aspiration that is (1) large (for instance X to Y on curve A) or (2) small (Y to Z on curve B) as long as the aspiration moves through some crucial point in the opportunity structure, that is, where the curve "suddenly" changes from flat to steep. These are the situations that are typically involved in movements *for* change—liberal or leftist movements. Case 1 is probably best exemplified by the "revolution of rising expectations" in developing countries, where through contacts with developed countries and internal social changes new reference groups are suddenly obtained. Case 2 is the situation in discontinuous stratification systems where for those in any given stratum there are somewhat severe hurdles that must be surmounted before the next higher stratum can be entered. Some examples might be passage from blue-collar to white-collar work, from worker to manager or owner, and from jobs and salaries usually available for women or for blacks to those that are available mainly for men and for whites (see Form and Geschwender, 1962, p. 237).

Since within any stratification system opportunities for realizing high aspirations have almost by definition been better for those who are not in the lowest stratum, these notions provide a possible theoretical basis for explaining the tendency for those who occupy positions well off the bottom (but still far from the top) of the stratification system to be more likely to be involved in social movements of aspirational deprivation than those in the lowest stratum. According to this reasoning then, different social strata have different opportunity curves, with the length of the flat, low portion of the curve representing the extent to which persons in a given stratum have had aspiration increases reinforced by experience. Thus the lowest social stratum would have a curve with a short flat, low portion like curve A, whereas a stratum well off the bottom would have a curve like B. Both groups encounter structural obstacles to mobility (i.e., points where the curve suddenly steepens), but the latter group has had more aspiration increases reinforced by fulfillment and is thus more likely to develop legitimate expectations that further aspiration increases will continue to be fulfilled, while the former group has not to the same degree had aspiration increases reinforced by positive experience. This same general line of reasoning is probably relevant in explaining why power movements are much more prevalent in underdeveloped countries that have made a genuine start toward development (Feierabend et al., 1969).

In addition, we can probably assume that the mobility hurdles to the next higher stratum become more difficult to scale as we go from the bottom to the top of the status hierarchy. Thus persons fairly well off the bottom but still far from the top of the hierarchy will, as they near a hurdle, experience a more rapid increase in blockage probability for a given increment in aspiration level than those on the bottom (as indicated in the relative difference in the steepness of curves A and B). The same is true, of course, for persons who are close to the top of the hierarchy, but the theoretical possibility for an increase in their opportunities for mobility is so small as to put severe reality limits on their aspirations—there is, realistically, "no room at the top," but relatively much more room in the middle.

Stating this somewhat differently and summarizing what has been said thus far, relative deprivation involves a special type of cognitive dissonance in which there develops the belief in a legitimate expectation and, simultaneously, the discrepant belief that there is a high probability that the expectation will not be fulfilled.[5] Since legitimate expectations are thought by their possessors to be "deserved," the specific feelings of dissonance that arise are that this situation is one of "injustice" or "inequity."[6] Such feelings can only come about when the belief in a high blockage probability comes about suddenly; otherwise, the legitimate expectation would not develop. For decremental deprivation the intensity of the dissonance will depend on the rate at which opportunities decline for a given level of aspiration. For aspirational deprivation the intensity of dissonance may or may not involve a great or sudden increase in aspiration, depending on the shape of the opportunity curve and where a person's aspiration level is when a higher aspiration is acquired. But in general the intensity of dissonance will be a function of the rate at which the perception of blockage probability for a legitimate expectation increases.

Dissonance is a psychologically upsetting state that generates attempts to reduce the dissonance. One possible alternative for lowering the dissonance created by relative deprivation is to interpret the blockage as due to individual shortages of talent, luck, resources, motivation, and so forth. This, in effect, amounts to a person saying that in his particular case the expectation is not legitimate, that his investments are not adequate. In this case a failure to achieve an aspiration is viewed, as Turner (1969, p. 391) says, as a misfortune rather than an injustice. Thus a person may simply lower his aspiration or he may engage in attempts to change his investments by trying to develop his talents, resources, or motivation. Another possible alternative for reducing the dissonance is to lower one's interpretation of the probability of blockage, that is, to believe that with a little patience one's investments will be adequately rewarded. Still another possible mode for resolving the dissonance is for a person to change his situation, to attempt to get into a context where one's investments are more likely to be rewarded, for instance, in rural to urban migration (in terms of Figure 1 this is to change to a more favorable opportunity curve).

When relative deprivation results in involvement in a power-oriented movement none of these alternatives for dissonance reduction is taken. Rather, both the beliefs in the legitimate expectation and in a high probability of blockage are maintained. The belief in blockage is translated into a belief in *structural blockage,* and attempts at dissonance reduction take the form of belief in a *structural solution.* Individuals come to see themselves as part of a *group* with legitimate expectations that are blocked by some aspect of the larger social structure outside the group; there is an attempt to remove the source of the dissonance by organized group action to change the structural source of the blockage.[7] Note, however, that it would be inaccurate to say that a power movement attempts directly or immediately to lower dissonance; indeed, a social movement depends on maintaining its participants in a state of tension and upset over their situation. The dissonance is not psychologically disabling for the individual because its effect is overridden by the belief that the blockage will be removed by group action (structural faith), and by the belief that some feature of the larger social structure outside the individual can be blamed for the blockage (structural blame).

The beliefs in structural blockage and structural solution are, then, simultaneously the psychology that emerges and develops when a power-oriented movement comes into being, the kinds of beliefs that are diffused to recruit persons to participate in the movement, and the major features of the ideology of the movement: the legitimate expectations of a group are substantially blocked, the source of the blockage is in the social structure, and the group acting in concert can and will change the social structure to remove the blockage.

The Structural Conditions for the Emergence of
Social Movements

We have already outlined the kinds of structural conditions that are related to high relative deprivation: rapid social changes of the sort that (1) increase contacts and communication between persons in different social strata and launch many persons on trajectories of upward social mobility (aspirational deprivation), or (2) decrease opportunities (decremental deprivation), or (3) (1) followed rapidly by (2)—the latter is the Davies' "J curve" notion (1962, 1969), called "progressive deprivation" by Gurr (1970, pp. 52–56).

The main structural conditions that increase the probability that beliefs in structural blockage and structural solution will emerge and spread when high relative deprivation is experienced (i.e., increase the probability of emergence of a power-oriented movement) would seem to be the following:

1. *A large population experiencing the relative deprivation* increases the chances that varying interpretations will be made of any given situation, and, particularly, that leadership potential will exist among some of those who develop notions of structural blockage and structural solution.

2. *Close interaction, communication, and proximity* are necessary so that similarity of situation can be better observed and so that interpretations of structural blockage and structural solution can be reinforced and refined into a coherent ideology when they arise. (Notions 1 and 2 together suggest that a certain "density" of relative deprivation is necessary for movement emergence.)

3. *High role and status commonality* is, of course, related to the "class consciousness" that is a part of all movements. It is more difficult to interpret a blockage as due to individual causes when many similar persons experience the same blockage. Moreover, when investments *cannot* be altered and rewards are inequitable, as with ascribed roles and statuses such as sex and race, individual solutions to blockage have inherently low appeal.

4. *A stratification system with clear strata boundaries and visible power differences between the strata* increases the likelihood that the blockages lie in the nature of the stratification system, that they will be

interpreted as such, and that structural interpretations of the necessary changes will develop accordingly.

5. *The presence of much voluntary association activity in a society* is important because the notion of a structural solution is not likely to emerge where there are no precedents for the view that society can be changed by voluntary group efforts. In addition, voluntary associations tend to create in any society a residue of leadership and organizational skills that are crucial for getting a movement off the ground.

Problems of Movement Recruitment, Growth, and Effectiveness

The essential psychological feature involved in the emergence of a power movement for the persons who bring the movement into existence is the substantial transfer of faith from individual to group solutions for relative deprivation. This does not mean that belief in the relevance of individual investments is discarded but, rather, adoption of the belief that individual investments are only necessary and not sufficient for reducing relative deprivation. What is involved, then, in becoming part of a movement is the unlearning of conventional notions for explaining the relationship between investments and rewards and the learning of new modes of explanation (structural blockage) as well as undertaking a commitment to group action to bring about the structural solution through the movement.

The decision to cast one's lot with *any* group that is seeking (rather than concretely providing) gains is, as Olson (1965) points out, a difficult one, since in a group endeavor the individual incurs costs over and above those he must bear in acting in an individual capacity and yet the increased benefits from the group activity are problematic. Indeed, Olson argues convincingly that a large group must (1) employ separate and selective incentives, that is, benefits other than the main ones the group is organized to seek (for instance, recreational, expressive, or insurance benefits in a union), and/or (2) coercion to get and keep members. Although Olsons's analysis is not intended specifically to apply to power-oriented social movements, his points are clearly relevant to such movements, perhaps even more so than to other voluntary groups. This is because the costs of participation in a power movement are typically very high in relation to immediate outcomes. In addition to the economic costs in the diversion of time, energy, and resources (often dues) away from individual routes to rewards in organizational and proselytizing activities, social costs and risks are incurred because movements involve an essentially unconventional—a radical—interpretation of social reality. And there is no guarantee that the structural solution will ever provide substantial benefits to the participants, much less short-run benefits or benefits greater than can be obtained by individual activity.

Thus, once a movement emerges—in the sense of a core of initial adherents who are in varying degrees the leaders of the movement—the recruitment of additional loyal adherents becomes the movement's immediate aim and, increasingly, its most perplexing problem. The recruitment of a relatively large number of loyal adherents is of central import because the power of the movement depends on the support it can command both in terms of sheer quantity of members and in terms of its ability to count on the supporters to act in concert. Recruitment is a perplexing problem because as the movement grows from its initial core of leaders the cost-benefit ratios of potential adherents rise sharply. This is because we can assume that movements arise and spread first to those who are most directly under the structural conditions conducive to high relative deprivation and to beliefs in structural blockage and structural solution. These initial adherents thus have the greatest faith in the structural solution and the least faith in alternative individual solutions to reducing relative deprivation, giving them relatively low cost-benefit ratios and thus a very high commitment to the movement, which is, of course, reinforced by well-known dissonance-reducing processes as they proselytize. In addition, these persons, by virtue of being the leaders of the movement, receive the attendant benefits of their power and prestige in and outside the movement—and often an income to boot; in short, they in some measure realize rewards and social mobility *in* the movement. In a sense, then, the leaders and early adherents of the movement are more like Olson's small group, for whom separate incentives are *not* necessary to maintain loyalty, whereas others who are in the movement or who are potential participators are more like Olson's large group.

This notion provides a basis for explaining goal-displacement, oligarchy, and coercive tendencies, including violence, in social movements. Those who are in power in the movement must use both separate incentives and coercion to bring in members, and, in turn, those who are brought in must be motivated by coercion to act in the disciplined ways necessary when power tactics are employed by the movement. However, since the use of coercion over time always carries the risk of losing members and of polarizing potential members and others against the movement, and thus risks loss of power by the leaders, there is a tendency over time for leaders to turn increasingly to separate incentives for the recruitment and maintenance of members. This makes radical action more difficult because of the increasingly conservative composition of the membership, the elaboration and rationalization of the organizational structure necessary to provide separate incentives, and the increasingly vested career interests of leaders that comes with their proliferation and tenure. Movements that do not take this route—or perhaps more accurately movements that have not yet reached the point of high goal displacement and oligarchy—often do not have the members needed to wield power to gain concessions from the structural targets with tactics short of extreme coercion, including violence. Furthermore, such extreme tactics are often employed on potential members or the structural targets by radical factions of the movement who are frustrated by the conservatism of the larger movement and its inability to gain or discipline members or achieve its original goals. Such tactics, of course, often escalate as the structural targets tighten their hold on power and strike back in kind.

Summary and Conclusion

Social movements create social change, but they are also created by social changes that take away opportunities or create expectations faster than opportunities for reaching the expectations are created, resulting in relative deprivation. Such a situation would appear to be particularly important in the developing countries where in almost Malthusian fashion expectations for modern life styles grow geometrically through contacts with developing countries, while opportunities grow arithmetically. Thus the "revolution of rising expectations" may only be a temporary euphemism for an impending explosion of discontent and power-oriented movements in these countries. It is also worth considering that this phenomenon operates for awakening and underdeveloped sectors of developed countries, such as the blacks in the United States (Feierabend et al., pp. 673–677).

Power-oriented movements are uniquely concerned with group, often "class," mobility and thus involve interpretations of structural blockage and structural solution. However, the social changes that create relative deprivation and the structural conditions that are conducive to interpretations of structural blockage and structural solutions do not affect potential movement benefactors equally. Therefore, movement members must be vigorously recruited and maintained by the leaders through incentives that are separate from the movement's goals and/or by coercion. The former results in the familiar phenomenon of movements becoming conservative and the latter results in the coercive tendencies of movements, including violence.

The connection of coercion with recruitment and member maintenance in this paper should not, however, imply that this source of coercive tendencies in movements is the whole explanation of the coercion that is often associated with power-oriented movements. Indeed, violence may be an integral and an effective part of the structural solution where the target structure is intractable by other means, or, conversely, violence may be a deliberate tactic the target structure uses to control the movement. Moreover, violence may simply be a nonprogramatic collective expression of frustration and aggression where relative deprivation is high and a power-oriented movement cannot or does not emerge. Thus the explanation of coercion outlined in this paper would seem to be particularly applicable in those societies where voluntary association activity is widespread and generally effective. To some extent this supplements Gurr's (1970) attempt to explain collective violence by relative deprivation by spelling out the way in which the inherent cost-benefit problems of organizing persons have a tendency to generate coercion by *and* within the movement.

Notes

1. Reprinted from the *American Behavioral Scientist*, May/June 1971. Michigan Agricultural Experiment Station Journal Article Number 5317.

2. See, for example, much of the literature summarized in Gurr (1970).

3. See Adams (1965) for an elaboration and an attempt at formalization of these notions.

4. By this conception two men with salaries of $6000 and $8000 who both want to make $10,000 have the same level of aspiration. Anticipating the discussion that follows, they may, of course, be on different opportunity curves, so that an increase in their aspiration from $10,000 to $12,000 may mean a sudden increase in blockage for one and not for the other. This conception of aspiration is different than the earlier one in Morrison and Steeves (1967).

5. See Geschwender (1968) for a thoughtful discussion of the relationship of relative deprivation to cognitive dissonance as well as status consistency.

6. It is also a situation of inequity, of course, when investments are over-rewarded. Thus it is worth considering the notion that feelings of social guilt are a product of overreward and that such feelings may help account for the frequent phenomenon wherein a movement receives considerable support, even leadership, from those who would not themselves benefit if the movement achieved its goals. For some relevant theory on overreward see Adams (1965) and Anderson et al. (1969).

7. Aberle (1962) has hypothesized that millenial movements arise when relative deprivation is high and structural blockage is perceived, but no chance of changing the social order to relieve the deprivation is perceived. It would seem to be the case, then, that participation-oriented movements arise when the deprivations are perceived to be of a personal nature, that is, when structural blockage is not perceived.

PART THREE

BASIC ELEMENTS IN THE CHANGE PROCESS: A MACRO VIEW

The three chapters in this section also focus on basic elements of social change. They have in common a more broadly conceived focus and emphasize somewhat different elements than are treated in other chapters; they are more social and social-psychologically oriented. For example, the discussion of attitude change is presented in terms of its implications for the design and management of social action programs.

Large-scale social action is a relatively recent phenomenon made possible by the scientific and industrial revolution and abetted by urbanization, mass communication, and technological progress. The chapter by Philip Kotler, "The Elements of Social Action," provides an important paradigm linking micro and macro elements of social change. Kotler defines social action as the undertaking of collective action to mitigate or resolve a social problem. In Kotler's conceptualization of social movements that produce change, it is clear that he wants to know not only about the leaders of change and their supporters, but also the targets, as well as the methods and channels through which the change agents affect those who are subject to influence. A paradigm of five elements—called the five C's—is advanced that comprehends a broad range of social action phenomena. A *cause* is a social objective or undertaking that change agents believe will provide some answer to a social problem. Three causes are distinguished: helping causes, which attempt to help the victims; protest causes, which attempt to discipline the offending institutions; and revolutionary causes, which attempt to destroy the offending institutions. A change agency is an organization whose primary mission is to advance a social cause. Change targets are individuals, groups, or institutions designated as the targets of change efforts. *Channels* are ways in which influence and response can be transmitted between change agents and change targets. A *change strategy* is a basic mode of influence adopted by the change agent to affect the change target. Each concept is subject to important distinctions which are expected to be useful in analyzing, predicting, and planning social action.

The reader is challenged by Kotler to take the next step beyond establishing a framework for distinguishing elements of social action. This next step is to study the dynamics of the overall process Kotler describes. For example, what interaction is there between strategies and channels? Is a given strategy differentially effective when pursued through different channels? Does the nature of the change agency or cause intervene in such interactions? Beyond giving an affirmative response wherever applicable, one must ultimately ask what the interaction among elements of social action actually are: How do they function and how do they manifest themselves? By distinguishing the important elements of social action Kotler moves us toward this greater undertaking.

The role of information processing and attitude formation and functioning as a micro level causal force in social change cannot be underestimated. Knowledge of these processes is indispensable in *explaining* social change, in *predicting* outcomes of ongoing social change phenomena, and in intervening effectively for purposes of *controlling* social change. It is especially important for the social planner interested in influencing the course of particular events to be sensitive to the psychological state of mind of his target groups in reference to the desired change and its related stimuli. He must also be concerned with the ongoing psychological processes accounted for by the interaction and operation of the relevant variables involved in the psychological state or states. These factors are major determinants of the strategies and tactics the social planner or change agent should choose for directing change. The chapter by John Maloney and Eugene Schonfeld on "Social Change and Attitude Change" is primarily concerned with identifying relevant psychological variables and describing their functioning with regard to social change. The chapter does not stop at simply identifying and describing important psychological variables related to thinking and attitude change. Considerable attention is also given to the implications of these factors for the design of social programs. Many comprehensive strategy guidelines for conducting social change are provided by the authors. Of particular interest is their discussion of a continuous information system which makes the change agent a participant in a multilevel system of communications and feedbacks as a program of social change passes through its life cycle. The chapter concludes with a provocative discussion and partial response to the question, "What if we *were* to have a scientifically precise political or social science of social change in place and ready to solve all the world's problems as we or others see them?" The reader is challenged here with the task of providing a response—his own design of a social organization or system—that would prevent the making of tyrants "out of those who merely aspire to clear up a mess."

Communication is a process that is at once individual and social. It is inextricably bound with both micro and macro phenomena; for example, it is both a cause and consequence of cognitive development at one level and of national development at another level. This is made very clear in Bruce Westley's chapter, "Communication and Social Change." Westley is careful to illustrate that both information exchange and information seeking may be causes as well as consequences of change. Communication is a social act regardless of the level of analysis; indeed it is a universal characteristic of all societies and it is not surprising that it is an essential ingredient of social change entering into that process in multiple ways. Westley challenges the reader with two related basic questions: "Is it the natural tendency of communication and of mass or public communication in particular to induce social change or to inhibit change?" and, "Is it in the nature of communications in general and mass communications where they exist to induce change in predictable directions?" Several research traditions bearing on these questions are reviewed with special emphasis on the diffusion of innovations and on national development. The traditions reviewed and the manner of their review by Westley provide considerable insight into the questions he poses. None of these traditions, however, provide unequivocal answers and the reader must reach his own conclusions about the *natural* tendency of communication as a facilitator or inhibitor of change and about the manageability of communication, that is, its yielding *predictable* effects under conditions of manipulation. Clearly very different policies and change strategies are suggested by the different possible answers to these questions. The reader cannot escape having to answer them. This chapter provides some of the ingredients for answers.

Philip Kotler

Graduate School of Management
Northwestern University

THE ELEMENTS OF SOCIAL ACTION

Social distress has always been a feature of man's existence. War, pestilence, poverty, and oppression have been so characteristic of human history that one is tempted to a functionalist explanation that they somehow serve the needs of the human or natural order. Yet this possibility can never quite be accepted, and one always finds some fraction of mankind engaged in organized collective efforts to banish—or at least mitigate—the amount of social distress.

The ideology of social action—that man can improve his society through organized collective effort—received its major impetus only in the last few hundred years. Before the scientific and industrial revolutions, there was a great amount of social distress but very little social action. Man's afflictions were treated as an inevitable part of the natural order and persuasively rationalized in religious or economic terms. The scientific revolution gave man new understandings of his world, mind, and body and spawned the idea of progress. The industrial revolution opened the possibility of increasing production so substantially that food, clothing, housing, and medicine would be available to all. Other developments—the growing middle class, increasing literacy, popular regimes—gave birth to a humanitarian consciousness which began to consider how social forces could be harnessed to help the needy, the sick, and the oppressed.

In particular, large-scale social action, as a species of social behavior, is a relatively recent phenomena. Today, large numbers of people join or support causes aimed at improving some aspect of society. They raise money for medical causes, give time to the needy, protest social injustice, and even challenge the established social order. Socially concerned people

169

are organized, aided, and abetted by a growing number of professional social actionists—lawyers, ministers, social workers, community organizers, social planners, teachers, radicals.

In spite of the increased outpouring and ministrations of concerned individuals and organizations, over the years, there is little evidence that man has reversed, or even held back, the amount of social misery. Social problems are very difficult to solve, resolve or mitigate. Etzioni (1969, p. ;749) suggested:

> If we observe a society faced with a problem—poverty, riots, unsafe cars— and formulating a program to deal with it, we can be sure that nine times out of ten the problem will not be solved. If we look again, ten or twenty years later, we shall find that the problem may have been trimmed, redefined, or redistributed, but only infrequently will it have been treated to anyone's satisfaction. Thus, we flatly predict that 15 years from now there will still be massive poverty in the United States (despite the "total war" devoted to its eradication), there will still be outbreaks of violence in the streets during hot summers, and there probably will still be tens of thousands of casualties on the highways each year.

Even when social action proves effective, it often succeeds in replacing one social problem with another. The Eighteenth Amendment destroyed the saloons and the whiskey trust but created organized crime. Better street lighting in one neighborhood often drives crime into the next. Many people who stop drinking alcohol start increasing their intake of cigarettes. Reducing the birth rate could lead to more affluence and in turn more pollution. Thus nature continuously confronts us with the fact that every change creates new social imbalances.

Yet we have no choice but to wage war against these problems. It is of interest that in spite of the magnitude of social action, no unified theory has been advanced concerning its nature, elements, antecedents, and consequences. The progress of theory is handicapped by the different vocabularies and perspectives of clergymen, politicians, educators, social workers, radicals, and others involved in social action. Each group has formulated situation-specific models of the social action process in which they are engaged. The structural and process similarities between the actions of angry students, Washington lobbyists, and ghetto organizers are rarely given theoretical recognition. Yet persons involved in social action —protesting the war, converting nonbelievers, motivating dropouts, and disabusing drug addicts—always find their problems are similar.

This chapter takes a look at the elements that seem to be common to all social action. The first section defines how the following terms will be used: social problem, social change, and social action. The following sections elaborate a paradigm called the five C's of social action: cause, change agency, change targets, channels, and change strategy. These five elements are the building blocks for understanding the phenomenon of social action.

Social Problems, Social Change, and Social Action

This section defines three important concepts used in the discussion that follows. The first is social problem, in the absence of which social action would have no meaning.

> **Social Problem.** A specific condition in society that is viewed apprehensively or distastefully by some of its members and is thought to be susceptible to mitigation or elimination through collective effort.

Thus social problems depend on the development of a group definition of a situation. Teenager drug use is essentially a private habit, but it becomes a social problem when a significant group begins to view it apprehensively or distastefully and to feel that some action should be taken against it. Poverty passes from being a personal affliction to a social problem when a significant group begins to view it apprehensively or distastefully and to call for social action. Alcoholism is a social problem because people think something can be done about it, but death from old age is not considered a social problem.

The next term we consider is *social change,*

> **Social Change,** The occurrence of an alteration in the form or functioning of a significant group, institution, or social order.

Social change takes place continuously as groups, institutions, and social orders receive, respond, and adapt to new stimuli. A useful distinction can be drawn between unplanned and planned social change. Social change will take place even in the absence of conscious change agents pursuing social goals. Inventions, crop failures, diseases, historical personages—all have a tremendous potential for altering the relations among people and between people and the natural habitat, perhaps more than the collective effects of planned social change.

Finally, social action has to be defined.

> **Social Action.** The undertaking of collective action to mitigate or resolve a social problem.

The aim of social action is social change in a direction deemed desirable by the agents of change. Success is seen in terms of overcoming or mitigating a social problem.

The Five Elements of Social Action

In every instance of social action, it is possible to distinguish five elements, which may be called the five C's of social action:

Cause. A social objective or undertaking that change agents believe will provide some answer to a social problem.

Change Agency. An organization whose primary mission is to advance a social cause.

Change Targets. Individuals, groups, or institutions designated as the targets of change efforts.

Channels. Ways in which influence and response can be transmitted between change agents and change targets.

Change Strategy. A basic mode of influence adopted by the change agent to affect the change target.

These elements are examined in the remaining sections of this chapter.

Causes

There are far more causes in society than there are social problems. Each social problem spawns a number of divergent solutions by different individuals and collectives. When a sufficient number of persons favor that solution, it becomes their "cause." If this cause is pursued with enough vigor, it may be turned into a *function,* that is, acquire functionaries who professionally handle it. The function may take on different forms, such as a social agency, a national organization, a social movement, or a political party. By the time the cause becomes institutionalized, it may no longer be clearly tied to the original social problem but represent a general solution seen to many social problems.

A Classification of Causes. A meaningful classification of causes would be helpful in a number of ways. It would show the underlying dimensions that unite or separate different causes. Each class of cause is likely to involve different relationships among the five elements of social action. Furthermore, each class of cause may suggest particular mixes of change strategies—power strategies, persuasive strategies, and reeducative strategies. "Lighter" social causes may call for primary reliance on persuasive strategies, whereas "heavier" social causes may require substantial doses of power or reeducation.

Insofar as causes arise to mitigate or eliminate a social problem, it is possible to develop the following three-way classification of causes based on the nature of the attack on the social problem: [1]

1. *Helping causes:* causes seeking to help the victims of the social problem.

2. *Protest causes:* causes seeking to discipline the offending institutions contributing to the social problem.

3. *Revolutionary causes:* causes seeking to eliminate the offending institutions contributing to the social problem.

Helping causes represent the mildest form of social action on behalf of the victims of a social problem. There is no effort to attack the social problem at its roots. This is deemed to be impossible, infeasible, or undesirable for that *agency* to do. The agency instead concerns itself with providing aid, comfort, or education to the actual or potential victims of the social problem. Helping causes direct their time and resources to the poor, drug addicts, juvenile offenders, the aged, and so on. The prime example of helping agencies are the social work agencies for whom social action meant, until recently, working with the victims of social maladies. Social action meant individual or group casework, with community action representing only a recent development.

Protest causes (also called reform causes) are primarily concerned with identifying the institutions that contribute most to the social problem and altering their behavior in a way that will improve the condition of the victims. The protesters may ask the offending institutions to distribute greater resources to the victims, share some of its powers, or to desist from certain practices. Consider the labor movement in this connection. The labor movement evolved from a helping movement to a protest movement. Early trade union activity consisted of the effort of laboring men to provide self-help to those among them in need. This was superseded by a protest movement which identified the company as a contributor to the plight of working men and sought to effect a redistribution of power and resources in favor of the workingmen. At the same time, most labor movements have not evolved beyond protest movements, being satisfied to discipline the "offenders" rather than eliminate them.

Revolutionary causes take as their social objective the elimination of those parties or institutions that contribute most to the social problem. They take the position that as long as the offending institution exists, no matter how cooperative or benign it may be, the social problem and its victims cannot be helped very much. The social problem is seen to be fathered by the existence of that institution, whether it be private property, the church, or the modern university. Revolutionary causes need not take on violent means to pursue their ends. Socialism and communism are both revolutionary movements, but the former wants to vote private property out through the ballot box and the latter sees violence as necessary.

Stages in the Life Cycle of Causes. In addition to distinguishing classes of causes, it is useful to distinguish cause stages. According to Cameron (1966, pp. 27–28):

> There is no characteristic life cycle of social movements. . . . If we quantify the development of a movement by counting members, amounts of income and expenditures, number of outside persons needed, number of pieces of literature, and so on, we find great variations. . . . Some movements grow very slowly . . . others seem blessed with the vitality and reproductiveness of a mushroom and accumulate personnel and property with great rapidity . . . some skyrocket into prominence and then almost as quickly decline.

Although there is great variation in the rates of growth and decline of social movements, many of them pass through certain well-defined *organizational* phases, or stages. Each stage is characterized by a particular set of problems, strategic options, and leadership styles. One of the more typical patterns is illustrated in Figure 1. This consists of four organizational stages—the crusading stage, popular cause stage, managerial stage, and bureaucratic stage.

Many causes start as crusades led by a few zealous individuals who have a knack of dramatizing a social ill. To the extent their message is effective, new supporters are attracted and the cause may reach the stage of a popular movement. As a popular movement, it is still led by the original leaders, whose primary quality is total absorption in the cause and concomitant charisma. But as the ranks of this movement swell, new problems must be coped with, such as developing clearer definitions of roles and responsibilities, and attracting adequate resources to keep the organization going. New types of leaders—those who have organizational skills—come into favor, and the cause passes into the managerial stage. The reins are tightened and more specific goal-setting, planning, and coordination take place. Nevertheless, with luck, the new leaders retain some of the original zeal. Finally, the movement passes into a bureaucratic phase in which the original zeal is lost and the cause is in the hands of functionaries whose main concern is organizational survival. The cause is run like any other business with a product to sell, with a rigid hierarchy, established policies, much functional specialization, and

Level of membership or resources

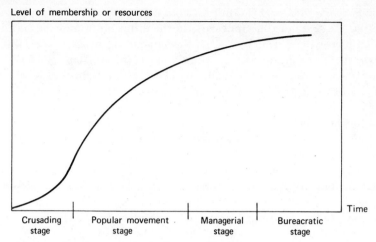

Figure 1.   Stages in the life cycle of a cause.

so on. Even the job of maintaining a following and support is handled as a specialist function.

These four stages are not inevitable or irreversible. The National Polio Foundation, after the successful development of the Salk vaccine, faced either a phasing out or an adoption of a new cause, and chose the latter course with a new zeal. In other cases, a new leader may appear to give new vitality to a flabby movement. The consumer protection movement was in a slump for years when Ralph Nader appeared and transformed it into a popular movement again. On the other hand, other cause organizations that once commanded power and public attention limp along, such as the Women's Christian Temperance Union, hoping but not being able to regain their former glory.

Change Agency

A change agency is an organization whose primary mission is to advance a social cause. The change agency might be an *informal group* (e.g., a concerned citizens group), a *formal organization* (e.g., a social agency or political party), or a *political unit* (e.g., a community, nation, or international body).[2]

Those who serve in some relationship to the change agency can be called change agents. This definition is broader than that advanced by the staff of the National Training Laboratory (Lippitt, 1958, pp. 10–14, 187–208, 226–238) or that appearing in the diffusion of innovation literature (Rogers, 1969) which defines the change agent as a specialist in change, such as a group worker, county agricultural agent, good government group, or community organizer. The broader definition is taken to permit a broader analysis of the roles played in advancing a cause.

Classification of Change Agent Roles. It is possible to distinguish two major roles, with several breakdowns, that change agents might have to the change agency.

The change agents fall into two groups, *leaders* and *supporters*. The leaders include six types of persons. The *directors* are those who started or head the organization and wield the power. Such names come to mind as Ralph Nader (consumer protection), Francis W. Willard (WCTU), and Eldridge Cleaver (Black Panthers). The *advocates* are those who wield the pen rather than the power but are close to those in power. For example, the peace movement has many leaders who write and speak to spread the cause of ending the war in Vietnam: John Kenneth Galbraith, David Riesman, Noam Chomsky, Paul Newman, Mary McCarthy, and so on. The *backers* are those who provide the purse. They supply the financial resources to keep the organization operating and are close to those who wield the power. Backers are typically wealthy individuals who become angels for the cause or who are excellent at raising money from others to support the cause. The *technicians* are those who provide professional advice or service—the expertise—to the directors. They may be hired, they may volunteer their services, or they may serve on the staff of the organization. Major technician types are public relation specialists, professional fund raisers, advertising practitioners, community organizers, lawyers, and management consultants. Their attitude toward the cause may range from high enthusiasm to simply the professional sale of their services. The *administrators* are those who run the day-to-day affairs of the organization. They make sure that letters are answered, bills are paid, publicity is developed. The administrators' commitment to the cause may range from intense enthusiasm all the way to "it's another job." Finally, the *organizers* are those who have effective skills in enlisting supporters and running programs and campaigns. These six groups—the directors, advocates, backers, consultants, administrators, and organizers—make up the agency's leadership. Certain persons may combine a number of leadership roles, especially in earlier stages of the agency, but these roles become more specialized as the agency grows.

Every cause that takes root gains a larger group of supporters or followers. Here three roles can be distinguished. The *workers* (i.e., "heelers") are those who are committed enough to the cause to give their time to it. They are the ones who ring doorbells in political campaigns, participate in demonstrations and marches, and help in mailings. *Donors* are those who make contributions of money rather than time to the cause. Finally, there may be a much larger group of *sympathizers* (i.e., fellow travelers) who neither work for nor give much money to the cause but give it lip-service support. They are willing to sign petitions, occasionally appear at rallies, and talk in social settings to friends about their feelings. One of the main jobs of the cause's leaders is to convert sympathizers into donors or active workers.

Thus making up any change agency is a range of persons who participate in numerous, complex ways to further the agency's cause. Moreover, many different change agencies may be involved in any particular area of social concern. As one example, Mackenzie (1962) has identified all of the following groups as active in educational reform: students; teachers; principals; supervisors; superintendents; boards of education; local community; state legislature; state boards or department of education; state and federal courts; foundations; industrialists; national government; noneducationalists; academicians; teacher training institutions; and professional teacher organizations.

Individual Motives for Participating in a Cause. People participate in social action for a variety of reasons. In addition to the good they might do, their participation presumably satisfies one or more psychological needs in the individual's makeup. They may be satisfying consciously or unconsciously an affiliation need, a status need, a power need, or a faith need.

Affiliation seekers have a strong need to be and work with others, and social causes represent one vehicle to satisfying this need. *Status seekers* have a strong need for respect from others and join causes that might advance their social status. *Power seekers* have a strong need for power over others. The cause presents them with an opportunity for attention and power. In the extreme, they become demagogues who use the cause to advance their personal ambitions. Finally, *faith seekers* have a strong need for something to believe in that will give meaning to their lives. The cause promises to fill an ideological void or vacuum. When the individuals are particularly frustrated and possibly self-hating, they become what Eric Hoffer (1951) calls the True Believers.

Phases of an Individual's Engagement in a Cause. Those who participate actively in a cause look forward to a certain degree of progress in accomplishing its aims. Disappointments and setbacks, which to some extent are inevitable, will test the real motives, fortitude, and maturity of the participants. Each individual will pass through several stages marked by growing or abating devotion. The psychological phase pattern in the typical case goes from *enthusiasm* to *frustration* to *reduced expectations* to *adjusted participation,* with occasional returns to earlier emotions with the ups and downs of the cause's successes. Some of the participants will drop out, usually those who joined the cause with unrealistic expectations or more personal motives.

The phase pattern in any particular case is complex and must be modeled carefully. The experiences of Peace Corps volunteers in the Philippines provide a useful example. In two short years, four volunteers resigned and twenty-six others were sent home because they were not able or willing to cope. Even among those remaining, some volunteers became cynical, or hostile, or relented in their efforts, and would have liked to find an honorable way to return home if they could face an overwhelming sense of personal failure. Volunteers typically passed through seven stages of coping with their environment (Fuchs, 1967, pp. 245–246):

1. The volunteer was curious and waited for signals as to what he should do.

2. He became impatient with the failure of Filipinos to give clear clues and developed a strong desire to accomplish something.

3. He started projects in school and community, sometimes with apparent success, often with failure, and began to realize how deep are the problems inherent in fundamental change.

4. He discovered that Filipinos might simulate change to please him but that nothing had really changed.

5. He reacted by working harder and by trying to push Filipinos to accomplish things his way.

6. He felt depleted and defeated in the realization that pushing did not result in real change.

7. He began to accept and enjoy individual Filipinos for what they were in an almost unconscious recognition that any change in skills and abilities depended on changes in values, and that such shifts could not be effected by action or words except through mutually accepting relationships.

These stages, which had several variations for different Peace Corps volunteers, underscores one of the key needs facing the top leadership of any movement, that of paying special attention to the recruiting, selection, training, and motivation of the cause's supporters.

Change Targets

The change targets are individuals, groups, or institutions designated as the targets of change efforts. The change agency seeks to influence a change in the behavior of the change target. This change is seen as an important step in the solution of the social problem.

Helping causes, by definition, designate the actual or potential victims of the social problem as the change targets. Consider the following examples:

Change agent	*Change target*
Social work agency	The poor
American Heart Association	Smokers, overweight people
Family Planning Association	Mothers, the public
Antidrug groups	Actual or potential users

These helping agencies often talk of the change targets as their clients. Their main target is a *client system*.

Protest causes single out offending institutions as the change targets. Labor movements seek to discipline companies; student movements, universities; and poor-people's movements, government. Their objective is not to destroy the institution but rather wrest concessions from it. They employ direct tactics (confrontation, harassment, negotiation) as well as indirect tactics (public rhetoric and coalitions designed to leverage their pressures against the institution). They describe their target as a *power system*.

Revolutionary causes also single out offending institutions as their change target, but their aim is to destroy or emasculate them. The change target is an *enemy system* which cannot be benign even if its leaders wished it to be. It is a root cause of social distress that has to be extirpated, either through the ballot box or violently.

Although the ultimate targets of a cause are "victims" or offending institutions, the change agency also seeks to influence intermediate targets because of their capability of influencing in turn the ultimate targets. There are four key intermediate targets for social action. The first is the *public*. Most social actionists attempt to arouse the sympathies of the public for their cause in the hope that this will influence other institutions or the ultimate targets. The second is the *government establishment*. Social actionists for helping and protest causes typically view the government as a major resource for mitigating the social problem, hoping for reform legislation to discipline the offending institutions or greater funding for the victims. The third intermediate target is the *business establishment,* or technostructure. When business is not involved as the offending institution, it is sought as an ally against the offending institutions. Or the support of noninvolved business firms is sought against other business firms that are the ultimate target. Still another frequent intermediate target is the *professional establishment* (educators, engineers, scientists, lawyers, doctors). Drug control programs enlist the participation of educators, lawyers, and doctors; pollution control programs enlist the support of engineers, scientists, and lawyers; and so on. In general, the development of a change program by a change agency requires identifying the key intermediate targets and mapping their interinfluence relations on the ultimate target.

Target Segmentation. Whether the change target is conceived as a client system, power system, or enemy system, change agencies attempt to apply *target segmentation* to aid their efforts. Target segmentation is a major step in effective social action. Too often the target system is stereotyped and its members and institutions are all approached in the same way. Yet the fact is that any target group contains persons at different stages of accessibility and susceptibility to the cause. The change agency must pay attention to these differences and search for the most meaningful dimensions of effective segmentation. The change agent can draw on demographic, geographic, psychographic, behavioral, and social structural variables for segmenting target individuals and institutions.

A notable example of target segmentation, where the public was the target, was performed by Pool and Abelson (1961) in connection with the 1960 political campaign of John F. Kennedy. The American voting population was segmented into 480 types by cross-relating identification data on region, city size, sex, race, socioeconomic status, party, and religion. For example, one voter type was "Eastern, metropolitan, lower-income, white, Catholic, female Democrats"; another voter type was "border state, rural, upper-income, white, Protestant, male Independents." The political analysts then took the further step of identifying 52 issue clusters (e.g., foreign aid, attitudes toward the United Nations) and cross-related each voter type's distribution of pros, cons, and indifferents on each issue. The result was the creation of an analytical and predictive mechanism for estimating the effects of different possible candidate stands on the likely number of votes.

The kind of segmentation variables that count vary with the cause class. In a helping cause, such as working with drug addicts, the change targets can be segmented by (1) the degree of their present addiction, (2) the number of years they have been habituated, and (3) the underlying motive(s). The first dimension leads to distinguishing four classes of persons in relation to drug use: (1) nonusers, (2) former users, (3) light users, and (4) heavy users. The first group, the nonusers, can be subdivided into the susceptibles and the nonsusceptibles. Only the former are a meaningful target group, and here the change agency's main effort takes on a persuasive character, particularly the use of fear appeals. The former users, on the other hand, need the type of support offered by individual and group therapy, that is, reeducative techniques. Finally, the light and heavy users may be reached with the previous approaches plus power tactics such as the threat of imprisonment. In addition, the heavy users (the addicted) require a higher counseling and medical input than the light users.

This preliminary analysis can be improved considerably by introducing the additional variables of the number of years of drug usage and the underlying motivational structure of the user. By cross-relating the significant segmentation variables, distinct drug user types can be identified and social action and treatment can be tailored to individual segment dynamics.

A different set of variables faces a peace movement group trying to identify its change targets. The relevant power systems include the military subsystem, the business system, the university system, and so on. The change agency's limited resources have to be allocated among these target systems to gain the greatest impact. Even the public is a target system, and a peace movement would want to distinguish at least among the following citizen types:

1. *Militant right.* My country is always right and I would like to beat the brains out of those who smear it.

2. *Patriots.* We should honor our country.

3. *Four-year voter.* I want to give the President a chance. His problem is a difficult one. Beside, we can vote him out at election time if he doesn't satisfy us.

4. *Spare time opponents.* I don't like our policies in Southeast Asia. I will express my opposition in my spare time but won't participate in anything disruptive.

5. *Peaceful dissenter.* I think my opposition to the war must be expressed in more substantial ways such as demonstrations, rallies, and other forms of peaceful dissent.

6. *Militant dissenter.* I don't feel we should tolerate a group of fascists who run this government and murder innocent people abroad. We must use all means to stop them, including sit-ins, marches on the Pentagon, and even terror and bombs if necessary.

7. *Revolutionary.* I think the whole country is corrupt and its institutions must be destroyed before we can enter a new age.

The peace organization seeking public support realizes there is little to gain from efforts directed at the first two groups because the chance of conversion is so low that too much effort per target is required. There is more chance of creating popular response by directing effort at group 3 and particularly at group 4. The rhetorics for each group must be appropriately chosen.

The segments chosen for major attention should meet three conditions. The first is *accessibility,* the degree to which meaningful channels exist for reaching the particular change target. Power centers such as the White House, the Pentagon, and the corporate oligarchy are very inaccessible on a direct basis. The second is *substantiality,* the degree to which the segment is large, powerful, or meaningful enough to be worth separate effort. The third is *susceptibility,* the degree to which the target segment is likely to be responsive to change effort. When the peace movement chose universities as their primary target system for change effort, they were influenced mostly by the accessibility and susceptibility of this institution, rather than its substantiality in the total power system.

Channels

Change agents face the problem of selecting effective and efficient channels for reaching their change targets and being reached by them. The task is to determine efficient social contact mechanisms. The channels may be subtle and complicated and various professionals—advertising men, publicists, press agents, local leaders—often are required to help the change agents make a careful determination and selection of channels.

A typology of channels is presented in Table 1. The basic division is

Table 1 Typology of Channels

I. Influence channels
   A. Media influence channels
      1. Mass media (television, radio, magazines, newspapers, billboards)
      2. Specialized media (the little magazines, newsletters, annual reports, announcements)
   B. Personal influence channels
      1. Mass meetings (rallies, demonstrations, assemblies, programs)
      2. Small groups (negotiation teams, threat squads)
      3. Individual visit (lobbying, personal phone calls)

II. Response channels
   A. Media response channels (telephone, telegraph, mail, paid advertisements)
   B. Personal response channels (visits to leaders, supporters, branch offices)

between influence channels and response channels, with further breakdowns of each. Influence channels describe ways by which change agents can reach change targets; response channels describe ways by which change targets can express their response to change agents.

Influence channels are subdivided in turn into media and personal influence channels. Media influence channels are those that deliver messages to the target audience detached from an interpersonal context. The first of these, the mass media, are print and electronic channels that reach great numbers of persons at home, work, or play, including many who may not have the slightest interest in the cause. Nevertheless, the mass media may be the most efficient way to spread the message in terms of cost per target audience exposure. The effect of any single exposure, or even set of repeated exposures, may not be sufficient to trigger the desired response in the target but may play an important role in conditioning his receptivity to other stimuli, particularly from a personal channel. The mass media are so encompassing and instantaneous in their sweep that they are the only media that make possible a mass distribution of influence.

Specialized media include those print and electronic communication vehicles that are addressed to particular audiences and are not likely to be received by others except by chance. Included are the specialized publications of the professions and the lobbyists and all the announcements, newsletters, and annual reports that are sent out by all organizations. The key characteristic of specialized media is that they are mainly a communication device within the change agency system—between leaders and supporters—rather than a channel to outside target groups.

Personal influence channels also offer varied possibilities for reaching change targets. Mass meetings are designed to develop or intensify enthusiasm for a cause. However, like specialized nonpersonal media, they are directed primarily at the cause's present supporters, to maintain or increase their spirit or knowledge, rather than being directed at other consumer targets. Mass meetings generally draw the current supporters and not those whose conversion is ultimately sought. Even mass media tend to reach current supporters more consistently than nonsupporters because mass audiences typically give selective, if not distortive, attention to the contents.

Small groups can be used effectively to reach a limited number of target individuals or groups. Although the large demonstration or meeting may prepare the Congressman to listen to an angry social action group, the small visiting committee who are admitted to his chambers may close the actual sale. Small committees or cadres are channels used by larger organizations for a multitude of purposes, including friendly persuasion, social modeling, negotiation, and threat.

Individual visits can be a highly effective method to reach and convert a target consumer. They signify personal attention and interest in the target consumer and allow a maximum tailoring of the message to the target. The more admired or the more matched the agent is to the target, the more effective the agent is likely to be. Even if the agent is a stranger, certain factors can make a difference in the effectiveness of this channel. The higher the agent's status relative to the target, the more favorable the target's likely response. Fund raisers use this principle in approaching a person who is financially able to give more money than he has been giving. The individual who gave $10,000 last year is approached by an individual who gave $50,000 last year. A second principle is that if the agent is to be on the same status level as the customer, he will be more effective the closer his characteristics match those of the target customer. Thus an insurance agent manages to sell more insurance to persons like himself than to those who differ (cf. Evans, 1963).

The change target who decides to respond to the change agent's appeal can respond through various channels, not necessarily those that carried the influence messages. Response channels are of two types: media response channels (telephone, telegraph, mail, and so on) and personal response channels (visits to the change agent). The probability of a positive response is enhanced by increasing the number and accessibility of response channels. This is illustrated in the celebrated U.S. bond promotion effort during World War II. The government made purchase as easy as possible by locating bond sales facilities in all post offices and most banks. On a special evening during the war Kate Smith appeared on a radio broadcast urging the American people to increase their bond purchases. A special response channel was set up: a citizen listening to the show could dial a special number and pledge to buy a bond. This additional channel served as a trigger-off mechanism and led to a tremendous sale of bonds in a single evening (Wiebe, 1951–1952, p. 679). Similarly, persons engaged in several other causes, such as in family planning and drug abuse, are beginning to appreciate the critical role played by response channels. In marketing terms, they are opening up new distribution channels for getting their product to the target system, including neighborhood storefronts, door-to-door service, the mails, and telephone.

Given the possible channels of influence and response, their feasibility and effectiveness will vary with different types of targets. The *influence channel mix* for reaching the urban poor (e.g., to sell them on better nutrition or inoculation) is different from the mix for reaching and influencing congressmen. The most effective media for reaching the urban poor are broadcast media and individual visits (D'Onofrio, n.d.). Television and radio are more effective than newspapers and magazines because of higher illiteracy among the poor and the cost of print media, especially magazines. Individual visits, especially by clergymen, social workers, physicians, and neighbors, have a higher chance of being effective than visits by strangers. Mass meetings have not been particularly effective in drawing large numbers of urban poor, although this may change. On the other hand, congressmen are most moved by incoming mail, group visits, surveys, and other channels that directly bear on the probability of their continuing in office.

Change Strategies

Change agents have many means or tactics at their disposal for trying to influence the change target; these include lobbying, petitioning, mail campaigns, publicity, advertising, harassment, and violence. All of these constitute alternative tactics for social action. Behind any set of chosen tactics should lie a more basic plan for achieving the desired social change. This plan should represent some conception of how the change targets are most effectively influenced. This core plan can be called the change strategy.

There are three basic ways in which a change agent can attempt to influence a change target. The change agent can attempt to *coerce, persuade, or educate.* Each change strategy works on a different premise concerning the best way to overcome the change target's resistance to the social object. Although an actual change program may combine two or all three strategies, here we will treat them as ideal types.[3]

A power strategy is a tactic that attempts to produce behavioral compliance or cooperation in the change target through the use of agent-controlled sanctions. Agents who resort to a power strategy are concerned primarily with changing the behavior rather than the beliefs or values of the change target. They seek to secure the desired behavior through agent-controlled sanctions such as authority, force, or payment. Change agents in a position of authority over change targets—parents (children), teachers (students), managers (workers), army officers (draftees), judges (defendants)—can attempt to produce change in the change targets by threatening to withhold rewards or to issue punishment. Change agents who have no authority over the change target, have two recourses. If the change agent views the change target as an enemy, the power strategy takes the form of force or threat of force—noncooperation, demonstration, harassment, or violence. If the change agent is neither an authority figure nor an enemy of the change target, the power strategy often takes the form of payment—gifts or bribes—to induce the desired behavior. In general, the resistance, inertia, or indifference of a change target often invites the use of a power strategy involving the use of authority, force, or payment.

A persuasion strategy is one that attempts to induce the desired behavior in the change target through identifying the social object with the change agent's existing beliefs or values. The change agent does not use any external sanctions but rather attempts to find arguments showing that the desired behavior serves the natural interests of the change target. Three types of persuasive arguments are possible, according to Aristotle: *logos,* or appeals to logic; *pathos,* or appeals to emotions; and *ethos,* or appeals to values. In the recent television campaign to discourage smoking, all three appeals were used. Some commercials were *logic-laden:* they attempted to prove that cigarette smoking was harmful to health. Some commercials were *affect-laden:* they sought to activate smoker's fears of death. Finally, some commercials were *value-laden:* they implied that the smoker was immoral or irresponsible to his family because his death would hurt *them.* Persuasion strategies do not try to create or change beliefs or values but rather to activate existing ones through identification with the social object.

A reeducative strategy is one that attempts to induce the desired behavior in the change target through the internalization of new beliefs or values. Here the change agent seeks a deep and lasting change in the behavior of the change target. He does not think that this can be produced through power or persuasive tactics. The key seems to be in attempting to change the beliefs and/or values of the change agent. The reeducative strategist in an antismoking campaign will try to formulate messages directed at modifying either the beliefs or the values of the change target. Many people have a primitive belief in their own immortality; they psychologically do not think death will ever touch them, although intellectually they acknowledge it. A *belief-modification* strategy would attempt to alter their psychological beliefs about death so that in coming to a felt awareness of their mortality, they will feel dissonance over continuing to smoke. The strain toward congruity of belief and behavior is expected to lead them to drop the cigarette habit.

Alternatively, the reeducative strategist can attempt to change a key value or its centrality in a person's value system. A *value-modification* strategy in the case of smoking is to make the issue of health more salient and cogent compared to other values held by the individual. It should be clear that reeducative strategies are the least direct, most ambitious approaches to behavioral modification. They are handled mainly by skilled practitioners such as psychotherapists in individual situations or milieu-therapists in group situations. It is doubtful that reeducative strategies are available or effective as an approach to the public as a whole or to offending institutions. Even in a totalitarian society with absolute control over media and official opinion, there are important limitations to how much thought control can be affected. The ability of these regimes to mold public opinion and especially to motivate citizens is not as great as was once thought (Pool, 1967).

Summary

Social action is the undertaking of collective action to mitigate or resolve a social problem. This essay proposed a framework that would comprehend a large range of social action phenomena—as found in social work, politics, reform movements, and revolutionary causes. A framework involving five elements—cause, change agent, change target, channel, and change strategy—provides a useful framework for social action analysis. Figure 2 summarizes this framework.

The direction of flow suggests a cause strategy that is carried through channels to various change targets. This direction of flow is somewhat arbitrary. From a planning point of view, the social action problem may better begin with the designation of change targets, the determination of change strategies, the choice of channels, and then the structuring of the change agency. This framework does not purport to get into the dynamics of the social planning process or the social change process. Rather it is designed as an initial framework for distinguishing the elements—the building blocks—as a prelude to effective social planning.

Notes

1. Two other types of causes will not be discussed here. *Escapist causes* are causes where the victims decide to withdraw psychologically or physically from the offending situation. Withdrawal cannot be considered a form of social action except in a very special sense. *Conservative causes* are causes involving an agency that denies the existence of the social problem or the desirability of

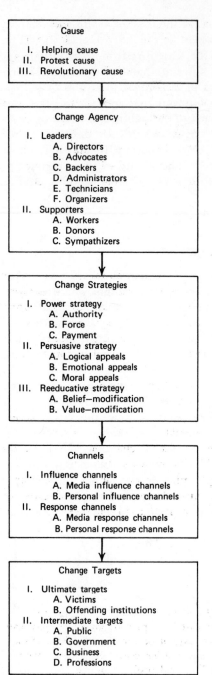

Figure 2. The elements of social action.

increasing social reforms or resources beyond the present level. Conservative causes typically rationalize the order of things and can be considered a form of social action to counter social action.

2. In rare cases, the change agency may consist of only one person. This person sets out on his own to correct some social problem, using legal, persuasive, or harassment procedures. Thus the anticigarette campaign received a tremendous boost in 1967 when John F. Banzhaf III, a young New York lawyer, filed a petition to the Federal Communications Commission asking them to require the television networks to provide equal time for anticigarette messages. He received a favorable ruling and this began the very effective barrage of antismoking commercials on television (Whiteside, 1970).

As another example, a mysterious individual called the "Fox" operates in Chicago's South Side to harass the steel companies for their pollution by dumping polluted water on executive carpets, jamming plant sewage systems, and placing antisteel signs throughout the area (Royko, 1970).

3. The concept of strategy goes beyond the choice of change instruments, including plans for timing and coalition formation. The choice of instruments is emphasized here.

John C. Maloney

Medill School of Journalism
Northwestern University

Eugene P. Schonfeld

Graduate School of Management
Northwestern University

SOCIAL CHANGE AND ATTITUDE CHANGE

Biological scientists have noted that the evolutionary progress of man has always had its ups and downs. Bertalanffy has described it as "a drama full of suspense, of dynamics and tragic complications" as "life spirals laboriously upwards to higher and ever higher levels, paying for every step" (Bertalanffy, 1956, p. 108). Social scientists are now discovering that potentially destructive oscillations also mark the technological and social progress of man (Milsum, 1969, p. 47) and that these can be controlled only by new or markedly reformed institutions and social structures (Buckley, 1968, p. 483).

We dare not count on famine or war to dampen the population explosion that has followed sharp reductions in infant mortality. We dare not assume that the "revolutions of rising expectations" which follow release from the bonds of illiteracy, apathy, and abject poverty will be peaceful and constructive revolutions. Nor can we hope that many of the other problems which accompany progress can be ameliorated by some "mind-bending" legerdemain of the social scientist. A social science that simply tries to shore up existing institutions and social structures with attitude-forming mass persuasion processes will not suffice. Functional human progress often demands new or revised channels of social action.

191

The Importance of Action Channels

The first concern of the social planner often must be with altering the behaviors of gatekeepers or power elites in existing channels of action in
order to establish new or revised channels. As cases in point, one cannot
"sell" a vasectomy program to an adult male population nor Medicare to
the elderly until the medical profession and certain support groups have
been persuaded to provide the facilities and services required.

It is only after the action channels are in place, at least on a trial
basis, that special public education or mass persuasion efforts can effectively be applied to bring about program or innovation acceptance by
the target population. Indeed, one of the most effective media of persuasion for the target population often is the accessibility and visibility of
the appropriate action channels. This is especially likely to be true when
a program establishes its own distribution or service centers.[1] In any case
social change agents have been rediscovering for 20 or more years the fact
that persuasion translates to action much more readily when the acceptance of an innovation may be accomplished with the greatest ease or
convenience (Wiebe, 1951–1952; Lazarsfeld and Merton, 1949).

Where a major physical distribution function is to be performed or
new facilities are needed, lead time must be allowed for the building of
inventories or facilities at points close to the target population. If money
or other forms of exchange are expected to flow back through the channels of action, accounting systems are needed to monitor transactions,
provide information on intrachannel exchanges, and prevent the seepage
of material (a new drug or other valuable commodity) and the theft of
funds. Systems may be required to train channel gatekeepers or program
employees and to audit their attitudes and performance to see that they
clearly understand the policies and goals of the program.

Marketing and management experts' corporate sales analysis, market
research, inventory control, distribution research, and personnel management practices can provide useful models for the social planner. Zaltman,
Kotler, and Kaufman have commented (1972):

> . . . the first step for the change agent is to have a clearly articulated set of
> goals and objectives. . . . When more than one change agent is employed, it is
> important that they have a common understanding of the change agency's goals
> and objectives. If goals are not understood or similarly perceived among differ-
> ent change agents, then their efforts may be poorly coordinated and possibly in
> direct conflict.

Channel-building or stage-setting communication and persuasion often involves a personal selling, lobbying, compromising, negotiating activity between social planners and members of an existing establishment or power elite. As Rogers (1973) points out, power elites typically have a vested interest in preserving the status quo and enhancing their positions within existing institutional structures. When evolutionary rather than revolutionary social change is the goal, it is often necessary to appeal to the self-interests of the power elite to enlist them.

We mention these issues at the outset of this discussion because we are convinced that many social change programs have failed for lack of an appreciation of the essential relationships between attitudes toward or expectancies of change in the minds of target populations and the actual availability of channels for action or change.

Kelman and Warwick (1973) have observed, with regard to the modernization of developing nations, that "The society's capacity to satisfy the aspirations (rising from 'modernizing' stimuli) tends to rise at a slower rate than the aspirations themselves." As a result there is likely to be severe pressure on the political system. Gurr (1971), Jacoby (1971), and Maloney (1972) have stressed the fact that attitude change without commensurate institutional change often leads to "goal gaps," stressful "want/get ratios," "relative deprivations," and ensuing "revolutions of rising expectations." Morrison (1973) cogently summarizes many studies of this phenomenon.

But if too little attention has been paid to society's capacity to satisfy aspirations, social planners have been more naive about the measurement or control of expectations, aspirations, or attitudes toward change. This is no doubt due, at least in part, to the fact that a good many social change programs in recent years have been predicated upon the principles of a behavioristic psychology, which denies the legitimacy of any concern for attitudes or other "mentalisms."

Behaviorism grew up under the influence of operationalism and logical positivism. As a result it has tried to avoid what it regards to be the unwarranted subjectivity of mentalistic phenomena. It has tried to confine its attention to stimulus and response (or situation and adjustment): the external and directly observable aspects of behavior occurring at the boundaries of the human organism. Whereas humanists, existentialists, and proponents of the "softer" psychologies have seen each man *acting upon* his environment in terms of his own constitutional uniqueness, the behaviorists have seen man *reacting to* his environment, with certain responses strengthened by environmental rewards and others weakened or extinguished by environmental punishments.

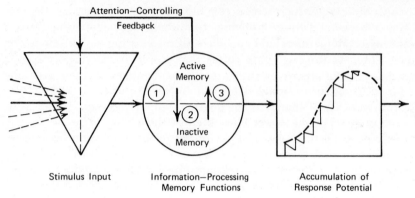

Figure 1. Surrogate model.

Long and bitter debates between those who subscribe to these two schools of thought have divided those concerned about the amelioration of human suffering into two warring camps (Platt, Black, Toynbee, and Skinner, all in the March–April 1972 issue of *The Center Magazine*). The debate has recently been intensified by Skinner's (1972) call for a highly developed behavioral technology which should go *Beyond Freedom and Dignity* to guide mankind away from ecological disaster.

It seems to us that these polemics obscure the obvious fact that man is part of his environment (Maloney, 1972); that he acts upon it *and* reacts to it. As we have implied, the social-political environment provides the channels of human action as well as shaping behavior by selectively rewarding and punishing various responses. But the slightest familiarity with motivation and attitude research also reveals that human beings are themselves selective in their noting, understanding, remembering, and responding to various environmental stimuli. We agree, then, with Kelman and Warwick (1972) when they imply that the study of attitudes, values, and motives demands an eclecticism which avoids the provincial arguments of one or another theoretical dogma. We thus subscribe to the surrogate model of human linkage to the environment implied by Figure 1.

This model stands in for a variety of theories concerning human linkage to the environment: the *stimulus-integration-response* paradigm of the behaviorists; the *input-internal processing-output* paradigm of the communications engineer; and the *independent variable-intervening variable-dependent variable* paradigm of experimental psychology. We see social values, attitudes and aspirations as uniquely human intervening variables—intervening between stimulus and response—but we do not see them to be neatly isolated from the lower order memory forms (sensations, perceptions, or cognitions) or the higher order memory forms (personality or public sentiments).[2]

All of the memory states implied here are both past and future oriented. They include internally stored images of past experience and images of, expectations about, or potential predispositions toward future stimuli or experiences. More specifically, the term *memory* applies to any functional, negentropic (organized or nonrandom) state within the organism which is self-regulating and selectively responsive to the environment. Memory includes all the organized residues or prior inputs to the organism that are available to mediate the processing or storage of subsequent stimuli or inputs. In this regard, these memory functions have much in common with Boulding's concept of *image* (1956). These memory functions serve a threefold role in the organism's response to environmental information or stimuli. They provide the mechanisms for (1) *stimulus decoding* (noting and understanding), (2) *internal storage* (remembering), and (3) *response encoding* (deciding and acting).

The solid arrow to the left of the Figure 1 diagram represents the input attended to at any one time. The dashed arrows represent the "noise" in the signal-to-noise ratio of the communications engineer, the background stimuli of figure-ground contrast of Gestalt psychology, and the exogenous and extraneous variables of the experimental psychologist's paradigm. The *accumulation of response potential* curve to the right in Figure 1 depicts the learning or attitude formation curve (the growth in acceptance of a social change program and readiness to act in accordance with it). The surrogate model also acknowledges a distinction between conscious, *active memory* forms, or mental states, and the unconscious or *inactive memory* forms. The active memory forms (the "executive" or "ego" functions of personality theory) are those that guide understanding-deciding processes going on at any one time. Inactive memories are "stored away but available for use" information residues within the system. They provide the templates or standards of comparison in the "reality testing" or "trial-and-check" phases of perception as things are "seen in the light of past experience." These are the "extra truths" which William James wrote of 70 years ago (1948, p. 161):

> We store such extra truths away in our memories, and with the overflow we fill our books of reference. Whenever such an extra truth becomes relevant to one of our emergencies, it passes from cold-storage to do work in the world and our belief in it grows active.

Learning, including those special forms of learning called attitude formation or change, involves the modification of memory forms. It occurs as memory structures strive for a steady-state balance. Bertalanffy's (1960) observations apply here as they do to other living structures: "Living structures are not in being, but in becoming. They are an expression of a ceaseless stream of matter and energy, passing through the organism and at the same time forming it." This is precisely the view of perception and attitude formation which Floyd Allport has taken in his classic review (1955).

Many different attitude formation theories describe this balanc-seeking phenomenon of the inactive memory structures as "strains toward symmetry" (Newcomb, 1953), seeking "cognitive balance" (Heider, 1956), seeking "congruity" (Osgood and Tannenbaum, 1955), or as an effort to overcome "cognitive dissonance" (Festinger, 1957). These dissonances, imbalances, incongruities, or anastasis rather than homeostasis within the memory structure give rise to certain doubts, interests, curiosities, sensitivities, and "needs for closure." Again, James (1948) anticipated the more cogent findings to grow out of these theories by half a century:

> The individual has a stock of old opinions already, but he meets a new experience that puts them to a strain. Somebody contradicts them; or in a reflective moment he discovers that they contradict each other; or he hears of facts with which they are incompatible; or desires arise in him which they cease to satisfy. The result is an inward trouble to which his mind till then had been a stranger, and from which he seeks to escape by modifying his previous mass of opinions. He saves as much of it as he can, for in this matter of belief we are all extreme conservatives. So he tries to change first this opinion and then that (for they resist change very vigorously), until at last some new idea comes up with which he can graft upon the ancient stock with a minimum of disturbance to the latter, some idea that mediates between the stock and the new experience and runs them into one another most felicitously and expediently.

The balance-seeking search for new ideas that might be grafted upon the ancient stock "with a minimum of disturbance" is represented by the *attention-controlling feedback* arrow of the surrogate model. This feedback regulates the stimulus input filter so that people *selectively attend* to those things that they are particularly interested in or curious about at any one time. This feature of the model resolves the paradox of how curiosity is *both* the cause *and* the effect of learning or attitude change as these processes gradually take place over time. Thus memory structure imbalances (questions) give rise to answers that raise new questions.

As James implies, the steady state of the memory structure is not solely maintained, altered, or restored by these feedbacks which seek wholly new information to resolve current imbalances. Both conscious and unconscious "mulling" of already received information may lead to new and satisfying, although somewhat delayed, forms of memory balance once the steady state has been disrupted. This is the essence of much humor, insight, creativity, and problem solving. Koestler (1964) describes such delayed insights as *bisociations,* the sudden coming together of cognitions or knowledge from two different "logical matrices" or planes of the memory structure.

There are two different kinds of attention-controlling feedback. *Continue-cycle feedback* is analogous to the "orientation response" of behaviorists' theories and involves a heightened sensitivity for certain stimuli already in the perceptual field. A more pervasive, persistent, or latent form of attention-controlling feedback is *renew-cycle feedback,* which inclines people toward attention to certain kinds of information at some later time, if and when it becomes available. The terms *attitude* and *motive* are usually reserved for this more persistent readiness to select out and respond to certain types of experience or information. But both types of feedback represent an input filtering arising from certain states of arousal in the memory structure, and both selectively involve the organism with certain kinds of environmental stimuli and certain kinds of actions rather than others.

The distinction between here-and-now, continue-cycle, attention-controlling feedback and the more pervasive renew-cycle feedback is a relative distinction, just as the distinctions among perceptions, cognitions, and attitudes are relative distinctions. There is a hierarchy of attention-controlling feedbacks and memory forms *with higher order forms of feedback and memory transcending and controlling the lower order forms.* Thus there is a logical homology between the behaviorists' and the existentialists' or humanists' theories of learning, attitude formation, motivation, and behavior.

From the behaviorists' point of view, everything starts at the bottom of the hierarchy with physical stimuli from the environment (see Figure 2). Sensations give rise to perceptions, which form cognitions (or recognitions). Cognitions are affectively charged to form attitudes, which shape personalities. Taken in the aggregate, attitudes of various sorts comprise public opinions, and so on, as lower order, building-block memory forms shape higher order structures. But from the humanist's or existentialist's point of view, everything starts at the top of the hierarchy and works down as higher order memory forms and feedbacks regulate the threshold levels for filtering of lower order information. As a result, the human organism is something more than a passive transducer of light and sound waves which become sensations, which become cognitions, which become attitudes, and so on. Higher order levels of integration provide the "boundary conditions" that harness lower order phenomena in the service of higher order phenomena. As Polanyi has remarked (1968, pp.

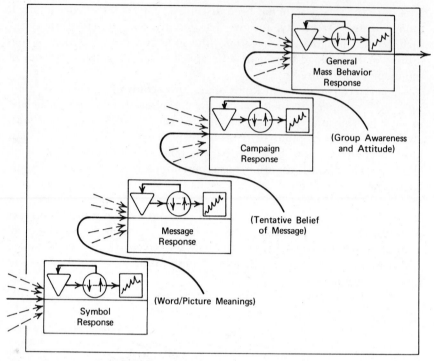

Figure 2.   The communication response hierarchy.

1308–1312), "The higher comprehends the workings of the lower and thus forms the meanings of the lower."

Thus, while higher order plans, social values, needs, and attitudes are formed and nurtured by things seen and heard, these higher order memory forms also determine the relevance, understandability, and attention value of information still to be seen and heard. Certain kinds of public opinions, once they are under construction, give employment to certain kinds of attitudes. These, in turn, create a need for certain kinds of cognitions and sensations. These, in turn, give rise to a hypersensitivity for certain kinds of information as the peripheral nervous system scans the environment for to-be-processed and to-be-ignored information. This active selection of inputs from the environment is the "free will" that existentialists and humanists tend to emphasize and behaviorists tend to ignore.

It may be noted that the communication response hierarchy is primarily oriented toward the *internalization* of actions and beliefs as people learn to merge new views with old attitudes "felicitously and expediently." That is to say that Figure 2 depicts a noncoercive, systematic use of symbols, messages, and campaigns of persuasion. However, as Kelman and Warwick (1973) point out, social change may also result from *compliance* or *identification*, and we do not mean to imply that social change programs cannot or should not employ either of these strategies. Indeed, the persuasive communications sources (message spokesman, media channels, etc.) should be chosen with some consideration of their credibility and appeal for the target audience (Weiss, 1971, p. 310). These information sources should offer behavior models with whom target audience members would be willing to identify. By the same token positively rewarding or action-facilitating compliance induction (special incentives) should be built into the action channels or situations in which the ultimate behavioral responses are expected to occur.

To the extent that initial trial of an innovation is induced by such identification or compliance strategies, the higher order behavioral responses may occur before completely congruent attitudes have been formed toward the innovation or change program. As the Figure 2 model implies, behavior may follow only moderately intense awareness or attitudes, or only *tentative* beliefs in the merits of the innovation or program.

When behavior precedes rather than follows complete attitude formation or change, the behavior may, in accord with the higher to lower order feedback principles described, lead to attitude change. We will consider these issues later but now we only stress our agreement with Kelman and Warwick's conclusion (1973) that "full-blown attitude change *prior* to the adoption of a new practice is neither a necessary nor a sufficient condition for social change."

Social Program Design

The communications response hierarchy demonstrates the need for coordinated change program objectives: immediate message objectives, intermediate campaign objectives, and ultimate mass behavior objectives that tie together in terms of part-whole or subsystem-system relationships. The setting of objectives should, of course, start with the ultimate behavioral objectives at the top of the hierarchy so that higher order strategies may dictate lower order tactics.

At the highest level of the hierarchy the desired mass behavioral responses dictate the need for (1) established channels of action and (2) those states of mind or memory forms that are predictive determinants of

behavioral responses; for example, awareness and acceptance of, and preference for the innovation. If such campaign effects are to contribute to
mass behaviors, they must follow from lower order noting, understanding, and at least tentative belief of lower order (third or message level) responses. These responses, in turn, must depend on effective perceptions of
word and picture or sight and sound symbols of communication. These
immediate, intermediate, and ultimate program objectives must all be applied to the same program-relevant population or target audience (Kiesler, 1973). The selection of communication channels suitable for the campaign objectives and the target audience composition can be facilitated
by the analysis of media habit topologies (Bass, Pessemier, and Tigert,
1969; Swanson, 1967).

Since the amount and prominence of coverage that mass media managers give to social change programs may well depend upon publishers'
or media managers' attitudes (Donohew, 1967), special persuasion efforts
may need to be developed to enlist their cooperation. Weiss observes
(1971): "While the essence of topical news can spread rapidly and widely
by word-of-mouth, knowledge of the national interpretation and evaluation of information requires contact with the mass media." Even in
press-poor countries, these interpretations may filter down as multiple
and out-loud readings of individual copies of printed media reach illiterates (Rao, 1967; Eapen, 1967). Broadcast media may similarly reach far
more people than simple radio and television ownership figures indicate,
since group listening and viewing is common in many countries
(UNESCO, 1968).

The overall media coverage of an issue or program is likely to involve a "bandwagon" effect (Maloney and Slovonsky, 1967) as media imitate each other's coverage and respond to the apparent degree of public
interest already achieved by the issue or program in question. The
"bandwagon" may move along slowly, for months or even years, with infrequent media coverage of an issue, until it suddenly produces a "critical
mass" of public interest and coverage. The formation of this "critical
mass" may be catalyzed by messages initiated by the change agent—press
releases or the staging of newsworthy events—as well as the process by
which less prestigious media come to imitate the coverage of more prestigious media.

Development of Basic Images. Having considered the communication channels that are at least tentatively available to him, the change
agent must develop persuasive messages which can be accommodated as
easily as possible by the memory (cognitive and attitude) structures of target audience members.

Qualitative research methods such as depth or group interviews, projective association tests, and related techniques can reveal much about relevant audience views. These methods, backed by quantitative psychometric research such as perceptual mapping (Sherak, 1969; Greenberg, 1969; Green and Carmone, 1970; Green and Rao, 1972), can help to identify ideal matches between message phrasing and audience segments.

We have found that a "mode of evaluation framework" can be useful for classifying motivational appeals (rational, sensory, social, and ego-supporting or self-realizing) and depictions of programs or innovations that might provide such appeals (direct experience with innovation, results of having used innovation, experiences incidental to overtly intended functional use of innovation) (Maloney, 1961). Thus, depending on the kind of interest, reservation, or concern a rural audience might show in adopting a new fertilizer, messages might emphasize the ease of applying the fertilizer, the increased crop yield resulting from use of the fertilizer, or the prestige of being an early, in-the-know adopter of the new fertilizer.

This search for optimal images or "basic selling ideas" must take into account the complexity of the target audience's innovation-relevant attitudes. Many theorists (Rokeach, 1960, pp. 54 ff; Schroder, Driver, and Streufert, 1967) have suggested that people with cognitively simple (one might say narrow-minded) attitudes toward a particular issue ward off or resist information that runs counter to their views. On the other hand, audience members with complex cognitive structures may seek out information on all sides of an issue to form a truly complete and balanced attitude set with regard to the social change. The most useful strategy will often be to segment the target population by media exposure habits to provide detailed information to the most interested audience segments who may seek exposure on all sides of an issue while protecting less interested persons from needless dissonance or "information overload."

Since people's opinions and attitudes are greatly influenced by group norms and values and by word-of-mouth corroborations or refutations of information carried in the media, it is essential to shape messages in accord with relevant group norms as well as individual attitudes. For almost any innovation one may find particularly influential opinion leaders within neighborhoods, communities, work groups, or other primary groups. Special attention to their interests is likely to make a considerable difference for the change agents' public education or persuasion efforts. There is a very extensive literature on this subject (Katz and Lazarsfeld, 1955; Rogers and Shoemaker, 1971).

As long as the message remains within the audience member's general "latitude of acceptance," which can often be determined only by research, communications research indicates that the message calling for the greatest opinion change in fact elicits the greatest change (Hovland and Pritzker, 1957). However, effective rhetoric usually calls for the linking of messages incompatible with the old views to ideas already known to be acceptable to the audience (Weiss, 1957). Most experts agree that a message with very explicit, action-suggesting conclusions are most likely to lead to idea adoption (Weiss and Steenbock, 1965), but there is mixed evidence concerning the importance of an explicit rationalization for such action. Despite the popularity of mass persuasion paradigms which stress message comprehension (awareness-*comprehension*-conviction-action), Haskins (1966) and others insist that literal comprehension of messages often has little to do with attitude change or behavioral effects of persuasive messages. This probably depends on the importance of rational considerations in audience members' relevant modes of evaluating an innovation, their already developed store of tangible information, and the exent to which behavior may be facilitated by simply increasing issue awareness or showing the issue in a more socially acceptable, pleasure-promising, or ego-rewarding light.

The interested reader may find many summaries of an extensive research on these and related message rhetoric issues. Karlins and Abelson's *Persuasion* (1970) is among the best of these.

Value Dimensions of Social Change Image. If the change agent's public information task is complicated by a need to present information incompatible with people's present attitudes, or a need to persuade those with cognitively complex attitudes, it is doubly complicated when he must overcome resistance at a higher order value level in audience memory structures. This is particularly likely to be the case when the long-term social good or necessity runs counter to short-term personal advantage of target audience members (Hardin, 1970) or when the principle beneficiaries of change are generations yet unborn (Boulding, 1970, p. 99).

In a preliminary effort to quantify such value dimensions, Robinson and Maloney (1971) applied the following content analysis categories to Chicago area residents' responses to an environmental attitude survey:

1. *Cognitive complexity.* The ability to understand the costs of change or the "tradeoffs" between private goods and a specific social good.

2. *Social circumference.* A continuum of concern for self, immediate family and friends, the community, the nation, and all of mankind.

3. *Time orientation.* A continuum of concern for the present, the immediate future, one's later years, and periods that will exceed one's own lifetime.

For example, those solely concerned with the effects of air pollution on their own immediate comfort and health were rated low on all of these value dimensions. Those concerned about the depletion of resources that may be needed for future generations, knowing that appropriate controls may slow economic growth, were rated high on all three value dimensions (Robinson, 1971).

At least one of these value dimensions, social circumference, has an impressive precedent in the concepts of "I," "me," "significant other," and "generalized other" orientations of Mead (1934). All show promise for the study of public acceptance of many different social change programs.

Social change calling for "altruistic," value-dependent behaviors may call for institutional (legal constraint, tax incentive, price structure, etc.) arrangements that will make people's self-interests accord with the necessary change. Some investigators (Rokeach, 1968) have successfully experimented with ways to bring about such change through manipulations of belief, attitude, and value congruencies, but sheer exhortation to "do the right thing" will not suffice when immediate self-interests conflict with the time-remote interests or needs of others.

The Accumulation of Campaign Effects: A Function of Message Repetition. Sociologists' studies of the diffusion of innovations emphasize the gradualness of innovation adoption as people go through various stages of the adoption process (awareness-interest-comprehension-conviction-action). (Robertson, 1971, provides an excellent summary and criticism of such paradigms.) When the decision risk is high, involving a significant expenditure of funds, a risk of embarrassment or serious inconvenience or a change in life styles, the process may take weeks, months, or even years. In the meantime, the tentative effects of individual message contributions to the persuasion process may be lost unless they are periodically reinforced.

This is the implication of the learn-and-forget pattern of response potential accumulation illustrated in the surrogate model of Figure 1. The general form of the response curve shown there is adapted from Zielske's (1959) and others' studies of message repetition and has been verified by the authors' own unpublished studies. When repeated messages within a campaign produce a cumulative effect, they do so by producing irregular "jolts" of effect following each message or persuasion-supportive learning experience. These jolts fade with the passage of time. But if subsequent messages or learning experiences come along hard enough on the heels of prior messages, building on the memory residue of those prior inputs, the response potential (awareness, interest, or attitude) accumulates over time.

The optimal long-term response curve is presumed to be an S-curve, rising slowly at first, then rising more rapidly until a point of diminishing return or maximal effect is reached. Finally, the curve is likely to drop off as the end of an innovation's life cycle is approached or as competing newer innovations erode its public acceptance. Shorter term response curves, which are really just portions of the curve stretching over the innovation's whole life cycle, may take a variety of forms. Curves based on just a few measures that happened to coincide with the peaks of a jolt or the troughs of a "fade" can take deceptive forms. The height of any given point on these response curves reflects the strength of certain structural bonds (attitude strengths or learning associations) within the memory structure.

These comments describe the sporadic accumulation of response potential within target audience memory structures *if and when* such accumulation occurs. It may not occur for many reasons. A flat or declining response curve may be expected when a competing campaign is reaching the same audience over the same time interval with greater frequency. A campaign may fail, without regard to competing message frequency, if its own message frequency is too low (if message repetitions reach the audience so seldom that the learning effects of prior messages have faded almost completely before they are reinforced by later messages). A campaign may fail if the repeated messages of the campaign lack mutually supportive congruency (if each message in the campaign is really a separate campaign unto itself). Such message congruency is defined, of course, by audience members' memory structures. Messages that seem consistent to the change agent as he encodes them may not seem consistent to audience members in terms of the way in which they decode them.

It is generally agreed that message repetition with variation is likely to be more effective than mere repetition of the same identical message. This strategy offers the advantages of both message familiarity (from repetition) and message novelty (from variation). But certain symbols or cues meaningful to the audience members' modes of message perception should be among the repeated elements of a repetition with variation pattern in order that audience members can "get it all together." This is the advantage often provided by advertisers' consistent use of brand-identifying trademarks, jingles, cartoon characters, or spokesmen.

Finally, a public information or mass persuasion campaign may fail because its individual messages, apart from any question of message-to-message congruency, are simply ineffective. As we have implied, persuasive messages may be ineffective because they are using inappropriate appeals or ineffective imagery; they may have "basic selling ideas" which simply do not accord with the audience members' decision-relevant attitudes or their "modes of evaluation" for the issue at hand. Or the messages may be poorly structured in terms of audience members' message perception processes.

Message Effects and Perception Processes. If a message is to be effective once the audience member is exposed to it, it must gain attention; it must be properly indexed, starting an appropriate train of thought; and its meaning must find a place in the "cold-storage compartment" of inactive memory (Maloney, 1963).

The attention value of messages is of two sorts, one having to do with the "stopping power" of the message and the other having to do with "holding power" or the ability of the message to trigger continue-cycle, attention-controlling feedback to keep the audience member locked onto the message until it is read, viewed, or heard to the end.

The stopping power of a message depends on the size, brightness, graphic simplicity, or (in the case of broadcast messages) audio and/or video tempo of opening portions of the message. The attention-stopping message has a not-to-be ignored intrusiveness, which is easily and immediately apparent to the audience member. What matters, of course, is the relative intrusiveness as compared to the stimulus properties of competing stimuli. It is not the number of square inches of a poster or advertisement that matters, for example; what matters is whether the poster is larger or smaller than surrounding posters or whether the advertisement is a half-page, full-page, or two-page spread without regard to total page size of the publication.

The holding power of a message depends on the layout of the printed message or the sequential flow of the spoken or broadcast message. The initial attention-stopping element of the message must be tied in time or space to other message elements of intrinsic interest (i.e., message elements which are "intrinsically interesting" vis-à-vis the preexisting expectations, attitudes, or memory structures of the target audience).

Too frequently the communicator will "borrow attention" by using message elements that are intrinsically interesting but irrelevant to the intended meanings of his message. The message is then likely to be "misindexed," activating a set of memories (starting a train of thought) unrelated to that portion of the memory structure which the message is intended to influence. This problem can be circumvented by the liberal use of sight and sound cues prior research has shown to be meaningful or relevant to audience members' issue-related attitudes or modes of evaluation. The effective message must speak the language of the audience both literally and figuratively—not just in terms of the way the audience sees things in general but in terms of the way in which they see or think about the specific change at hand.

The message that finds its way to the relevant portion of the inactive memory structure may find a congenial resting place there. This is likely to be the case if it is simply a "reminder" message designed to reinforce message-compatible attitudes or outlooks. But when the message meaning is inconsistent with prior memory or meaning structures, a competition between message and old memory forms ensues. Memories or attitudes may be changed to accommodate the message meaning, or the message it-self may be distorted so that it will fit in with the old points of view without creating that "inward trouble" to which James referred.

Message distortion is most likely to take one of three forms. The message may be *reindexed* as attention shifts from issue-related to source-related considerations. The audience asks, in effect, "What's wrong with these people that they would expect me to believe a thing like that?" The message may be *sharpened* as the audience draws upon old memory elements to supplement message elements, thereby adding unintended meanings to the message. Or message elements that are incompatible with old views may be *ignored*. When all but a few message elements nicely fit the meaning templates provided by old memory structures, the novel or unfamiliar elements are easily overlooked.

The likelihood of unfavorable reindexing can be minimized by the use of message channels or spokesmen likely to have high credibility for the intended audience or by using spokesmen with whom the audience members may easily identify themselves. Unfavorable sharpening and lev-eling of messages may be minimized by explicit treatments of those novel meanings the audience is most likely to overlook or those meanings the communicator does not want the audience to read into his message. The need for such accommodations to the audience's old points of view can be anticipated, at least in part, by the prior explorations of audience memory structures described earlier in connection with basic image or "selling idea" research. Such needs may otherwise become apparent only by the process of message pre-testing or post-testing.

We do not mean to imply that the communicator's intention is always ill served by audience members' tendencies to add their own meanings to mass communications. When the audience is already quite favorably disposed toward the issue in question, implicit or "cool" communications (to use the McLuhanesque term) may be best simply because they encourage the audience members to read their own favorable meanings into the message. Neither do we mean to imply that effective message communication must always leave the audience with explicit comprehension of a rational message meaning. Advertising practice has clearly shown the place for messages that do little more than enhance attitude salience or encourage a "friendly familiarity" with the issue, innovation, or program in question. Nor do we suggest that the audience's failure to completely accept or endorse any one message should be taken as a sign of ineffective communication.

Disbelief versus Curious Nonbelief. Change agents evaluating responses to persuasive messages must remember that significant attitude change involves a complex and richly interactive process. It often takes place gradually, over a considerable period of time. As people "unfreeze" old attitudes and move toward the acceptance of new ones, they inevitably go through dissonant stages of doubt about the old and curiosity about the new.

When the audience finds a particular message "hard to believe" they may be reflecting outright rejection or disbelief of the message *or* they may be indicating *curious nonbelief.* The latter, which often implies "That sounds too good (or too bad) to be true; I won't believe it until I see it," may be the best possible response from the communicator's point of view. It reflects the fact that a curiosity has been established which should predispose the doubter to pay greater attention to subsequent information about the issue in question. (Maloney, 1962, 1963). In terms of the implications of our earlier discussions of Figures 1 and 2, such curious nonbelief is evidence that a higher order, renew-cycle, attention-controlling feedback has been established.

Krugman's observations about "learning without involvement" (1966) bear importantly upon this point. As Krugman points out, persuasive information may change perceptions without changing attitudes in terms of the usual definition of attitude change. Krugman suggests that such perceptual change (latent or tentative attitude change) often becomes actual attitude change only after audience members are called upon to act on the information which has been given them.

The change agent-communicator should not be concerned, then, about the message which "sounds too good to be true"—*so long as it is true.* Responses of this sort must be considered in the light of message-confirming or message-refuting information or experiences to which the audience is likely to be exposed later. The change agent who starts his audience down the path toward acceptance of nonexistent innovations or reforms is simply asking for trouble. He is building the "goal gaps," "want/get ratios," and "relative deprivations" which turn awareness-comprehension-conviction-action into awareness-confusion-conflict-apathy. Curious nonbelief may become cynical disbelief or a new "revolution of rising expectations."

Wildavsky (1969) has described such ill-advised and overzealous change agentry as a "prescription for violence." On the basis of his analysis of civil unrest in the United States in the late 1960s, Maloney (1972) offers a special prescription for violence to mass communicators:

1. Call attention to serious social problems while suggesting that such problems can and must be alleviated at once.

2. Suggest that the problem in question exists solely because of the selfish way in which establishment factions set priorities or because of their intentional stupidity and cupidity.

3. Imply that the establishment scapegoats will see the evil of their ways and reform if only enough pressure is put on them.

4. As a protest movement grows and becomes unruly in the face of establishment confusion or buckpassing, publicize statements which attribute the unrest to (a) the intransigence of the establishment scapegoats and (b) the naturally understandable impatience of the protesters.

5. Ignore any detailed analysis of the origins or complexity of the problems, the resources and time it may take to overcome them, and the probability that solutions to these problems will give rise to other problems. (That is to say, ignore the "tradeoffs" problems.)

6. Assume that any confusion, apathy, or violence resulting from steps 1 to 5 will mystically be resolved (a) by covering protests and other pseudo-events staged by change agents, (b) by publicizing interpretations made available in speeches or press releases of social activists, and (c) by relying on the "self-righting tendency in the free marketplace of ideas."

The Need for a Hierarchical Information System

The social-psychological study of attitude formation and the study of relationships between attitude and behaviors calls for a considerable variety of measures and methodologies (Kelman and Warwick, 1973). As the communications response hierarchy implies, those measures and methodologies must be mutually complementary in their abilities to reflect part-whole or subsystem-system interactions. Without the guidance of such a hierarchy, researchers have tended to ignore crucial time frame considerations (evaluating behavioral or campaign effects without close enough attention to the timing of message inputs); they have chosen lower order message measures without regard to the extent to which they could or should predict campaign or behavioral successes; they have overlooked the extraneous variables that inhibit or facilitate level-to-level interface and interactions.

It has been common practice, for example, to evaluate messages or program interventions with laboratory procedures that "rub respondents' noses" in the message and obtain immediate response to the message, often using highly reactive measures or leading questions. Such practices short-circuit the selective-attention, selective-perception, selective-recall phenomena that naturally inhibit message effects in the field (Hovland, 1959). As a result, laboratory measures of message effects typically provide gross overestimates of attitudinal effects which will later occur in the field (Day, 1972). At the same time, while tentative attitudinal effects of messages often fail to carry over to actual attitude change from campaigns, the researcher is often chagrined to learn that campaign-induced attitude change fails to carry over to behavioral change (Wicker, 1969).

The answer to such problems, we feel, is to be found in the development of a continuous information system, such as that implied in Figure 3, which makes the change agent a participant in a multilevel system of communications and feedbacks as the change program runs its course. In the proposed system, the change agent continually takes in information from the social environment he seeks to influence. He processes this information in the light of prior plans and past experiences and sends out new communications and action channel manipulations. He thus *decodes* (notes/understands) a continual stream of inputs, stores information (mulling over past successes and failures), and encodes responses (decides and acts), just as the target audience and each member of the target audience does.

The information coming to him is of two general sorts: (1) *inferential* feedback and (2) *synthetic* feedback. Inferential feedback (the solid-line external-loop feedback of Figure 3) may be observed in the normal course of events such as birth rates, pollution indices, or other "ultimate criterion" measures related to the goals of the program in question. Synthetic feedback (the dashed-line feedback of Figure 3) would not occur unless generated by research which monitors the states-of-mind correlates of target audience action.

Although the highest order, inferential feedbacks are the most meaningful in the sense that they reflect ultimate program success and failure, the lower order, synthetic feedbacks are likely to be much more sensitive to the change agent's short-term efforts. The synthetic feedbacks are therefore a vital part of the change agent's evaluation, planning, and control functions in that they allow the change agent to learn as he goes and to steer (in the literal cybernetic sense) his innovations and programs to eventual success.

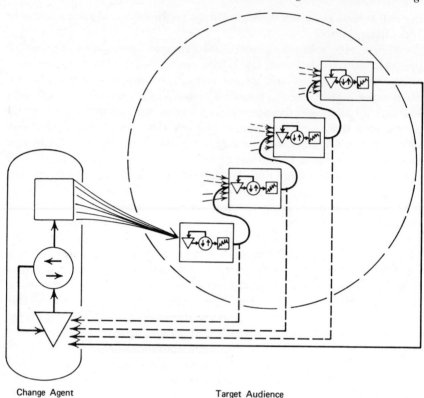

Change Agent   Target Audience

Figure 3. An ideal change agent to target audience linkage with external loop feedbacks.

The development of a synthetic feedback system of interrelated, interfacing measures for monitoring the total hierarchy of response is required so that program failures at every level may be corrected before erroneous or conflicting information is passed up the hierarchy of response and higher order top-down feedback "turns off" attention at lower levels. The measures and methods for this type of hierarchical system already exist, although refinements and adaptations are needed for most social change applications. This technology draws upon those theories, concepts, and social science disciplines most relevant for each level in question.

At the bottom of the hierarchy, the symbol level, feedbacks may be obtained by special experiments or laboratory measures to evaluate the attention value and meaningfulness of partial or tentative messages and individual communication symbols and cues. Autonomic arousal measures (pupil dilation and galvinic skin response), controlled exposure measures (tachistiscopic methods), and rating scales might be used.

At the perceptual level in the hierarchy, whole messages may be measured for intrusiveness that overcomes selective attention, clarity of the intended basic "selling" idea (when this is important), memorability of salient details such as where-to or how-to perform the suggested behavior, and potential or tentative attitude effects as evidenced by content analysis of open-end responses that indicate both a favorable disposition and personal involvement or internalization.

At the attitudinal or state-of-mind level in the hierarchy, periodic surveys of the target population can be used to construct profiles of innovation demand; for example, unaided awareness, acceptance of or preference for the innovation, trial and satisfaction among those who recently tried the innovation (Maloney, 1966). These surveys may also include secondary measures of program performance: approval measures, overall trial, length of interval since previous trial, repeat trial, and perceived convenience of the channels of action measures.

The validity of the interrelated, interfacing measures of performance in an information system such as that suggested in Figure 3 can be established by empirical demonstration of level-to-level measurement linkages. Each level's measures should be correlated with higher order performance measures to provide a basis for ultimate projections of mass behavioral response. Maximal predictive efficiency from one level to the next is likely to require multivariate procedures and special algorithms which take into account the higher order "noises" or "extraneous variables" such as behavior inhibiting or facilitating environmental or situational factors.

In this effort to establish the empirical, between-level linkages, the response measures at each level in the feedback or measurement hierarchy automatically provide criteria for validating the immediately lower order measures. This is of considerable importance for validating lower order measures and linkages. Symbol and message level measures can seldom be expected to predict complex mass behaviors over considerable periods of time. But if symbol level responses predict message level responses, if these predict campaign level responses, and if these, in turn, predict top level mass behaviors—given available and properly functioning channels of action—one need not worry about the validity of symbol-level measures for predicting mass behavior.

In an information system such as that described here, the theory of change and the measurement of change are simultaneously refined by continuous attempts to maximize level-to-level prediction. Once the validities of the feedback measures are generally established, and once the research team determines how responses at each level are mediated by extraneous variables operating at the next level, the deviations from expected or predicted performance at each level become highly instructive. It is the ability to identify such surprises or residual error variances that permit continuous refinement of the system as it operates through time. The importance of this feature of information system operation, as contrasted with conventional experimental approaches to the study of change or communication effects, can hardly be overemphasized.

In the experimental or piecemeal approach to research, the *ceteris paribus* assumptions are seldom valid; the "other things" often have a greater effect on higher level response then the change agent's own efforts. Gross (1966, p. 185) points out that the information system approach (such as we suggest in Figure 3) prevents the *ceteris paribus* from becoming the *ceteris incognitus*. We reiterate: the change agent must look down the hierarchy of response and take a "big picture" view of the social system he is trying to influence.

In the final analysis, the validation of any social change decision model or monitoring system requires that someone apply it in a "real world" test for a sufficient period of time and incur the associated financial, social, and political risks. This is a process likely to put to the test the researcher or change agent's integrity as much as the research methodology.

Most researchers experienced in large-scale change strategy evaluations in either commercial or political settings can attest to the pressures they have experienced to produce the "right" (i.e., reassuring) answers. As Campbell has observed (1969, p. 410):

> If the political and administrative system has committed itself in advance to the correctness and efficacy of its reforms, it cannot tolerate learning of failure. To be truly scientific, we must be able to experiment. We must be able to advocate without that excess of commitment that blinds us to reality testing.
>
> This predicament, abetted by public apathy and by deliberate corruption, may prove in the long run to permanently preclude a truly experimental approach to social amelioration. . . .

We live in a time when objectivity is denigrated as a myth, a lack of commitment, or a sign of the same technocratic insensitivity that gave rise to so many of our social problems (Roszak, 1969; Shaver and Staines, 1972). Such criticisms often have validity. But the researcher should keep in mind the fact that *feigned* objectivity is not only likely to lead to eventual frustration and failure for himself but also frustration and failure for the intended beneficiaries of social change.

Organization for Social Change

Throughout this discussion we have spoken of *social planners* and *change agents* as though anonymous and diabolically clever fellows could coopt a reluctant group of reactionary *gatekeepers* among an existing power elite all in the interest of hawking social reforms to a *target population*. The very language required to set forth our thoughts gives us cause for pause and reflection. The intent of our general approach is clear and even to us (or especially to us) our own language is a bit shocking.

What if we *were* to have a scientifically precise political or social science of social change in place and ready to solve all of the world's problems as we or others see them? In *Brave New World Revisited* (1965, p. 23) Huxley wrote: "In politics the equivalent of a fully developed scientific theory or philosophical system is a totalitarian dictatorship." He warned that "The Will to Order can make tyrants out of those who merely aspire to clear up a mess. The beauty of tidiness is just a justification for despotism." Fair warning for those who would move too fast toward scientific and overzealous social reform!

Huxley went on to express our own biases on these matters:

> Organization is indispensable; for liberty arises and has meaning only within a self-regulating community of freely cooperating individuals. But, though indispensable, organization can also be fatal. Too much organization transforms men and women into automata, suffocates the creative spirit and abolishes the very possibility of freedom. As usual, the only safe course is in the middle, between the extremes of *laissez faire* at one end of the scale and total control at the other.

How do we find that "safe course in the middle"? It is not easy. Since 1964 a group of Harvard scholars has been studying the effects of technology upon democratic processes. Their fourth annual report (Methvin, 1969, p. 463) posed the problem as follows:

> If you go the full way to the technocratic elite, you'll wind up with a technocracy. But if you go the way of those who want full participation, you'll wind up with chaos. The question is how to take advantage of the knowledge necessary to run a big, complex society without giving up the values of participation. The answer we are looking for is a third way. We haven't found it yet.

We would suggest that the "middle course" or the "third way" is to be found in the judicious application of the principles we have been espousing.

The stage-setting phases of social change, those complex negotiating operations required to establish effective action channels for social change, should no doubt be set up by elites, but not the secretive, technocratic elites locked behind the closed doors of think tanks; rather the elected elites, the informed citizen elites, the journalistic and academic elites—those whom Michael (1968, p. 1182) has called the "concerned citizens," or those whom James Reston (1966, pp. 101–108) has referred to as the "saving remnant" of society. These people must have clear access to channels of decision making which guarantee a hearing to everyone who has done his or her homework and has a well considered view that he or she wishes to express.

We are *not* talking about the well-ordered despotism to which Huxley refers nor the "tyranny of the expert" against which Dubos (1970) and Dickson (1971) warn us. Neither are we talking about a simple-minded "participatory democracy" or a blind faith in a "self-righting tendency" in the "free marketplace of ideas." The former would, in our view, be intolerably dehumanizing; the latter, our recent experience warns us, could lead to utter chaos, to unrealistic expectations, and to "goal gaps," frustrations, and the increased likelihood of nihilistic violence.

We *are* speaking, then, of a democratic elitism, a nonsecretive elitism open to all who have the time, talent, and skills required to participate in higher level decision making; an elitism whose reforms or innovations must in all cases be approved and endorsed by the voluntary actions of the majority.

The "field experiment" and "selling" stages of social change must, of course, involve a broader base of the citizenry. We refer to the *target population.* Some call them the "client populations," a term we eschew since they do not, in fact, bear the relationships to the change agents or social planners that a lawyer's clients or any other profession's paying clients would bear to the professional. The target population's views must be reflected in their acceptance or rejection of social change alternatives—in their willingness to adopt the birth control practice, to use the new mass transit facility, to support the referendum. More particularly, their views must be reflected in the attitude research feedbacks we have discussed.

Finally, it seems to us that social change procedures, the social indicators and attitude measurement procedures that must accompany them, must be open to the scrutiny and criticism (a judicious and patient scrutiny we might hope) of the nation's press. This could lead to embarrassment or even some degree of harassment of social planners, change agents, and attitude researchers, who will surely feel harassed enough simply trying to cope with the complexities they must face. But this is the price that democratic elites must be prepared to pay if we are to avoid the likelihood that "the Will to Order can make tyrants out of those who merely aspire to clear up a mess."

Notes

1. In studying gasoline, fast-food service, and comparable markets in the United States, the authors have noted that variations in sales and brand share for various companies or brands correlate so highly with numbers of outlets that the residual sales variance attributable to advertising or other forms of persuasion is often quite limited. Such correlations are typically nonlinear, taking a form which suggests that a high share or concentration of outlets builds brand image or "share of mind" as well as share of distribution. We would expect that a comparable phenomenon would occur with regard to the attitudinal effects of channel visibility for many social innovations.

2. Our orientation is not to be taken as a rejection of more widely held views of attitudes or attitude formation. Indeed, the informed reader will see a good deal of conventional theory reflected in the remarks that follow. Other selections in this volume give an excellent explicit account of those theories.

Bruçe H. Westley

Department of Journalism
University of Kentucky

COMMUNICATION AND SOCIAL CHANGE

Perhaps no aspect of social change has been as extensively researched as the relationship between communication and change, individual and social, and in particular the part played by the media of public communication in the process. Yet the research has proceeded from so many different assumptions, has predicted behavior at so many different levels, and has been contributed by so many different disciplines that it cannot be said that there is *a* perspective in this field. There are in fact many, and part of what this essay attempts to do is to sort the perspectives and attempt to give the subject some order.

This book understandably assigns the communication perspective to the microscopic level. However, this chapter will argue that to assign the process to the level of stimulus and response only perpetuates a bias that misses the critical point of communication and *social* change. Human information processing demonstrably occurs at many levels. It may be studied at the neurological level, at the level of human individuality, at the level of face-to-face interaction, at the level of the neighborhood, the community, the complex organization, the national state, the language community—even the human community. It is argued that communication and change may be described and predicted at all these levels, and none is exclusively the domain of social change.

Finally, communication may be seen as both cause and consequence. It is not exclusively a matter of generating messages and measuring some change in a receiver. Both information-exchange and information-seeking behavior are significant communicative acts that may be either causes or consequences of change.[1]

217

System Levels

Let us first examine the question of the appropriate levels at which to study the dynamics of communication and change. The biological organism may be viewed as an information system. Young (1951) defines communication as an interchange of information between two self-regulating systems. Any biological organism may be treated as a self-regulating system, and, although infrahuman species are evidently wholly incapable of language, they demonstrably influence each others' behavior in the manipulation of signs (though perhaps not symbols) by virtue of a language of gesture. DeFleur (1970) has given an account of some of the ways animals interact by means of what he calls a "natural sign." Von Frisch (1962) demonstrated that the gestural "language" of bees conveys information about the location of sources of nectar; Guhl (1956) demonstrated that pecking order in chickens is maintained by a gestural language. We know that neurons as information carriers within the human organism are binary communicative systems. Wiener (1950) has emphasized that the difference between the communication system of an insect and a human is to be found in the kind of programing capability each has. Insects appear to have a limited set of single-purpose "tapes" and virtually no memory; human beings have a few of the former and a great many of the latter.

Are these phenomena "below" the level of society and social change? The interesting thing about the "language" of the bees and the chickens is that in each case the exchange of information is *for a social purpose*. It is the hive that requires the information about the location of the nectar, and it is the social order of the chicken yard that is served by the language of pecking order. We cannot therefore say that communication phenomena are irrelevant to social life and, by extension, irrelevant to social change, at any level.

It might be even more readily accepted that cognitive systems of human beings and the limits they place on individual members of social systems contribute to an understanding of social process. In the version of Osgood and Tannebaum (1955), for example, the source's relation to the receiver is obviously a social one, for the receiver can have an image and an expectation of a source only on the basis of past communications. In fact, most human expectations may be seen as social in origin.

Interpersonal communication is clearly a social behavior and, as Newcomb (1953) has theorized, it is the microscosmic foundation for consensus, which might be called the basic condition for the existence of society. Hickey (1968) has demonstrated that information control in the problem-solving group is critical to the group's perception of the controller, thus pointing up the fact that communication acts in face-to-face groups influence and are influenced by the social structure of the group.

To summarize, communication may be studied at various levels and macro-micro does not really distinguish them. It is a social act at all levels.

However, it is only at the level of the community or the social system that all aspects of communication may be treated in a single model. Particular reference is made here to the impersonal or mediated or public or "mass" communication media. Although it is quite true that these may be treated as the carriers of stimuli to the individual receiver to be processed at the cognitive level, the complications that public, one-to-many, institutional communications introduce into the communication system of the modern society suggest that these require us to study the communication processes of social systems, rather than treating them as competing or reinforcing stimuli at the cognitive level or as sources of information to the individual or to the group information seeker at the interpersonal level. The suspicion is that mediated or machine-interposed communication (Deutschmann, 1956) is related to social change in unique ways. The exploration of these issues is the concern of the next few pages of this report.

Communication and Mass Communication

When we speak of communication and mass communication as aspects of human society we need to remind ourselves that the former is a universal characteristic of societies and the latter a unique characteristic of certain societies. "Mass communication" implies an assumption about societies that to the writer is unacceptable—that societies which have mass communication are "mass societies."

The concept may be traced to the perception of a "mass man" arising from an urbanized and bureaucratized society, one in which the supportive interpersonal communication characteristics of *Gemeinschaft* were replaced by an organized *Gesellschaft* and then through the depersonalized communication system of the urban society became "mass society." Although we know that today's Western societies cannot properly be called "mass societies," the concept "mass communication"—also a misnomer—casts a semantic cloud over much of our thinking about modern society and its communication systems.

The distinction between social, or interpersonal, or face-to-face, or one-to-one communication, on the one hand, and societal, or impersonal, or mediated, or one-to-many communication, on the other, is an important one, if for no other reason that that the former normally permits instantaneous and subtle feedback where the latter permits only a highly constrained and attenuated feedback. One-to-many communication can occur in societies that have no modern media; jungle drums and smoke signals reach everyone who can hear and see. Media are multipliers of signals but they also impose constraints on messages. Machines can, however, also conquer distance without multiplication (telephone and telegraph). They can provide monopolized private channels (closed-circuit television) as well as channels open to anyone with a receiver (network television). They can be aimed at a highly specialized subculture (*Women's Wear Daily*) or compete for the widest and most undifferentiated audience they can attract (prime-time television). Our literature suffers from the fact that phenomena as diverse as these are so often lumped under the single, loose rubric "mass communication."

Communication Effects

Is it the natural tendency of communication in general and of mass or public communication in particular to induce change or to inhibit change? Although these phenomena have been extensively studied at many levels and from the viewpoint of many different disciplines, this question remains essentially unanswered. Some research traditions assume that an act of communication is a necessary condition for change. Others assume that communication can only inhibit change; still others assume that it tends to be a stabilizing factor after change has occurred. New disciplines treat information processing, especially feedback, as a necessary condition for *the maintenance of adaptive change* and assume that there is no other kind.

In the early years of this century, Charles Horton Cooley (1902, 1909) thought of the mass media as the communication instrument that human society needed to expand its frontiers, both intellectual and technical. Just as the primary group humanized the child, the mass media could humanize society, to extend its capacity to cope with new problems, to provide a common context for democratic decision making, and to break the aristocratic monopoly of knowledge. For him, mass media made mass society a viable institution.

A few decades later another view arose which was no less convinced of the power of media but provided a less optimistic view of its consequences. The concept of propaganda assumed that under certain conditions of control, mass and interpersonal communication—but especially the former—could be manipulated to achieve conformity. All that was needed was to control access tô the media and to monitor its effects through interpersonal surveillance. In fact, the control of communication channels was thought to be the primary means of controlling a society (e.g., see Doob, 1950).

Marxism-Leninism treats propaganda (the propagation of ideas among significant elites) and agitation (the dissemination of ideology among the masses) as distinct processes (Inkeles, 1951) but relies heavily on the idea that society can be controlled—that is to say, the revolution can be managed—by controlling the instruments of communication (Pool, 1963). Self-criticism is seen as a means of control which permits and encourages feedback within a carefully controlled range of possibilities (Inkeles, 1951).

C. Wright Mills (1959) took the view that power elites control the masses by controlling access to the mass media. The mass, he writes, is characterized by a low ratio of opinion giving to opinion receiving. The mass media fulfill significant needs for the individual—to give him identity, aspirations, and techniques for their realization and escape from the consequences of disappointed aspirations. All this permits the elite that controls the media to control the behavior of the mass.

Mills' reliance on the idea of mass society is similar to that which characterized the "Chicago school" of sociology. With its emphasis on urbanism, it tended to emphasize the "teeming masses." Louis Wirth (1948) said that modern society takes two basic forms, organized groups and detached masses, the latter characterized by great numbers, widely dispersed, heterogeneous, and anonymous: thus, as Blumer (1956) puts it, "devoid of the features of society and community: no social organization, no status structure, no sense of community, no ideology, no customs, no established leadership." For Blumer this made the mass the captive of the mass media and permitted the controllers of the media to control mass behavior.[2] But Wirth saw that mass media could be a social instrument for welding a system-wide consensus as society became more differentiated into interest groups.

All of these perspectives assume or assert that mass communication has effects; their differences concern whether and how these effects are functional for society. They also differ in their view of whether the mass media are instruments of control capable of reducing dissent or instruments for attaining the goal of consensus. By and large, they have yielded no evidence on the question at hand: Is it in the nature of communications in general and mass communications where they exist to induce change in predictable directions?

Several powerful research traditions have grown up in the intervening years. One will be treated only briefly, for it makes the contrary assumption that communications reflect the conditions of society and therefore cannot shape them. Typically this approach analyzes mass media products as cultural artifacts. For example, Lowenthal (1943) analyzed biographies in popular magazines during four periods of time to test for ideological differences. Johns-Heine and Gerth (1949) similarly tested mass periodical fiction for ideological change; Berelson and Salter (1946) studied magazine fiction to relate majority-minority status to role assignment. The problems associated with inferring such connections have been extensively explored by Martel and McCall (1964).

A second research tradition grew out of the wartime studies of the effects of propaganda films (Hovland et al., 1949) and under Hovland's leadership brought the study of mass communication effects into the learning laboratory to study order effects (Hovland et al., 1957), personality correlates of persuasability (Janis et al., 1959), and a variety of other determinants of persuasion, including group membership, content factors such as fear appeals, and order of arguments (Hovland et al., 1953). In the captive audience situations in which these studies were conducted, incidentally, there was rarely any difficulty in producing persuasion.

A third tradition in a sense grew out of and tended to replace the second. It concerned itself with the structural component of cognition. In brief, its central thrust is that stimulus characteristics interact with the existing state of the receivers' cognitive structure (Osgood and Tannenbaum, 1955; Festinger and Brehm, 1960; Festinger, 1964). The tendency is to shift the emphasis from the stimulus side to the response side, from environmental control to stability of cognitive systems, from attitude change to attitudinal stability, and—in the case of post-decision dissonance—from information receiving to information seeking. It helps explain why change is more readily induced when it is in the direction of the receiver's predispositions and precognitions. It also helps explain why persuasive change, although easy to induce, is often fleeting.

A fourth tradition dealt more directly with the question of mass media effects. The "Columbia school" set out to determine how people made up their minds in a political campaign (Lazarsfeld et al., 1944), then continued their concern with communication and decision by studying other elections (Berelson et al., 1954) and other decisions (Katz and Lazarsfeld, 1955; Katz and Menzel, 1955). The burden of this research is that interpersonal influence plays a large part and the mass media a relatively small part in transmitting information and changing attitudes. Information and influence proceed through a two-step process, from an opinion leader to another member of his peer group. The opinion leader influences his peer by shaping the communication to be consistent with the group's perception of the world and by being a respected opinion leader and hence a credible source.

This position has been called into question on a number of grounds. First, numerous studies (e.g. Larsen and Hill, 1954; Danielson, 1956; Deutschmann and Danielson, 1960; Greenberg, 1964a, 1964b; Mendelsohn, 1964; Sheatsley and Feldman, 1964; for a summary, Greenberg and Parker, 1965) find that major news stories are in fact diffused directly by the mass media to a far greater extent than by personal sources. Hill and Bonjean (1964) found that the greater the news value of the event, the more personal communication figures in its diffusion. An unpublished study by the present author supported a different generalization: The more important the event *to the recipient,* the more personal communication contributed to its diffusion. (Great news events were diffused by personal communication to a greater degree than lesser news events; but a very minor "news event"—a routine fire—occurring in the neighborhood in which the study was conducted was largely diffused by personal communication, and the closer the recipient to the event, the more this was the case.) Of the various news diffusion studies following the assassination of President Kennedy, the only one that showed a preponderance of interpersonal sources of first knowledge was conducted in Dallas itself (Spitzer and Spitzer, 1965; the others are cited above). Budd et al. (1966) present data that support the "importance" hypothesis of Hill and Bonjean (1964) that class differences, which many studies found to be positively related to mass media use and knowledge of public affairs (Steinberg, 1949; Cottrell and Everhart, 1948; Davis, 1949; Nafziger et al., 1951; Campbell et al., 1954; Hero, 1959a, 1959b; Patchen, 1964; Westley and Severin, 1964; Rogers, 1965; Robinson, 1967) are less influential in determining when important news reaches a member of the audience. The finding is, instead, that persons of higher education got the news earlier than persons of lower education.

This brings us back to the Katz and Lazarsfeld position, which holds that persons influential on others tend to belong to the same status levels as those they influence. This is important because it attacks a widely held view that ascribes influence primarily to status. But close examination of the Katz and Lazarsfeld (1955) data suggests that in public affairs and certain consumer goods choices, high-status people received more nominations as influentials than lower status persons. (There is an interesting exception in fashion, where young women tended to nominate women in the age group just above them whereas older women chose younger women as influentials; Katz and Lazarsfeld, 1955, p. 258). The finding on status calls into question the two-step flow hypothesis. The support is based on the finding that influentials are more likely to be heavier users of the mass media. But if they are of higher status than those they influence, and, as is well known, higher status people use media more, the whole proposition comes tumbling down.[3] Tichenor et al. (1970), in fact, show that information flows reach the best educated most readily, and unless the campaign is continued at a high level of input, there is an ever-widening "knowledge gap" between these informational elites and what has been called "the chronic know-nothing" (Hyman and Sheatsley, 1947). This could not be true if knowers fed information toward nonknowers as the two-step flow model suggests.

Perhaps the data of Troldahl and Van Dam (1965–1966) are the most damaging to the two-step flow hypothesis: "Opinion giving in public affairs topics seems to be reciprocal to a great extent . . . opinion sharing rather than opinion giving." Opinion givers "were not significantly different [from seekers] in their exposure to relevant media content, their information level on national news, their occupational prestige, and four of five attributes of gregariousness" (Troldahl and Van Dam, 1965–1966, pp. 633ff).

The matter is of some importance to the way change agents view the part played by communication in the change process and will be reexamined later.

Studies have shown that massive information campaigns fail to produce attitude change. Although these are not usually reported as diffusion studies, they go directly to the heart of the question posed here: Can mass media produce widespread changes in knowledge and attitude? Perhaps the best known is the study of an information campaign in Cincinnati to increase knowledge of the United Nations (Star and Hughes, 1950; Hyman and Sheatsley, 1947). In this and other campaigns—to increase understanding of the purpose of war bonds (Haire, 1956), to change attitudes toward oil versus gas (reported by Klapper, 1960, p. 17), and a political telethon (Schramm and Carter, 1959)—no effects could be discerned. These and other findings have been summarized by Klapper (1957–1958, 1960, 1963) and reinterpreted by Fisk (1959). The general conclusion is that mass media rarely have direct effects; they influence change only through interpersonal processes and then only when predisposition to change exists. The point that predisposing conditions must be present is supported by Hovland (1959), Klapper (1963, p. 70), and Smith et al. (1956). However, Greenberg (1964) has found evidence that "the more one learns, the greater the magnitude of the attitude change will be —*in either direction.*"

In a recent study, Douglas et al. (1970) reported an information campaign that had large and widespread effects on public knowledge of and attitudes toward mental retardation. We found significant differences in both knowledge and attitude items between experimental and control communities and significant before-after changes in attitude. The largest information gain was made by persons of lowest education, where predispositional factors should also. be lowest. When sources were correlated with information level after the campaign, the largest difference between experimental and control correlations was "friends," and the next largest was "local newspaper." Although the campaign information was fed largely into local media, it was supported and reinforced by word-of-mouth. Information obtained in the media was evidently relayed to others as the two-step flow hypothesis predicts, but the effect was to supplement and extend the campaign. Rogers and Sverring (1969, p. 222) made the same point in summarizing the weaknesses of the hypothesis: "it implies a competitive rather than complementary role for mass media and interpersonal channels."

It cannot be doubted that media influence is affected by the process of group validation, just as cognitive constancies affect the way individuals process new information. The treatment given to group processes by Katz and Lazarsfeld (1955, pp. 48–65) states the case very well. But the *direction* of the effect must be predicted from some other source. If the group norms are strongly shared and contrary to the new information, then the effect of the medium bearing the message should be blunted; if consistent with prevailing norms, the media effect should be enhanced. We should expect groups to function, thus, *as information-processing systems,* as cognitive systems do. This will be discussed later.

Diffusion of Innovations

A sixth research tradition—research on the diffusion of innovations—has made a substantial contribution to our knowledge of communication and change. It has tended to blend together with the communication-and-influence research tradition just discussed. It is treated here only in relation to what it tells us about the relation between mass and interpersonal communications in the induction of change. This tradition owes much to Rogers, who developed a coherent theory of the process (1962) and has summarized the literature in light of that theory (with Sverring, 1969), including much of the literature of the communication and development research tradition that will be treated here.

The diffusion-of-innovations viewpoint stresses stages in the adoption process, usually described as awareness, interest, evaluation, trial, and adoption (Rogers, 1962, p. 306). Decision makers are categorized according to time of adoption, usually as innovators, early majority, late majority, and laggards (Rogers, 1962, pp. 160–164).

On the basis of his research in Turkey, Frey (1966, p. 32) said that "if contemporary research is agreed upon anything, it is that both the mass media and interpersonal communication are integral parts of the diffusion process."

> Our data seem to show that the mass media in Turkey have a broad impact on many attitudes and behaviors of the nation's peasantry . . . In some ways the planner can get more mileage from the mass media as a development instrument than can the planner in a developed society (1966, p. 30).

Planners no doubt have greater control over the media in underdeveloped areas if they are also relatively authoritarian. But authoritarian relationships do not necessarily produce commitment to change, even when they are able to induce acceptance (Coch and French, 1948; Lewin et al., 1939; Lippitt et al., 1959).

Evidently we are not as nearly unanimous on this point as Frey believes. Rogers, with Sverring (1969, pp. 128–130), has concluded that mass media play a relatively minor role in the change process in developing nations. It should not be surprising that mass media are not a significant bearer of new tidings to Andean peasants, considering that the media are relatively an elite consumer item in "underdeveloped" parts of the world. Myren (in Rogers with Sverring, 1969, p. 130) has stated the obvious: "The hypothesis concerning the impact of the mass media can be applied only in areas where media circulate widely and where . . . they command attention and deal with questions of interest."

Rogers (1969, p. 132) found no evidence of any media influence at any stage of the adoption process in his Colombian peasant sample, whereas a sample of Iowa farmers credited media sources more than any other at the awareness (or first knowledge) stage and to a much lesser degree at the persuasion stage (Rogers with Sverring, 1969, p. 131). Similarly, Van den Ban (1965) found that nearly three-quarters of a sample of Dutch farmers attached "the greatest significance" to mass media as a means of learning of the existence of new products but almost none of them assigned importance to the media in deciding whether to adopt them. In such a well-developed nation, media reach nearly everyone.

Deutschmann et al. (1961) found that media used by elite populations of 11 Latin American countries was comparable quantitatively to that of North Americans of similar status, but the Latin elites used books and technical publications more heavily than their northern counterparts.

In another study, carried out in an Andean peasant community,

Deutschmann and Mendez (1962) found that mass media use, although it accounted for little initial awareness of new consumer products by comparison with interpersonal channels, was highly characteristic of early adopters. Waisanen and Lassey (see McNelly, 1966; Rogers with Sverring, 1969) report that Costa Ricans who bought stock in a cement plant as a development venture were heavier users of print media but less heavy users of radio, which in this and other studies in Latin America has proved to be a popular medium for those less modernized, lower class, and more traditional (e.g., see Deutschmann, 1963; U.S. Information Service, 1961; McNelly and Deutschmann, 1963; Deutschmann et al., 1961; McNelly and Fonseca, 1964); the opposite trend, however, was found in Chile (Carter and Sepulveda, 1964).

Rogers (1965–1966; Rogers with Sverring, 1969) has proposed and tested a most ingenious explanation for the relationships between mass media use and other predictors of readiness for modernization. He treats functional literacy, education, social status, age, and "cosmopolitanness," as antecedents (since they are prior in probable time order) and empathy, agricultural and home innovativeness, political knowledge, achievement motivation, and educational and occupational aspirations as consequences, these being the usual indices of readiness for modernization. Mass media exposure, which normally is found to correlate with both sets of variables, is treated as an intervening variable. Using data from five Colombian villages, three relatively modern and two relatively traditional, Rogers found that the relationship between functional literacy and the consequent variables was reduced when mass media exposure was introduced as a partial correlate, indicating an intervening relationship. Thus functional literacy predicts readiness for modernization, as does mass media exposure, but the two in combination are stronger than either taken alone. It is reasoned, then, that functional literacy increases mass media exposure and the two taken together increase empathy, achievement motivation, political knowledge, and the like.

Little attention has been paid to the congruency between the innovation under study and the life and work situation and cultural values of the proposed target. This is odd, considering the emphasis given the question in recent years at the cognitive level. Brandner and Kearl (1964) have shown that when persons evaluate an innovation's congruency with a favorably evaluated existing practice the rate of acceptance is affected more strongly than most of the usual predictors—age, education, income, and the economic importance of the innovation—combined. On the basis of other studies summarized earlier, it is probable that personal communication should play a larger part than mass media in congruency evaluation, although this is not known.

Witt (1972) found additional evidence for the congruency idea. When he examined Wisconsin counties for news coverage concerning adoption of shoreland regulations, he found that it was positively associated with progress toward adoption and negatively associated with the development of shoreline housing. He takes this to mean that communities, like individuals, exhibit a kind of "selective perception" in making their information congruent with significantly related conditions.

Bebermeyer and Rogers (reported by Rogers with Sverring, 1969, pp. 134–136) have pointed out that media channels can be utilized in combination with interpersonal communications, both "cosmopolite" and "localite," by the use of *media forums*—discussion groups led by change agents and participated in by target individuals. The advantage of combining these communicative instruments of change is fairly obvious. They extend the reach of the change agent in permitting him to deal with groups of target individuals rather than one individual at a time. This point is also made by Spector (1963). The assembled audience also permits the change agent to bring consensual influence to bear upon people unwilling to accept influence from alien change agents or from the medium. Media-borne messages can be restated and evaluated in the terms of the culture of the target group.

Behavioral Contagion

A new research tradition appears to be developing in the wake of widespread urban ghetto and campus riots. It is concerned with the conditions that produce spread of riots and crises out of concern that mass media may be culpable. These may be called studies of communication in behavioral contagion.

Singer (1970) interviewed a sample of persons who had been arrested during a riot. He found that this group received first information of what was going on from interpersonal sources (48%) more than from direct experience (27%) and radio and television (26%). A similar result was obtained by Nwankwo (1971) in a study of communication in a campus crisis. But Singer's subjects were at least as likely to pass the word to others when their own sources were the mass media as when they were interpersonal or direct.

Those who got their information from interpersonal sources got information that was more explicit, more inflammatory, more conducive to participation, and more in terms of their own ways of perceiving the situation. Thus when sources were personal, the event was more likely to be categorized as a riot at a particular location than when sources were the media (Singer, 1970). Media sources tended to categorize the event (more than personal sources) as looting and stealing, as a raid, and as the occasion for a curfew. Hence the media cast the event in the terms and categories used by the authorities, whereas personal sources cast it in the terms used by soul brothers.

Of course the media can create the initial conditions for behavioral contagion, as the Orson Welles broadcast of "War of the Worlds" demonstrated, but, as Cantril (1940) has shown, apprehension grows into panic only when the fearful perceive the actions of others as supportive of the idea that the feared event is real.

National Development

A final research tradition that has shed light on the questions raised by this review is that of communication and national development, although it too is merging into a general tradition of communication and social change, using data from a broad range of cultures. What is distinctive about this tradition is that it has dealt with the conditions for broad social change in the direction of modernization not, as in the rural sociology tradition, the adoption of particular concrete behaviors consistent with modernization. At the same time it has been peculiarly subject to the charge of cultural imperialism.

For example, "fatalism," (Rogers, 1969, p. 291) the belief that events are preordained and the individual cannot control his own future, is found to be a barrier to modernization. The lack of fit between this view and readiness for modernization is apparent. Bonilla (see Rogers with Sverring, 1969) found fatalism among Colombian villagers to be negatively related to literacy, mass media exposure, empathy, cosmopolitanism, innovativeness, achievement motivation, aspirations for the future, and political knowledge. It did not, however, prove to be a negative intervening variable in the same way that mass media exposure proved to be a positive intervening variable.

The change agent in the international sphere has his own ideological biases. He exports empathy, the achievement motive, and the work ethic. Lerner (1958) is largely responsible for the notion that mass media and interpersonal contacts, but especially the former, produce a critical precondition for the developmental sequence—empathy—defined more or less as the ability to perceive oneself in the role of another. Rogers (1969, p. 210) found that in Colombia empathy was indeed predicted by mass media exposure to a substantial degree. Only it and functional literacy accounted for a significant amount of variance. He also reports that empathy predicted agricultural innovativeness among his Colombian peasants. Empathy in turn predicted achievement motivation, political knowledge, having political opinions, opinion leadership, and aspiration. However, it is acknowledged that all of these attributes are associated with high social status.

McClelland (1961) has produced evidence that in many cultures, East and West, past and present, achievement motivation precedes and is associated with economic growth. The position has been challenged by Hagen (1961) and Rogers (1969), among others. It closely resembles the classic work of Weber (1930).

Mishra (1970) has reported two interesting findings in his study of mass media use and modernization in the basties of greater Delhi. Membership in groups was found to be positively correlated with use of the newspaper, a result also found by Westley and Severin (1964) in a mid-western state. Thus those who seek information in informal groups also seek it in the media, contrary to the widely held folk-urban conception that attaches importance to social congress in folk societies and emphasizes media in urban societies. Mishra also found a positive association between mass media use and family dependence. Since family dependence and group dependence are traditional virtues, these findings also attack the notion that readiness for development is a matter of substituting transitional for traditional values.

Since motives seek gratification, Lerner is among those who are concerned about inducing motives for change when economic development does not quickly follow psychological readiness, producing a disruptive want/get ratio, to use Lerner's term (e.g., in Pye, 1963). In a more recent essay, Lerner (1970) has pointed out that when social change proceeds smoothly the research and development rhetoric emphasizes "positive programs," but when they go sour the emphasis shifts to communication as a scapegoat. Communication, Lerner says, is both a proper panacea and a proper scapegoat; a scapegoat because "grievous errors" have been committed in its name in two decades of work in underdeveloped areas, "a proper panacea because it manages the only process that offers hope for remedial action and for constructive attitudes to future issues." In the same review he stresses the importance of implanting a "work ethic." Communication "will have to teach many millions of simple folk around the world to associate personal reward with personal effort, to acquire a work ethic appropriate to what they want and what they get." The risks of cultural imperialism are more apparent than ever in efforts to procure development in underdeveloped nations, as the present author has pointed out (Westley, 1966).

Opler (1968) has called attention to the unfortunate results of human engineering when change agents accept "the doctrine of inescapable evolution and inevitable progress." Examples abound in the southeastern United States, where Indian tribal units are forced to accept modern (and to them meaningless) political boundaries and where Indians were "civilized" by being forced to abandon their traditional hunting and gathering in favor of a settled agriculture, even where they knew (although the agents did not) that the land was wrong for that purpose.

Another concern is that the same popular media that produce empathy (and a desire for Western-style consumer goods) will instead tend to produce apathy; or that an unfavorable want/get ratio will produce alienation.

The escape hypothesis (Katz and Foulkes, 1962) is a sort of anti-effect from the viewpoint of a change agent, who wants to use media to induce rational problem-solving behavior but finds that the same instrument is being used to avoid facing issues. Although their own hypotheses were not supported by their data, McLeod et al. (1965–1966) shed some interesting light on the question. They reasoned that alienated persons should use the media to escape from the problems of the day more than the unalienated. Their study yielded correlations between education and alienation on the one hand with preference for sensational and nonsensational content (represented by headlines) on the other. What was expected, of course, was that education would correlate positively with preference for nonsensational news and that alienation would correlate positively with sensational news: the alienated should be more likely to use the media to seek vicarious experience as a means of escape, whereas the educated should use the media to seek information necessary to rational problem solving. Of the four resulting correlations, only one was statistically significant (.001): alienation was negatively correlated with preference for nonsensational headlines. The data seem to support a more interesting and more obvious hypothesis: the alienated reject the real problems of a world more than they seek means of engaging in fantasy about it. (There was no correlation between alienation and preference for sensational content.)

If it were possible to extend these predictions to non-Western cultures (and this is doubtful, owing to the culture-bound character of both sides of the correlations reported here, alienation and media preference), it might suggest that the media cannot be counted on to bring the marginal worker or peasant into the part of media content that could yield empathy (the fantasy content), as Lerner might hope, since the alienated do not seek fantasy; and the media cannot bring him into the reality content either because the alienated reject or avoid the problems of their own society.

It is interesting that the leaders of Communist China's national development specialists distrust the mass media and at the same time are optimistic about their capacity to produce positive effects (Liu, 1966). Out of fear of their capacity to disrupt, the media are controlled by the Party. But films are used to exhort people to work harder (Liu, 1966, p. 324), and the media system is designed to build links between the technological revolution and the ideological one. Where non-Communist underdeveloped nations are being urged to become more materialist, the Chinese masses are urged to immerse themselves in a collective happiness above material things. It would seem that the West adjusts the want/get ratio by increasing the "get," whereas the East adjusts it by decreasing the "want."

The usual way of looking at communication and change is, in oversimplified fashion, the following: If we are to introduce change in something, we must communicate something to someone. The question then is: What shall we communicate, to whom, through what channels?—the oft-quoted formula of Lasswell (1948). This is simply the persuasion model (if I can make you think as I think, you'll do as I do). This model turns up frequently in the modernization literature. For example, McNelly (1966) says that "in order to influence the climate of modernization," the media must be available, contain content relevant to modernization, gain the attention of mass audiences, and have effects predisposing to "modern ideas, methods and products." It treats societies as aggregates of individuals rather than as a structure for disseminating and acting upon information relevant to problem solution.

Cartwright (1949) proposed a similar set of propositions concerning "mass persuasion" in summarizing research on the sale of war bonds. Its dynamics were all cognitive. But shortly thereafter he produced a radically different change model (Cartwright, 1951) whose dynamics were those of the group. It is just one step further to suggest that the dynamics of a culture, including the way a culture provides for the resolution of problems in decision-making groups, must be understood.

This writer has suggested elsewhere (Westley, 1966) that societies, like cognitive systems and problem-solving groups, are systems, and systems attempt to maintain a stable state. Information from outside the system keeps it informed as to changes requiring adjustment, and such information often is carried by public communication channels (Westley, 1970). But this information must be processed to test for its congruence with existing states; if hopelessly incongruent, it will tend to be rejected; if prospectively congruent, it will be modified to make a mutual adjustment to the existing culture. This is, of course, the model of diffusion of cultural traits as the anthropologist sees it.

The change agent knows better than to attempt to persuade or to attempt to introduce incompatible innovations. His role is that of catalyst of group communications processes, not as the expert and not as the wise man (Lippitt et al., 1958). Functioning groups need to overcome initial apathy (Poston, 1950), to learn to face problems not previously recognized or problems customarily left to others (Cannell et al., 1953), to avoid the resistance built into the kind of constituent groups whose function it is to maintain the status quo (Ogden and Ogden, 1946), to avoid widespread public scrutiny until they have developed a capacity to produce relevant alternatives for wide dissemination and dialogue. Instead of a persuasion model, much concerned with what form of communication produces the greatest persuasion, communication scholars interested in producing planned social change should be studying the capacity of social systems to adjust to new conditions by improving their capacity for collective problem solving (Lippitt et al., 1958).

According to this model, mass and interpersonal communication are not competitors in persuasion, but each has a distinctive role. Mass media provide the inputs from outside the system, much in the manner of the "sentinel role" proposed by Lasswell (1948), that warn of new conditions requiring adjustment. To some extent they provide information concerning successes and failures in coping with these new conditions. But interpersonal communication is the means by which society gives cultural response to the new inputs, validating them in terms of the unique characteristics of that culture, legitimizing them, and fitting them into the existing scheme of things, accepting and rejecting and modifying them, much as a cognitive system does for the individual (Westley, 1966).

This interplay between the alien and the traditional is the hard fact of change. According to this view, it is not sufficient to persuade or to induce empathy or readiness for modernization. Hitler's idea was to obliterate cultures and replace them with *Kultür*. The modernizer tends to ignore culture and evangelize for Western methods of thought and articles of faith. Yet every social system provides for group decision making in one form or another. Lasting change cannot proceed person by person or article by article. It must be brought about by the orderly, human process that societies provide. Mass media cannot alone inculcate change. Change agents (Lippitt et al., 1958) must either utilize existing social mechanisms or help provide new ones if persistent change is the goal.

Culture is not something apart from life. It is the manner in which a certain kind of organism asserts its humanity. Planned development is the translation into action of the determination to use human capacities productively, morally and wisely (Opler, 1968, p. 34).

Notes

1. Causal analysis has, until recently, eluded the student of the relationship between media inputs and social change. Questions of the kind that can be reduced to the laboratory, such as those raised by Hovland (1953) and by Hovland and his associates (1949, 1957; Janis et al., 1959) seem to have little bearing on the question. When the issues are taken into the field, with rare exceptions (Douglas et al., 1970) correlational data result and these are notoriously difficult to interpret causally, again with exceptions (Brandner and Sistrunk, 1966; Rogers, 1965–1966). However, new methods have been proposed (Blalock, 1961) and one new method—cross-lagged correlation—has been applied to mass media effects studies (McCombs, 1972). In testing the principle of relative constancy—that economic support for the mass media is a constant function of gross national product—McCombs tests alternative causal hypotheses (that media prosperity influences national prosperity and/or that national prosperity influences media prosperity). The method, tied to correlations over time, may free us from some of the obvious limits of correlational analysis and avoid the *assumption* that media have social effects (Blumer, 1946; Doob, 1950; Robinson, 1967), the contrary assumption that society has effects on media content (Lowenthal, 1943), and the cop-out that everything affects everything else (Berelson, 1948).

2. It was, interestingly enough, a study coming out of the Chicago sociology department that questioned the proposition that the mass media are the product of a mass society. Janowitz (1952) found in his study of the community press of Chicago, both in "emergent" communities within the urban core and "survival" communities in the outer parts of the city, that "significant proportions of the residents of the urban metropolis are not 'rootless' individuals. . . . Despite the growth of mass communications and large-scale organization most individuals are not living in a 'mass society.' . . . Rather, the growth of large-scale organization has been accompanied by a proliferation of . . . social arrangements and communication patterns. The local urban community appears to be a complex of social interactions which tends to identify a local elite and local institutionalized patterns for controlling social change." The urban community newspaper served as a humanizing and socializing agent, no matter where it was found in the city.

3. The original proposition is based on a different interpretation of the same tables. One which shows influentials in all strata are nominated as influentials is the basis for the statement that influence is exerted at the same status level, not across status levels. But the same tables show influentiality increasing as a function of status level, which is the basis for the interpretation given here.

PART FOUR

SOCIAL SECTOR PERSPECTIVES ON CHANGE

It is important and even necessary to view social change in various social sectors in order to gain a better appreciation of the manifestation of social problems and change processes. Three special sectors are presented in Part Four. One is the public policy area, which stresses the problems of evaluative research in the area that is particularly germane as governments play increasingly strong roles in social change. Another sector is education, certainly an enduring and important factor moderating change in all other sectors. The final area is population, which is clearly one of the crucial problems facing the world today.

One of the major sources of social change are the micro and macro policies pursued by national and regional governments. These policies are sometimes as important for the second-order consequences as they are for their first-order or intended consequence. For this reason at least it is particularly important that public policies be assessed in methodologically sound ways. This is a difficult task with many confounding factors. The chapter by Henry Teune, "Public Policy: Macro Perspectives," confronts the problem of evaluating empirically macro policy predictions. This chapter also includes some treatment of micro policy. Teune discusses types of macro policy predictions, confounding factors in policy assessment, and designs for macro policy analysis. His observations and conclusions are not particularly encouraging, at least with regard to formal analysis and evaluation in the area of macro public policy. He sensitizes us to the problems inherent in macro policy evaluation which, although a source of frustration, is a first positive step since it establishes some standard to strive for and alerts us to weaknesses that may be inherent in the evaluative work attempted in this area. Given the dominance of macro policies in the actions of governments, particularly in the developing areas of the world, Teune's implicit message is that it is difficult to

235

underestimate the importance of allocating more effort toward construction of macro policy evaluation mechanisms. The reader is challenged to
develop his own research design for evaluating public policy in his area
of interest. What are the confounding factors? What design would minimize or control their effect? What are the criteria for evaluating the effectiveness of the public policy? These are only a few of the challenges
Teune sensitizes us to.

The education sector of society is as crucial a social sector as one can
find. It is indeed a problem area. The educational sector has a causal relation with many other social sectors; change in education precedes and
helps produce change in such areas as science and technology, health and
social services. At the same time the education profession is notoriously
oriented toward maintaining the status quo. It has been pointed out by
educators—in self-defense—that no other profession has as much reason
to be skeptical or doubtful about things labeled "new" and "innovative."
There is substantial evidence supporting this claim. Nevertheless, leadership for educational change, as the educational sector is currently constructed, must come from without rather than from within the profession.
The chapter "Change in Education," by Lindley Stiles and Beecham
Robinson, discusses with great insight and boldness the reasons for this,
that is, the sensitive factors which inhibit change in education. Stiles and
Robinson also respond positively by discussing forces for change and the
means available for producing change. The political, research and development, and systems models they describe are unique and provide very
good perspectives for viewing social change in education. Clearly the
challenge laid down in this paper is to develop remedial, implementable
strategies for moving the locus of leadership in educational change fom
outside the sector to within the sector. At least strategies that would facilitate the development and direction of social change in education by educators should be implemented.

Population growth ranks among the most serious social problems in
the world today. As Timothy Sprehe and Joseph Speidel state in the introduction to their chapter, "Population and Social Change," "The world
today is waking to the fact that one of the most critical areas of social
change requiring massive efforts at management is the simple growth of
numbers of people." The negative social and psychological effects of this
simple growth are massive and in many countries it is difficult to see how
the problem can be brought under control short of using methods repug-
nant to most of mankind today. The reader will recall the chapter by
Rogers dealing with incentives in family planning. This issue of incentives
is probably one of the most ethnically controversial issues in family planning, although it falls far short of techniques forecast for the future. The

Sprehe and Speidel chapter also explores the case of incentives and solutions for alleviating population problems and evaluates their potential effectiveness in both the short and long run. This chapter also provides an excellent overview of the demographic aspects of population growth and the implications of these conditions for other areas of human life as well as a very good sketch of the demographic aspects of population growth. The reader is presented with the argument that "family planning is the best available alternative today for coping with the fertility factor in the population." The reader should be challenged in many ways by this position. What rationale does the reader have for supporting or not agreeing with this position? What are the alternatives and their costs? How can family planning be implemented effectively while still preserving the maximal degree of individuals' freedom of choice?

Henry Teune

Department of Political Science
University of Pennsylvania

PUBLIC POLICY:
MACRO PERSPECTIVES

Public policies are instrumentalities of political collectivities for inducing, guiding, accelerating, or slowing down social change.[1] In this behavioral sense each policy contains at least one and usually a set of predictions that can be evaluated empirically. For this discussion policies will be grouped into two major types: micro policies, which are relatively specific and have isolatable targets; and macro policies, which have global coverage or a global target, the system itself, or both. A further distinguishing characteristic of these two types of policies is the expected time interval of their effect: short term versus long term.

The problem is to evaluate empirically macro policy predictions. In principle social science has well understood standards and procedures for evaluating the consequences of micro but not macro policies, whose scientific study has been avoided for various reasons.[2] The extension of the principles of experimental design to natural settings, treated as quasi-experimental designs, has provided a context for micro policy evaluation. But policies that have (1) a specific instrument, an educational program, (2) a specific target, isolatable school children; and (3) a short time period, one year, are only a small fraction of the efforts to induce social change in large-scale social systems, such as are seen in massive national development programs.

In common sense terms the problem is: What can one nation learn from another about macro policies? A number of such national policies have been marketed as lessons for other systems: national medical programs, worker participation in industrial decisions, public housing, and entire educational systems. Most of the details of such policies are so complex that even if there is conscious adoption from another system it is nearly impossible to draw inferences from one system to another. Despite the lack of sound evaluation, many attempts are made, out of pragmatic or ideological motivations, to export policies to other systems.

Macro and Micro Policy

One component of a public policy is a set of goals, including a target population, some instrumentalities, and some predictions linking the instrumentalities to the goals. In a general sense a policy decision of a collectivity is the introduction (or change in) instrumentalities to induce change (including stopping changes that are taking place). These predictions may be theoretically based, such as the relationships between savings and growth or interest rates and inflation; ideologically derived, such as predictions about decentralization and innovation or differentials in incentives and productivity; common sensically fashioned, as is often the case, for example, in the predictions that increasing expenditures on law enforcement will reduce crime or providing day care centers for children will increase national productivity by adding mothers to the work force; or simple extrapolations, such as pollution programs based on projections about the number and density of population.

The instrumentalities of change selected will be constrained by the nature of the collectivity making the decision. For most governments of industrialized countries these include prescribing, proscribing, or permitting some existing institutions, groups, or individuals to act; directly or indirectly rewarding or punishing certain classes of behavior; establishing new institutions; paying for some service or project; or actually engaging in some activity. Any one of these general instrumentalities, when specified, can be appropriate for almost any general public policy.

Micro policies are "relatively" micro. They have policy targets that are "relatively" isolatable within a system, such as the poor, banks, or schoolchildren; they have "relatively" specific instrumentalities, such as increasing welfare payments, changing the interest rate, or allocating money for school lunch programs; and they contain "relatively" short-term predictions, changes in months or usually a year. Further, these policies are likely to be "clean" in that it is possible to match the goals, instrumentalities, and the target population.

Macro policies are relatively "macro." The target is often the entire system, such as the whole country; the goal often global, such as industrialization; the instrumentalities general and diffuse, such as unspecified allocations to an industrial development bank, a tax incentive plan, subsidies for industries; and the predictions are long term, such as a five- or seven-year plan. Further, macro policies usually have multiple rather than single predictions, such as changing the settlement patterns, the life style, and the family structure of the population.

Of course, micro and macro policies are linked. "Macro" and "Micro" are relational concepts defined in terms of some specific context (just as "to the right of" is a relational property that must be defined in terms of a spatial context). Thus the same policy may be a macro policy for one system, such as a literacy program to improve the educational level of some population strata, and a macro policy for another, such as a literacy program as a stimulus to general social development. The effectiveness of micro policy components can be "deaggregated" from a macro policy and independently evaluated. Road construction for development, for example, can be deaggregated into roads and movement of agricultural goods to the market and evaluated. The problem, however, is that the macro effects of micro policies cannot be evaluated through an examination of deaggregated micro policy components alone. The multiplier, spillover, side-effects, and, indeed, the dynamics of small changes evolving into large-scale general system changes constitute crucial characteristics of macro policy predictions.

Evaluating Micro Policies: Quasi-Experimental Designs

Donald Campbell has comprehensively and influentially discussed the analogy between experimental designs and certain types of "real world" situations in order to show that the consequences of introducing changes can be judged in terms of experimental principles.[3] These naturalistic settings, however, impair the flexibility of research required to obtain the ideal conditions of experimentation. Two prevailing conditions of naturalistic settings are the points that discriminate these "quasi-experimental" designs from experimental designs proper and weaken the validity of experimental inference: randomization of observations, the cases being treated, and randomization of treatment. The major advantages that naturalistic settings have over experimental settings are, first, the reactive effects of pre-test measurement before the experimental treatment are not usually present, and, second, certain kinds of experimenter biases are less likely to intrude because the treatment takes place in a familiar way and the data are usually organized independent of the experimenter (Campbell and Stanley, 1966). Nonetheless, even with some violations of the principles of "good" experimental design, there are natural cases where experimental principles can be used in such a way that conclusions can be made at least about the lack or presence of disconfirming evidence.

The extent to which principles of experimental design can allow for inferences in naturalistic settings depends on the extent to which the observations are random and isolatable from a general social context. This isolatability principle is essential for quasi-experimental design and the lack of it is a source of many of the "threats" to the validity of the results. Experiments conducted on the negative income tax (a sliding scale of taxes or payments based on a minimum income level) in the United States assumed, for example, that low-income or welfare families can be isolated as units, and thus a sample of families was selected from urban areas in one state with little regard for the contexts in which the families lived. These contextual effects are aggravated insofar as the principle of randomization is not met.

Despite the problems of isolating the consequences of events and the difficulty of identifying the randomization of the events that have taken place, even if this randomization is argued for "theoretically" rather than demonstrated empirically, it is possible to evaluate micro policies more systematically in the context of experimental design than is possible through informal observation, accumulation of self-reports, or analysis of the dialectical processes found in the arguments of detached historians.

Evaluating Macro Policies: A Comparative Context

Scientific evaluation of macro policies departs more significantly from quasi-experimental design than quasi-experimental design departs from experimental design. A macro systems design requires entire societies, nation-states, countries, or social systems to be treated as independent observations in a way that historical and comparative data can be systematically brought to bear on the predictions contained in public policy. Historical and comparative variations become the surrogate for experimental conditions.

Generally all public policy can be broadly interpreted as *ex post facto* interrupted time series experiments where it is possible to obtain data before and after the event, the inauguration of the policy. This is true even for the large number of policies that simply affirm in a series of actions particular trends by making them explicit and legitimate, such as the "policy" of the United States to become an industrialized country in the second half of the nineteenth century. The critical data become system states before and after the policy, which express certain kinds of changes: what kinds of changes, if any; to what extent did these changes take place: how fast were the changes; and what was the change in the rate of change. These data then become the foundation for the evaluation of the predictions of macro public policy.

Macro Policy Predictions

There are three general kinds of macro policy predictions: under all conditions policy X will have consequences y in time t; for certain classes of systems policy X will have consequences y in time t; or in this particular social system (a set unspecified conditions) policy X will have consequences y in time t. The first can be found in general development policies formulated by United Nations agencies; the second in policies designed for particular types of systems; and the third in nationally defined programs. If precisely formulated, the first is relatively easy to disconfirm with any one case; the second is more difficult in that errors can be made regarding which systems have the defining characteristics, that is, those characteristics that circumscribe the validity of the policy predictions; and the last can be disconfirmed only in a system-specific context. The last is not a general hypothesis at all; rather it is a "descriptive prediction" and invulnerable to disconfirming evidence from other systems. Although the validity of the system-specific hypothesis is confined to a single case, it is nonetheless possible to transform some of the system-specific characteristics into system variables, such as "democratic," "industrialized," "large-scale," in order to translate the specific hypothesis into one of the first two types, which are subject to general evidence.

The critical problem in evaluating macro systems policy predictions, or, for that matter, the results of quasi-experimental designs, concerns the measurement of the system state before and after the event as well as the nature of the policy intervention. Although this problem will not be discussed here, measurement is decisive for macro policy evaluation, especially in a comparative context in that the data are likely to be specific to each system (e.g., the definition of employment). However, one advantage in macro system measurement of change is that the policy predicts changes in a system-specific context—the degrees of difference between at least two time periods—and to some extent the problem of the comparability of measurement can be circumvented by the use of rate or amount of change in employment, productivity, and so forth, from a given base even if defined specifically by each system. The major danger to this kind of change measure is that the systems themselves often change their definitions.

There are several types of macro predictions, depending on whether the treatment or the predicted consequences or both are global. The first is a global treatment and a specific response of the system, such as massive increases in research and development support and specific predictions about the rate of innovations, the export of research-oriented products, and the time lag in manufacturing new products. A second type concerns specific treatment and the expectation of a global response, such as in the construction of roads and the development of a market economy or an increase in the amount of money and an increase in the pace of economic growth. Finally, there is the global policy and the global expectation: a policy of industrialization and the creation of an industrialized society, or public welfare and taxation policies and general social equality. (Specific policies and specific predictions have been defined as micro policies.)

Most policies contain hypotheses about the time needed before system changes can be observed, the sequencing of events before the impact of policy intervention can be observed (increased supply of money, which leads to less costly loans, which lead to . . .), the critical mass of effort required for effectuating any change (the amount of subsidies for housing needed before a noticeable improvement in the distribution of housing can be observed), and, finally, the linear or nonlinear nature of the relationship between policy effort and policy results (a linear relationship is usually assumed between money allocated to public schools and the quality of schools; a nonlinear one between savings and growth).

Although macro policy predictions are difficult to test, even very loosely, several general kinds of hypotheses may be amenable to some incursions of systematic data to disconfirm or perhaps even to establish low-level probabilities.

"Any-Impact" Hypothesis. The most general hypothesis is that the policy has had an impact—whatever the specific nature of the impact. Of course, the activity of introducing the policy will itself have some consequence, even if only that of diverting resources from other sectors. In order to assess the any-impact hypothesis, a minimum condition is to project what would have been the case if the policy had not been introduced or to compare at least one system with such a policy with one without. These projections will be confounded by many factors, such as the tendency of policies to be introduced "too late"—the policy takes effect at some "natural" discontinuous point, where corrective measures are not needed.

"Any Policy Will Do" Hypothesis. Even if it can be established that a policy had some macro level effect, another problem is to generalize

about a particular type or class of policies. Thus any welfare policy might have the same redistributive effects and the prediction that is being tested is simply that all such policies rather than any specific policy are equivalent treatments in terms of their effects. Moreover, the process of formulating a policy may be sufficient to cause a change.

"Policy X" Hypothesis. If after examining these two hypotheses, the conclusions are that this type of policy had some effect, or, more properly, at least it was not followed by no change, the practical payoffs of the empirical analysis would be embarrassingly lean. This kind of conclusion would be far removed from engineering predictions, recommending a policy, that is, predicting desired change will occur with specific costs. Specific predictions are needed rather than the general ones that this class of policies will increase or will not decrease industrialization. The degree, rate, direction, and amount of specific changes must be specified to be subject to social engineering.

Assessing Policy: Confounding Features of Macro Public Policy

The strategy of structuring observations for evaluating macro policies is to reduce the complexity of factors that make comparison across cases difficult. This requires measurement of those characteristics of the system that are hypothesized to be the necessary conditions for the policy effects to take hold, measurement of the consequences of the policy, and especially an assessment of the nature of the policies to determine whether or not they are "equivalent" treatments across systems. The policy-making process in contemporary political systems, especially in nation-states, makes comparative assessment of policy and determination of equivalence of policy "treatment" especially difficult.

The most general of these confounding factors is that macro policies usually have multiple components. These multiple attacks on a problem are often political insurance for success: a broad-based program to improve the technological capacity of a country by investments in higher education, funds for research, tax rebates for research and development costs, special instructions to embassies to encourage scientific exchange, and so on.

All of these specific components are not likely to be found in all systems. Further, the administration of the policy often is not only different but is given to agencies with competing goals. The problem then is to determine which of these components are critical or whether the entire package of activities must be taken as the policy treatment. Because of the complexity of policy components, what is often done for comparisons is to use some features common to all, such as total expenditures per capita, the number of people working to apply the policy, the duration of the program, and the publicity of the policy. But the use of such general dimensions of policy do not aid in the evaluation of specific kinds of policy.

Second, developmental trends in political systems lead to a bunching of particular policies in particular types of systems. Industrialized countries have similar governmental programs, differing for political reasons only in timing and in specific features. Thus medical care programs are paid for by institutions in some systems and by individuals in the form of a tax in others; some are local and locally administered, others are national. In addition, there is the tendency of democratic systems to endorse trends by making them into law. The amendment giving the right to vote to women in the United States made national what was in effect in many states, and the amendment requiring popular election of senators was already the practice of almost all states. Thus to examine the impact of women voters on national policies or the popular election of senators on national politics would be confounded by determining when the treatment actually took effect.

A third problem is that of time equivalency. Most political systems have different decision-making cycles and different "start-up times" for implementation. Predictions of how long is required before the policy produces the intended result will differ. Furthermore, groups take charge of specific aspects of the policy before it becomes "official."

Systems differ with respect to the decentralization of their decision making. A national macro policy thus will have different effects, depending on the related policies of various territorial subunits. National civil rights laws in the United States came after several similar laws were in effect in several states. Further complications of comparison arise if the administration of a policy, such as a national welfare program, is parcelled out among local units at local discretion.

Moreover, most systems will continuously modify a policy according to the experience that is being evaluated. Not only must the observations of effects take place while the "treatment" or policy is in force, but, as is well known, the bureaucracy will not only modify the intention but in some cases even substantially subvert the intention of the original policy.[4]

Finally, due to extraneous factors such as the time of the policy-making cycle, the number of other issues on the agenda, and international events, new policies will have varying degrees of saliency. The saliency of the policy can be expected to have an impact in and of itself, but it will be nearly impossible to isolate this factor and remove its influence when comparing across systems.

Some Designs and Data for Macro Policy Analysis

The nature of the observations determine which of several possible designs are appropriate to evaluate the consequences of macro policies. The following discussion is based on some hypothetical data, without suggestions of statistical tests and without requirements of measurement statements more sophisticated than dichotomies.

Strong Evidence. Ideally, what would be required to recommend or not recommend a policy without careful scrutiny of the circumstances in which the policy takes place? Such recommendations would be possible if the following conditions were met:

1. A random distribution of policies across systems, including some frequency of the policy being evaluated as well as alternative policies with the similar macro predictions of consequences.

2. At least one hypothesis that would compete with the policy hypothesis, such as whether the system is democratic or has a market economy.

3. Relatively error-free observations.

For this discussion, policy X will be designated as the policy being evaluated; policy Y as all other policies that have the same predicted results as policy X; and "no policy" for systems without any explicit policy in effect, although this can be interpreted as a policy. One system characteristic will be assumed to be a competing hypothesis; all systems with this characteristic will have this system state, the macro consequences, regardless of policy (industrialized countries will have increasing urbanization without regard to national policies concerning urbanization). Those systems that have such a characteristic will be designated as similar systems; all others as a group of dissimilar systems. Finally, it will be assumed that whether the policy had the predicted effect or something other than the predicted effect over some period is known.

One type of strong evidence would be the rejection of evidence that any policy whatsoever mattered. The error-free distribution of the data is shown in Table 1. This distribution of observations suggests that general social processes underlying whatever has been called "similar systems" are at work and that policies are largely extraneous or ironic manifestations of these general processes. There is no evidence in favor of any policy,

Table 1

	Policy X	Policy Y	"No" Policy
Similar systems			
Predicted results	✕	✕	✕
Results not as predicted	O	O	O
Dissimilar systems			
Predicted results	O	O	O
Results not as predicted	✕	✕	✕

since the predicted policy consequences occur without regard to policy. An example of this is the debate about income policy and the actual level of economic equality. One position is that the political system can effectuate redistribution; the contending position is that equality of income is a function of the affluence of the system; that is, scarce resources lead to income inequality despite governmental intervention. In the foregoing example, similar systems would be wealthy systems; dissimilar systems, poor.

A second case is one in which the policy, and not the circumstances of the system (the competing hypothesis), matters: wherever the policy is in force the predicted consequences obtain. This is found in the distribution of observations, shown in Table 2, again assuming randomization of

Table 2

	Policy X	Policy Y	"No" Policy
Similar systems			
Predicted results	✕	O	O
Results not as predicted	O	✕	✕
Dissimilar systems			
Predicted results	✕	O	O
Results not as predicted	O	✕	✕

policies and error-free observations. The evidence is against any policy but policy X and against the system characteristic hypothesis. Support for the lack of evidence disconfirming the policy would be strengthened to the extent that the same result obtained with different groupings of systems based on alternative "nonpolicy" hypotheses. An example of this is a policy limiting the size of private land holdings in order to shift agricultural production to collective or "industrial" farms. No matter what the circumstances, a limitation on the size of land holdings affects the behavior of farmers everywhere. The prediction that a limit on the size of land holding will reduce the proportion of private agricultural production increase to total agricultural production increase is not disconfirmed by the evidence.

A third case (Table 3) would show that any policy has the same effect

Table 3

	Policy X	Policy Y	"No" Policy
Similar systems			
Predicted results	X	X	X
Results not as predicted	O	O	X
Dissimilar systems			
Predicted results	X	X	O
Results not as predicted	O	X	X

regardless of the nature of the policy or the circumstances of the system. The differences observed would be simply whether there was a policy or not. An example of this might be policies to improve the lot of discriminated strata. The general improvement of discriminated strata and their participation in the system would be a function of whether the system had a policy to improve, without regard to whether the discriminated strata were blacks in the United States or low castes in India or whether these policies were oriented to individuals or to "communities of people."

Other cases include laissez faire, where no policy produces the results intended by those systems with a policy and the various policies adopted produce results other than predicted; there is also the "bad policy," where any policy other than the one being evaluated is associated with the predicted results. All of these cases, however, assume a large number of observations of systems, or a number of observations substantially larger than the various policies being examined, and some random distribution of the policies. In fact, this rarely occurs.

Weak Evidence. Because of lack of randomization it is necessary to revert to statement of association rather than have evidence that would not be inconsistent with a plausible causal implication. Policies clustered in certain kinds of systems will have been accumulated over a long period of time, making it difficult to know, for example, to what extent social insurance programs are a function of the system's development or whether the system is the way it is because of the policies. The cluster of characteristics associated with industrialization makes it difficult to deaggregate macro policies from macro system characteristics.[5] It would be difficult to extract from this cluster a policy component to recommend to a less industrialized country. It is nearly impossible to move beyond simple statements of descriptive association.

Another factor is that political systems, being rather imitative, all have similar or nearly similar policies with different or indeterminable results. Almost all countries from the poorest to the richest have similar policies on social welfare, education, and banking, often with very similar administrative structures. Since there is little or no variation in treatment, what remains are associations of characteristics across countries with little reference to the policies.

Nonrandomization of policy or near uniformity of policy, insofar as the policies can be measured, destroys any but the weakest kinds of implications of causation of which policy predictions are made. It is this situation that argues for detailed examination of specific systems and specific policies: to fall back on case studies in order to get knowledge about policies that appears practically impossible from the perspective of quasi-experimental design, no matter how quasi.

Case studies are informal data on which many social science recommendations are founded. In case studies there is little control over the method of observation or the kind of variation in the policies being examined: only those kinds of systems that have had a policy "experience" are likely to be observed. In a single case study, of course, there can be no control observation or control group. The details concerning the setting of the case provide a practically unlimited number of alternative hypotheses to the policy hypothesis, as each item recorded is in effect an item suggestive of a general hypothesis. The case, after all, is by definition rich in observation but improverished in variation.

Because of these problems with cases, one central question is whether a case or even a few cases are better than nothing. What can be learned that is generally true about medical care systems and the general level of the population's health from two cases, for example, Great Britain and the United States? The problem with a case is that what is general—the general hypothesis—is rarely spelled out; the focus is on specific phenomena. In a very limited way, if the policy predictions are seen to hold true in the case, there is very limited evidence and an abundance of alternative hypotheses that at least the case did not negate the prediction.

As a substitute for limited case studies, several cases can be structured in such a way that a redundancy of observations may provide a basis for inferring to a population of systems. What can be done are "comparative" case studies over some period of time. It may be possible to study system A, B, C, and continue to find that increases in investment in university research is a direct function of the technological productivity of the society. The conclusion would be that in every case heretofore examined, or in almost every case, increases in university research lead to an increase in technological productivity. One of the additional arguments for this approach, especially when there is doubt about the processes by which policy gets transformed into consequence, is "functional linkage" findings. The redundant observation might be that students with research experience in universities are more likely to take research positions than those who do not and those with university research experience are more likely to be productive than those without, and these individual contributions somehow aggregate into societal level technological productivity. Thus the detailed case study, if constructed in such a way as to provide for some reliability of assessment across cases, might allow for redundancy to serve as a surrogate for a sample of systems, and also might yield information about the processes that create policy impact.

A third approach, which must be considered a case study approach, is to use subsystems or subnational policy units as substitutes for macro system policy observations. This is part of the old argument for local units as laboratories. Because the general system setting is the same for all, held constant, these units are obviously appropriate for micro policy analysis; for example, one might look at variations in laws to determine impact on individual behavior. Further, this approach can be used for macro system policies that are appropriate for the local territorial units and have so been used.[6] But if the national unit is the macro system of analysis, the subnational units are a series of potential cases. There are advantages to this approach if the macro system consequences can be deaggregated into territorial units.

The problem here, however, is that these subunits are not free to vary on these policies and, more important, are not "equally free" to vary. Thus although a local unit may adopt an employment policy, it is not clear that unemployment is due to factors operating at that level, and in comparing across subunits, it is even less clear that each of them, for example, agricultural versus industrial units, is equally capable of adopting such a course. If, however, some national policy has predictions that can be deaggregated into differential responses among local units, then it is obvious that this differential impact can be assessed and several hypotheses tested about the differences in impact. Grant-in-aid programs

are one such example: Why does one city or local unit use national housing funds and another not? But the long-term macro effects, such as how
such local responses change the nature of urbanization in the country,
cannot be judged solely with data from subunits.

A fourth kind of "case" is the "hard" case and the "test" case. Both of
these, however, require theoretical prediction (as contrasted to extrapola-
tion), and in general, if theoretical prediction is possible, then it is very
likely that general observations to establish general propositions either
have been or can be made. In the social sciences, there are so many alternative explanatory factors that the hard case and the test case are likely
to remain instructive in principle rather than with example. The hard
case requires predictions about the conditions necessary for the policy to
have an effect. Then, if it is possible to find an instance or "case" which
barely meets the minimal conditions, and the policy does have the predicted result, the implication is that the policy should have the same effect for those systems that easily meet those conditions. If Ghana can
make a national health plan work, then the United States certainly can.
This test case most easily meets all of the conditions necessary for the policy to have the intended result. If the policy does not work as intended,
the implication is that it probably cannot work anywhere else. Thus if
the United States with its wealth, institutions, and so forth, cannot meet
the challenge of housing, then surely the future is dim for all less
wealthy societies. But both of these cases require more than common
sense understanding of what the conditions are: they require precise, theoretically based prediction, which if possible allows for the organization of
better evidence than either a hard case or a test case.

Alternative Evidence: Prediction. The requirements of experimental
design, even if compromised, are harsh; they allow in principle only statements that a particular set of evidence does not disconfirm the hypothesis.
The results at best do not disconfirm. Sensitivity to the cannons of scientific evidence in an experimental context must be conservative and thus
the recommendations most tentative. But macro policies are recommended
and their consequences, although generally ambiguous, are often conducive to increasing confidence in the policy hypotheses or assumptions
underlying the recommendations.

The key to this is the number and precision of theoretically based
predictions, especially if many of the predictions are intermediate to the
general macro system result. Thus it is necessary to be precise not only
about the end states that the policies might produce but also about some
states of the system before the end state. Econometric models, in addition

to giving long-term predictions based on sets of "if then" statements, expressed as functions such as the relationship between inflation and interest rates, can also produce statements about the state of the economy at the end of the next quarter. General systems models not only predict the state of the world's pollution at the end of the century but also pollution levels for several intervals of time (Forrester, 1971). Further, these general models have multiple predictions about items that can be measured, such as population, consumption, and investment levels.

With multiple, precise, time-specific predictions, it is possible to have many observations on a single system or on several systems. Each of these predictions can be evaluated against observation and each in a sense is a test of the general model. One component of such models can be a set of "if-then statements about policy." Unfortunately, those policies that can be precisely measured for use in such general theories is limited. Many of the policies of interest, such as the macro consequences on country's development of recruiting a professional cadre of civil servants, are too imprecise to provide precise prediction. Not only is it difficult to assess professional cadres, but the macro consequences are not time specific. Further, the developmental theories on which macro policies for several countries are or have been based are general and tentative.

Although the way out of the difficulties of macro policy evaluation that are caused by nonrandomization, complexity of measurement, and the effort required for observation is theoretical prediction, most of the models that offer predictions are neither general nor theoretical. It is commonplace that different approaches to economics can end up with similar predictions about the future state of the economy, that the correct models are open to question, and that a model for one country is hardly transferable to another. The lack of generality, and thus the ability to disconfirm strong competing hypotheses, is due to the fact that the functions that generate the predictions are for the most part projections from the past behavior of the system. Furthermore, even "precise" predictions often are not precise enough. Thus various econometric models predict slightly different results, but those small differences finally amount to great differences, spelling success or failure. The different models have different track records; some are better than others in some regards and in some years. Each is continually calibrated to the most recent observations. Nonetheless, if policy recommendations have a facsimile of a theoretical foundation, predictions should be numerous and precise enough to determine whether the recommendations are right at least half of the time and at least for more than one system.

A theoretical approach is a solution to the problems of evaluating macro policies. But this statement says nothing more than that a lot more knowledge is necessary before the predictions inherent in macro policies can be systematically tested.

Summary and Conclusion

The practical question raised at the beginning was what can one system, or set of leaders of the system, learn from other systems about what policies will be instrumental to certain goals. On an informal level, perhaps a lot of information can be gathered; on a formal level, the scientific requirements are most difficult to meet.

Several kinds of general recommendations always have been possible. One is to do nothing, since there is no evidence that doing nothing is any worse than doing something. Alternatively, one can do nothing but say something, if there is evidence not hurting the first alternative. Second, if there is evidence that any relevant policy appears to have the intended results, one can recommend that since there is no evidence about what is working, do many things at once. (Perhaps as a matter of general incentive, perhaps because of the combination of activities, perhaps because various activities neutralize each other, there is some evidence that all kinds of policies do not negate the goal.) Fourth, and most desirable, would be to pinpoint specific policies that have the status of propositions with predictive power. But then those predictions may stimulate requests for alternatives. Policy predictions are a risky affair that might someday be responsibly done with the use of macro level theories; in the meantime they might be better left to forecasters with institionalized protection.

Notes

1. This definition assumes a political system that can be differentiated from the social system. There are many "developmental" and political developmental ideas about the circumstances giving rise to such a differentiation.

2. Donald T. Campbell and Julian C. Stanley (1966, p. 63) refer to a "true parable" about a college receiving half a million dollars to study the impact of the college on the students. They observe that no research reports were produced and conclude that perhaps no scientist would be curious about the effects of such a "global X." These global X's, however, are defined here as macro policy.

3. See, for example, his, "Reforms as Experiments," *American Psychologist*

(April, 1969), pp. 409–422. Campbell has inspired scientific study and thought about public policy.

4. For a famous case of this, see P. Selznick, *TVA and the Grassroots* (Berkeley: The University of California Press, 1949).

5. A number of cross-national studies have shown the "industrialization wealth cluster and its correlation with political and social factors." See, for example, I. Adelman and C. Morris, *Society, Politics, and Economic Development* (Baltimore: The Johns Hopkins Press, 1967).

6. See some of the research on U.S. states; for example, T. R. Dye, *Politics, Economics and the Public* (Chicago: Rand-McNally, 1966).

Lindley J. Stiles

Beecham Robinson

School of Education
Northwestern University

CHANGE IN EDUCATION

Change in education typically generates from outside rather than from within.[1] This basic characteristic gives education a kinship with other social, political, and professional enterprises, all of which tend to hold deeper commitments to the status quo than they do to progress. Differences prevail, however, in the degree to which education can be manipulated by external forces and also with respect to the processes by which changes are brought about. Additionally, education is set apart from other social and professional fields by its differentiated responses to change, which stem from the fact that schools and colleges generally are locally controlled and oriented. Then, too, unlike law, which uses Supreme Court decisions as national guidelines, or medicine, which has a scientific base to validate health theory, education has yet to develop an effective research component to point the way. Thus change in education always is more political than professional, more impromptu than rationally derived, and, as a consequence, more susceptible to failure than success as well as more controversial than accepted.

To understand the nature of educational change it is necessary to realize, first, why professionals are unable to shape progress to the extent that their counterparts do in other fields. The change factors unique to education need to be considered. Deeper insights come from an examination of the basic forces that promote change, the key means by which changes are produced, and the change models that predominate. Finally, attention in this chapter will be given to how educational change is currently being managed and measured.

257

Blocks to Professional Leadership

Educational professionals, perhaps more than experts in other fields, es-
pouse change but do not lead in change.[2] So infatuated are educators
with the idea of change, in fact, that some school systems actually employ
special "change agents" and "innovators."[3] Some students of educational
change even assert that the scarcity of change agents in schools and colleges is a key factor in the slow rate of educational change (Carlson, 1965,
p. 4). Clearly, educational administrators and teachers are expected to be
leaders for change. When looking for a middle or top administrator,
boards of control typically make "ability to lead change" a high priority.
Similarly, classroom teachers—when judged for employment at least—are
expected to be creative innovators.

When considering the roles of educational professionals in advancing
change, a distinction needs to be made between *initiation,* the function
of conceiving and introducing new practices, and *implementation,* a process of enacting changes that others have instigated. By this type of comparison, it is a myth that educational administrators, supervisors, teachers, and professors are leaders for change, despite the fact that they are
always involved when changes occur. What school and college personnel
do is implement or carry out changes imposed by outside forces. In some
cases, educators are sufficiently sensitive to emerging external mandates
for change and so skillful in adapting to them that they, like good politicians, actually take credit for new developments. Riding the groundswells
of change, however, involves a kind of brinkmanship that few educators
are willing to risk. To move ahead of public opinion is to lose the game,
which may mean loss of employment. Chances of failure are so great that
most education professionals choose to react to and implement, rather
than to lead, change.

Contrary to popular stereotypes of educational personnel, their failure to lead change is not necessarily due to incompetence or lack of cour-
age. Their behavior is shaped more by the nature of the educational enterprise itself, the roles it prescribes for educational workers, than by
individual characteristics. Schools are social agencies, created and maintained to achieve social purposes. What such purposes are, and the priorities assigned to each, are defined by majority opinion. In practice, representatives selected by the majority (school board and trustee members)
interpret constituency goals and attitudes into educational objectives,
programs, and in many situations, even instructional procedures. Educational personnel are employed to follow the prescriptions. Traditions of

local control of education tend to mitigate against state and national agreements about what education is supposed to do and how it should accomplish its purposes. Majority opinions that shape the nature of education, although influenced by state and national policies and trends, may be highly individualistic. To illustrate, one community may favor sex education in its schools while a neighboring school district opposes it. New instructional technology may be used in one college but not in another. Whatever the issue, school personnel must respond to the wishes of the majority.

So potent is the majority mandate in shaping the direction of education that professionals find it difficult to enact changes that are not supported. Even in colleges and universities where professors have tenure, the tendency is to abide by the prescriptions of the institution's clientele, even when they are felt to be wrong. Being a maverick is too lonely and hectic an existence for most people who work at educational pursuits. The safer and more rewarding course, both socially and professionally, is to wait for change to be dictated by outside forces and then adapt to it.

Social majorities support what is best for them. Having achieved such an advantage, they defend it at all costs. Thus schools and educational personnel are charged with maintaining the status quo rather than with producing changes that might upset existing social, economic, or political equations. Only in communities where a close balance of power prevails, or in instances where the demands of minorities are so persistent or violently supported that concessions must be made, are changes likely to win support. Thus education professionals, by the nature of their employment, are enslaved to the status quo; they are not free to advocate change, except, of course, to keep schools aligned with majority changes in the society itself.

Most education practitioners confront another type of majority commitment to the status quo that is an even more powerful influence than public opinion in negating leadership for change. They are enslaved by their own professional organizations. The conservative posture of professional associations, of course, is not unique to the field of education. But the influence of such bodies on educational professionals is intensified by their links with the majority rule of the society itself. The public decides what education should be and the profession, by and large, accepts its decision. Thus professional organizations find their own directives in the social, economic, and political views of the establishment. They survive by walking in the footsteps of the majority. Their commitment to conserve what is becomes doubly reinforced. Their majorities are composed of administrators, supervisors, and teachers who are conditioned to accept the status quo mandates of their communities. Thus associations of educational personnel tend to adapt to rather than lead change, as do individuals in education. Because their commitment to the status quo is a double one—in their schools 'and within their professional associations—educational personnel tend to be even more conservative than citizens. As a consequence, they often find themselves defending the status quo long after majority opinion in their communities has shifted.[4]

Occasionally, of course, a professional maverick emerges in a school, college, or professional organization to challenge the status quo. When this occurs, professional bodies typically unite either to discredit the rebel or else to force an admission of error and a return to the established doctrine. Only when the changes espoused are successful in enlisting majority public support does the heretic have a chance of surviving professionally. Even then, professional groups rarely forgive such challenges to the status quo even though the public does. Little wonder, then, that leadership for educational change must come from without rather than within the profession.

Change Factors Unique to Education

In contrast with such fields as law, medicine, public health, industry, and agriculture, educational change is influenced by a number of unique factors. As we have seen, changes tend to be forced upon professional personnel rather than generated by them, as is more typical in other fields, not because educators are less competent or less committed to change but for the basic reason that education is more closely intertwined with and controlled by society itself. Predominant social values and majority agreements prescribe the nature and direction for education more than they do for other social and professional endeavors. The control often extends to matters of instruction and teacher-student relationships—strictly professional concerns—as well as to curriculum policies, school organization, administration, and finance. Thus to generate change, educators have to first change the society and then convince their colleagues that change is permissible and possible.

In promoting changes within the society, educational personnel are at a disadvantage. Educators work for institutions, either public or nonpublic, rather than engaging in private practice. They are seen as employees to be instructed (originally teachers were slaves, and the image lingers on) rather than professionals to be followed. They do not have the scientific research to identify better professional procedures; hence they tend to follow dogma and custom or popularized proposals for change. This being the case, laymen compete easily with professionals for leadership; when the pattern involves only translation of unrefined theory into practice, power and persuasion are more effective than logic or so-called professional opinion. The nonprofessional, in fact, often has the advantage in winning public support for new ideas, because of the growing tendency for laymen to lack confidence in professional educators.

In addition to the social interactions that set education apart in terms of the factors that influence change, certain characteristics that are internal to the educational establishment itself tend to inhibit change.[5] In addition to the fact that education, as contrasted to fields such as medicine or engineering, has no research component and consequently tends not to give a high priority to new inventions or documented techniques, educators are inclined to be individualistic in their professional practice. They do not meet often to study educational problems, nor is there a close working relationship between teachers and educational leaders. Teaching is seen as a highly personal creative endeavor, a view that makes many teachers reluctant to adopt or adapt practices that others have developed. Even the communications between educational personnel are generally haphazard and ineffective. Teachers are not in tune with new inventions for education; they often see innovations as threats to their professional independence. Thus the rapport they feel with colleagues frequently generates from resistance to rather than support for change.

The education establishment does not maintain close working relationships with cognate professionals in fields such as psychology, sociology, anthropology, science, economics, and politics. As a consequence, it is isolated from vital resources that might both promote and validate change. The separation from specialists in the behavioral sciences and allied professional fields is by design rather than accident. Educationists, who over the past century have been heavily and persistently criticized, often unfairly and unprofessionally, by representatives of academic disciplines and other professional fields, have withdrawn unto themselves. The defenses they have built against alliances with others interested in improving education rest on legal prohibitions, such as certification requirements, as well as common distrust and animosities. Current efforts to reduce the isolationism of educational personnel from colleagues in allied fields by developing interdisciplinary approaches to educational change have yet to achieve widespread impact.

The educational establishment has developed its own defenses of the professional status quo that inhibit or influence change. Examples are legalized prescriptions for licenses for practice; detailed formulas for the accreditation of preparing institutions; unionized approaches to personnel policies, which provide for uniform salary scales based exclusively on amount of training and years of employment; negotiated working arrangements; a system of tenure that protects incompetence but not the leader for change; a loose conception of academic freedom that allows no challenge to the teacher; and a subtle system for indoctrination of new members to accept and defend the status quo. Such practices and characteristics obviously influence teachers, supervisors, and administrators when changes are considered. Their most devastating impact, however, is found in their selective influence on personnel who choose to enter and remain in the education professions. They function effectively to repel change-oriented persons from the choice of educational work and to drive into other fields those who give education a try only to find their commitments to change unwelcome and unencouraged. Thus education more than other fields continues to be dominated by professionals who are committed to guard against rather than promote change.

Forces for Educational Change

Despite the fact that educational programs and processes as well as the professionals who operate them are controlled by majority opinion of sponsoring groups, change does take place in education. In recent years, in fact, changes have been occurring so rapidly that neither the public nor the professionals can keep pace. The modifications occurring touch all aspects of education, ranging from goal priorities, financial provisions, organizational and administrative arrangements, curriculum, and instruction, to teacher and student personnel policies. Change might be said to have become so much a way of life in education that no self-respecting school, college, professional association, state or national educational agency would be caught without one or more innovations to boast about. The spirit of educational change has even permeated the halls of state and federal governments to the extent that innovation has become the magic word in policy legislation and budget appropriations for schools and colleges.

To understand the widespread interest in educational change, it helps to identify the forces that are most capable of producing educational modifications. From such insights it is then possible to analyze the impact that particular forces are having on the climate for change that prevails.

Pressure from Minorities for Rights and Justice. A key force for modifying majority opinion are pressures exerted by minority groups for equal rights and human justice. Our system of democratic self-government abides by the majority, but it has a commitment to protect the rights of minorities. The goal of according equality of treatment, opportunity, and justice is a basic tenet that is both espoused and, more important, supported by law. Minorities not only are free to work to become the majority, as they can do by grouping together, but they are entitled by law to the same rights and privileges accorded by the state to the majority. Thus majorities rule, but they must be fair to minorities.

In the past, majorities that controlled schools and colleges were not always sensitive to the rights of minorities. Since 1960 many minority groups have called attention to educational injustices: racial, ethnic, religious, and economic groups; parents of children who are mentally, emotionally, or physically handicapped; and a new voice of a segment of the population that has received unfair educational treatment, women. Students represent another kind of minority; they protest both social injustices and national policies and the fact that they have been excluded from the policy-making processes of the society. The tendency has been for the majority to treat educational institutions as vested social services for those in control. The policy survived on the ancient political dogma, "To the victor belong the spoils," which in educational terms was translated to mean a program of education designed to serve the needs of children of the controlling majority. The needs of children of minorities were given low priorities or ignored. Thus equal educational opportunity —in terms of needs and cultural backgrounds—for children of the poor and racial and ethnic minorities became more of a neglected ideal than an operational reality. Such an educational status quo, however strongly supported by the majority and its enslaved professionals, was ripe for reform—because of its failure to provide equal educational opportunities.

Traditionally, minorities have sought equality of educational treatment principally through appeals to the conscience of the majority. In situations in communities or states where enlightened leadership prevailed, such rational processes often worked, at least sufficiently to appease the petitioners. As social decision-making processes have become more pressure prone, however, with speedy negotiation tending to replace deliberation and power dominating politics, appeals of the minorities carry less weight. Denied their educational rights, minorities have undertaken to develop pressures of their own to force the majorities to change educational policies and programs to meet the needs of their children. A key tactic has been to appeal to the courts for equal treatment under the law. When the courts have been slow to act or obviously prejudiced toward the majority, minority frustration and disillusionment has turned to various forms of public protest—both peaceful and violent. The result is the social revolution that is now taking place, which is forcing changes on education.

Crisis Conditions. When a society confronts a crisis, it typically turns to appropriate organized institutions for help in finding a solution. When this occurs, confidence in the status quo is shaken and established controls are weakened as new solutions are demanded. The effect of such a crisis on education was dramatically demonstrated in 1957 when the Soviet Union launched the first satellite into space. The United States, which prided itself in being the leader in scientific developments, immediately was engulfed by nation-wide panic. Mass fear that an "enemy" nation had outdistanced this country scientifically caused the people to first condemn the schools and colleges for failing to keep the nation strong, and, second, demand that educational institutions change their programs and procedures to prepare the kinds and numbers of scientifically trained experts needed to win the "space race." Such a mandate for change was soon reinforced by legislation passed by a frightened U.S. Congress, the National Defense Education Act of 1957, which provided funds to train and retrain science and mathematics teachers, teachers of modern foreign languages, and guidance counselors, as well as to provide instructional scientific equipment and language labs for schools—all of which were judged to be in the interest of national security. Within months, changes in schools were under way—all dictated by an anxious and united society as a result of the crisis conditions.

The space race crisis turned schools in the United States—from kindergarten through graduate schools—toward the central goal of producing high-level scientific personnel. The mandate was to discover and develop the gifted student. All else was secondary. Not until black minorities began burning cities and bombing and blockading schools and college campuses—which signaled a new kind of social crisis—did the society question whether the course it had set was valid. Again, crisis conditions produced crash changes in schools and colleges. Again the federal government prescribed the changes that would take place by enacting in Congress the Elementary and Secondary Education Act of 1965, which allocated funds to support supplementary educational services and educational innovations for children of the poor. These funds were specifically aimed to make equality of educational opportunity a functional reality.

New Discoveries—Of Knowledge and Technology. Change in the field of education, as in other areas, is produced by new discoveries. As knowledge is verified and refined, it leads to modifications in both curricula and instruction. A recent example is the expansion of knowledge about the space sciences. It presses for inclusion in science programs at all levels of the school system. New knowledge about how children learn to read or respond to particular kinds of reinforcement can alter teaching procedures. Similarly, knowledge about the cultural characteristics of different types of students can shape goal priorities and educational services as well as invalidate the results of culturally biased intelligence and achievement tests.

Technological inventions prescribe changes in educational techniques as well as the roles of teachers. Television coupled with satellite transmission makes it possible for one teacher to literally teach the world. Programed instruction, whether by books, machines, or computers, can monitor many different kinds of learning, which brings about changes in both the organization of courses and the work of teachers. When all children are able to master skills and knowledge, the single variable being the time required, as programed learning makes possible, changes are mandated in standards for assessing student achievement as well as in the way schools organize educational services.

New knowledge and technology, however pertinent they may be to educational operations, can produce change only if put to work. As contrasted to other fields, education is slow to adopt new discoveries to modify practice. To illustrate, many schools and colleges have yet to adopt the new curricula in science and mathematics despite concentrated efforts of science scholars and teachers and substantial expenditures of government money to perfect the programs over the past 15 years. Many teacher training institutions are not yet preparing personnel to work in such programs. The new curriculum knowledge exists, but it has yet to change educational programs in many school systems.

Radio, motion pictures, slide projector equipment, tape recorders, and other types of audiovisual resources have verified contributions to make toward improving instruction. Most of these instructional resources have been available, at comparably reasonable costs, for a quarter of a century, yet many schools and colleges operate daily as if they did not exist. Newer types of instructional technology, such as educational television and programed instruction, have the potential of revolutionizing schools and colleges, as has already been demonstrated, but they have had only token use so far.

Putting new discoveries to work in the field of education, as with other forces for change, requires changes in values, attitudes, and traditions for both the general public and members of the education professions. It requires, also, the definition of new roles and performance skills for teachers and other educational personnel. Costs may be an inhibiting factor inasmuch as educational productivity of a school cannot be measured in direct and immediate financial returns to the community. In the final analysis, the changes that the use of new discoveries make possible will come only if the majority of constituents of a school so rule.

Economic and Political Conditions. Change in education may be furthered or frustrated by economic or political conditions. Generally speaking, changes cost money—initially at least. Innovations usually do not replace traditional practices immediately; they get established as extra expenditures until they become generally accepted. In the absence of documented evidence that the new is superior to the old—which is usually the case in a field that has no real research component—the practice is to let the two compete with the hope that the innovation will ultimately win public and professional support. Only when crisis conditions or social pressures dictate otherwise do innovations not come as added costs in the educational budgets. When money is lacking, change is limited.

However, reductions in school and college budgets can bring changes in school practices, many of which are retrogressive. When cuts come, the new and the experimental are sacrificed to preserve the traditional. The reason is simple: Innovations rarely have widespread public or professional support and they may be highly controversial. Majority decisions dictate the priorities to be preserved; hence when money is scarce schools tend to revert to generally accepted programs and instructional procedures.

The changes that took place in educational philosophy and practice during the economic depression of the 1930s constitute an exception to this rule. With unemployment running high, the society could no longer motivate learning by the promise of rewards to come; yet students had to be kept in school. The policy followed was to try to make learning fun and satisfying as an end in itself. The focus was on promoting creative talents, individual initiative, and selfhood. The changes effected were called *progressive education* (Cremin, 1961, pp. 358–359). Not surprisingly, the economic recession of the early 1970s produced momentum for the return to progressive education (Silberman, 1970).

Political conditions bring about educational change because schools, particularly those that are public in control and support, are a part of the political system. The obligation to serve and preserve the political system is a mandate that cannot be ignored. What's more, schools depend on political decisions for their existence and survival. Their financial support, basic goals, as well as curricula and even instructional procedures, in some cases, are influenced by political actions.

Means of Producing Change

Forces that shape educational policy operate in particular, predictable ways. When change takes place, one or more of these processes is always operating. Those who seek to advance change understand the means by which educational modifications are accomplished.

Allocation of Funds. As research has proved, one of the most successful means of effecting change in schools and colleges is the infusion of funds.[6] With sufficient money, just about any kind of educational change can be purchased—provided of course the innovation wins majority public support. Dramatic proof of how the allocation of funds produces educational changes is found in the advance of such organizational and instructional arrangements as team teaching and modular scheduling, supported by the Ford Foundation (Woodring, 1970). Moreover, the Master of Arts Program to prepare teachers, also a Ford Foundation implantation, is being used in practically every college or university that trains teachers as well as performance contracts, an innovation that is currently being supported by the federal government.

In higher education, the allocation of funds is the primary means of producing change, both within institutions and on a nation-wide basis. A classic illustration is the establishment of the land grant colleges and universities by the appropriation of support by the federal government in 1862. In some states, such as Illinois, Wisconsin, and Minnesota, existing state universities accepted the money and established schools of agriculture and mechanical arts in order to qualify for federal grants. In others, including Michigan, Iowa, and Virginia, the state universities refused to make the change, which resulted in the creation of separate land grant institutions. As is often the case, the funds provided by the federal government to purchase training and research programs in the field of agriculture were minimal compared to the total costs of the institutions.

Modification of Policies. Changes come with the modification of policies, by institutional boards of control, a state, or the federal government. This is the most typical way in which majority opinion is translated into educational practice. When policy changes occur, they may or may not have the support of education professionals. When adopted by an official agency, however, they have the effect of law: compliance is compelled.

Policies adopted by boards of education for elementary and secondary schools may be highly prescriptive. Customarily, school boards set the organizational pattern followed, prescribe standards for personnel, define curricular offerings, approve textbooks, assign pupil populations to schools, and may provide formulas for internal placement of students in class groups and endorse particular teaching strategies.

At the state level, policies usually relate to pupil attendance, curriculum, student services, teacher qualifications, school buildings, and financial arrangements. State policies may be highly specific, such as the requirement of credit in particular college courses for teacher licensure or the prescription that all students in high school must pass given subjects, such as American history or physical education, in order to graduate.

Policies made by the federal government usually are general in nature and apply to particular problems whose solutions are being sought by the infusion of federal funds. Guaranteeing that schools and colleges produce manpower to meet national needs for defense or to maintain given segments of the economy, for example, agricultural or scientific personnel, is an aim of federal policies for education. Recent and current concerns are protecting civil rights, promoting school integration, and the teaching of reading. Providing appropriate educational experiences for children who are handicapped either by physical and mental limitations, or by economic and cultural environmental influences, is another base for policy at the federal level. Traditionally, national policies have been implemented through negotiated agreements with state departments of education. In recent years, however, there has been a tendency for the U.S. Office of Education and other federal agencies to deal directly with school systems, as is being done in the area of school integration.

Legal Enactments. When a state or the federal government passes a law dealing with an aspect of education, it prescribes changes that must take place. Such legislation may be far-reaching; for example, the law may prescribe how teachers must be prepared and licensed, as was the case in recent legislation passed by the State of California. In some instances, changes in schools come from legislation in other areas, such as human rights enactments at the federal level.

Whether directly or indirectly related to education, legal enactments set the pattern for educational services that allow no options. Legislation is a quick way of effecting change on a state- or nation-wide basis. It has the disadvantage, however, of being difficult to change, even after the majorities that originally supported its adoption have dissipated. Thus legal enactments may be the instruments of initial change and ultimately become the guardians of the status quo. For this reason, political and educational leaders generally counsel caution when legislative power is employed to force change.

Court Mandates. A relatively new process for producing change in education, one that has always been available but only recently has come to be employed extensively, is the appeal to the courts for direction. When people cannot agree on policies for their schools or when minority needs are ignored, it becomes necessary to appeal to the courts for a resolution of the conflict or injustice. The issue of public support for religious education is one that can be settled only by the U. S. Supreme Court. School integration was mandated by that body in 1954 and progress toward achieving this goal has been monitored by the lower courts in a series of subsequent rulings.

The trend is for courts to broaden their influence on educational policy and practice. A dramatic illustration of the expanding influence of the courts on educational change is the recent ruling of Circuit Judge J. Skelly Wright in the U. S. Court District of Columbia (Hazard, 1971, pp. 163–187). This decision was against the use of the "track system," a method of classifying students according to their ability to learn, which the court found to be discriminatory along economic and racial lines. Its historical significance lies in the fact that for the first time internal instructional arrangements in schools were prescribed by legal action.

Another educational change has been prescribed by the courts in recent rulings in California and Minnesota (similar actions are pending in most other states and in the Supreme Court) stating that the system of financing elementary and secondary schools which depends heavily on real estate taxes of each school district denies equal educational opportunities. How far the ruling of the courts can reach in influencing educational processes is illustrated in a growing number of cases prohibiting school authorities from limiting the rights of students to particular styles of grooming or the wearing of symbols to express political views (Hazard, 1971, pp. 252–276). In all such rulings the authority has derived from the civil rights of the individual, as prescribed by the U. S. Constitution and subsequent congressional legislation.

Research. In fields that have developed dependable research components, such as medicine, engineering, and agriculture, changes tend to generate from applying the results of scientific investigations. However, before scientific inquiry became an accepted method of solving problems in these fields, majority public opinion and political decisions played key roles in shaping direction and practice—just as they do now in the field of education. As people have gained confidence in the scientific method, however, the tendency is to trust professionals to make the changes in their fields that knowledge dictates. Confidence in the use of scientific research to prescribe needed change in such fields has evolved, largely over the past half century, as the method of science has increasingly demonstrated its effectiveness. Thus when a new disease afflicts society or the farmers' corn crop, or when a space vehicle is to be designed, the people have learned to send researchers to their laboratories rather than to simply vote on what should be done.

Unlike medicine, engineering, agriculture, or even business, education has yet to develop an adequate and effective research component, or public and professional confidence that the scientific method can improve schools. Some progress has been made toward the use of research to solve educational problems in the past decade, but it is largely token in nature. To illustrate, business invests from 5 to 15% of its annual expenditures in research. Medicine and public health allocate about 5% to research and development. In contrast, education is now spending less than 0.5% on research and development. Ironically, the impetus for more research and development in education comes from the public more than it does from educators themselves. People who have learned what research and development can do for health, agriculture, engineering, and business tend to have confidence that the same scientific process can solve educational problems. Educators, on the other hand, who have not been trained to employ research and development and who are not leaders for change, are slow to make research a primary means of effecting changes in schools.

What research we have done in education suggests that it can be an effective means of changing practice—both in individual classrooms and for institutions as a whole. A teacher, for example, can try out new content organizations and instructional procedures under conditions that permit their benefits to be appraised. When improvements are documented, the innovations can win public and professional acceptance. School systems can test proposed changes under controlled and limited conditions before communities are asked to make heavy financial commitments to their implementation. Thus research and development can both save money and protect children against untested theories or politically prescribed modifications. Another advantage to the teaching professions of depending on research and development to guide change is the fact that professionals are in charge of the process.

Models for Educational Change

As has been seen, the predominant model for educational change in the United States at the present time is a *political* one. However, as schools and institutions of higher learning as well as the public place greater emphasis on scientifically derived knowledge, two types of research and development models are coming into use. The most visable of these is *regional* in influence and is supported almost entirely by federal resources. Only beginning to be employed by individual school systems is a *systems analysis model,* which aims to take the risk out of innovation.

Political Process Model. In the absence of research-documented directives, change in education is accomplished by political processes that mold direction out of public opinion. Since vested interests are at stake, it may be highly traumatic as well as temporary. Change in this model begins, typically, with the process of criticism, which ultimately evolves into organized protests and legal mandates to force action to service unmet educational needs. In most cases, such challenges are directed toward specific educational goals and practices that have been endorsed by public majorities and are defended by educational personnel.

The component steps through which educational change moves in the political process model are shown in Figure 1. The first step is for

Development	Diffusion	Legitimation	Adoption	Adaptation
Marshaling of force for change	Criticism and protest	Court decisions Legislation Allocation of funds Modification of policies	Public and professional compliance	Professional implementation

Figure 1. Political process model for educational change. Steps through which educational changes move identified by Hobbs as characteristic of social changes. [See also Egon C. Guba, "Diffusion of Innovations," *Educational Leadership, 25* (4), (January 1968), 292–295.]

forces such as the unmet needs of minority-group children or crisis conditions to be marshaled. When complaints or proposals for change have been identified, diffusion is accomplished by public criticism and protest. The role of the critic is to synthesize and dramatize the appeal for change. Critics are usually self-appointed and may or may not be closely associated with the particular minority group whose complaints are voiced. Educational criticism has become a rewarding endeavor for individuals skilled in either writing or speaking. A competent critic with a cause whose time is ripe can command high fees and gain widespread public visibility. Often philanthropic foundations looking for innovations to sponsor will provide sustaining support for the critic's activities.

The role of the critic is a double one: to solidify the force for change and to attract general public attention. The concentration at this stage is more on dramatizing educational deficiencies than on proposing solutions. In the political process model for change, the critics' effectiveness is usually short-lived and related only to a particular campaign. A few individuals who have had success as spokesmen for particular minority causes have tried to make careers out of educational criticism.[7] Their success, however, tends to be limited to the duration of the popularity of the particular issues with which they originally became identified. It is almost impossible for the education critic, who must dramatize and often tends to overstate his case, to maintain public and professional confidence as an objective spokesman for educational change.[8] Hence every new proposal for change must find its own spokesman.

As criticism stimulates organized protests, the change momentum focuses on the legitimation process. The force and nature of protests usually depend on the rigidity of the defenses of the status quo by public and professional groups. If due process procedures are effective with policy modifications and reallocations of funds are made at the local level, peaceful petitions are likely to be the pattern. When resistance to change is entrenched, the attacks tend to become aggressive and appeals for legislative enactments and court decisions become the course of action.

Critics typically attack educational professionals, implying that they alone stand in the way of change. Ignored is the fact that however an administrator or teacher may feel personally about an issue, he is powerless to lead change until the public can be persuaded that modifications are either desirable or unavoidable. Shrewd critics know this, but the public is anonymous and the need is for a villain to attack. Professional personnel, particularly top administrative officers, are visible symbols of the status quo. Consequently, the cycle of persecution of educational leaders continues with one after another being discredited or discharged for failing to make the changes they are helpless to effect. Then their replacements face similar indictments for the same reasons.

Education professionals tend to move into the change process at the adoption stage, after legitimation has taken place. Their role at this point is more that of a midwife who helps with the delivery than that of a mother who gives birth to new life. Once a change is born, however, the professionals take responsibility for nurturing its development. The behavior of professional organizations tends to follow the pattern set by individual members in schools and colleges. Such bodies tend to defend the status quo until change has been legitimatized and then adopt the modification and help adapt it to function successfully in schools. One might assume that a professional organization could give leadership to change, even though its individual members cannot. However, this is not the case: Such bodies depend for their survival on the dues collected from members. They dare not deal in controversial matters for fear of loss of revenue.

In the political process model, strong impetus for adoption and adaptation come from individual and institutional tendencies to imitate and compete. Let one school or college try something new, such as team teaching, modular scheduling, or televised instruction, and others will either imitate the effort or develop a competing procedure. No better example can be found than the kind of imitation and competition that motivates change among midwestern universities associated with what is called the Big Ten Athletic Conference. The competitive spirit that characterizes athletic contests between the institutions extends to educational policies and practices. When one adopts a new innovation, it is safe to predict that the others will do the same, often without taking the time to test whether the change is appropriate to their own goals and student clientele.

Imitation and competition are poor motivations for educational change, even though they may be powerful forces in altering public opinions that control policies and programs. Following such superficial motives, as educators are prone to do when they adopt and adapt new innovations, is hardly a sound method of improving education. Yet the bandwagon, as it is properly called, is more the process for educational change within the political process model than the public and professionals like to admit.

Research and Development Model. The research and development model for educational change is less than 10 years old but it already is providing an alternative to the political process model, particularly in the areas of curriculum change and the improvement of instructional techniques. This knowledge-based model, at present, is found in the operations of 11 regional research laboratories, which are bringing the results of basic reasearch conducted in 17 university research centers to help solve educational problems in the schools. The resources of state departments of education, of the education industries, and of the newly formed National Institute for Education are utilized as well. The format for this type of regional research and development model is shown in Figure 2, with the flow of the research and development process of change being illustrated in Figure 3.

In this model, the concern is with objective validation of better pro-

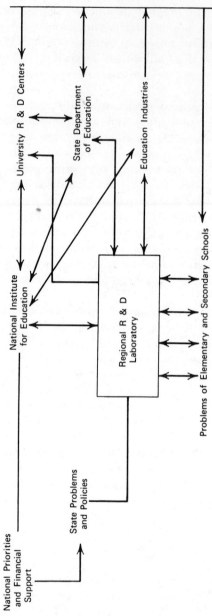

Figure 2.   Format for research and development model.

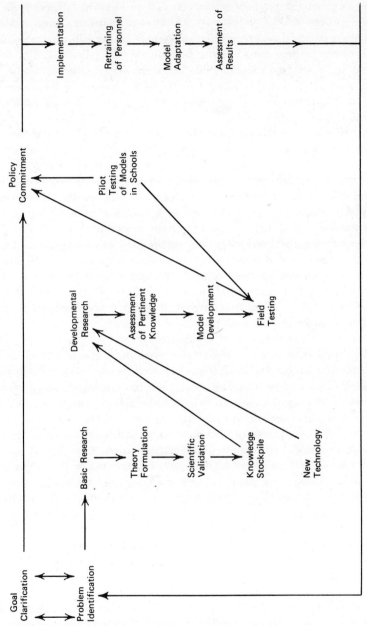

Figure 3.   Research and development change process.

cedures to meet the goals of schools. It is a process that differs from the political process model in many ways: change generates from evidence rather than political power; professionals give leadership throughout; innovations are verified before being introduced into schools; policy modifications are based on demonstrated effectiveness; and educational personnel are retrained to make changes work. A by-product of following this model is a concern for accountability that often is lacking under the political process operation.

For this kind of research and development model to be effective, educational goals must be carefully and precisely defined. Problems tend to relate to the objectives pursued. Since goal formulation is a social process, aspects of the political process model are likely to always function in educational change. It is significant, however, that with research results available, public decisions can deal more with evidence than with emotions. Once problems have been identified, basic research becomes concerned with discovering the knowledge and technology to resolve them. In the future the basic research in university centers is expected to be supplemented by programs operated directly by the National Institute for Education, which will allocate funds to university centers and regional laboratories. About 20% of its investments in research are expected to go to the study of priority problems that are nation-wide.

Developmental research is conducted in the regional laboratories, but also by state education department personnel, the education industries, and by colleges and universities as well as the schools themselves. Its function is to draw from the results the basic research solutions that fit specific educational problems in particular school situations. The process involves the construction and testing of alternative models to the point that best solutions are documented. A subsequent step is the field testing of the model in schools under natural conditions. When the success of the model has been verified, schools can make the decision to adopt it on the basis of demonstrated performance. An aspect of the research and development approach to educational change is the retraining of teachers and other educational personnel to operate successfully the new innovations. This is essential because we now know that much of educational change fails not because it is not valid in itself, but because school and college personnel are either antagonistic to it or professionally incompetent to make it work.

Systems Analysis Model. A promising model for educational change that is particularly suited to individual school systems is the systems aproach, which has been pioneered by business and industry. Utalizing research and development principles, the systems analysis model, as

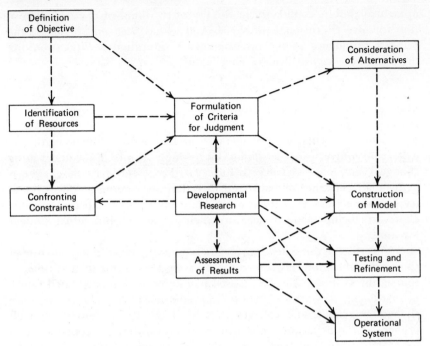

Figure 4.   Systems analysis model.

illustrated in Figure 4, provides a sequence of steps beginning with the development of clear-cut agreements with respect to the educational ob-jective, and moving to marshal the human and material resources needed to achieve the objective and to develop and test working models that will achieve the outcomes prescribed. Refinements are made as needed during the model-testing phase to achieve the essential level of proficiency. The successful model is then tested on a larger population and ultimately, when completely validated, introduced into the entire school system.

In the systems analysis model, as with the regional research and de-velopment model, the definition of objectives is a policy priority that people and professionals must decide. If the goals relate to the overall direction of the educational program, such as whether or not to provide vocational training or black studies in the curriculum, the decision is likely to rest largely with the constitutents of the school. If they pertain to instructional procedures, such as the best way to teach minority group children to read, the decision may be left primarily to professionals. An anticipated outcome of the use of the systems analysis model is the development of public confidence in the use of this kind of planned innovation to solve educational problems. And as has been noted, raising the public's confidence in the professionals in education is vital to giving them the necessary leadership for change.

Managing and Measuring Change

Education, particularly in elementary and secondary schools, with colleges and universities becoming increasingly involved, is undergoing change faster now than ever before. To the extent that the change is being managed, the influence and direction are coming at the national level. Not only are dramatic changes being encouraged, but concentrated efforts are being made to measure their impact on individual student learning.

The role of the federal government as a manager and evaluator of change in education has emerged only after 1957. Prior to that time, of course, the United States had passed legislation and appropriated funds, primarily in the area of vocational education, that brought about changes in schools and colleges. Not until the 1950s, however, did all branches of the national government—administrative, legislative, and judicial—become involved so directly and collectively in shaping the nature of educational operations. Never before have presidents of the United States, particularly President John F. Kennedy and President Lyndon B. Johnson, or the U. S. Congress been so concerned with promoting innovations in schools. Nor have the courts ever before taken such an interest in examining both the purposes and the performance of educational institutions. The federal government has the means of producing change, and it is putting them to work. It is doubtful if a school or university exists anywhere in the United States—public or nonpublic—that has not made changes in its program as a result of federal influence. The amount and rates of change can be expected to accelerate from this type of federal management and evaluation.

Current motivations for stimulating and managing educational change stem from its diligent monitoring of civil rights in all aspects of life. Equality of educational opportunity is the benchmark from which federal influence is taking its direction. The means employed include court decisions, legislation, policy prescriptions, research and development, and, of course, the allocation of funds.

With respect to measuring change, efforts are being made to make accountability a feature of all programs supported by federal funds. Provisions of the Elementary and Secondary Education Act of 1965 prescribed that (1) a national commission be established to monitor the effect of programs supported to improve the learning of poor and minority group children, (2) states administering the funds must require school systems to present plans for innovations and define procedures for measuring changes in student performance, and (3) the total impact of the investments must be assessed by the national committee and its conclusions must be transmitted to the Congress and the people.

Interest in the problem of measuring change itself, in such areas as personality, mental abilities, achievement, and attitudes, is growing among educational researchers (Harris, 1963). The concern is with gain or loss in learning or adjustment of individuals as well as what might be called forward movement or regression in institutional organization and educational processes. Rate of change as well as amount is considered. Attention also has been given to the prediction of change (Lord, 1963, p.27).

Management and measurement of change can be expected to receive more attention in the future as research and development models become more predominant in the change process. A high priority will be to learn how knowledge can be disseminated and translated into educational programs in ways that are both efficient and productive of desired results. Particular concerns will be with the success professional educators are able to achieve in managing change and the accountability they manifest in doing so.

Notes

1. It is generally conceded that administrative leadership is a key factor in educational change. See Donald E. Tope, "Summary of Seminar on Change Processes in Public Schools" (in Carlson, 1965, p. 89). If the top administrator in a school or university is not supportive of innovations, few are likely to be tried. Administrators, however, because of the unique relationships of educational institutions to social and political processes, tend to function as what John Useem and co-writers call the "men in the middle" rather than leaders for change. (See John Useem, John D. Donoghue, and Ruth Hill Useem, "Men in the Middle of the Third Culture," *Human Organization, 22* (1963), 169–179.

2. According to John Goodlad, only 5 or 6% of the schools of the nation are making concerted efforts to solve the problems administrators and teachers say they confront. (See John I. Goodlad, "Lag on Making Ideas Work," *The New York Times,* January 1970, p. 67.

3. Richard O. Carlson (see Richard O. Carlson, *Change Processes in the Public Schools,* Center for the Advanced Study of Education Administration, Eugene, Ore., 1965, p. 4) defines a "change agent" as "a professional who has as

his major function the advocacy and introduction of innovations into practice."
H. G. Barnett (see *Innovation: The Basis of Culture Change*, McGraw-Hill, New
York, 1953) defines an "innovator" as a person who promotes any thought, behavior, or thing that is new because it is qualitatively different from existing
forms. A distinction appears to be that a "change agent" is a person employed
especially to promote change, whereas any teacher or educational worker may
be an innovator. Everett M. Rogers lists the characteristics of educational innovators as youthful, high social status, impersonal, cosmopolite, and deviate
thinkers (in Carlson, 1965, pp. 58–59).

4. According to the Gallup International, Inc., *Study of Parents' Reactions to Educational Innovations* (May 1966, p. 25), "the public is ready to accept innovations which would change substantially the present type of education their children receive. In fact, it is accurate to describe their views as
revolutionary."

5. For a more extensive analysis of such factors, see Ronald Lippit, "Roles
and Processes in Curriculum Development and Change," in *Strategy for Curriculum Change*, Association for Supervision and Curriculum Development, Washington, D.C., 1965, pp. 11–28.

6. Simply increasing school budgets or the amount expended per pupil
does not produce change; additional funds have to be earmarked to support
particular innovations (Carlson, 1965, p. 7).

7. Arthur Bestor, James Koerner, John Holt, and Jonathan Kozol.

8. Examples of distinguished public figures whose images for objectivity
were tarnished by their roles as education critics include Admiral Hyman Rick-
over and James B. Conant.

J. Timothy Sprehe, Ph.D.

J. Joseph Speidel, M.D., M.P.H.

Office of Population
U.S. Agency for International Development

POPULATION AND SOCIAL CHANGE

The world today is waking to the fact that one of the most critical areas of social change requiring massive efforts at management is the simple growth of numbers of people. The growth of population and the spatial distribution of people, with all the human problems these factors bring, is breaking at last into the consciousness of the world population itself and that of the people and institutions that influence the course of world affairs. For the first time governments are showing such concern over population growth that actions are being taken to reduce the fertility of individual citizens. In 1967, 30 nations were signatories to the United Nations Declaration of Population, a document which proclaimed as a basic right access to the means for families to plan and control their own reproduction (Population Council, 1967, 1968). Each year since 1967 has brought a new series of benchmarks to witness the growing awareness of the population problem. Abortion laws are gradually becoming liberalized in the United States. In 1971, India enacted a liberalized abortion law. The Philippines, acting in the same year, established a five-year plan for dealing with population growth. Indonesia moved with increased vigor to implement its own program. The Italian Constitutional Court handed down a decision that prohibiting dissemination of family planning services and information was unconstitutional (Agency for International Development, 1971). In Africa, some 30 countries began preparations for participation in the United Nation's African Census Program, some of the countries taking censuses for the first time in history (U.N. Economic Commission for Africa, 1970). France legalized the intrauterine

281

device (IUD). In March 1972, the Commission on Population Growth and the American Future began issuing its final report on the relation between population growth and the quality of life in the United States. Also in 1972 Mexico reversed a long held position and announced the adoption of a national family planning program (International Planned Parenthood Federation, 1972). The United Nations, appealing for concerted international attention to the population question, declared 1974 a World Population Year (U.N. Population Commission, 1971).

The growing awareness of population as a principal twentieth-century world problem in the management of social change has obviously not meant automatic solution of the problem. Willingness to cope with the problem on a national and international level, although it may mean a major part of the battle is won, is a long way from detailed, well-thought-out policies and vigorous, wide-ranging programs. Focusing world-wide attention on the congeries of social conditions encompassed by the population problem may well result only in the conclusion that we know very little and have seen but the tip of the iceberg.

In this paper, we attempt to survey the dimensions of the population problem. We do this initially by setting forth in outline the demographic aspects of population growth and then by looking briefly at consequences of demographic conditions for other sectors of human life. Given the statement of the problem, one then wishes to know something of the state of knowledge that can be employed in the search for solutions. We examine selected correlates of human fertility in the light of what such correlates reveal for strategies of social change management. Finally, we examine the kinds of solutions that are currently being pursued and attempt to evaluate their potential for alleviating the population condition of the world in either the near or long-run future.

The World Population Crisis

Demographic Aspects. As of January 1, 1970, world population stood at approximately 3.7 billion, with a world average of 36 births and 15 deaths per thousand population in that year. At this rate, there are 133 million births and only 55 million deaths per year, resulting in a world population increase of 78 million per year or 1.5 million per week. In comparative terms, this annual increase in world population is roughly equal to the entire 1971 population of the seven countries of Central America. The weekly increase of 1.5 million means that the 1971 population of the country of Panama is being reproduced every seven days.

The world's population increases daily by 210,000 persons, the equivalent of a medium-sized city. It increases at an annual rate of about 2.1%.

Table 1 Percentage Contribution to Total Growth Among Developing Countries, 1970–1980, by Country (30 of 97 countries are listed, excluding mainland China)

India	31.68
Pakistan and Bangaladesh	7.47
Brazil	6.30
Indonesia	6.24
Mexico	3.78
Nigeria	3.10
Philippines	2.97
Thailand	2.71
Turkey	1.95
Iran	1.94
Egypt	1.67
Korea	1.61
Colombia	1.47
Burma	1.26
Morocco	1.14
Sudan	1.10
Ethiopia	1.09
Vietnam	1.01
Algeria	.96
Congo	.93
Peru	.91
Afghanistan	.81
Venezuela	.80
Taiwan	.74
Malaysia	.74
Kenya	.70
Tunisia	.70
Ghana	.65
Ceylon	.60
Nepal	.46
Total	87.49

Source. Projections made by International Demographic Statistics Center, U.S. Bureau of the Census, Department of Commerce.

Given this constant rate, in the year 2000 the world's population will be more than 7 billion; 10 billion by the year 2020, and 20 billion in 2070 (Hauser, 1971).

This population growth takes place disproportionately in those countries which are conventionally termed "less developed" or "developing" and which are least able to absorb great numbers in a manner that increases the quality of human life. Of 97 less developed countries (excluding mainland China), 5 will contribute 55% of the total growth in less developed countries in the decade of the 1970s, as Table 1 shows. India alone will account for nearly one-third of the growth. The top 30 will contribute seven-eighths of the projected growth during the decade.

These figures loom even larger when seen in historical perspective. In 1650, 11 or 12 generations ago, the world's population could be estimated at a mere 500 million. As Table 2 indicates, growth rates have accelerated rapidly since that time (Hauser, 1971). As rates of growth increase, the doubling time for population growth decreases (cf. Figure 1). Clearly the world is not simply at the beginning of a snowball process, it is somewhat further forward. Whether it has passed the brow of the hill to the point of uncontrollable head-over-heels momentum is a matter of debate and perhaps even of philosophy, but these data must surely sober the most determined optimist.

Table 2   Representative Growth Rates and Doubling Times, 1650–Present

Years	Annual Rate of Growth (%)	Doubling Time (years)
1650–1750	0.3	231
1850–1900	0.6	116
1930–1940	1.0	69
1971	2.1	35

Source.   Extracted from P. M. Hauser, "World Population: Retrospect and Prospect," in National Academy of Sciences, *Rapid Population Growth*, Baltimore: Johns Hopkins Press, 1971.

Historically there have been two waves of rapid population growth. The first, occurring among the European population and those of European descent, took place in the three centuries from 1650 to 1950, during which time the world population multiplied about fivefold. The population of North America was multiplied by 168 and that of Latin America by 23. Africa only doubled during this period, while Asia increased by a factor of four. Since World War II, the second wave of growth has occurred. In Asia, Latin America, and Africa, the disparity between births and deaths has rapidly increased. Whereas North America and Europe are now characterized by crude birth rates (i.e., births per 1000 population) of less than 20 and similarly low death rates, most of Africa, Asia, and Latin America have crude birth rates of over 40, accompanied by rapidly decreasing death rates. Where low death rates and high fertility prevail, as in these latter continents, annual growth rates are almost al-

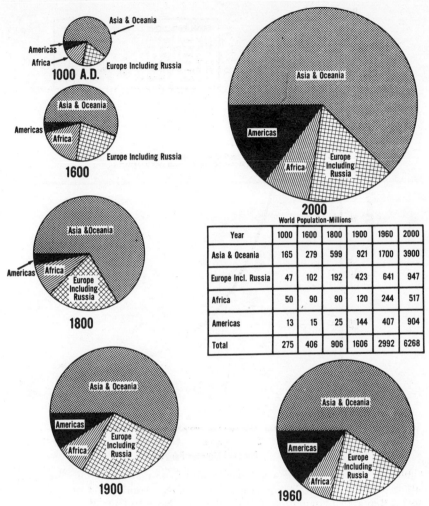

Figure 1. World population by historical periods past, present, and future. (*Source.* A. Desmond, "How Many People Have Lived on Earth?" In L. K. Y. Ng and S. Mudd (eds.), *The Population Crisis.* Bloomington: Indiana University Press, 1966.

ways above 2% and sometimes above 3% (Hauser, 1971; Nortman, 1970; Agency for International Development, 1971; Desmond, 1966).

Figure 2 shows changes in the relative distribution of population since the year 1000. At that time Asia counted for 60% of world population, Europe including Russia 17%, Africa 18%, and the Americas 4%. By 1960, Asia's percentage had declined to somewhat under 60%, Europe

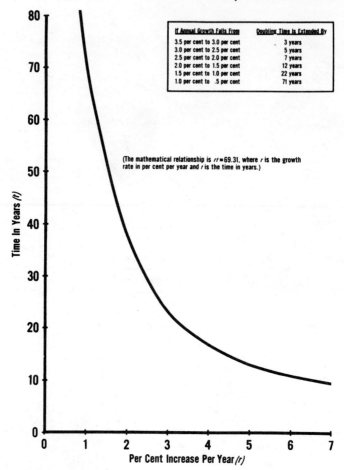

Figure 2.   Relation between population growth rate and time on which population doubles. (*Source.* "Population and Family Planning Programs: A Factbook," Reports on Population/Family Planning, No. 2, July, 1970.)

and the USSR decreased to 22%, the Americas were 14%, and Africa was
8%. Figures 3 and 4 show the situation for 1970. By the year 2000, however, Asia will constitute a little more than 62% of the total, Europe and
the USSR 15%, the Americas 14%, and Africa 8%.

These changes, particularly in the developing areas of the world, are
the result of continuing high fertility accompanied by rapidly decreasing
birth rates. Decreased death rates can be attributed to several causes. One
cause is increased productivity, particularly in the agricultural sector, but

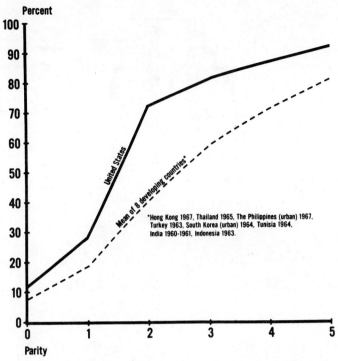

Percent

Figure 3. Percentage of respondents not wanting more children, by parity. (*Source*. B. Berelson, "The Present State of Family Planning Programs," Studies in Family Planning, No. 57, September 1970.)

also in industry. Higher productivity leads to higher levels of living, a higher earning capacity for the land, and less starvation and malnutrition. A second major cause of decreased death rates is the improvements in preventive medicine and public health programs. Environmental sanitation and personal hygiene have improved throughout the world, resulting in decreased contamination of food and water and a corresponding decrease in infant and child mortality. World-wide preventive medical campaigns to eliminate communicable and insect-borne diseases such as smallpox and malaria have decreased mortality. In this, the development of modern medicine, including chemotherapeutic antibacterial agents and immunizations, has played a strong role, even though modern medicine is not directly available to a high proportion of residents of less developed countries (Agency for International Development, 1971; National Academy of Sciences, 1971). In considering today's greater life expectancy

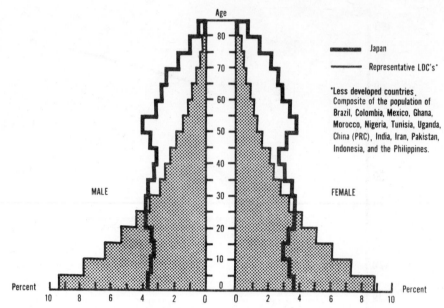

Figure 4. Projected population by age groups. Selected less developed countries and Japan, 2000. (*Source.* Projections of the International Demographic
Statistics Center, U.S. Bureau of the Census. Projections assume constant fertility and declining mortality.)

for residents of developing countries, it should be borne in mind that
most of the differential in death rates is to be found among the very
young, particularly infants under the age of 1 year (Coale, 1964; Densen,
1965).

Compared to the management of the kind of social change that will
bring about reductions in birth rates, the problem of lowering death
rates throughout the world has been comparatively simple. This contention is made credible only when one understands that preventive medicine generally can be applied to mass groups with little or no involvement on their part. The introduction of water purification or the use of
insecticides required relatively little initiative on the part of the persons
whom the technology was intended to benefit. On the other hand, within
the range of viable alternatives available today (described in the final section of this paper), it is not possible to introduce birth limitation measures without intimately involving the populations for whom they are intended. The management of decreased death rates involves principally
the mobilization of technology. The management of decreased birth rates

requires mobilization of technology plus the mass participation of the target populations. Furthermore, the benefit to the individual of improved
health care is by and large obvious, whereas the benefits of family limitation are far less apparent in many cultures.

Consequences. One result of the interplay between fertility and mortality rates is a variation in the age structure of populations. A factor that
is affected significantly by age distribution differences is the *dependency
ratio,* the proportion of a population who are dependents; that is, under
15 or over 60 years of age. Most developing countries are in what is
termed a transitional stage: their death rates have declined radically, but
birth rates have yet to begin a significant drop. In these societies, the proportion of the population under 15 may approach 50%, and those over
60 constitute approximately 5%. These figures stand in contrast to the
developed countries where those under 15 make up perhaps 25% of the
total and those over 60 may be 15% (Hauser, 1971).

This means that in the less developed country the dependency ratio
approaches 100; that is, there is one dependent for every member of the
population aged 15 to 59. In developed societies, a dependency ratio of
70 is more typical. In general, the higher the dependency ratio, the
greater the proportion of societal resources that must be expended simply
upon sustaining the living portion of the population, and the less that
can be devoted to the social and economic development which will benefit future populations. The contrast between developing and developed
countries can be seen in Figure 5, which gives the projected age-sex structure of selected developing countries and Japan, a low growth rate country.

Employment. An important result of high fertility relates to employment. Large numbers of young people enter a job market where relatively few older persons are leaving employment because of death or
retirement. This undoubtedly contributes to the high rates of unemployment and underemployment found in the less developed countries (National Academy of Sciences, 1971).

Economic Development. It cannot be said that high population growth
rates have actually prevented economic development, nor have they led
to widespread starvation in developing countries. What can be argued is
that too rapid growth in population retards development, that per capita
incomes in countries with high growth rates have risen much more slowly
than they might have under conditions of lower fertility. Similarly, standards of living and per capita food production have not risen as fast as

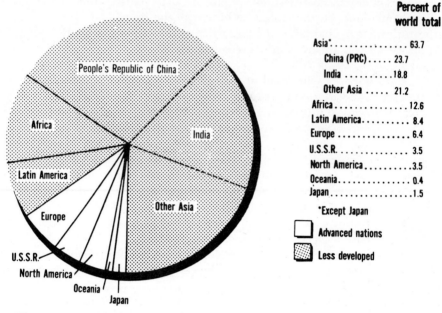

Figure 5. World births, percentage by region, 1970. (*Source.* Estimates of the International Demographic Statistics Center, U.S. Bureau of the Census.)

they might have otherwise. The Green Revolution has seen to it that the world will not face an immediate major food crisis, but beyond 10 or 20 years the future of food supplies is uncertain. National economic growth rates have continued to increase rapidly, so that reductions in fertility, were they to occur, could quickly result in increased individual and family welfare for the populations of those countries most affected by rapid growth in numbers (National Academy of Sciences, 1971).

Urbanization. The spatial distribution of people, particularly into cities, is both a cause and a consequence of the population problem. Urbanization has already progressed into mature stages for the developed countries. In the developing countries, the last 20 years have witnessed great changes in cities. Overall percentage increase in urban populations for 1950–1970 was 177% for Africa, 135% for Asia, and 136% for Latin America (National Academy of Sciences, 1971). From 45 to 90% of the populations of developing countries still live in rural areas. The rate of growth for cities in these countries far exceeds that of the overall population. Between 1950 and 1960, among 24 countries with per capita income of less that $250 per year, cities of more than 100,000 inhabitants grew 60% more rapidly than the total population. The average rate of growth of these cities is over 4% a year, resulting in a doubling time of only 17 years (Browning, 1971). The city of Jakarta is said to be increasing in size at an annual rate of 6% or more, despite laws restricting in-migration. Jakarta is likely to double its size in less than 15 years. Severely overcrowded conditions could shortly become intolerable.

Migration to cities means that formerly rural populations become absorbed gradually into the urban industrial labor force. However, the process of assimilation into the urban labor force is much slower than the rate of migration. The consequences are high rates of urban unemployment or underemployment together with problems of providing adequate housing and public health facilities. Many analysts urge that developing countries adopt policies restricting migration to cities.

Education. Growth in population, entailing growth in urbanization and the industrial labor force, requires growth in education. From 1950 to 1965, the number of children enrolled in primary schools of less developed countries rose by 150%. The percentage of all children 6–12 years of age who are enrolled increased from less than 40% to more than 60%. And yet the gains are insufficient to offset the onrush of population growth. The fact is that, despite worldwide strenuous efforts, the proportion of the world's people who are literate is declining (Jones, 1971). Teacher shortages in the near future will be critical; one estimate places the teacher-pupil ratio in primary schools at 1:68 for Pakistan and 1:102 for Singapore (Jones, 1971). And this is only a theoretical potential, not an actuality; it is only for primary schools, not for secondary and higher education.

The nearly universal value placed on education, particularly by urban populations who understand the increased economic rewards of education, places great demands on governments. Population growth seems to advance somewhat irrespective of advances in the GNP, and only gradually can countries raise their allocations to education. Current population growth rates make it difficult for developing countries to raise their enrollment ratios without spending a far greater proportion of GNP on education than do developed countries. Reductions in fertility would enable educational systems to set and fulfill much more realistic goals for educating their populations.

Public Health. Although a great deal has been accomplished in public health throughout the world, much still remains to be done, particularly in the developing countries where the most optimal conditions do not approach unacceptable conditions for developed countries. In a study of physician manpower needs for 31 developing countries, it was shown that simply to maintain the physician-population ratios of 1955 would require a 25% increase in physicians because of population growth. To increase the ratio up to 21.1 physicians per 100,000 population, 50% more doctors would be needed for the period 1955–1965 (National Academy of Sciences, 1971). Rapidly growing populations are young populations in which medical needs are largely for mothers and children. Close spacing of pregnancies, coupled with high parity, makes for unfavorable health demands, which most systems in developing countries cannot meet.

The most common form of birth control in many developing countries is abortion. As societies begin the transition to lower fertility, abortion reaches epidemic proportions. A committee of the Indian Parliament, investigating the matter with a view to liberalizing India's abortion law, reported in 1970 that there were an estimated 4.5 million abortions per year in that country (Agency for International Development, 1970). A high incidence of abortion, even while reducing requirements for maternal and infant care, places additional demands on the health system.

Trends toward overcrowding, poverty, poor nutrition, poor housing, and pollution, trends exacerbated by rapid population growth, tend to be injurious to public health. Although effects of overcrowding upon human health are not yet well measured, it is clear that severe health problems accompany rapid urbanization.

The Family. Other things being equal, it is generally conceded that children in smaller families enjoy greater material and perhaps psychic advantages than those in larger families. Infant mortality is higher in large families and higher in families where birth intervals are short. Malnourishment is less common in smaller families than in large. When one controls for social class, children from smaller families score higher on intelligence tests (Wray, 1971). Inasmuch as intelligence correlates roughly with one's performance in the educational system and position in the occupational structure, a predominance of larger families in a society, particularly among the less advantaged, is an indicator that the human capital wherewith a society develops may be of relatively lower quality. The deleterious effects of large families upon individual welfare have some aggregate effect upon overall societal development.

Environmental Quality. How population pressure impacts upon the quality of the physical environment is as yet imperfectly understood. Economists are only beginning to tally up the "social costs" of products such as automobiles and airplanes. Certainly rising population pressure in less developed countries results in some deterioration of the environment, as in the Middle East where farming has been extended into areas in which the soil is suitable principally for grazing only, resulting in further deterioration of the land through erosion (National Academy of Sciences, 1971). Extreme overcrowding of cities in many developing countries has led to serious pollution and public health problems.

In developed countries, the impact of population growth upon the environment is now receiving much increased attention. There the problem is somewhat different. The individual with a higher level of living in a developed country contributes more to ecological problems than does his counterpart in developing countries. The upper income person in a developed country may consume hundreds of times the energy, industrial production, and fossil fuels as does the person in developing countries. The United States comprises a very small percentage of the world's population, and yet it consumes 30% of the world's production.

The topic of environmental quality is perhaps a fitting place to draw some contemporary conclusions concerning the description of the world population crisis. Even in the most developed societies, awareness of the population problem is just now verging over into coordinated endeavors to conceptualize the problem in all of its ramifications. Not only do we not yet have good measures, for example, as to how much an additional automobile costs society in terms of additional pollution, congestion, opportunities foregone for other alternatives, public safety, and eventually littering the country with junkyards—we have not yet thought out the problem or its ramifications. As the report of the Commission on Population Growth and the American Future (1972) points out, population is a long-run problem requiring long-run perceptions and solutions; it is a problem that is susceptible to many interpretations ranging from doomsday warnings to calm pride in national growth; it affects every facet of life, yet we have not made a beginning even at uncovering the character of its effects; its effects are undramatic, without the headline-getting appeal of other social problems, and yet pervasively related to every other problem. If this combination of qualities did not already make the population problem an unappealing platform for action on the part of politicians and public officials, the remedies proposed for the problem run counter to long-ingrained values in many cultures of the world.

Fertility Correlates and Management of Change

In seeking out the kinds of social change that will result in solutions for population problems, one can separate strategies roughly according to

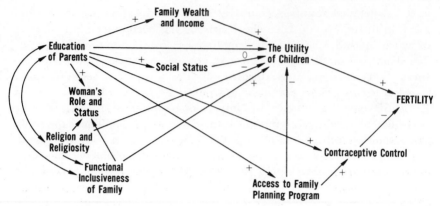

Figure 6.   A caused model of social and economic factors affecting family fertility. (*Source*. Adapted from K. O. Mason, A. S. David, et al. (1971). *Social and Economic Correlates of Family Fertility: A Survey of the Evidence*. North Carolina: Research Triangle Institute.)

whether they are population-responsive or population-influencing. Population-responsive strategies tend to look to the present and past, attempting to develop policies and programs to cope with existing consequences of previous and current high growth patterns, such as urban migration and overcrowding. Population-influencing strategies focus more on what can be done now to assure a better future in terms of lower growth rates and less uneven spatial distribution of the population.

In this section, we adopt the viewpoint of population-influencing strategy and pose the query: What do we need to know in order to influence future populations in the direction of lowered fertility? The most immediate answer would seem to be that we must look at factors associated with differential fertility rates and ask whether a change in one of these factors might not eventuate in changes in fertility.

One approach to the analysis of what affects fertility has been to employ a model of all events that may contribute to fertility. Davis (1967) and Freedman (1970) have focused on the "intermediate" or "intervening" variables, such factors being as disparate as frequency of sexual intercourse and the lifelong cultural conditioning concerning the value of children.

Table 3 gives a selection of largely confirmed hypotheses concerning fertility and three other variables: the family as a productive unit, the role of women, and education. The hypotheses were derived from the model shown graphically in Figure 6 (Mason et al., 1971). The model assumes that a cost-benefit calculus is operative in family decisions concerning fertility and that fertility is a function of potential net utility of children to parents and parental ability to control fertility behavior. Although the model deals with seven variables, we have selected only three for consideration here.

We review the illustrative findings of Table 3 with an eye toward the planned management of change. We seek not only to find solid relationships between fertility and other variables, but also to find which of these relationships are most amenable to manipulation through policies and programs of planned social change. Our bias is to look especially for relationships that are open to direct, short-run intervention. To look to the long run is, we believe, to court disaster in the form of even more adverse demographic and social conditions than now confront the world. Or, to put the matter another way, the long-run perspective is the same as awaiting the demographic transition from high to low birth rates which accompanies general social and economic development. If, as the evidence previously quoted seems to argue, high rates of population growth are a hindrance to development, then one does not wish to wait for the advent of full development in order to accomplish reduced population growth. This would in effect be to await the resolution of a vicious cycle. Rather, one seeks avenues which are less dependent on the entire development process itself. In a sense, the test of a strategy for managing the planned reduction of fertility is whether fertility is reduced at least semi-independently of the general development process. In all probability, the case will never be clearly made in one direction or the other.

It should be noted that the massive intervention needed in the realm of "social management" to dramatically reduce fertility is and will remain controversial in many cultures and societies. Even if the technical means for lowering fertility were more obvious than it is today, the requisite social mobilization would remain problematic in some settings.

The Family. For the long run, one could expect that increasing urbanization and the accompanying shift to nonagricultural occupations will diminish the relationships presented in part A of Table 3. In developed countries families do not generally act as units of economic production, children are not an important source of labor and are not a major source of old age support. For the short run, one could enact child labor laws which, if enforced, would at least remove children from the labor force and might possibly, although not necessarily, alter high fertility. Or it could be made more desirable through intensive mass media campaigns that the labor of children be foregone for a higher value, such as their education. As long as families remain economic productive units, however,

Table 3   Selected Correlates of Fertility: Strength of Relationship ·and Adequacy of Research

Confirmed Hypothesis	Strength of Relation	Adequacy of Research
A. The family as a productive unit		
1. The greater the extent to which families utilize children for labor, the higher the fertility		
Controlling for agricultural versus all other occupations	Medium	Fair-good
Controlling for rural/urban residence: yields an *inverse* relationship	Low	Fair-good
2. Families which act as units of economic production will have higher fertility than other families dependent on wage-earning of adult family members		
Controlling for agricultural versus all other occupations	Medium	Fair-good
3. Families which depend on adult children for economic and social support of the aged will have higher fertility than other families	Low-Medium	Poor
B. The role of women		
1. The greater the participation of women in economically remunerative activities, especially in the "labor force," the lower their fertility		
For developed countries	High	Good
For developing countries, hypothesis is either weakly confirmed or no relation found	Low	Fair-good

they are likely to resist the enforcement of child labor laws, and the value of education presupposes the development of an educational system in which these values can be realized, integrated with an industrialized occupational structure where education's benefits can be reaped. All too frequently in the developing countries college graduates cannot find jobs that use their training. Increased mechanization of agriculture is one intervention that might reduce the desirability of child labor, but again this is a major step in the process of economic development, not easily or surely pursued as an independent step in fertility reduction.

An old age social security system might assist in decreasing the dependence of parents on their children in old age. As it becomes institu-

Confirmed Hypothesis	Strength of Relation	Adequacy of Research
2. The higher the wage-rate a woman worker can command, the lower her fertility	Medium	Fair-good
3. Participation of women in extrafamilial activities of a noneconomic nature will bring about lower fertility	Unknown or mixed	Poor
4. The more egalitarian, companionate, and communicative the husband-wife relationship, the lower the fertility and the higher the contraceptive use and efficacy	Unknown or mixed	Fair-poor
C. Education		
1. The higher the educational level of the husband or wife, the lower the fertility	High	Good
2. The greater the education of husband or wife, the greater the use of contraception or other effective means of controlling fertility	High	Good
3. Educational attainment will be negatively associated with fertility only when the curricular content of the education is largely western or "modern" rather than traditional (e.g., religious education)	Unknown	Poor

Source. Adapted from Karen O. Mason, Abraham S. David, et al., *Social and Economic Correlates of Family Feritility: A Survey of the Evidence,* prepared by the Research Triangle Institute as Project SU-518 for the Near East-South Asia Bureau of U.S. Agency for International Development, September 1971.

tionalized and legitimated, such a system might result in reduced fertility (although frequently such dependencies are also buttressed by strong religio-cultural beliefs). The ability of governments to institute social security systems is itself a function of the development process. Nevertheless, some promising efforts in this direction are being initiated. On certain tea estates in South India, an experiment is under way to provide families with an old age annuity in returning for foregoing higher-order pregnancies.

The Role of Women. The set of hypotheses in part B of Table 3 represents in some measure an attempt to extrapolate findings from developed to developing countries. The fourth hypothesis assumes that the husband and wife have the goal of reducing fertility, which they may well not have, and combines a number of variables that may not exist in positive association.

Nevertheless, were the relationships solidly founded, what would be the implications for management of social change? The evidence does show that, in developing countries where ample employment opportunities for women exist, the age at marriage has steadily risen, and this factor can be expected to have an impact on fertility. In general, however, conditions of unemployment and underemployment in developing countries do not augur favorably for expansion of female employment opportunities. It should be recalled that major participation in the labor force by women occurred relatively late in the development of Western societies. Major long-term governmental intervention, as perhaps in China and the socialist countries of Europe, may result in changing roles for women; in the short run, prospects seem less promising.

Education. The third hypothesis in part C of Table 3 is aimed at searching out more precisely what it is about education that reduces fertility. The assumption is that traditional religious education could well reinforce higher fertility, as appears to have been the case with parochial school education in the United States. Too little research has been done to pronounce conclusively concerning this hypothesis, but the others in part C reaffirm that education is strongly related to lowered fertility.

The fact that increased education is associated with decreased fertility leads to the suggestion that it is the middle and upper classes of a society that will first be receptive to the notions of birth limitation, child spacing, higher age of marriage, or family planning in general. This appears to be the case, despite the fact that it is the lower socioeconomic classes that have the greatest "need" for family planning (in terms of allocating scarce family resources for the welfare of family members). Thus the idea of limiting family size seems to suffer the fate of all "innovations." Studies in the diffusion of innovation have consistently shown that new ideas and technologies are first embraced by the higher socioeconomic classes and gradually trickle down to the lower classes (Rogers and Shoemaker, 1971). One of the tasks of a short-run strategy for easing the world population crisis should be to seek ways to break through this generalization and to mobilize those sectors of the population that are contributing most heavily to rapid population growth.

In this section we have tried to suggest that, where we do have some solid knowledge concerning the determinants of a major component of the population problem such as fertility, we do not often have the basis for short-run strategies of social change management. A management approach to population control needs knowledge not simply of fertility correlates but of those correlates that are themselves most susceptible to change by planned intervention. Fertility is so intricately bound up with the institutional fabric of society that a major change in fertility might well be called a societal change, not just social. The short-run solutions may very well have to be piecemeal until the variety of such solutions increases in weight to a major tipping point. This may not mean that the outlook is bleak. Kirk (1971) has argued recently that new "thresholds" of declining natality are appearing in developing countries and that once past the thresholds the countries will experience much more rapid decline in fertility than was historically the case for developed countries. Ravenholt et al. (1972) have detailed these trends of declining fertility in the 1960s.

Solutions to the Population Problem

Without doubt, unchecked growth of population and the resultant changes in the spatial distribution of people, if allowed to continue at present rates, will constitute increasingly severe social problems and be indirectly responsible for major social changes. The report of the Commission on Population Growth and the American Future (1972) notes that one cannot point to a single U.S. social problem that would be alleviated by population growth.

The onrushing character of the population crisis means that societies will be forced to cope with greatly increased numbers ànd densities of people in all of their economic, educational, environmental, political and cultural ramifications. Even with rapid declines in fertility—declines which seem highly unlikely in view of present efforts—the numbers and densities will be there; an immediate transition to the two-child family will bring the United States 50 million more people by the year 2000 (Commission on Population Growth, 1972). Although the problem is most vitally urgent in developing countries, it is of great significance in developed countries also. Because of geometric increases in absolute size—a change of 1% in 1 billion is no different from a change of 0.1% in 10 billion—with any given rate of increase there is a high premium on early rather than later corrective action. Of all current social problems, population is perhaps the most clearly time-related, the one in which it is most easily seen that passage of months and years of inaction amounts to a decision to aggravate the difficulties.

If the results of inaction are manifest, the strategies for action are not. Various elements within society, including population experts, observe the kinds of evidence presented in previous sections and look at current programs and individual efforts to control fertility. They arrive at differing perceptions as to which social actions might best address the problem. Different parties opt for different points of entry into the complex determinants of fertility and accordingly give different emphases in priority actions. Taking only the fertility aspects of the population crisis, similarities and differences revolve around three general areas of activity:

1. *Provision of the means for controlling fertility,* that is, making fertility control services widely available. Proponents of this approach assume fertility control services, like health services, are universally in demand.

2. *Increasing demand for, and use of, fertility control measures,* that is, educational and motivational efforts. Proponents of this approach tend to view society and man as responsive to economic pressures and self-interest.

3. *Regulation of behavior,* that is, controlling fertility via constraints on sexual activity such as raising the legal age for marriage. Individual responsibility and morality are emphasized by proponents of this approach.

The categories are not mutually exclusive. Proponents of the provision–of–fertility–control–services–approach frequently consider motivational efforts and control of sexual activity to be only ancillary strategies. The differences lie in where priorities are located, and these are differences in philosophies of social change.

Some interests, notably religious groups such as the Catholic Church, have placed principal emphasis on the regulation of sexual activity (Noonan, 1965). Many speculative discussions have focused on the second and third items above, and encompass a sizable number of largely untried proposals—sometimes called "beyond family planning"—which would presumably reduce fertility. There is, however, no universal agreement concerning what is encompassed by the term "family planning." Few would disagree that family planning includes provision of information and contraceptive services and in general aims at influencing fertility in a downward direction through voluntary cooperation of individual couples (Saunders, 1970). However, some authors who cite the failure of the family planning approach employ a definition that excludes certain aspects such as postconceptive means of fertility control (abortion) or use of economic incentives. These, they say, are not part of family planning, and indeed many family planning programs have excluded these aspects for a variety of reasons. We feel that the most useful definition of family planning is a broad one which includes provision of preconceptive and postconceptive services as well as extensive motivational efforts.

It is instructive to follow Berelson's (1970) definition of the four components essential to provision of family planning services and to solution of population problems. They are: (1) political will or policy; (2) motivation of people to accept family planning services; (3) available technology; and (4) organization for delivery of necessary services.

1. *The Role of Policy.* In many countries the possibility of action directed to the solution of population problems is highly dependent on conscious development of a policy or action strategy. This is particularly true in developing countries where large-scale social change more frequently stems from governmental action programs. In developed countries, fertility has often been reduced in almost total absence of formal population policies initiated by national governments. A few governments of developed countries are now creating population policy apparatuses such as that which the Commission on Population Growth and the American Future (1972) calls for in the United States.

Unfortunately, often only the most rudimentary information is available concerning the demographic status of less developed countries. Therefore the fundamental data to guide policy makers are absent or inaccurate. Also lacking are hard and convincing data with respect to population dynamics and the relationship of such dynamics to other development goals such as improved health, education, and industrialization (Freedman, 1970; Speidel, et al., 1971). Competing considerations—economic, political, religious—have too often relegated population policy and its resulting programs to a position of low priority. The nature of the population problem is such that the problem is not visible with immediacy and drama and not remedied by swift and decisive action; the nature of the problem does not appeal to the direct self-interest of the politician concerned with staying in office tomorrow.

Even so, recent years have witnessed considerable progress in formal policy statements (Lyons, 1971; Berelson, 1970). The creation of an action program to control fertility, it should be noted, may proceed with or without an explicit or public policy statement. Strong policy statements have all too often been followed by inaction on the program level. However, in 1970, 79% of the people in less developed countries were in nations with either a population policy or a family planning program.

Lyons (1971) has defined the existence of a population policy on the part of the government in terms of governmental action precisely because of the lag between words and deeds. By his definition, only an implemented population policy could be considered a real policy. Inaction

may reflect a deliberate covert policy, even though it is in direct conflict
with stated objectives to provide services and take other measures to reduce population growth. According to Lyons' definition—"publicly announced policies of fertility limitation coupled with subsequent action to
implement these policies"—some 22 governments in developing countries
have a population policy. These countries encompass 49% of the world's
people. Such a commitment to the solution of population problems, al-
beit limited, is a remarkable change from the situation in 1960 when
only three countries had antinatalist policies and very few programs existed.

In addition, the great efforts of donor countries seeking to foster development have, until the past decade, ignored population. As little as
nine years ago only one developed country rendered foreign assistance to
developing countries for population problems. In recent years, however,
funding for population activities by developed countries has increased remarkably, virtually "taken off," and reached approximately $175 million
in fiscal year 1972. Contributions of the U.S. Agency for International
Development, the largest single donor, are shown in Figure 7.

Thus developed countries have in recent years made a policy decision that population program assistance is a valid and desirable goal for
their agencies which seek to foster social and economic development
(Ravenholt, 1969; Carter, 1968). Although establishment of a population
policy is not a necessary concomitant to decreased fertility, there are numerous advantages to such an action. Lyons (1971) has noted that a population policy (1) allows for government resources to be planned for and
budgeted toward achievement of certain goals which usually result from
instituting a policy; (2) tends to encourage cooperation among many
branches and agencies of the government, a necessary condition for successful programs; (3) legitimizes program activity for the doubtful and so-
lidifies support of the uncommitted; (4) promotes more open relationships concerning the problem with other governments and international
organizations and groups, thereby allowing a freer exchange between official actors; (5) presents symbolic if not real evidence of the national plan
to achieve a predetermined, well-thought-out goal; (6) removes doubt,
where doubt of governmental position may bring irregular or even contradictory approaches in national planning; and (7) tends to give equal
status with other areas of high priority.

Of course even with a stated policy there may remain a great deal of
ambivalence and timidity, resulting in reluctance to initiate actions and
continuing low priority for such activity. Even with an official national
policy, key groups within society such as government officials and religious leaders may fail to endorse population programs. Traditionally,

Table 4 Developing Countries with National Population Policies and Programs

United Nations Data	Population Council Data	IPPF Data	T. C. Lyons, A.I.D. Data
Africa			
Botswana	—	—	—
Ghana	Ghana	Ghana	Ghana
Kenya	Kenya	Kenya	Kenya
—	Mauritius	Mauritius	Mauritius
Morocco	Morocco	—	Morocco
Tunisia	Tunisia	Tunisia	Tunisia
Egypt	Egypt	Egypt	Egypt
Asia			
Ceylon	Ceylon	Ceylon	Ceylon
India	India	India	India
Indonesia	Indonesia	Indonesia	Indonesia
Iran	Iran	—	Iran
Korea	Korea	Korea	Korea
Malaysia	Malaysia	Malaysia	Malaysia
Nepal	Nepal	Nepal	Nepal
Pakistan	Pakistan	Pakistan	Pakistan
—	Philippines	Philippines	Philippines
Singapore	Singapore	Singapore	Singapore
Taiwan	Taiwan	Taiwan	Taiwan
—	Thailand	—	—
Turkey	Turkey	—	Turkey
Latin America			
Barbados	Barbados	—	Barbados
Chile	—	Chile	—
—	—	Colombia	—
Costa Rica	—	Costa Rica	—
Dom. Republic	Dom. Republic	Dom. Republic	—
—	—	Guatemala	—
Honduras	—	Honduras	—
Jamaica	Jamaica	Jamaica	Jamaica
Nicaragua	—	Nicaragua	—
Trinidad and Tobago	Trinidad and Tobago	Trinidad and Tobago	Trinidad and Tobago
Total 25	23	24	21

Source. Thomas C. Lyons, Jr., "Social / Political / Cultural Considerations in the Population Policy Process." Paper delivered at African Population Conference, Accra, Ghana, December 1971.

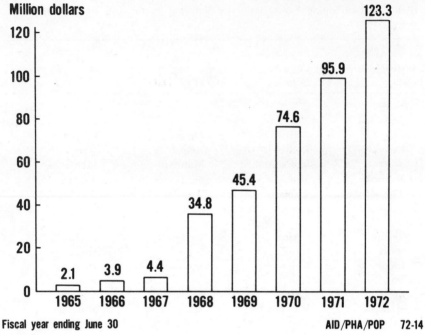

Million dollars

Fiscal year ending June 30   AID/PHA/POP   72-14

Figure 7

population action programs have been located within ministries of health, bureaucracies which often possess little "clout" in the competition for resources. In short, policy does not insure program effectiveness in the absence of other factors, and the existence of reasonably effective programs in the absence of stated policy seems possible. Policy would also seem to be an essential component of the many changes advocated in the strategy to solve population problems which are advanced as "beyond family planning."

2. *Motivation to Limit Fertility.* The question of motivation for family planning services has created controversy among family planning strategists and program administrators. Unfortunately, the question is often placed in an either-or context, with one group, frequently scholars and academicians of social science background, calling for increased emphasis on engendering motivation within the population of potential acceptors of fertility control services. On the other hand are most program administrators, frequently coming from backgrounds in the medical professions,

preventive health services, or government civil service, who feel confident that existing programs have come nowhere near exhausting available demand. These observers place the extension of family planning services as the highest priority.

There is at present no definitive information to resolve this debate, and in the last analysis much of the difference between the two groups may stem from the experiential prejudices of their different backgrounds. There is considerable survey data from existing KAP (Knowledge, Attitudes, and Practice) surveys of fertility-related behavior, which suggests that in many countries the still young and frequently rudimentary family planning service programs have a considerable distance to go before existing demand is satisfied (Berelson, 1970). On the other hand, there is the testimony of program administrators in some of these countries that their service programs, imperfect as they are, are not reaching as many of the population as they had been led to expect. Even though desires for low fertility are correlated with high education, urbanization, affluence, and other evidences of modernization, public attitudes in less developed countries are becoming more favorable to family planning, and fertility desires appear to be less than what might be expected.

In the long run this controversy will probably resolve itself with a more rounded concept of what constitutes adequate family planning services; that is, with the inclusion of motivation-generating devices within the concept of these services. Most successful programs have had an integral means of informing the target population, using mass media, posters, traveling shows, and other devices. In most developing countries, the quality and quantity of personnel to work at the clinic level is so questionable that one cannot surely say the existing program is being fully implemented. Experience from several programs suggests that the continued presence of a sufficient number of field workers at the clinic level is of key importance (Berelson, 1969). Lack of success in other programs has similarly been attributed to failure to put into place a cadre of trained field workers (International Bank for Reconstruction and Development, 1969).

In a growing number of countries a new motivational approach is being integrated into family planning services. This is the use of material incentives for acceptors to encourage their acceptance and continuation of family planning (Sprehe, 1971). The use of incentive payments has long been known in business and industry, as well as other areas of human life. Only recently, however, have incentives begun to play a role in family planning, although they were suggested by Enke (1960) over a decade ago. Basically there are two distinctions operative as to how incentives figure in family planning. First, there are *acceptor incentives* versus *administrative incentives:* incentives paid either to the person who accepts the family planning, or paid to someone else who is involved in acceptance such as nurse, physician, field worker, or "motivator." Second, there are *immediate and delayed incentives:* incentives paid on the spot, or incentives delayed to some future date.

A recent example of an integrated program of services and motivational efforts, including large acceptor incentives, has met with great success in India. In the district of Ernakulam, state of Kerala, a Family Welfare Festival was held during July 1971. Organized by the District Collector, Mr. Krishnakumar, the month-long festival was a masterpiece of public administration. Every organization, interest group, and other collective entity within the district was approached; teams of canvassers were organized; appeals were made by prominent persons. The purpose was a male vasectomy drive, and the 30-day goal was 20,000 acceptors. Using over 500 committees, continuous provision of services, and large incentives in money and goods, the festival managed to far overreach its target and accomplish some 63,418 acceptors. These figures represent several years of program objectives, accomplished in the space of four weeks (Krishnakumar, 1971).

Several attempts to copy this campaign, relying principally on increased incentives but lacking the entire Ernakulam spectrum of organization and services, were moderately successful, thereby demonstrating that an impact from incentives alone is possible, but also highly important is the intensive and well-organized informational and service program (Rogers, 1972).

An Ernakulam-style festival, offering a full range of services and motivational efforts, was repeated in the state of Gujarat from November 1971 to January 1972, and despite the disruption of war, 220,000 acceptors were reached, again for vasectomy. Twenty more such festivals are now planned in India, and the idea is spreading abroad.

At Ernakulam, four-fifths of those accepting vasectomy had monthly incomes of less than 100 rupees. Incentives distributed to acceptors amounted to approximately 130 rupees in cash value, more than a month's pay for most. Not surprisingly, such a large incentive, coupled with the highly organized program for delivery of services and a festival atmosphere, attracted high acceptance from the lower socioeconomic classes. Although we reported (in connection with discussion of Table 3) that innovations tend to be adopted by the upper classes and then trickle down to the lower classes, it appears that incentives—or perhaps one should say incentives-cum-organized-campaign—offer a device for breaking this pattern. Of course the payment to a poor man of the equivalent of more than a month's pay for a possibly irreversible sterilization may be considered exploitative in many cultures, and the possibility of a public opinion backlash exists.

Several programs have also begun using delayed acceptor incentives. Their rationale is somewhat different. Generally, immediate acceptor incentives perform as a kind of advertisement or immediate inducement for the undecided acceptor (although in the Ernakulam case this "nudge" was extraordinarily strong). The delayed incentives serve a different function; they provide an old age annuity for the acceptor. In return for foregoing additional children who might provide old age support, the family receives essentially an old age pension.

One such program, which owes its origins to Ridker (1971), is in operation on the tea estates in South India. The association of tea estate owners instituted a program in which, for every month in which a women in the program remains nonpregnant, several rupees are deposited in a blocked bank account. The account continues to grow and earn interest, but the woman can gain access to it only at a much later date, say when she reaches age 45. Intervening pregnancies result in progressive penalties to her account, or, if too many occur, cancellation of the account. A similar program on Taiwan capitalizes on the high value Taiwanese families place on education. The Taiwan educational bond program developed by Finnigan (1972) utilizes essentially the same program strategy as the tea estates, with the exception that the money is placed toward a bond for the education of existing children in the family; that is, the bond can only be "cashed" in terms of education.

Administrative incentives, which are basically a piecework form of payment and are principally of the immediate variety, have become an integral part of family planning programs in a number of countries, notably India and Pakistan. The Pakistan program claims that it could not succeed without such incentives; physicians can nearly double their incomes from insertion of IUDs.

Acceptor incentives, at least as practiced on a large scale and as an integral part of programs, are young to family planning. For many administrators, they pose problems of ethical acceptability and openness to fraud and graft. A key problem is the low "quality" of acceptors, the fact that many persons patronize the family planning services only to receive the incentives and will cease family planning as soon as payments cease (Sprehe, 1971). To the extent that low quality of acceptors continues to plague incentives programs, incentives are an expensive alternative not likely to persist over the long run, except perhaps in the case of irreversible family planning methods such as sterilization, where a continued relationship with the client is obviated. In principle, however, there is no reason why the problem of low-quality acceptors cannot be ameliorated with proper structuring of the incentives program. For example, if incentives can be given for avoiding pregnancy, incentives might also be given for attending instructional and motivational lectures concerning family planning.

An additional problem relating to the use of acceptor incentives relates to their cost compared to other program strategies. For example, to achieve sterilization coverage in India equivalent to that in Puerto Rico in 1965, that is, 34% of the 100 million eligible couples, would cost $562 million for acceptor incentives at the rates paid in Ernakulam. Total expenditures for family planning in India over the past decade totaled about half this amount (Speidel et al., 1972; Robinson, 1971).

The cost effectiveness of a program using incentives to recruit acceptors to the use of reversible contraceptives could be much less than for a sterilization program, since a considerable dropout rate can be expected with these means. And it may turn out that large acceptor incentive payments are only practical in a sterilization program.

Debates over incentives in family planning programs may be proving increasingly nugatory. Incentives apparently appeal to program administrators with their promise of dramatic leaps in service statistics and publicity value. Prior to widespread application of more incentive schemes, research is needed to examine cost effectiveness, political acceptability, and organizational feasibility; this should be the careful experimental type of research recommended by Rogers in his recent survey (Rogers, 1972b).

3. *The Role of Fertility Control Technology.* Availability of adequate means of fertility control is a crucial factor in the success of family planning programs. Experience in many cultures suggests that for some individuals some methods are easy to use and others are difficult (Berelson, 1970; Ravenholt, 1969). The interrelationship between existence and availability of various means of fertility control technology and programatic requirements is outlined in Table 5.

It has proven easier to introduce modern and easy-to-use means of fertility control than to increase motivation to the point where the more difficult methods can be used. This situation has been most clearly demonstrated in countries where delivery systems are adequate to meet the needs of the society. In the United States, only with the advent of the pill and the IUD was it possible to extend fertility control services to many members of the poorer segments of the U.S. population. Planned Parenthood clinics, which service a low-income clientele in the United States, noted a doubling or tripling of their patient population when the pill and the IUD became available (Ravenhold et al., 1971). Only with the advent of these methods have reasonably successful mass programs become possible among unsophisticated populations. Pills are easy to administer and require no relationship to sexual activity. The IUD, although requiring a more clinical procedure for insertion, does not require sustained motivation.

Many individuals, particularly in developing countries, have been successful in using foresight means of fertility control (contraceptives). For many others in all societies the motivation and ability to deal with the established reality of pregnancy or the suspicion of pregancy is much greater. Consequently it is felt that access to hindsight (postconceptive) means of fertility control is imperative for controlling fertility (Ravenholt et al., 1971; Speidel et al., 1971; Potts, 1970).

Moreover, it has been demonstrated that there are an appreciable number of failures associated with the use of all reversible means of contraception, either because of lack of use or failure of the contraceptive. Even when used properly, a not insignificant number of contraceptive failures will result over perhaps 20 years of sexual activity per woman, and access to hindsight means is thus essential to maintain satisfactory control over fertility (Speidel et al., 1971).

Although relatively neglected by most official family planning programs, surgical termination of pregnancy may reach more than 30 million women annually. This method, abortion, is probably the single most important means of fertility control on a world-wide basis (Hauser, 1971; Potts, 1971; United Nations, 1972). With the passage of India's medical termination of pregnancy act on August 2, 1971, and the availability of improved knowledge of the nature of fertility control activities in the People's Republic of China, it can now be estimated that a majority of the world's population lives in areas where abortion is legal.

Inevitably, we are on the threshold of greatly increased use of abortion in the less developed countries. When legal barriers guarding access to hindsight means have been removed, their popularity has amply demonstrated itself. Following the pattern of Eastern Europe and Japan, the tremendous surge of abortions in Great Britain and New York in the past few years has placed heavy burdens on medical facilities. These burdens will only be compounded in less developed countries, where lack of an adequate clinical delivery system is a serious bottleneck to extension of presently available means for surgical termination of pregnancy. Realization of this condition has stimulated research programs on the part of some organizations such as the Agency for International Development to perfect a hindsight, self-administered means of fertility control independent of clinical delivery systems (Speidel at al., 1971).

A synergistic relationship seems to exist between each of the various

Table 5 Birth Control Technology and Implications for Family Planning
Programs

Technology Tiers	Advent of Method	Methods Generally Available	Family Planning Program Needs
5	1970s?	Methods listed below plus: "a nontoxic and completely effective substance or method which when self-administered on a single occasion would ensure the nonpregnant state at completion of a monthly cycle"	Minimal regulation of sexual activity. Reduced need for education. Main emphasis on ensuring availability of contraceptives and postconceptives through medical and nonmedical facilities
4	1970s	Methods listed below plus legal surgical abortion	Slight regulation of sexual activity; less emphasis on education, main emphasis on provision of contraceptive services through medical and nonmedical facilities and abortion services through medical facilities

modern fertility control methods and the population at risk. Younger,
lower parity women prefer use of the pill. Women in their 30s and 40s of
higher parity prefer IUDs, and those who wish to terminate fecundity
often select sterilization (Ravenholt, 1971). At present, those obtaining
sterilization operations do so at advanced ages and high parities, so that
the demographic impact of this method is less than ideal (Presser, 1970).
However, much evidence suggests that it is the program requirements
concerning the number of children a woman must have had before the
operation is allowed which accounts for this situation (Presser, 1970; Speidel, 1972).

Programs relying on only a few methods of fertility control have
usually been less successful than those offering a variety of techniques.
This finding is completely understandable in view of the preferences
mentioned in the previous paragraph. The removal of barriers to availability, particularly through the private sector, has proven to be an im-

Technology Tiers	Advent of Method	Methods Generally Available	Family Planning Program Needs
3	1960s	Methods listed below plus oral contraceptives and intrauterine devices	Some regulation of sexual activity; continued emphasis on education and provision of contraceptives and family planning services through medical and nonmedical facilities
2	Before 1960	Methods listed below plus condoms, diaphragms, vaginal chemicals, rhythm, and surgical sterilization	Considerable regulation of sexual activity; emphasis on education and provision of materials and services through medical and nonmedical facilities
1	Before 1870	Abstinence, coitus interruptus, delayed marriage and non-marriage, crude vaginal barriers (e.g., sponges) douching, and illegal abortion	Strict regulation of sexual activity; emphasis on education

Source. R. T. Ravenholt, P. T. Piotrow, and J. J. Speidel, "Use of Oral Contraceptives: A Decade of Controversy," *Int. J. Gyn. Obst.* 8:94 (November 1970).

portant change strategy in opening up the availability of contraceptive technology, and a very valuable adjunct to official family planning programs. In this regard, it is interesting to consider Brazil, which has no official family planning programs, although BEMFAM, a private organization, has worked unopposed. It is estimated that 3.25 million women in Brazil (22% of those married) use the pill. About 2.5 million of these users (17% of married women) buy the pill from physicians' offices, drugstores, and other commercial outlets (Sanders, 1971; IPPF, 1971). Annual outlays of $80 million in India (fiscal 1970–1971) have been required to achieve program coverage of 12.7% of eligible couples (Government of India, 1972). Yet India has failed to introduce oral contraceptives into its program, preferring to rely on sterilization, IUDs, and, more recently, the condom. The impact of the recent change of abortion laws in India is as yet minimal, although it is estimated that some 4:5 million abortions, mostly illegal, occur in India annually (Agency for International Development, 1970).

4. Organization, Administration, and Personnel for Family Planning Programs. The development of adequate institutions and organizations to insure delivery of family planning services is one of the most difficult tasks relating to solution of population problems in developing countries. Sollins and Belsky (1970) have shown that the private sector contributes an appreciable proportion of family planning services in all countries, even those which are less developed. If abortion services were included in Table 6, the percentage of services delivered through official organized programs would be considerably lower.

Success of organized family planning programs in developing countries has varied considerably. Coverage ranges from 0.3 to 45% of eligible women aged 15 to 44 (Nortman, 1970; Berelson, 1970). Table 7 gives an indication of this coverage, and Table 8 shows an estimate of total world use of fertility control means.

The true impact on fertility made by these programs is difficult to assess. Many countries with so-called successful family planning programs —Hong Kong, Singapore, South Korea, Taiwan—experienced a trend to decreased birth rates prior to initiation of family planning programs, yet undoubtedly the programs have accelerated this trend and increased its

Table 6 Percentage of Family Planning Services and Supplies Provided to Users by Official Governmental Program (January 1969), Selected Countries

Country	Percentage
India	87
South Korea	84
Ceylon	76
Tunisia	66
Egypt	60
Malaysia	57
Turkey	57
Thailand	56
Taiwan	53
Iran	50
Kenya	50
Morocco	40
Singapore	24

Source. B. Berelson, "The Present State of Family Planning Programs," *Studies in Family Planning, 57* (September 1970).

Table 7 Proportion of Married Women of Reproductive Age Provided Family Planning Services in National Programs in Developing Countries

Country	Percentage
Hong Kong	45
South Korea	42
Singapore	37
Taiwan	31
Chile	22
Pakistan	13
India	10
Tunisia	10
Kenya	7
Dominican Republic	7
Ceylon	6
Malaysia	6
Thailand	6
Colombia	4
Turkey	2
Iran	1.5
Morocco	0.8
Nepal	0.3

Source.   B. Berelson, "The Present State of Family Planning Programs," *Studies in Family Planning, 57* (September 1970).

Table 8 Estimated World Use of Means of Fertility Control in 1971 *(a)* (prevalence in millions)

Method	Users in Developed Countries	Users in Less Developed Countries	Total
Surgical sterilization	10	15	25
Oral contraceptives	20	10	30
Intrauterine devices	5	7	12
Condoms	12	13	25
Diaphragm, spermicides, withdrawal, rhythm, and other methods	18	34	52
Surgical termination of pregnancy *(b)*	10	22	32

Source.   J. J. Speidel, R. T. Ravenholt, and M. I. Perry, "Non-Clinical Distribution of Oral Contraceptives," *Advances in Planned Parenthood,* Volume VIII (in press).
(a) Excludes Mainland China.
(b) Annual incidence.

magnitude appreciably. A crude assessment of the current status of fertility control efforts can be seen from the fact that the current annual birth rate per thousand population for the world is about 34. To achieve a stable population or zero population growth, this birth rate must be brought down to match the annual death rate per thousand population, which on a world-wide basis now stands at about 14. Since there exists a theoretical maximum of about 60 births per thousand, these figures suggest that current world fertility is about halfway to its goal.

Lest one become too pessimistic about the current status of family planning programs, it should be borne in mind that a tremendous amount has already been achieved at very low cost. Robinson (1971) estimated the cost per acceptor of family planning services to be somewhere in the order of $10 to $15 per acceptor per year. Judged by this standard, it is obvious that total allocations for family planning services have been very low in relation to the need. Per capita governmental allocations for family planning programs can in fact be counted in pennies: in countries such as Kenya, Morocco, and Nepal, less than 2¢ per year. Other countries—Iran, Turkey, Malaysia, South Korea, Taiwan, and Egypt—have ranged from 2 to 8¢ per year, and only in India and Pakistan have per capita allocations been 9¢ or more per year. In countries with national family planning programs, budgets for these programs may range as high as 25% of the health budget, as in Pakistan, or even 50%, as in India. More typically, they are about 0.5 to 5%.

The total funds allocated to family planning by developing countries and donor nations is estimated at around $350 million annually. Approximately 50% of this amount comes from the donor nations in developed countries (Ravenholt, 1972). This figure may be compared to the budget of approximately $15 billion spent annually for health in less developed countries (Howard, 1971). The 1960s saw the growing awareness of the population problem and the establishment of national family planning programs, but the total monetary support for these programs remains low in comparison to needs. Looking at the total governmental budget, only India is placing as much as 1% annually into family planning. More typically the figures range from 0.01 to 0.1%. One optimistic note is the fact that donor agencies from developed countries have rapidly increased their support for family planning services in less developed countries recently (Nortman, 1970).

Any assessment of the current status of national family planning programs finds obvious lacks in coverage. In Africa, services are simply unavailable for the majority of the population. Even in India, with annual inputs of $80 million annually, the network of field workers and those required to deliver services cannot serve the 80% of the population who are illiterate and rural. India has established the very modest target of one field worker per 50,000 population and yet has only one worker per 100,000 population in place (International Bank for Reconstruction and Development, 1969). Successful pilot projects in India indicate that perhaps as much as one worker per 10,000 population is necessary for satisfactory results (Speidel, 1971; Majumdan et al., 1971). In other words, India might need up to ten times its current coverage in order to provide adequate services.

Beyond Family Planning. Family planning programs to date have had limited success. Their lack of convincingly demonstrated success in relation to the enormous need for fertility control has caused critics to suggest that societies must turn to other alternatives. In general defense of family planning, it may be said that current programs are new, functioning in extremely difficult settings with very limited resources and often only a marginal national commitment to their success.

Only a few developed or less developed countries have established reasonably accessible and well publicized family planning programs offering the best currently available means of fertility control. These programs have experienced high utilization of such services and significant declines in fertility, particularly when abortion is available. Therefore present experience suggests that whatever measures may actually be necessary to reduce fertility current, family planning programs have not yet satisfied existing demand.

Proposals put forward by the critics of family planning are often drastic and coercive and infringe on the human rights of persons. From the critics' point of view, there is the urgency of time, the fact that present programs may only be helping us to lose ground more slowly, but still to lose ground against a truly formidable problem.

The principal strategy for managing reduction in population growth still appears to be the family planning approach. Other strategies suggested in this paper—use of incentive payments, improvement of fertility control technology, a push for better policies, attention to organization and administration—all hinge on the assumption that they are to be integrated into family planning.

Critics have made some telling points against this strategy. The difficulty lies in the provision of equally attractive alternatives. Berelson has suggested six criteria by which to evaluate the alternatives: (1) scientific readiness; (2) political viability; (3) administrative feasibility; (4) economic capability; (5) ethical acceptability; and (6) presumed effectiveness. Against these criteria one can measure some of the alternative proposals to family planning (Saunders, 1970).

Table 9 Selected Measures of Family Planning Program Performance

Country	1961	1962	1963	1964	1965	1966	1967	1968	1969	1970
	Equivalent Dollar Expenditure per Eligible Couple									
Coverage										
Chile	—	—	—	0.17	0.31	0.79	0.75	1.22	—	—
India	0.04	0.07	0.07	.12	.22	.23	.43	.47	—	—
Korea	—	.10	.17	.32	.39	.70	.73	1.00	.64	—
Malaysia	—	—	—	—	—	—	.41	.56	—	—
Pakistan	—	—	—	—	—	.35	.56	.76	—	—
Taiwan	—	—	—	.09	.33	.29	.33	.42	.44	—
Tunisia	—	—	—	—	—	—	—	1.13	—	—
	Percent of Eligible Couples Contracepting via the Program at End of Year									
Acceptance										
Chile	0.4	0.5	—	1.2	4.6	7.2	8.8	12.7	—	—
India	—	0.5	1.1	1.6	3.0	4.4	6.3	8.1	—	—
Korea	—	.1	.7	8.1	13.2	18.8	20.4	20.1	23.0	—
Malaysia	—	—	—	—	—	—	.9	4.3	7.0	—
Pakistan	—	—	—	—	—	2.8	7.9	14.0	17.8	—
Taiwan	—	—	—	2.3	6.2	8.9	11.4	13.1	14.0	—
Tunisia	—	—	—	.3	1.8	3.1	3.4	3.9	5.0	—

Births Averted as Percentage of Births Expected in Absence of Program

Effectiveness

Chile	—	—	—	—	1.3	5.2	8.1	9.8	14.0	—
India	0.2	0.4	0.5	1.0	1.5	2.8	4.1	5.9	7.5	—
Korea	—	—	.1	.6	6.2	10.5	15.2	16.2	15.7	18.1
Malaysia	—	—	—	—	—	—	—	.9	4.4	7.2
Pakistan	—	—	—	—	—	—	2.3	6.5	11.6	14.9
Taiwan	—	—	—	—	1.9	4.9	6.8	8.6	9.5	9.9
Tunisia	—	—	—	—	.3	1.9	3.2	3.5	4.0	5.1

Cost-effectiveness

Equivalent Dollar Expenditure per Birth Averted

Chile	—	—	—	13.99	11.03	19.08	14.30	17.76	—	—
India	11.54	16.35	10.94	12.26	10.88	8.01	8.67	10.60	—	—
Korea	—	47.43	13.90	7.79	7.66	9.36	11.70	19.57	—	—
Malaysia	—	—	—	—	—	—	113.84	33.20	32.99	—
Pakistan	—	—	—	—	—	28.67	16.62	10.68	—	—
Taiwan	—	—	—	10.04	17.30	13.76	14.07	17.20	17.81	—
Tunisia	—	—	—	—	—	—	—	58.63	—	—

Source. Population Program Assistance, Agency for International Development, Washington, D.C., 1971.

Table 10 Illustrative Appraisal of Proposals by Criteria

	Scientific Readiness	Political Viability	Administrative Feasibility	Economic Capability	Ethical Acceptability	Presumed Effectiveness
Extension of voluntary fertility control	High	High on maternal care, moderate to low on abortion	Uncertain in near future	Maternal care too costly for local budget, abortion feasible	High for maternal care, low for abortion	Moderately high
Establishment of involuntary fertility control	Low	Low	Low	High	Low	High
Intensified educational campaigns	High	Moderate to high	High	Probably high	Generally high	Moderate
Incentive programs	High	Moderately low	Low	Low to moderate	Low to high	Uncertain

Tax and welfare benefits and penalties	High	Moderately low	Low	Low to moderate	Low to moderate	Uncertain
Shifts in social and economic institutions	High	Generally high, but low on some specifics	Low	Generally low	Generally high, but uneven	High, over long run
Political channels and organizations	High	Low	Low	Moderate	Moderately low	Uncertain
Augmented research efforts	Moderate	High	Moderate to high	High	High	Uncertain
Family planning programs	Generally high, but could use improved technology	Moderate to high	Moderate to high	High	Generally high, but uneven on religious grounds	Moderately high

Source. B. Berelson, "Beyond Family Planning," *Studies in Family Planning* (February 1969).

Some have suggested extension of voluntary fertility control by link-ing family planning services to other programs, for example, agricultural extension services. Others urge making family planning an integral part of some form of curative medical care; maternal and child health services are most frequently mentioned. These proposals do not go truly beyond family planning. Rather, they extend the concept or graft it to something else. In the case of the two proposals just mentioned, the key questions are perhaps administrative feasibility and economic capability, both of which bear on presumed effectiveness. In other words, could the "host systems" of agricultural extension services and maternal and child health care bear the increased burden of family planning, and if they took it on would it really lead to more effective family planning?

Other proposals are somewhat more drastic. The establishment of in-voluntary fertility control by mass use of as-yet-undeveloped fertility con-trol agents has been suggested; this is the "put something in the water supply" approach. Others have urged licenses for having children, legal limits on the number of children, or complusory sterilization after a stated number of children. The politico-legal-ethical aspects of these pro-posals bar their serious exploration for the short-run future. Less drastic means are going in these directions already: legal barriers to availability of family planning services, including abortion, are gradually being re-moved, and more countries are reexamining pronatalist laws such as those relating to income taxes and maternity benefits.

In conclusion, it appears that the family planning approach is likely to continue for some time to be the principal strategy for planned social change in the area of fertility reduction. Much remains to be done in the adequate implementation of the strategy. In many places it is too nar-rowly conceived: the full range of contraceptive and postconceptive tech-nology is not available, and the organization and administration are con-stricted by lack of sufficient qualified personnel and a full panoply of educational and motivational devices. Yet, within Callahan's (1972) limits of "excluding social repression and mindful of maximizing human freedom," family planning is the best available alternative today for coping with the fertility factor in the population problem.

PART FIVE
SOCIAL ISSUES IN SOCIAL CHANGE

This concluding section contains three chapters. The first concerns the need for evaluative research to provide remedial feedback for social action programs. The second chapter discusses the partisan nature for social programs including programs of research, intervention, and evaluation. The final chapter in this book focuses on the ethics of planned and unplanned intervention in social affairs. There seems to be a general consensus among social scientists that these three issues are among the most significant issues in social change today and it is appropriate that we conclude with these significant chapters.

Despite the great prevalence of privately and publicly supported programs of planned change and the vast resources expended for their implementation, we are still in a stage of infancy in terms of learning about the effectiveness of such programs. This has been noted earlier by Teune. Technically sound evaluative research built into programs of planned change is a rarity. Moreover, it is certain that progress in the social technology of conducting effective programs of planned social change will be slow until scientific evaluative research is made an integral part of change programs. Charles Kiesler in his chapter "Evaluating Social Change Programs" discusses some of the reasons why true experiments are seldom performed in change programs. He also presents needed guidelines and suggestions for conducting evaluative research, pointing to particular hazards and raising important questions often left out of discussions of evaluative research. His ideas concerning the "bargain alternative" and his concept of "middle-level testing" are most intriguing. Equally interesting and laudable is his insistence that greater attention be given to substantive theory in evaluative research. "Any statement whatsoever of a way to implement an objective of a social change program is a theoretical statement whether explicitly recognized or not." We need clear statements not only of the objectives of a program but why a program should work—

what the theory is which is being tested. The evaluation of a program of social change is inherently an evaluation of a theoretical cause and effect relationship.

The challenge to the reader is clear: Make true experiments out of your social change efforts. This is a task requiring much ingenuity, particularly in natural environments where perhaps much more ingenuity or creativity is needed than in any other experimental situation.

Although scholars would like to believe otherwise—and surprisingly large numbers do believe otherwise—the notion of a value-free social science is a myth. Scholars and their research are not value free nor is the utilizations of their work value free. It is no less important to keep this in mind during the process of diagnosing social problems to be researched than when involved with research itself. This is the major theme of the provocative chapter by Alan Guskin and Mark Chesler, "Partisan Diagnosis of Social Problems." As they write, "The academic researcher cannot assess accurately the human meaning of crisis and conflict in communities, schools and so forth, because his distance is a barrier to seeing the critical issues to be studied. It is only through close involvement that one can really understand and therefore conduct effective scholarship for social problems and issues. Mutual involvement in diagnosis then makes such scholarship and the scholarly process partisan. . . . The questions are: 'Whose side are you on? and, Do you know it?'" The human character as well as scientific research methodology make value neutrality impossible. It becomes a must for scientists to be conscious and deliberate about their partisanship. In developing this theme Guskin and Chesler discuss differences between social diagnosis and social research, methodological issues in partisan scholarship, the use of diagnostic methods and information utilization issues.

For the reader, perhaps the major challenge among many in this chapter is: Are you aware of your own partisanship in your selection of social problem areas for study, in your definition of social problems in that context, and in the research you carry out as a response to the problem? Diagnosis of one's own partisanship is a difficult task but may well be an obligatory one for scholars. At the very least it may be an obligation owed to the consumers of research.

There are either latent or manifest ethical issues involved in all instances of social change. Alterations in the structure and/or function of any aspect of society may bring about changes in reward structures and in other systems in which value and ethical systems are rooted; in fact, changes in value systems may be requisites for change in the structure and functioning of society. In the first instance the change agent may not deliberately seek alterations in value systems, whereas in the later instance he does. The ethical issue, however, is of equal importance in both contexts. Donald Warwick and Herbert Kelman in "Ethical Issues in Social Intervention" explore a number of the ethical and value dimensions of social change. They define social intervention as "any act, planned or unplanned, that alters the characteristics· of another individual or the pattern of relationships between individuals." Note that they include within their purview unplanned as well as planned change, and they discuss alternative strategies of social change. In their discussion of ethics of social intervention they cover such topics as value preferences and value conflicts, choice of goals, definition of target, choice of means, and assessment of consequences.

The concluding chapter may well be the most provocative in this book, since it concerns a topic which is a vital part of the activities of all scientists. The questions raised demand answers, although the answers do not come forth very readily. The reader is challenged to identify in his own work the manifestation of the issues raised by Warwick and Kelman, to look at the position he takes, and to ask what the consequences are. Even those who disdain active participation in social change are not free to turn away from the issues and questions posed, since abstinence is a form of social intervention.

Charles A. Kiesler

Department of Psychology
University of Kansas

EVALUATING SOCIAL CHANGE PROGRAMS [1]

How does one evaluate social change programs? There are two main approaches, one philosophical and one scientific.[2] The philosophical asks questions of values: Is this change desirable for society? Is it morally defensible? Are the values and goals of one part of a society being imposed on another? These are issues of conscience, and perhaps no one individual is better able to speak on them than another. Such moral questions should and hopefully will be raised regarding any program for social change.

There are also scientific evaluations of social change programs: Did any change whatsoever occur? Who changed? Why? Which parts of the program were critical in producing the effect? What is our theoretical understanding of the change? Could the same effect be produced in other, perhaps less expensive, ways? Will the change generalize to other settings or programs (e.g., does learning letters from *Sesame Street* facilitate acquiring reading skills later?)?

The present chapter discusses only the scientific issues. Did change occur? How much? To whom? Why? Does it generalize? Are there theoretically equivalent ways to reproduce the same effect?

A complete treatment of these issues would involve a thorough discussion of social science theory, experimental design, and statistics. The issues are very complex, and no single chapter could hope to cover all, or perhaps any, adequately. We can and will skim only a few highlights that strike the author as important. For readers wanting a more complete treatment, there is a new *Handbook of Evaluation Research* now in preparation (Guttentag and Strunening, in preparation), and judging from the chapter titles and authors, it will be excellent. Also, for anyone interested in evaluation research, Campbell and Stanley's *Experimental and Quasi-experimental Designs for Research on Teaching* (1963) is a must.[3]

Let me also confess my bias, and hence the slant of this chapter. I am an experimental social psychologist with interests in both method and theory. I am not an expert in evaluation research and make no pretense of so being. But the perspective of the experimental social psychologist can be useful to the evaluation researcher. I cannot circumscribe the area, of course, but the issues to be raised in this chapter are important ones, and they are often left out of discussions of evaluation research.

Caro (1969) suggests that there is general agreement that in principle evaluative research is no different from other forms of social science research in terms of methodology: *the classical experimental design is the accepted basic model.* Indeed, it is this ultimate reliance on the experimental method that distinguishes the social scientist's approach to evaluation research from the more impressionistic methods of administrators and journalists. It is within this context of the experimental method that an experimental social psychologist might have something of interest to say.

However, many sophisticated social scientists feel—and rightly so—that the problems of experimental method represent only some of the difficulties facing the evaluation researcher. There are many other complex issues and problems specific to evaluation research about which the outsider is naive. For example, there are questions of relationships to administrators and others within social action programs; whether an evaluation researcher should be an insider or an outsider; problems in gaining cooperation from agencies; and issues relating to publication of sensitive data. The laboratory social psychologist is unlikely to have much worthwhile to add here. This chapter ignores all of these complicated issues not because they are unimportant but because many others have considered them at length.

In the discussion to follow, we will touch on a few selected issues of experimental method that are related to problems typically found in evaluative research. We will discuss some persistent problems of statistics and design, raise some issues relevant to theory, suggest the use of the concept of the "bargain alternative" in evaluative research, bring up the idea of middle-level testing, and end with some general discussion.

Statistical Design Issues:
Did the Treatment Have Any Effect?

Randomization

As mentioned, the logic of experimental design underlies evaluative research and distinguishes it from more impressionistic interpretations. Particularly for the social sciences, the core of the experimental method is random assignment of subjects to conditions. *Absolutely nothing* is more important to precise experimentation than the random assignment of subjects. One cannot have a true experiment without randomization.

Human activity is very complex, and human behavior is multiply determined. One cannot select small segments of a given person's life and make confident predictions about his future behavior or feelings, because of other potentially important variables related to these small segments. When differences other than controlled treatments exist between groups we cannot be absolutely certain that effects are due to treatments or to the associated variables. If, for example, experimental and control groups differ intellectually (e.g., in IQ), demographically (e.g., in social class), or in psychological environment (e.g., parents may volunteer their children for a study because they are interested in their achievement or development and may treat them differently at home as well), then the inference regarding treatment effects is limited.

These variables may also interact with one another. Suppose one tests a high-IQ group and a low-IQ group of first-graders and finds a two-month difference in reading level between the two groups. Does this mean that in the absence of other treatments or events the two groups will differ by two reading levels two years later? No, it does not; further, it is likely that the difference between the two groups will become larger over time. If we treat the lower IQ group with a remedial reading course and find that two years later they still differ by two reading levels, may we say that the remedial reading course was successful since the two groups would have been further apart without it? No, we may not, if we have no evidence about how far apart they would be without the treatment. We also could not say that the remedial reading course would benefit even lower IQ groups.

It is plausible that the treatment variable (the reading course) statistically interacts with both the levels variable (IQ) and a temporal variable (whatever could produce differences in effects over time without treatment). To make a straightforward inference of treatment effects, it is necessary to randomly assign subjects to conditions within IQ levels. The best way to test the effect of a remedial reading course is to randomly assign children within each of several levels of IQ to either the remedial reading course or a control group. There is no other impeccable way to test the effect of such a treatment, except random assignment. One can attempt to approximate an experiment (using, e.g., some of the quasi-experimental designs suggested by Campbell and Stanley, 1963), but there are serious problems with such attempts, as discussed later. We shall also mention later that there can be serious problems with the experimental method using randomization, but in spite of these problems, there is really no satisfactory alternative.

When we attempt to evaluate a social program (or anything else, for that matter), what we want and need first is a clear-cut answer to the question, "Did the program have an effect on the recipients?" If one wants a clear-cut answer to that question, then one should use the best methods he has to bear on it. Underlying all of those methods is the principle of randomization.

The importance of randomization is obvious, but few seem to attend to it. An enormous amount of time, energy, and money is wasted in half-hearted attempts to evaluate social change programs. One can say on *a priori* grounds that the vast majority of such attempts are doomed to failure before they commence. For example, McDill, McDill, and Sprehe (1969) reviewed 66 attempts to evaluate the Head Start Program carried out between the years 1965 and 1967. Of these, they excluded 35 from the discussion because they presented no evidence pro or con on cognitive growth, but instead took the form of testimonials or subjective impressions by the investigator. Of the remaining 31 studies, 14 used before-after comparisons but did not include control groups. Only 17 of 66 studies used a before-after design with control groups, less than 25% of the total batch of studies reviewed. "However, even in the 17 studies employing control groups, random assignment of students to one or the other category was the exception." (p. 19) Even the large national study (Cicirelli, 1969), which used almost 2000 children as subjects, did not randomly assign them to conditions.

McDill, McDill, and Sprehe found that only 11 of the 31 studies presenting evidence on cognitive development demonstrated any clearly positive effect of Head Start experiences. Campbell and Erlebacher (1970) claim that five of these 11 studies used randomly assigned control groups and that all five showed significant gains on some cognitive measures. They further say that of the five with quasi-experimental controls (i.e., not randomly assigned), only one study showed a significant effect, suggesting that "the most plausible explanation [of the lack of results] seems to us to be the bias of the superior control group in the quasi-experimental studies."

It is only by a random assignment of subjects to conditions that the effects of other variables related to the dependent measures (aside from the independent variable) can be cancelled out. True experiments are far more informative than quasi-experiments or *ex post facto* designs. Campbell and Erlebacher say that data ". . . from 400 children from such an experiment would be far more informative than 4,000 tested by the best quasi-experiments, to say nothing of an *ex post facto* study." Everyone seems to acknowledge that the true experiment is the most powerful evaluative device that the researcher has at his disposal. Why don't people use it more often? Why did only five of 66 studies designed to evaluate Head Start programs use the minimally acceptable procedure?

There are a number of reasons given why true experiments are seldom done:

1. *Time.* Social action programs are often approved at the last minute and designed to be implemented immediately. The evaluative researcher has to scramble to do the best he can under the circumstances.

2. *Political pressures.* The mechanics for evaluation are often politically determined and occasionally even written into the executive order or law. Thus an order implementing a given program can, by its very wording, prevent the researcher from employing a random procedure. The Title I program explicitly prohibits using control groups in evaluation, for example.

3. *Convinced actionists.* Many people involved in implementing a program (e.g., remedial reading, Head Start, Upward Bound) begin the program by being convinced that it will have an enormous impact on the recipients. Being convinced of this in advance of evaluation, the actionist is loathe to have any control group—to prevent anyone from receiving the "beneficial treatment." However, effects of treatments are empirical questions, and in the absence of a control group, one cannot even claim an effect, beneficial or otherwise. Such altruism is misplaced, since the treatment could be harmful or replaced by a more effective program.

4. *Antiscientific attitudes.* Many actionists are not involved with obtaining the best evaluation possible, because they believe that social science methods are neither reliable nor valid. One could only say that if it were really true that on the average five out of every 66 evaluation studies employed randomization, then one could understand the actionist's doubts about the reliability and validity of the results.

5. *Contamination.* Many argue that experimental groups often con-

taminate the control groups; that there is communication between the two groups, rendering the control group "partly treated." This sometimes is the case, but if one is sampling from a large enough group of subjects, one can usually control communication between small groups of experimental and control subjects. It is instructive to point out that a contaminated control group may provide a more conservative test of the hypothesis. If the control group is contaminated but there is still a difference on the dependent measures between the control and experimental groups, one could only conclude that if the contamination had been contained, the difference on the dependent measures would have been larger. However, this is after the fact, and any interpretation depends upon clean results. Contamination should be avoided and perhaps the best method is having small numbers of individuals participating in the research, but randomly drawn from a (numerically and geographically) much larger population.

Evans and Schiller (1970) present the case for the status quo as follows:

> Our experience leads us to conclude, though reluctantly, that in the actual time pressured and politically loaded circumstances in which social action programs inevitably arise, the instances when random assignment is practical are rare; and the nature of political and governmental processes makes it likely that this will continue to be the case. Unfortunately, the political process is not orderly, scheduled, or rational. Crests of public and congressional support for social action programs often swell quickly and with little anticipation. Once legislation is enacted, the pressures on administrators for swift program implementation are intense. In these circumstances—which are the rule rather than the exception—pleas that the program should be implemented carefully, along the lines of a true experiment with the random assignment of subjects so that we can confidently evaluate the program's effectiveness, are bound to be ignored (pp. 217–218).

Campbell and Erlebacher argue for dramatic change. They recommend that a national group be formed, recognized as having the requisite competence and objectivity to rule on evaluation programs. They suggest that instead of acceding to the political pressures of the moment, that social scientists as a group organize against them and educate the politicians about the importance of impeccable evaluation designs. From this point of view, a national council could insist that social change programs be evaluated consistent with acceptable methodological and experimental techniques drawn from the social sciences. When the government or agencies in question do not accept a reasonable method of evaluating a social change program, Campbell and Erlebacher suggest that the social and behavioral scientists withdraw from the evaluation—that no scientific evaluation be done at all. They say that it is fundamentally misleading to lend the prestige of science to any report in a situation where no scientific evaluation is possible. Evans and Schiller refer to this view as remarkably naive.[4] In this controversy, the present writer, although recognizing some of the difficulties of convincing people to allow adequate evaluative research to be carried out, stands firmly on the side of Campbell and Erlebacher. Of course, it is difficult for science to insist that adequate research methods be used in evaluative programs. But as long as science acquiesces to unnecessarily less rigorous techniques of evaluation, the situation will certainly not change.

These issues refer only to the feasibility of randomization. In a personal communication, Thomas Cook has suggested to me that there are also several problems associated with the implementation and maintenance of any randomization procedure. For example, if one is dealing with large units such as organizations, the number of available units may be so small as to preclude pretreatment equivalence through randomization. Moreover, some treatments may be difficult or costly, and subjects may either refuse to participate in a particular condition or show differential attrition rates between conditions. Cook also suggests that authorities may be incompetent to randomize adequately, and he cites the 1969 draft lottery as an example. Cook's analysis of these issues is very penetrating. Randomization is difficult from all perspectives—initial procedure, implementation, and maintenance—but unfortunately there usually is no adequate substitute.

Selected Problems with Nonrandomization

The model underlying evaluation research is the experimental one. A critical underlying assumption of the experimental model is the random assignment of subjects to treatments, including control conditions. After reviewing the literature on the evaluation of social change programs, one could pragmatically say that one decent study with randomized assignment of subjects gives about as much or more information than 20 studies of any other variety. This is not a rule of thumb of research design. Rather it is an observation on the state of evaluation research, and what has taken place under that guise.

Of course, it is not always possible to employ randomization. However, in reviewing the literature, it is my impression that in over half of the evaluation studies, randomization could have been used when it was not. It was not used either because the investigator was not tenacious or ingenious enough to think of a suitable method, or he set his sights too low and was willing to settle for a less acceptable research method without giving the matter sufficient thought. Funding agencies should not allow the issue to be settled so easily and should demand detailed explanations of why randomization is not proposed in any study. A surprising amount of evaluation research should have been considered worthless on *a priori* grounds and never seriously considered for funding.

If it seems obvious that randomization cannot be used, then there are several methods available to the researcher to approximate the control of the experimental method. Campbell (1957; Campbell and Stanley, 1963) in particular has written brilliantly on the topic of quasi-experimental design. But perhaps some of the warnings he has raised regarding specific design issues have not received sufficient attention, and it may be worthwhile to bring them up again here.

Matching. One method often used to attain statistical equivalence between experimental and control groups is to try to match them on relevant characteristics. For example, suppose one wished to measure the impact of psychotherapy. If one believes that psychotherapy has significant impact, then one perhaps would be unwilling to prevent people from undergoing it, or even to hold them in abeyance until the efficacy of the treatment is demonstrated. Hence one might not want to assign equally sick people to psychotherapy and control groups. Therefore, one might do as has often been done in such outcome studies: One would use as the experimental group people who showed up asking for psychotherapy and then search for an equivalent control group. But equivalent how? If one considers psychotherapy to deal with treatment of neuroses, then one method might be to find a control group whose neuroticism scores on some personality test matched those of the experimental group.

As Campbell has pointed out, this is a highly suspect procedure. It is never an adequate method of control unless either the population means and variances of the matched variable are the same for the two groups (sick and well), or the index matched on is perfectly reliable (i.e., unlikely to change with retesting). [5] Regression effects usually contaminate the results with such a precedure.

Most psychological indices do not have perfect reliability. That is, an individual will not receive the identical score on a second testing as on the first, whether the test involved is a personality test, IQ test, reading level, judgments of teacher competence, satisfaction with one's environment, or whatever. The tests have some error in them and it is assumed that over the total population this error in a given testing is randomly distributed. However, if one selects out a subgroup of the total population on the basis of test score—particularly an extreme subgroup

—then the assumption that the error in the test score is random is no longer tenable. In a given testing, extreme groups are likely to have error in their test score associated with the extremity. Retesting will cancel out this error, and the second scores will be closer to the population mean. Therefore, if one selects out the five children receiving the highest scores on an IQ test in a high school and gives them the same test again, he finds in general that their scores are lower on the second testing. If one selects out the five people with the lowest scores on the test, he finds that they gain on the retest. When one nonrandomly selects people on the basis of almost any test score, he finds that the error in the original score is not random either.

Returning to our psychotherapy example, by judicious selection of the "matched" normals, one could find that psychotherapy had a positive or a negative or a neutral effect. If one selected out normal subjects whose neuroticism scores matched those of the people requesting psychotherapy, then one would expect the scores of normals on a second testing to regress toward the mean of the normals—a "positive" gain. One might conclude that the normals, without treatment, were getting better. In this manner, even though psychotherapy might have a beneficial effect, decrease in neuroticism scores could be greater for the normals than for the people in psychotherapy.

One might also obtain the reverse outcome in the following manner. Suppose one's feelings of neuroticism vary from day to day, much on the order of Lewin's "quasi-stationary equilibria." Presumably, it would only be on a day when one felt especially neurotic that one would be motivated to undergo psychotherapy. If so, then the neuroticism scores of people undergoing psychotherapy would be biased in an extreme direction and one would expect them to appear more positive on a second testing. In this manner, even if one were comparing equally neurotic people, the decrease in neuroticism score for those undergoing psychotherapy could be expected to be larger than the controls. The first example in which psychotherapy appeared to have a negative effect involved regression toward the (normal) population mean. In the latter example in which psychotherapy appeared to have a positive effect, day-to-day fluctuations in test score happened to be correlated with an important behavior—volunteering for psychotherapy. In a sense, the individual's score is regressing toward his own true mean.

In any event, one typically does not know what the population means and variances are of indices used in evaluation research. Further, one does not often know which variables to match on. Suppose we are trying to compare children participating in a voluntary Head Start program with those who are not. It is not sufficient to match these two groups on IQ, race, sex, and the usual demographic variables. We know on *a priori* grounds that there can be any number of differences between the two groups. Parents who are interested enough in their children to enroll them in Head Start programs may be also interested enough in them to treat them differently from the control children in many other ways as well. In general, matching is a fallible technique which, to use Campbell and Stanley's phrase, has been vastly oversold.

Differential Growth. We said that parents who enroll their children in Head Start programs may also be very interested in their children's welfare and treat them differently than do parents who do not enroll their children in Head Start programs. As a result of such differential treatment, we might expect greater changes over time in the experimental than in the control condition, whether or not they were enrolled in a Head Start program. We made the point earlier that these two groups of subjects might differ on a pretest. Now we add the fact that their growth over time, even without the benefit of treatment, might be expected to be different as well. This question of differential growth is a problem for any study that is not a true experiment. Recall the example given previously of remedial reading for a low-IQ group. We might well expect differential growth rates in reading level between IQ groups. Therefore one would expect the difference in reading competence between high- and low-IQ groups to increase over time. If so, a remedial reading treatment might be very effective if it simply kept the difference between these two groups constant over time. However, in the absence of independent information that the growth rates are indeed different, a claim of effectiveness could not be made. We note that random assignment to condition would solve this problem.

Problems with Covariance Techniques. Just as matching as a technique has been oversold, so has covariance. Covariance is a statistical technique designed to equate between experimental and control groups on variables that are related to the dependent measures and on which the two groups differ before treatment. For example, if one were interested in gains in reading skills as the result of a remedial reading course, one might wish to covary on prior differences in reading skill (or IQ, etc.) between experimental and control groups shown on a pretest. This technique is also fallible, and its fallibility has seldom been noted.

One of the main assumptions of the covariance technique is that the relationship of the covariate to the dependent measure is the same from cell to cell in the experimental design (more specifically, that the groups in the design are drawn from populations having the same correlation

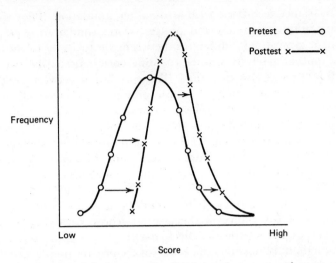

Figure 1. Hypothetical frequency distributions of pretest and posttest scores, showing a negative relationship between pretest and change and attenuated variance in the posttest. Arrows indicate degrees of individual change as a function of pretest, with low scorers changing most.

between covariate and dependent measure). People do not treat this assumption seriously and often covariance is used without checking the correlations. In my experience in experimental research, it is often the case that the correlation between the covariate and the dependent measure is substantially different from cell to cell, particularly when control cells are compared to experimental cells.

For example, posttest scores may have smaller variances following experimental treatment. Often (but not always) those subjects having lowest pretest scores change most. That is, following a remedial reading course, the gain in reading level might be greatest for those with the lowest pretest scores. Figure 1 shows such an effect. The correlation between pretest and posttest is attenuated for the experimental group and is due to the decrease in variance of posttest scores. The correlation between pretest and posttest would therefore be smaller in the experimental group shown than in a control group. When this occurs, I know of no way to handle the problem statistically, and indeed there is not even a constant bias that one may take into account. Depending on the array of correlations from cell to cell, the covariance technique may either overcorrect for pretest differences (or covariate differences) or undercorrect.

Campbell and Erlebacher illustrated a different source of fallibility of the covariance technique with a computer simulation. They compiled two distributions of pretest and posttest scores similar to experimental and control groups. The difference between the two groups on the pretest was approximately two units; the difference between the two groups on the posttest was also two units. The correlation between pretest and posttest was approximately .5. Both groups then changed the same amount over time, and if we were to analyze these data using change scores, we would conclude that there was absolutely no difference between the groups. If we simply look at the posttest difference and ignore the pretest, we would find a highly significant difference ($F=375$). It is interesting from the point of view of the present discussion that if one analyzes these data using covariance—which would presumably equate the groups on the pretest—there would be a serious undercorrection. The analysis of covariance of the posttest scores, covarying on pretest, still yields a highly significant effect ($F=91$).

Although it is possible that the covariance technique can lead to overcorrection of differences between groups, it is much more likely, pragmatically speaking, that it leads to an undercorrection. For example, Campbell and Erlebacher say with regard to Head Start "that had the Head Start programs actually produced no effects whatsoever, the mode of analysis used in the Westinghouse/Ohio University study would have made them look worse than useless, actually harmful" (p. 197). These same issues apply whether the covariate is such a typical measure as a pretest or even if it's a demographic variable such as social class. For further discussion of ways to get around these problems, the reader is referred to Campbell and Erlebacher (1970), Lord (1960), and Porter (1967). However, the reader should be warned that under a rather wide variety of practical conditions, one simply cannot correct for the biases in the analysis of covariance, and the researcher should not depend on covariance as a dependable way of avoiding true experiments. In general, covariance is an inadequate procedure, but it should be noted that it will decrease pretest differences, and even when it does not provide equivalence between groups (Cronbach and Furby, 1970).

The ex post facto design. With a suitable amount of pretesting and a sizable amount of information about other variables that might relate to one's dependent measures, one can construct a very informative quasi-experiment. The problems with *ex post facto* designs (designs in which randomization did not occur and in which one does not have access to suitable covariates such as pretests) are substantially more numerous and serious. In fact, they raise such serious problems that one wonders whether *ex post facto* designs should be tolerated at all. As others have noted, it is often the case that in evaluating government programs, the researcher is not offered any choice. He is presented with a *fait accompli* after the program is well under way, and his only alternative is to do the best he can with an *ex post facto* design. That he does so is to his credit, and we have no quarrel with individual investigators who get caught in this way. Perhaps the only way out of this dilemma is to have a representative national council for evaluative research which would urge the early entry of methodologically sophisticated social scientists into social change programs. One suspects that such a council is likely to ban *ex post facto* designs.[6] Government programs cannot exist without evaluation, and if it were clear that a scientifically acceptable evaluation would not be carried out unless the researcher were allowed the freedom to do it, perhaps the issues would resolve themselves over time.

Let us take a brief example of some of the difficulties inherent in *ex post facto* designs. The Educational Testing Service evaluated the *Sesame Street* television program. They did not use an *ex post facto* design, but their data are illustrative of what might have happened if they had. Their subjects were tested on certain cognitive skills (letters, numbers, etc.). They pretested a large sample of subjects prior to exposure to the program. They subsequently obtained data on how frequently the subjects watched the program. It was found that children who watched the program more had the highest posttest scores on these cognitive skills. Could one conclude in an *ex post facto* design that the program was effective in teaching cognitive skills? Obviously not, since these children might well have had higher pretest scores as well. In this case (see the "Age Cohorts" study of Ball and Bogatz, 1970) that is actually what happened. The children who watched *Sesame Street* more often had higher scores on letters and numbers tests before watching the program. Further, even though they had higher scores initially, those who watched the program more gained more on these tests than did the children who watched the program less frequently. Such information would never have been picked up by an *ex post facto* design.

The investigators were also able to estimate growth rates. For example, the posttest scores of children who had watched the program in the year from age three to four were compared to the pretest scores of the four-year-olds. The posttest scores for the children having experienced the program were substantially higher than the pretest scores for the comparable age group, substantiating the claim that the program indeed had a beneficial effect. It is important to note that neither critical comparison could have been made with an *ex post facto* design. It is necessary to substantiate that people who watched the program more changed more, and that the change thus evidenced was not due to differential growth rates but is higher than that of children of comparable age. From what is described in the Ball and Bogatz article, the ETS evaluation of *Sesame Street* appears to be an excellent example of quasi-experimental research. Using the data in their article, it would be very difficult indeed to argue that *Sesame Street* did not have a beneficial effect on those who watched it and further that the degree of effect could be related to the amount of watching. Any conclusion of this sort based on an *ex post facto* design without the pretest scores of the separate age groups would have been highly suspect, and one could not have made similar claims from the data.

The ETS evaluation of *Sesame Street* is an example of reasonably good quasi-experimental research. What would a true experimental design have added? A small point, but an important one, given the goals of the program. In the quasi-experimental study, frequency of watching the program is confounded with level of cognitive skills. Other variables associated with higher cognitive skills are also confounded: IQ, parental encouragement to watch the program (and to acquire further skills), parental participation in watching the program, and so forth. Consequently, we cannot say on the basis of these data whether children of lesser cognitive skills induced to watch the program more often would show substantial gains or that amount of gain would be directly related to frequency of viewing.[7] The present data are suggestive on both points, but they cannot be regarded as impeccable evidence. This is an important point since helping children possessing lesser cognitive skills is a central goal of the Children's Television Workshop. But one would need a true experiment to document the point.

The Acceptability of Quasi-Experimental Designs. The question of when a quasi-experimental design is acceptable cannot be adequately answered in a short manuscript. Whether the design is acceptable depends upon questions such as the following:

1. What are you prepared to accept? To generalize to other programs or other methods or to estimate costs requires precision not usually associated with quasi-experimental designs. If a low-level conclusion is acceptable—for example, one only wishes to know *if* there is an effect and is less concerned with the degree of effect—then perhaps the quasi-experimental design could be useful.

2. What are the plausible alternative explanations or rival hypotheses for an effect, if it should occur? Is there information available that could help to rule them out? Plausible alternative explanations cannot be enumerated in detail without considering the specifics of the

study. Campbell and Stanley categorize many potential sources of such hypotheses (e.g., instrumentation, maturation), but they obviously cannot deal with any based on theory (see, e.g., Aronson and Carlsmith, 1968, for detailed discussion of ruling out other theoretical hypotheses).

3. What is the conclusion you want to draw? A colleague asked, "If a university wished to change from a system of letter grades (A, B, C) to pass-fail, is a quasi-experimental design sufficient? Why evaluate at all?" It depends on the question you are asking of the data. If the decision to change is irrelevant to the effects of the change ("We're morally against comparing students"), then no evaluation is needed because no question is asked. If one is changing, say, as a result of student demands, then one might not wish to evaluate. What do you hope to accomplish with the change? is the central question. If nothing, then don't evaluate. If you wish to please the students but not affect intellectual habits, then a study checking average syllabus length, number of books checked out of the library, number of people entering the libtary stacks, class attendance, book sales, and so forth, before and after the change (and at a university not changing) would be relevant.

Let us consider another example of question asking. Suppose one is starting a racially integrated preschool. If one is doing so out of the moral belief that children of different races should not be segregated and they should be accustomed to interacting with each other, then no evaluation is necessary (unless some special importance is attached to "accustomed"). The existence of the program accomplishes the goal—physical interaction. If, however, one asserts some effect or impact of this experience (reducing prejudice, increasing "cultural awareness," learning tolerance), then evaluation is necessary. And the evaluation takes the form of "Did these effects occur and why?"

In quasi-experimental research, as in experimental research, the specific question(s) asked determine design details. The exact nature of the control conditions and procedural specifics depend on the nature of the plausible alternative explanations of effects. Only some of these can be discussed without reference to the specific study. Campbell and Stanley provide a useful discussion of certain kinds of rival hypotheses. Inevitably, however, questions of theory arise.

Theoretical Issues

Earlier we discussed some statistical and design issues related to the question of whether a program has an effect and, if so, what the effects were.

This section deals with the closely related problem of *why* the effects occurred. Or, stated in terms of *a priori* methodological considerations: What effects should occur and why?

There is apparently some feeling among evaluation researchers that questions of theory are at worst irrelevant and at best not directly applicable to programs of social change. Moynihan (1969) argues that "social science is at its weakest, and its worst, when it offers theories of individual or collective behavior which raise the possibility, by controlling certain inputs, of bringing about mass behavioral change. No such knowledge now exists" (p. 39). He goes on to say that "the role of social science lies not in its formulation of social policy, but in the measurements of its results" (p. 41).

There is rampant confusion in applied social research about what theory is and what it is supposed to do. Moynihan, for example, confuses the philosophical and scientific evaluations of planned social change. To say what the general objectives of a social change program should be is a question of values, as we have stated previously. The statement of general objectives is a task in which every citizen should participate, and the social scientist should play no more prominent a role than any other similarly educated or concerned citizen.

However, one can differentiate between general objectives and specific objectives. A general objective reflects one's values; for example, reducing the educational disadvantages of certain ethnic groups. A specific objective reflects an outcome or implementation of the more general objective such as raising the children's reading level of an ethnic group or having more of their members graduate from college. The social scientist is simply another citizen in stating general objectives or values, but he has an expert's role to play in the development of specific objectives or potential outcomes of social change programs. Regarding specific objectives, he should use existing knowledge to help state what the range of specific objectives or potential outcomes is, which outcomes are more easily implemented and what they cost, how dramatic the effect might be on individuals, how many individuals are likely to be reached, and so forth.

Once stated, the question of how to implement general objectives is not a simple one of the values of the citizens in the society. To a certain extent, the question of how to achieve a certain social objective is a question of theory. It is a question of "what leads to what?" Partly because social scientists with some justification have declined to engage in a statement of general objectives, they have also been left out of discussions of ways to implement them. *But any statement whatsoever of a way to implement an objective of a social change program is a theoretical statement whether explicitly recognized or not.*

Suppose our general objective is to decrease or eliminate the frequency of malnutrition among children of the poor, a value upon which we can all agree as citizens. However, any statement of how to achieve that objective involves at least in part some implicit assumption about human behavior. This assumption is an implicit theorietical statement, and evaluation research would be more respected today if this were explicitly recognized. Suppose we decide to decrease the malnutrition among the children of the poor by giving the poor more money to buy food (e.g., the negative income tax). There are some obvious assumptions about human motivation and human behavior inherent in the statement that if one gives another money, he will buy food; further, that he will purchase a nutritionally balanced diet; further, that this method of accomplishing the goal is the most efficient one.[8]

Each potential program of social change has hidden implicit assumptions that directly reflect one's unstated theoretical approach to human behavior. To the extent that social science understands human behavior, it should speak on these issues. There is no question that social science does have a body of knowledge and theory related to such choices. This body of knowledge and theory is not perfect—it does not predict accurately in every curcumstance—but it nonetheless has distinct advantages over uninformed opinion. From this point of view, although social scientists should play a no more prominent role in the selection of general objectives than any other group of people, they should be intimately involved with the selection and design of programs to achieve specific objectives. As Suchman says,

The statement of an evaluative hypothesis, we conclude, is almost as closely tied to an understanding of "causal" theories as is a nonevaluative hypothesis. While this condition is accepted as a *sine qua non* of basic research, it is often overlooked by the evaluative researcher who may tend to forget that a test of "does it work?" presupposes some theory as to why one might expect it to work (1967, p. 86).

There are three main outcomes of this lack of attention to theory in evaluation research. First, since questions of *why* a program might work tend not to be taken into serious consideration, one cannot generalize from a specific program to (accomplishing the same objectives in) a slightly different kind of program. Second, in order to bring a theoretical perspective to bear upon specific objectives, it is necessary to state very clearly and precisely what the objectives are. I submit that as a result of avoiding theoretical questions in social change programs, there is not enough emphasis on a clear statement of objectives, and the objectives are not specific enough.

It is my contention, and I think it can be documented, that in those social change programs where objectives are not clearly and specifically stated, little if any value can be documented coming out of the program. It is precisely those Head Start programs with fuzzy objectives (e.g., increasing cultural awareness) that developed fuzzy methods of implementation (e.g., visiting museums), and that show little evidence of having accomplished anything. If one were more theoretically oriented and concerned about what leads to what, then one would be very intolerant of a stated objective such as increasing cultural awareness. Before one could design a program to accomplish such an objective, one would have to state very specifically and exactly what it is.

A third negative implication of a lack of attention to theory in applied programs is that since we have not stated the objectives of the program clearly, we cannot understand why the program works. Therefore we almost inevitably end up with inadequate programs, inefficient programs, or both. An inadequate program is one that does not implement the stated objectives. An inefficient program is one whose objectives could be accomplished better by other means (more cheaply, by reaching more people, causing less turmoil, and so forth).

Hovland, Lumsdaine, and Sheffield (1949) distinguish between program and variable testing in evaluation research. Program testing refers to the typical evaluative project—trying to test whether some overall, complex program had any effect at all. Variable testing refers to testing a causal inference. With respect to evaluation research, variable testing can refer to determining which parts of the program are critical in producing the effect. Programs are very complex independent variables, and their generality often is very low. Unless we know why a particular program works, we either cannot generalize from that program to other situations or, in the few instances that we can generalize, the generalization is very inefficient.

Questions of generality and theory are particularly applicable to pilot studies. It is often the case that the government will fund a pilot project very richly. It employs Ph.D.'s as counselors, uses highly selected and well-motivated subjects, is broadly advertised and well regarded by the community; it has the distinct advantage that it is considered by both participants and outsiders as an exciting experiment ("the Hawthorne effect"). Many of these pilot projects are highly successful in the sense that they have substantial impact on the participants. But without further documentation or further research, one cannot generalize from them to a national setting. To generalize to other settings, one must first clearly state the objectives and state exactly why this program should accomplish those objectives. The research evaluating the project then must document the causal or critical variables in accomplishing the objectives, the "whys" underlying the end-product. Unless one can document these critical variables and rule out the plethora of alternative hypotheses for the effect, the program provides little evidence to generalize to other settings.

In short, theory is intimately intertwined with evaluation research whether we wish it or acknowledge it. To leave theoretical issues implicit in evaluation research destroys the validity of the research by limiting the generality of the effects. It also has unintended negative side-effects in that when we do not consider theory seriously, we also tend not to state our specific objectives clearly and precisely, as well as ignoring alternative ways to accomplish the same ends. A few aspects of this argument are discussed in more detail in the next section.

Proper Comparison Groups—the Concept of the "Bargain Alternative"

When we ignore theory in planning social change programs and their evaluation, we tend to ignore other ways of accomplishing the same ends. When we are concerned about the theoretical underpinnings of an effect, the comparison of the experimental group with the control (the treated group with the untreated) is only a first step. Normally, to tease out why a particular effect occurred and to rule out plausible rival hypotheses, we need other comparison groups, whose treatment includes some but not all of the variables in the main experimental group. Frequently such comparison groups lead us to accomplish much more than we thought possible when we began.

The social change program often originates as a demonstration project. Typically in applied settings, when we want to accomplish a certain end, we throw the whole book of potentially effective variables at the recipient. In some projects where expense, time, and other factors, are of no consequence, we do everything we can that is conceivably related to the desired outcome. If the college sophomore wants to impress his girl friend, he brings out his whole repertoire of variables potentially related to such an outcome. His manners, his dress, his behavior (being gallant), his financial investment (taking her to dinner), and more, are all brought to bear on the same problem. If he accomplishes his goal, perhaps he doesn't care which of these variables was critical in attaining the goal. Particularly if there is only one girl in question, the expenditure of such a vast amount of resources in pursuit of a desired outcome could be considered irrelevant. However, if he is a Don Juan and has a sizable number of girls in mind, then he becomes much more interested in which variables are most important—which control the greatest variance in the behavior of the other. If a candlelight dinner is the critical variable, then he will not bother with all of the other effort and expense.

In social change programs, particularly demonstration programs, we often engage in a similar sort of overkill. We are concerned less with which variable produces the effect than we are with obtaining the effect. However, there are more laudable causes today than society can hope to fund. Hence the most efficient way may be the only way for a given program to be implemented, or, if not, it will at least allow a certain amount of money and time to be diverted to other worthwhile programs.

In evaluating any project, whether demonstration or otherwise, we should as a matter of course demand that in addition to the experimental and control groups, another comparison group—a less expensive alternative—also be included. I call this the "bargain alternative." If the bargain alternative is relatively ineffective, we have that much more knowledge about which critical variables underlie the effect for the experimental group. However, if the bargain alternative is equally effective as the more complex experimental treatment, then we are in the best possible position. Using the bargain alternative, we can accomplish the same goals more efficiently, more inexpensively, and more effectively, while at the same time perhaps reaching a larger group of people.

Consider the example of some Upward Bound programs, where disadvantaged high school seniors are brought to a special summer program to prepare them for entrance into college. This program is often lengthy, highly expensive, complex, and of necessity it reaches only a small proportion of the potentially eligible people. The program usually involves a number of full-time counselors who have already graduated from college (who indeed may have Ph.D.'s) and a number of other counselors who are still in college but originally came from the same disadvantaged group. The program includes learning the ins and outs of college (e.g., how to find things in the library), some instruction about reading, how to write term papers, how grading systems work, and so forth. The program often continues into the college years with the beginning freshman being assigned a roommate who is from the same group but who is obviously successful in the system.

The main problem with the program as it stands is that it is expensive, and because of its expense and complexity (involving potentially a whole summer) it would be very difficult to apply to the large number of eligible applicants (roughly 50% of disadvantaged youth could potentially be eligible for the program on the grounds that 50% of youth in general go to college). There are many separate projects indicating that the Upward Bound program has been successful, particularly from the point of view of the grades earned by the recipients in college and by the relatively infrequent withdrawals from college. In short, the recipients stick it out, and they are reasonably successful. However, since the program is so complex, we don't know which aspects of it are critical and which aspects contribute the greater amount of variance. One possibility is that disadvantaged youth are unaccustomed to the groups that they will be interacting with and essentially don't know how the game is played. To the extent that this is true, any situation which allows them to learn the game would be effective. Perhaps one might then construct a bargain alternative (in addition to the control and regular experimental groups) in which only certain potentially related elements are retained.

One could construct a bargain alternative emphasizing the following. The student might go directly into college but would be assigned to a roommate from the same group who was already successful in the system. The roommate actually might be paid to spend extra time with the subject, helping him and "clueing him in." Regular meetings between counselors and subjects could easily be carried out (as they often are in Upward Bound programs as well) to help the subjects share experiences and to solve any unusual problems.

The bargain alternative has the advantages that it is much less expensive; it involves much less time on the part of the subjects; and in theory at least, it could be applied to a much larger group of people. If the bargain alternative is not successful compared to the regular experimental and the control groups, we can dispense with the hypothesis that these elements contribute substantially to the success of the subject. On those grounds they might be excluded from future tries with the experimental group.[9]

If, on the other hand, the bargain alternative is as successful as the experimental group, the implications are quite clear. Other things being equal, the program should go with the bargain alternative and forget about the more complex and expensive regular experimental treatment. If, as is more likely, the effect of the bargain alternative is somewhere between the experimental group and the control group—that is, it is more effective than the control but less effective than the regualr complex experimental treatment—then at least one has the basis on which either to make programatic decisions or to follow up with more research. One could compare, for example, the relative frequency of success and the expense of the two separate treatments and make an administrative decision on that basis. The regular treatment might have 10% more success than the bargain alternative; on the other hand, it might cost four times as much. The implications could be clear in any event.

The bargain alternative has several advantages. It helps us clarify theoretical aspects of the regular treatment by more clearly specifying what it is about the regular treatment that produces the effect (accomplishes the objective). Second, the bargain alternative may actually have some effect of its own, which in turn might lead us to abandon the experimental treatment in favor of the less complex and less expensive bargain alternative. Third, the presence of a bargain alternative in an experimental design helps to clarify administrative decisions by clarifying not only what leads to what, but how much it costs.

The Concept of Middle-Level Testing

Demonstration projects are just that—demonstrations—and they cannot be construed as a direct test of any hypothesis. In bureaucratic parlance, they test the "feasibility" of some programatic notion. To say that something is feasible is usually to say that it is possible; if we construct a situation in which a large number of variables potentially contributing to a certain effect are juxtaposed, we obtain the effect. Some of these juxtaposed variables are relevant to the hypotheses in question, but some are irrelevant. The Hawthorne effect, highly trained and highly skilled program leaders, the participation of the most highly motivated subjects, and so forth, are variables that could produce an effect in a pilot study but probably would not be present in a larger national program. In almost any situation, it is an untenable conclusion that the effects of a demonstration program would also hold true for an extrapolated larger national study. At the very least, one must acknowledge that a great many things assist in producing effects in demonstration studies that would not be present in a larger study. Consequently on a priori grounds one must expect any larger study to have less effect on the subject population. That is to say, at minimum we must expect it to have less effect. Quite frequently there is no reason to expect any effect whatsoever.

Without pointing our collective finger at anyone in particular, each of us is aware of demonstration programs that were expanded into national programs without any demonstrable effects. This is a very expensive loss, particularly in the sense that the money could have been used to good effect elsewhere. As long as we make the jump from complex demonstration projects to national programs, however, we must be prepared to accept the fact that many very expensive national programs are going to be at best ineffective and inefficient.

There is an alternative, however. That is what I call "middle-level testing." We should never jump from a demonstration project to a national program without an intermediate step of middle-level testing. The middle-level testing should consist of a well-controlled true experimental study based on a fairly small national sample. Insofar as possible, the circumstances, events, and related issues should be the same in the middle-level testing as might be expected to occur in a national program. Such an experiment might provide a very conservative test of any theoretical hypothesis, but it would allow for a much more straightforward generalization to a national program.

It sounds more expensive because it involves an extra step, and indeed middle-level tests would not be cheap. On the other hand, if such middle-level testing were to occur routinely, we would have few if any ineffective and inefficient national programs. The savings from that standpoint would be enormous.

The real drawback to middle-level testing is the time lag. Since we are requiring a well-designed, small national experiment as the middle-level test, there could be a lag of two or three (or more) years between the demonstration project and the feedback about whether the project is feasible to implement on the national level. One could see many objections to middle-level testing coming from actionists, potential recipients of the beneficial treatment, government officials, and Congressmen who demand immediate action. However, these pressures should be actively resisted by the scientific community. It is a disservice to all to give less than what social science has to offer—the most effective and efficient national programs that can be designed. A national council of evaluation research could be helpful in effecting such badly needed changes in the process of evaluation research.

Tinkering within Programs

This is a short chapter on a complex problem and misinterpretation is possible on several issues. Therefore let us consider some pragmatic issues of program testing.

The "Whiz Kids" Approach to Program Evaluation. An adequate program evaluation depends on an intimate knowledge of the situation: the participants' feelings about a potential program; their expressed needs; how they might view a potential testing situation; and so forth. If I have given the impression that one can develop a cadre of content-free evaluators—who, like white knights, dash in and dash off a program evaluation, and then ride off into the sunset—that is quite incorrect. A competent investigator might spend months setting the stage for a proper evaluation. Through being immersed in the situation, he would try to develop a thorough understanding of it by talking to agency officials and potential participants, and perhaps by surveying them systematically. In this stage, one might develop hypotheses regarding the impact of the program and build a test of them into the evaluation. One might also conclude that an evaluation of a particular program would be a waste of time.

Pretesting Parts of Programs. Sesame Street programs are pretested (presumably) before airing, to determine whether an individual program is effective and entertaining. This procedure should be applied wherever feasible. Its main advantage is that it reduces the risk of failure of the overall program. Pretesting parts of programs would be especially advantageous and plausible in almost any educational program. Of course, some programs form such an integral whole that the pretesting of parts would be neither desirable nor feasible.

Changing Parts of Programs. Often programs are not implemented exactly as planned. Certain pragmatic difficulties may become obvious only after the program is under way: accounting procedures may be cumbersome; participants may misinterpret the intent of the agency and/or the actions of the agency; participants may prefer certain changes to make it easier for them to participate; and so forth. Some program leaders intentionally make such changes and regard them as an integral part of program development. The actual program as implemented may be quite different from the program as planned—particularly with regard to theoretical issues of why one should expect the program to have impact.

These changes are important for an isolated instance of a programatic concept and may play the central role between success and failure. They help tailor the program to the needs of the participants, and, through participation in development, the staff is likely to be enthusiastic. An enthusiastic staff meeting the needs of participants should, theoretically, lead to a successful outcome.

However, these changes may be very subtle and may make it difficult to evaluate the program for several reasons. One is not certain what program is being evaluated. Is it the final program as described by the leaders? Or, rather, did the *esprit* generated by participation in development and change play a critical role in outcome? Can anyone even describe the program objectively? Is the "final" program as perceived by the leaders similarly described by the participants?

These issues are not important unless one wishes to generalize to other settings. If it is a one-time program, geared, for example, to a particular town, then success itself is important, and an objective view of the underpinnings of success is secondary. However, if one wishes to extrapolate—to take the program because it is successful and apply it to a different community—one does so at great risk. One certainly would not want to extrapolate from a single instance of such program development to a national implementation of a large number of instances based on the same concept. At least one more replication is necessary; some middle-level testing is preferable.

Empirically Based Programs. Many correctly contend that social science theory is not sufficiently detailed to allow one to choose a specific implementation of a program concept over others. One way to proceed is with Scriven's (1967) concept of formative research. In the initial stages of program evaluation, one might try several different programs—each a plausible strategy for implementing the same concept. Subsequently, one would choose the more successful alternatives for refinement and further testing. In this way one could empirically derive a program with a high probability of success.

Who Will Do It?

One of the reasons that evaluation research has not progressed theoretically and methodologically, more than it has is that you, I, and our colleagues have not placed a sufficiently high premium on its accomplishments. As Evans points out, "we as social scientists are in the untenable position of continually criticizing the government for not basing its judgments and decisions on social science research while at the same time being unwilling to provide the practically oriented professional talent necessary for this to occur" (1969, p. 251). There is no question in my mind that evaluation research is very complex and very difficult to do adequately. To be a good evaluation researcher, one needs not only an excellent broad grounding in social science theory, but one also needs much better methodological and statistical skills than it takes to work effectively in the laboratory. There are two problems then: how to induce the government to take better advantage of social science theory and method; and how to train more people interested and competent in evaluation research.

Perhaps the first goal could be accomplished by a collective push toward a national council for evaluation research. Such a council would not only lend prestige to the accomplishments of evaluation research, but it could also lead to evaluation research of higher quality. To help evaluation researchers improve the quality of their research, it is neces-

sary to help them win the battle within the agencies: to be in on evaluation research from its very inception; to have a role in stating potential
ways to implement or accomplish objectives; and to be in a position sufficiently superordinate to insist upon the basic elements of proper research.

Training people to carry out this complex research is perhaps even
more difficult. Interest in "relevant" topics in graduate schools is increasing throughout the country. But an interest in relevance is hardly sufficient for an evaluation researcher. We do not need to train actionists in
social science. Perhaps social scientists are not even good actionists. As
Campbell once jocularly commented, as an actionist a Ph.D. in social science could be advantageously replaced by a randomly selected college
sophomore. Any citizen can and should speak up about policy formation.
But the unique contribution of social science to policy is in terms of theoretical statements, the measurement of complex psychological and sociological variables, and the design of complex but precise experiments. It is
true that the interest in social issues is increasing at both the graduate
and undergraduate levels, but unless these students are interested in and
highly sophisticated about theory, measurement, and design, they are of
no more use to social science or society than is any other interested citizen. We do not need more graduate community action programs in social
science in which our students and junior faculty only get experience in
the ghetto. What we do need is more graduate community action programs where our students also learn about relevant theory and about the
complex measurement and design problems related to implementing and
evaluating social action programs. To say that social scientists should be
more involved in action is nonsense—we should be no more or less involved than any other group of concerned citizens. However, we should
be much more involved in sharpening our unique set of skills that pertain to the design and evaluation of programs in social change.

Summary

We have only been able to highlight some selected issues facing evaluation researchers today. These can be summarized quite briefly.

1. There is no satisfactory substitute for true experiments, which include the random assignment of subjects to conditions. It has been the
premise of this essay that not only should more true experiments be
carried out in the field of evaluation research, but they are feasible—and
easier to do than people apparently think. Several salient problems with
quasi-experimental and *ex post facto* designs were briefly discussed.

2. The question of theory seems to have slipped away from us in evaluation research. We have argued that there is no way to avoid theory, and to avoid discussing it really means implicit theorizing rather than explicit theorizing. In the final analysis, explicit discussions of theory will lead not only to better programs but to more efficient programs. Several drawbacks of implicit theorizing were mentioned. The concepts of the bargain alternative and middle-level testing and their potentially important role in understanding social change programs were outlined.

Implicit throughout this chapter has been the assumption that the evaluation researcher fights a lonely battle. Often he is called in at the last minute, as if evaluation research could be separated from the design of research. It cannot be. Often I am consulted about particular laboratory experiments in the same way. People describe to me experiments with tragic design flaws and ask how best to analyze their data. I find that question particularly annoying and am tempted to reply simply that they shouldn't have done the experiment in the first place. I am sure that the evaluation researcher must find it equally annoying to be called in on a social change project at the last minute, as the poor boy sweeping up the trash. Obviously social science must develop better ways to back the evaluation researcher and make it easier for him to do a competent job. We have endorsed Campbell and Erlebacher's suggestion that some national body competent to speak on such issues—perhaps a national council for evaluation research—be formed as a highly credible special interest group to urge more adequate and accurate use of social science theory and method.

Notes

1. This chapter was prepared while the author was partially supported by N.S.F. Grant GS 29722X. My thanks to Donald Campbell, Thomas Cook, Paul Gump, David Holmes, Kent Houston, and Sara Kiesler for criticisms of an earlier draft.

2. Political evaluations occur as well, emphasizing such considerations as the "feasibility" of a program or its potential acceptance by the electorate.

3. See also Suchman (1967), Caro (1969), Hyman and Wright (1967), Festinger and Katz (1953), Zurcher and Bonjean (1970), and many others.

4. Of course Evans is not advocating sloppy research. He has been a key figure in developing better methods of evaluation research and gaining their acceptance at the national level, as chief of the evaluation division of the OEO Office of Research, Plans, Programs and Evaluations. The real question is how obstinate social scientists should be about this important question.

5. At minimum, one should match only on variables that correlate equally with pretest and posttest.

6. We do not take the stand here that the only reasonable research to do is either experimental or quasi-experimental. In evaluation research, as any other, a good deal of preliminary work is necessary before a decent experiment can be done. Observations, extended discussions with participants and administrators, and so forth, are integral to this preliminary stage of the research process. We believe that such preliminary evidence cannot stand by itself, particularly if one wishes to generalize to other settings and other participants.

7. Actually, Ball and Bogatz did "encourage" some subjects to watch more, attempting a true experimental design. The variable was imperfectly implemented, and encouragement was confounded with watching. The study may still be considered a quasi-experimental design.

8. I do not mean to imply that these assumptions are false, but rather that they should be made explicit.

9. Actually, all we would know is that the bargain alternative is ineffective by itself. It still might play a critical role when combined with the regular treatment.

Alan E. Guskin

Provost
Clark University

Mark A. Chesler

Department of Sociology
University of Michigan

PARTISAN DIAGNOSIS
OF SOCIAL PROBLEMS [1]

The study of American society clearly requires scholarly endeavor. Most social scientists approach this task with cautious confidence in their methods for generating or deriving objective, value-free findings. The tasks of utilizing social scientific knowledge are seen as more problematic than study itself, and they are felt to raise serious value dilemmas. It is our view that the dilemmas of neutrality or partisanship pervade the scientific enterprise—both in methods and uses—and we seek to explore the outlines of these issues in this chapter.

American social science is embedded firmly in the culture of the society it serves. Its practitioners overwhelmingly come from and live in certain strata of that society, and its institutions must interface with other major social systems. As a result, the psychological styles and methods of individual scientists, the social structure and traditions of the profession, and the political context of the society make scholarly objectivity or neutrality impossible. If the study of our own culture and institutions necessarily is "valuecentric" and politically partisan in character, objectivity means careful rather than neutral or value-free scholarship.

Scholarly analyses of American institutions can be considered as either research or diagnostic efforts. It is our view that social diagnosis differs from social research in several important ways. Research, especially pure research, and most efforts at applied research as well, starts from researchers' needs to acquire knowledge. This beginning is essential to the historic assumption of autonomy the social sciences have appeared to embody; in practice, of course, autonomy is no more possible than is neutrality. It also has contributed to the lack of social relevance and the public nonaccountability of professional works. Diagnostic efforts, on the other hand, start with practical needs for specific knowledge, and they require inquiry to be tuned and accountable to the assessment of human needs and the solution of social problems. The diagnostician's job demands he connect specific requests to broader and more fundamental questions, but the trend of payoff is very different. Social scientists' stress on the proper use of a scientific methodology hypothetically makes possible replication and leads to a series of theories which reflect the accepted truths of the field. Since methodological purity is a prime value in scientific research, other concerns for breadth or depth of data must respond to this priority. In a diagnosis, the intent to serve and to gather data relevant for use is a prime value, and concerns for methodological rigor or theory-testing must respond to this priority.

Research is conducted primarily to answer certain questions or test certain theories about the workings of key variables in a social system. The attainment of these answers is ostensibly its own reward. A diagnosis usually is the first step in a change process which includes goal setting, analysis and interpretation of data, generation of change plans and programs, creation of change and evaluation (or rediagnosis).

The professional social scientist rarely acts as a diagnostician; the personal priorities and skills involved are very different, as are the reference and reward systems. The training of most social scientists is strictly controlled by master scholars who encourage adherence to established standards and aspirations. Such training also discourages any primary concern in the research process with the utilization of results (although application is permissible and even desirable if it follows carefully conceived and instrumented research). Direct involvement in action programs where clients' needs take precedence over the discipline's accepted theoretical and research concerns is considered "second class" or "too applied." Within elite academic institutions those involved in diagnosis and/or utilization are clearly of lower status and not quite legitimate. They receive most of their rewards from external social or political status, and/or from participation in movements for social reform. The social researcher is more likely to seek rewards from professional colleagues and from satisfaction of his intellectual curiosity and theoretical perspectives. The publication and dissemination of research results, rather than their use, is the reward for intellectual achievement in the guild's showcases of journals, and books.

Historically, the prime focus of social science research has been developed from the interests of the profession, not from those of any client group. In effect, the profession is a class with specified interests and preferred styles of life. The interests are the practice of an "objective" methodology, acceptance of certain theories, and preferred styles of life reflected in an elite academic university environment, acceptable publication rate, a job market in favor of the professional, and an academic freedom which permits the maintenance of these styles with minimum interference.

The maintenance of these interests and life styles requires adequate funding for desired research projects. Over the years, particularly since 1960, these funds have been forthcoming in ways and at a rate that permits much of the type of work professionals desire. For most of the 1960s, universities had an abundance of money and positions and the major private and public funding agencies were very generous. Even during budget scarcity the science lobby pursued and received a generous federal allocation. If the locus of social accountability or funding patterns were different, the social scientist's output and life style would vary greatly. For instance, if professional researchers were accountable to blacks or poor people, they would have spent most of their efforts assessing the forces that maintain a ghetto, the bizarre rationale for a school with a 100% black student population and a 90% white teaching staff, the nature of institutional white racism, and the factors that limit the employment opportunities of blacks and other minority groups. Since professional social scientists have been accountable to themselves and to elite private and public funding sources, they have studied the "deviant," "neurotic," and "psychotic" behavior and "deficient" maternal and paternal behavior of ghetto families and youth, the learning deficits and antisocial behavior of black youth, and the motivation and job skills of black adults. Thus they supply the rhetoric and rationale for other professionals (teachers, social workers) who "cool out" their clients' political demands and reinforce requests for welfare paternalism.

The results of all these interactions is that the professional social scientist's values of safe, nondiagnostic, nonactivist research, "objectivity," and a high publication rate have been reinforced. It is only now that the society is in severe crisis and elitist or mainstream values are being questioned seriously that significant groups of young social scientists are aware of and questioning these interests. But it should be clear that such inquiry still demands considerable cost; a professional interest group does not take lightly the challenge to its cherished standards and values.

Throughout our discussion of the issues in research and diagnosis we try to focus on "social problems"; we elect not to concern ourselves with problems of individual pathology in adjusting or accommodating to the nature of the American society. The problems addressed here are collective in character and fundamental to the society's existence. Structural constraints and opportunities, as well as people's feelings, need our attention. However, the "overpsychologization" of social science leaves major social structures mysterious and therefore invulnerable to serious question. Here the organization of judicial systems and reward allocation draw our attention, not the characteristics of poor people or delinquents. Furthermore, we are not limited to a negative orientation; problems do not necessarily mean overt maladjustment or glaring inadequacy. An organization's failure to achieve its stated goals, or the effort to improve an already positive quality of life, each represents a problem in the sense of changes to be made. In this context, problems also may be taken to mean the essential dilemmas a system must solve or tasks it must perform to survive—governance, resource development, resource use, division of labor, allocation of rewards, manpower training, loyalty, social control and defense, and so on.

It is impossible to relegate these dilemmas to abstract arguments engaged in by a group of ivory-tower academics. The professional scientific tradition has had serious ramifications for public policy and program. The kinds of research and conceptual frameworks that scholars have presented have created or reinforced the masses' and policy makers' myths and perspectives about minority groups, students, women, and counter-elite interest groups. Moreover, these studies and programs often have exhausted public funds that could have been utilized by opposing interest groups to support their own cause.

In the remaining portions of this essay we examine these issues. None of the examples considered are accidental, nor are they cases of individual malpractice. It is the definition and structure of the social research profession that creates these standard practices and standard dilemmas. The second section focuses further on ways in which the methods of social research and social diagnosis differ, and how partisan social values are built into these processes. The third section focuses on issues of utilization, per se, and how research and/or diagnosis establishes and can alter certain utilization patterns. Finally, we discuss alternative roles and styles for scholars committed to the utilization of partisan diagnoses.

Methodological Issues in Partisan Scholarship

The "objective" character of standard methods is a fundamental proposition in scientific inquiry. The assumption is made that when applied with care, approved methods lead to value-free findings. However, this is a dubious base for strong tradition, since the methods and procedures utilized in research on social problems are not neutral, and they tend to create partisan outcomes. It is not just that a good researcher can use good methods to overcome his personal biases; standard methods themselves are subtly biased. If these trends were acknowledged, they could be countered; they could not be avoided but perhaps neutralized. Since these biases are assumed not to exist they are all the more dangerous.

There are several arenas of social scientific inquiry suitable for illustrating methodological biases that have partisan political consequences. Most glaring, however, are studies where the American culture and ideology are subtly assumed or taken for granted rather than queried. Research on race and racism, male chauvinism and sex biases, cultural and political attitudes and values are especially fertile grounds. Three methodological problems affecting basic value issues typically are at stake: (1) the choice and simplification of the phenomena being investigated; (2) the choice and simplification of the criterion variables; and (3) the bias built into the data-gathering situation itself.

Some particularly blatant examples of bias can be found in the area of "cultural deficits" and "deficiencies" in the language development of minority children (Baratz and Baratz, 1970). The phenomena studied are basically the adjustment problems of a deviant group, not the lack of pluralism in the dominant culture and institutions. Researchers typically collect data from low-income black children by taking speech samples or by requiring verbal responses to pictures or statements presented in a testing situation. Analyses of these samples are then compared with the criterion variable, standard English. Statistical comparisons that indicate low-income black youth are "deficient" mean simply that the language of many low-income black youth is different from the language of middle-class white youth. Is this a deficit? It is only if one places a greater value on the standard dialect. Hence the concept of deficit is a result of researchers' values regarding desirable language patterns. This difference is interpreted as a deficit because it is important for the security of the American middle-class to see itself as superior to blacks and the lower classes; scholars borne of this cultural tradition serve its maintenance unconsciously or consciously.

The nature of the testing or data-gathering situation itself also represents a major methodological issue. Typically the poor or black youth is tested by a white middle-class adult. In addition to the obvious middle-class bias built into these tests the situation creates further methodological partisanship because of (1) the relationship between the researcher and respondent, (2) the types of situational constraints placed on the youth, and (3) the relationship between the types of responses the researcher is seeking and what he supposedly is measuring. The researcher usually is white, middle-class, adult, verbal, part of the school or agency extablishment and generally a feared object. Black youth often are not comfortable dealing with white adults in these settings and their consequent anxiety or alienation alone could produce limited speech patterns. Katz (1964) and Ledvinka (1969) have demonstrated the different effects white and black testers and interviewers have upon blacks in white, black, or interracial settings. Any adult white study of black youth builds in a further language bias because of anxieties and constraints upon youth's natural language responses. When the respondent is unable to utilize his sophisticated nonverbal language (so readily understood by his peers, family, and people in his neighborhood) to express himself, his apparent abilities are downgraded. The testing situation ostensibly established to increase the objectivity of the data often has distorted the true faculties of black youth.

Since language is a form of communication that occurs on a natural basis between individuals, it has some clear purposes for the parties concerned. The types of responses elicited in non-natural settings are restricted samples of the *potential* speech of the respondent as a communicant. Therefore the relationship between the variable being studied—language—in a non-natural setting and the actual presence of this variable in a natural setting may be quite minimal. The assumption of the researcher is that the relationship is great, but that is only because the phenomena of language have been reduced to a too simplistic form.

These criticisms force us to ask whether low-income black youth have a language deficit or whether the research merely fulfills the prophecies of white middle-class researchers. The black youth uses language in multiple ways and is asked to respond to a researcher in only one way; he speaks one dialect of English and is judged on the basis of another, which is considered culturally more desirable; he is placed in a setting with people he mistrusts and with whom he finds it difficult to relate; he is made to respond in unfamiliar ways and the forms of communication he normally utilizes to express himself are deemed inappropriate.

The barriers between subject and researcher are highlighted by, but not limited to, a cross-cultural situation. Barnard (1967) refers to the constant battle of wits between these parties as a generic phenomenon in all scientific research. Although this battle obviously affects the research findings, and despite the fact that the cultural or political biases built into the methods used in these studies are clear and considerable, consensus exists as to the legitimacy of the conclusions. One of the ways scholars have avoided confrontation with the outrageous implications of these studies or with the societal conditions that perpetrate this mythology is to find elements of poor and black culture that "explain" poor language patterns. By explaining it they continue to assume and confirm its existence.

Herzog (1970) analyzes a series of studies on the role of the family in "culturally deprived" youth, and the ways in which these studies have been methodologically biased in the direction of supporting the cultural deprivation hypothesis. The causal analysis that supports the superiority of the prevailing culture is overdetermined, and typical methods do not overcome these tendencies. One of the fundamental methodological biases Herzog stresses lies in the scientists' needs for methodologically secure and "tidy research." In order for research to be "tidy," "real life" variables must be reduced to a manageable number of dimensions and variables or to a simple continuum. Built into this conceptual and methodological reduction is distortion which may often reflect value dimensions. For instance, Herzog recounts the tendency for studies to present male dominance and female dominance as mutually exclusive family conditions. At the same time studies show that fathers are likely to be dominant in some areas and mothers in other areas; to discuss a complex family pattern as a simple matriarchy or patriarchy is to distort reality.

The bias built into research studies appears most clearly when one looks at patterns of studies. One of the questions in deviance research is, "Do fatherless homes cause delinquency?" Herzog's review showed that "a clear association is not to be taken for granted." She reports:

> Bordua has suggested that conclusions about factors contributing to juvenile delinquency depend on the theory of causation espoused. If the hypothesis is that father absence itself leads to delinquency, the general climate and functioning of the family tend to be ignored. If family climate and functioning are hypothesized as causal, environmental factors tend to be disregarded. If the cause is attributed to community factors, individual family process tend to be left out. If delinquency is attributed to the opportunity prevailing in the society at large, other factors receive scant consideration. . . . A highly structured experiment can show whether previously identified factors are associated with previously identified reaction. But it is less likely to reveal that some other factor or factors, not included in the research design, are more crucial and determinative than the ones under investigation (1970, p. 120).

Thus the researcher interested in the effects of the functioning of the family on tendencies toward juvenile delinquency develops his minitheories to reflect this interest. In doing so he leaves out other major factors that may influence juvenile delinquency.

The results of these acts cannot be said to be neutral. Rather, such a series of developments is fertile ground for the inclusion of the value-biases of the researcher and those of other researchers pursuing similar issues. The consensus that develops among researchers may seem to represent the "real world" but more than likely is a trans-subjectivism heavily invested with value biases. As Agger points out,

> . . . investigators simply work with a set of concepts that happens currently to be prominent in their field. The very act of accepting an empirical domain together with some set of dimensions for the purpose, perhaps, of testing a hypothesis inadequately tested heretofore, or of testing a hypothesis under newly chosen conditions with a view to further specify the limits of its generalizability, or of testing a new hypothesis derived from existing theory is in itself a value-choice. This is necessarily the case whether or not the investigator is conscious of it (1964, p. 213).

The specific hypotheses that are the outcomes of the conceptualization process severely delimit the methods to be used. They are to be tested and other potential areas are in effect excluded. Essentially, the accurate perception of a complex reality is less important than the way that perception is created. This is a constant price of theory-directed research as it is currently practiced.

The bureaucratization and isolation of the social research profession creates other serious methodological problems in experimental and survey research. A researcher who directs field studies may study the racial attitudes or life styles of blacks and whites in many geographical areas without leaving his office. Will he or they be able to adequately develop questions that tap the deep-seated feelings of people on these issues? He may hire a black staff member—who is supposed to represent "his people"—but the representation is done without a constituency: thus the results of his efforts often are antiseptic. How will these researchers understand the true feelings of blacks and whites? By aggregating their survey responses? But how does that relate to other criterion variables, such as their behavior on the job, in their social club, in the street, or in their homes? Is their behavior the same in such groups as when they were interviewed? Given the highly politicized and volatile nature of black-white relations, will the respondents give answers to the conservatively dressed black and white interviewers? How can anyone familiar with today's racial scene assume blacks will answer research questions openly and honestly? Or that whites even know what they feel? Or is such a research study implicitly built to avoid the raw nerves of the present relationships between blacks and whites? Is it possible to do research at a distance on critical social issues about which social science has little prior knowledge?

If so, then doesn't such research create results in line with the past traditions or value biases rather than the present reality?

An example of how these factors can affect research is the recent forced termination of a study of black youth in Roxbury (Boston) conducted by two white social research directors with their black staff (*Behavior Today*, 1970). Black community leaders apparently decided that the key issue was not how many black staff members were on the project but who controlled it. If whites control it, it would likely end up being a white study. And they were probably right, not because the whites were overtly bigoted and wished to harm blacks; on the contrary, they may have been fairly open-minded and well intentioned. But the nature of the questions being asked and how they would be analyzed and interpreted could lead to racist results undesirable for Roxbury. Or, Roxbury residents might consider them undesirable. It is quite unlikely that white researchers can understand the complexities of the black community and culture. Lacking such understanding, error is highly probable. The history of white-directed social research does not belie their argument: language deficit, cultural deprivation, fatherless homes leading to juvenile delinquency, and so forth—these types of research results provide ample evidence for the reasonable mistrust of the partisan values built into research studies carried out by well-intentioned white social scientists on black people. The scientists' focus on blacks and "black problems," rather than attention to whites and to the majority culture's racist roles and styles, confirms this mistrust.

What is apparent from the social research literature is that the most commonly used methods are built to provide scientists with the answers they generally want. The experimental design and the correlational interview survey both by themselves or even together have built-in tendencies in directions of such confirmation. Let us examine these methods in greater detail.

The experimental design has been employed by evaluation researchers in an attempt to assess the effectiveness of action programs. Such evaluation attempts generally have accepted as criteria the assumptions and value biases of action program creators and managers. Recent articles by leading evaluation researchers (Weiss and Rein, 1970; Weiss, 1970) have emphasized the failures of these efforts.

One basic issue highlighting the general inadequacy and partisanship of the experimental method as presently used lies in the process of establishing phenomena to be studied and criteria amenable for study. We have already reviewed some problems in this area with regard to language patterns. The orientation of the evaluator utilizing the experimental design is to develop specific criteria that can be carefully measured in experimental and control situations. If accepted by program administrators, such delineations severely constrain the evolutionary tendencies of action programs when dealing with specific environments, people, or communities. Moreover, such predetermined efforts at criteria development, when part of an experimental before/after design, seriously reduce the measurement and evaluation of unanticipated or emergent consequences. Given the present meager state of social science theory about desirable social action programs, the main results of any change effort may be these unanticipated outcomes.

The experimental design tends to overemphasize the fact that some treatment did or did not achieve a specified goal. This reflects the concerns of the social scientist for corroboration of his conceptual notions; it also fulfills the desires of funding agencies which are concerned with showing immediate effectiveness. These partisan research and political values may very well be counter to the long-range effects of the program. As Weiss and Rein (1970) point out, and Campbell (1970) supports, we need to know how these programs operate; we need to look thoroughly at their internal functions, what they do and why; we need to know what not to do; and we need to learn how to manage and plan such programs. The experimental design, as presently utilized, does not emphasize collection of such process data and therefore only rarely helps fulfill these needs.

The type of data collected using the experimental design tends to focus on individuals and not collectivities. This methodological bias once again feeds into a tendency to derive concepts that psychologize rather than deal with sociological variables. Further, those who utilize the experimental design tend to overemphasize the collection of quantitative data and underemphasize the importance of qualitative data. They tend to ask questions of individuals and look at the attitudes, values, and aspirations of individuals and not the documentary records, job opportunities, data from community meetings, and so on. Such types of data collection tend to emphasize those action program concerns dealing with bettering or changing individuals rather than collectives or institutions. This bias toward studying changes in the victim and not the actions that create victims reflects a clearly partisan orientation to what are relevant or potent phenomena.

In practice, then, the experimental design tends to limit seriously the scope of evaluation efforts. Although these limitations are not necessarily inherent in the method itself, its uses both as a field evaluation tool and in laboratory settings indicate the strong tendency for the social scientist using such a method to look at limited approaches to the problem being studied. The limitation most often results from the need to clearly specify and exclude variables so that proper controls may be utilized.

Another major research tool is the interview survey. While interviews or surveys often are utilized as part of an experimental design, many of them attempt to make correlations among different variables across specified populations. The key to the survey is the use of sophisticated probability sampling procedures which develop representative samples of the population under study. The use of probability sampling techniques may not be questioned seriously as a tool when one is attempting to specify demographic characteristics or to assess innocuous attitudes about general social issues; however, when dealing with sensitive political and social issues, the best sampling techniques can and do feed into the partisan approaches and interests of researchers. For instance, in a hypothetical study of student activism in high schools the major research question might be the degree to which the demands of student activists reflect widespread student feelings. The rather direct implication of this research question is how seriously should the school and the public consider the views of the activists; are they demanding changes which are generally desired by all students, or are they held uniquely by them? Let us consider such a hypothetical study.

After reading prior literature and conceptualizing the problem, researchers would begin to plan their sampling techniques and to test their quantitative instruments. The sample probably would be chosen randomly within each grade to reflect the whole school population; the questions in the individual interview or questionnaire would attempt to tap the most salient interests and values of students. In all likelihood results of such a study would indicate that 5% of the students were very alienated and between 25 and 33% of the students held highly salient values and interests similar to those of the "student activists." The majority of students would be concerned primarily with more personal concerns and only secondarily with demands for changing the school. The conclusion of such a study might be that there is limited support for activists' demands for massive educational reform. Yet two weeks later 5% of the student body might disrupt the school, and well over 70% of the students might do nothing to discourage the disruption. A small minority of the students might attempt to counter the disruptors.

The sampling techniques utilized in such a study would generate results that could not predict the potential for such disruption, might not predict the tacit support by the overwhelming majority of the students, could not specify the intensity of feelings expressed by most students, could not understand the political dynamics of the student groups, and, perhaps most critical, could not easily specify the type or degree of educational reform desirable or necessary in the school for the school to be more responsive to students' educational and personal needs. In short, sampling techniques that emphasize randomness and representativeness often overlook the intensity and degree of advocacy of student activists. Such techniques dilute political demands into technical issues of *how many feel what* rather than *who feels what, to what degree,* and *what is the content* of potential change. Thus they aid the dominant forces of social control to the detriment of minority forces for change, by emphasizing the quantity of feelings rather than the accuracy of the analysis of school conditions. As we have noted in several other contexts, individual attitudinal data may not reflect organizational or collective conditions in the social structure of the school and community. Organizational conflict is a collective experience involving differences in goals and procedures among different roles or organizational units. The use of structured interviews tuned to quantitative analyses make it extremely difficult to pick up issues that the researchers did not think about specifically ahead of time.

The point to be made is not that we are opposed to quantitative research and sampling per se. Rather, we are concerned with specifying the potential and actual partisan value positions implicit in the research methodology itself. When the quantitative survey is utilized exclusively within the context of sampling procedures which emphasize the total system, the results usually downgrade the importance and effectiveness of minority political groups that may actually tap the deep-seated feelings of large sectors of a population. To compensate for the partisan approach reflected in the use of such techniques, social scientists must employ a qualitative approach as well; an approach which tends to emphasize the roles of the more influential, more articulate, the more demanding subgroups. The quantitative survey further emphasizes the psychological aspects of individuals' adaptations to a social system, not the characteristics of the system that may be liberating or degrading to them. Compensations must quantify or at least review the bases of complex organizational forms and processes that lead to members' views and reactions.

The Use of Diagnostic Methods

Thus far our discussion has focused on methods used by social scientists in pursuit of their professional research and evaluative aims. But some scientists also use their skills to perform diagnoses of social and organizational problems. Diagnosis and research are two different activities, although they may call upon some of the same skills.

Diagnostic efforts clearly begin with specified value and service positions; their conduct deals directly with some problems and biases that evolve from the lack of scientists' accountability and consequent public hostility and suspiciousness toward science. The inaccessibility of certain groups, the potential inaccuracy of data collected, and the difficulty of specifying and assessing all relevant subgroups and people for study are key issues undermining traditional research. Without accessibility, no study can hope to present an accurate overall picture of the events or organizations observed; without some surety of the honesty or accuracy of responses no study can proceed; without being able to specify the groups or individuals to be studied an inappropriate sampling bias would severely dilute actual events.

All research studies require preliminary conceptualization of a topic and reduction of these concepts into workable or testable hypotheses. We have discussed the ways in which such simplification or "operationalization" may distort the natural complexity of organizational life. Diagnostic studies deliberately seek to preserve the nature of this reality and to resist premature conceptualization or reduction of the field of variables for methodological purposes. Evaluative studies often constrain this open inquiry posture to preserve some appearance of clarity and objectivity. Of course, in doing so they fall prey to many of the researchers' dilemmas noted earlier.

Inherent in any diagnostic effort dealing with real life issues is the necessity to specify criteria against which the data are to be judged. Social diagnosticians are interested not only in language use, for instance, but in how such verbalization relates to some other behaviors. As in any research activity, in diagnostic work the criterion problem is essential, but the question is: Whose criteria are utilized? Are the criteria of success to be defined by the funding agency? Or by the clients of the program staff? Who is to define the program goals? To what extent are the social scientists concerned with process goals of the program (staff development, staff management, type of staff-client contacts)? Decisions related to the development of criteria—in terms of who selects them and measures them—are the result of the values of the evaluators or those who control the evaluators. The importance of such decisions is that the funding agency, the program staff, and the target group may have totally different and partisan conceptions about what constitutes legitimate criteria. As Weiss (1970) notes:

> Evaluation has always had explicitly political overtones. It is designed to yield conclusions about the worth of programs and, in so doing, is intended to affect the allocation of resources. The rationale of evaluation research is that it provides evidence on which to base decisions about maintaining, institution-

alizing, and expanding successful programs and modifying or abandoning unsuccessful ones.

Weiss' clarity about the purposes of diagnostic and evaluative research clearly distinguishes it from traditional research. Its political clarity and service to program goals will affect the ways various methods are utilized. Unfortunately, many social scientists purporting to do evaluative research behave as if they were doing basic rather than service or field-oriented research.

The conduct of research is in itself an intervention into the life of an organization. The researcher often cares about such intervention only insofar as it distorts the data. The diagnostician also is concerned about the quality of life in that system. Therefore he is willing to minimize the intervention even at the cost of gaining less rigorous data. This difference often makes the diagnostic researcher vulnerable to sanctions from scientists holding to traditional norms. What is at stake here is only partly a matter of different research methods; it is a different value placed on the way respondents should be treated and the kinds of data gathered.

The awareness of the partisan perspectives unintentionally built into the use of scientific techniques does not necessarily reduce the difficulties facing survey researchers working on important issues, particularly those issues related to such minority groups as low-income blacks and students. Awareness without change in method, views of the data or relation to clients will not make a difference. In fact, Goering and Cummins report that "conventional survey research operations have failed recently to achieve acceptable levels of response in low-income areas. . . . An OEO survey of non-whites in Topeka, Kansas reported a 21 percent refusal rate and an inability to contact 31 percent of assigned households" (1970, p. 49). The suspicion and hostility of minority groups toward survey research are considerable and have some basis. With middle-class techniques and methods scholars have examined and often degraded the minds and culture of minorities. When done in the name of political debate and preferences, such statements can be met and reacted to in the public arena. When such distortion is draped in the cloak of truth and value-free science, minorities have difficulty defending themselves. Thus science itself must be rejected by these groups.

Diagnostic efforts may be able to avoid such traps. For instance, Goering and Cummins (1970) maintain that in a study they did with similar groups they had no such problems. The major reason for success evidently was that their survey was closely articulated to the goals and life styles of the population studied. The first steps in the study involved discussions with community leaders and members. Members from community agencies exerted pressures on the researchers for the utilization of local citizens as staff of the study. When these arrangements were agreed to the project was approved by the community. In reference to these experiences the authors state:

> One of the most manifest reasons for the rejection of researchers relates to the broad context of the participatory revolution which has as its central axis the decentralization of control to the local neighborhood level. The poor, by attempting to get a handle on the power needed to control their own environment, are informing social scientists that their "specific" tools are seen as part of the configuration of power which built and maintains the ghetto. Reform and evaluation at a distance are unacceptable to the new forms of community organization and control which are arising in association with the moves toward black separation and minority group power (Goering and Cummins, 1970, p. 51).

The message is that people, particularly black and poor people, are refusing to be used for research purposes. They refuse the one-way exploitation of their minds for abstract scholarly purposes and desire programatic help or employment in return. The role of the diagnostician clearly acknowledges this dynamic and seeks to avoid such exploitation. In order to carry out such diagnostic research Goering and Cummins (1970) propose the following procedures:

1. Use community representatives as interviewers.

2. Establish legitimacy and accountability based on the potential for the research to end in community problem solving.

3. Use the language of the ghetto.

4. Continue the interaction between community representative/interviewer and researcher, which "sensitizes the interviewers to research strategies and the researchers to community problems and issues."

Suchman (1967) and Galtung (1967) also suggest using program recipients in more than an interviewing capacity; they should be involved in creating the study design, interpreting data, and deriving implications for program direction. This means they must have continual access to the data and its use. It is our view that they should be able to control use of the data as well.

If the diagnosis is then fed to indigenous advocates, the diagnostician-scholar is unavoidably involved in the generation of community change. Direct two-way involvement in the community change process permits the diagnostician to contribute to the betterment of the human condition as well as to collect data relevant to particular issues. Sanford (1970) emphasized the critical importance of such involvement in the life of the community. Direct participation in an action-research process is essential for understanding many of the most exciting and crucial events of our society. The academic researcher cannot assess accurately the human meaning of crisis and conflict in communities, schools, and so forth, because his distance is a barrier to seeing the critical issues to be studied. It is only through close involvement that one can really understand and therefore conduct effective scholarship for social problems and issues. Mutual involvement in diagnosis then makes such scholarship and the scholarly process partisan, but we have argued this is true of all research in such settings. The questions are: (1) Whose side are you on? (2) Do you know it?

Utilization Issues in Partisan Diagnosis

All attempts at inquiry into the nature of social systems carry with them a variety of implications for the eventual utilization of this knowledge for a variety of clients in a variety of ways. Scholars who do not pay strict attention to the potential utilization of their data by varied consumers may ill prepare their data for such consumption and unwittingly collude with consumers or clients they do not wish to serve. Scholars who desire their inquiries to be utilized for the improvement of the human condition must attend to these concerns in the development of their instruments and methods and in the interpretation of their data. It is too late to tack on a concern for utilization at the end of a social research process.

An initial proposition in our consideration of the utilization of social scientific knowledge, then, is that such knowledge or system diagnoses are always utilized by one or many sets of consumers. A scientific report published in even the most obscure academic journal or limited mimeograph will nevertheless find its way into the hands of people who desire to put that knowledge to work for their own gain or for their partisan definition of social welfare. This is to be expected, and scholars who do not understand this proposition are attempting to bury their heads in the sand. The naivete of such efforts to avoid reality is well reflected by the "Oppenheimer syndrome," a condition describing a generation of well-meaning physical scientists who decided either not to worry about, or that they could not control, the utilization of their research. Utilization cannot be denied; since it is likely to happen it becomes an ethical responsibility of the scientist, especially the social scientist, to be concerned about utilization.

Diagnostic information is most likely to be utilized effectively if findings are prepared and presented at a relatively low level of specificity and if generalizations remain narrow (Suchman, 1967). But even fairly low-level generalizations must be mined for their concrete implications in a field setting. One of the requirements here is that the scientists collect and share data and interpretations that the practitioner can use. (Chesler and Flanders, 1967). As we noted previously, this concern usually has low priority for the traditional researcher; for him, usable findings are not nearly as important as basic knowledge. But usability is partly an issue of specifying the use and/or the user; without defined users, usability is difficult.

There is a further step beyond generating findings that may have interesting implications; that is, to move from these implications to specific programs and action recommendations. But specific findings do not necessarily become policy recommendations unless they are clarified mutually by policy-oriented scientists and science-oriented practitioners. For instance, we may consider the research finding that white teachers consistently underestimate and often are ignorant of the human potentials and learning abilities of their black students. Such a finding does not provide us with clear policy recommendations; we also need to know the degree of information these white teachers had about their black students, the way the black students in that class or community perceive their white teachers, the extent to which students resist or are willing to collaborate with these teachers, the social structure of faculty and student-faculty relations, and the school's interface with the local community. With these data one could begin to prepare a set of policy recommendations about teachers' need for greater information, for antiracism training, for termination of their contracts, or for the hiring of black teachers to whom black students might be less resistant. Diagnoses will be most relevant to social policy if concerns about utilization and a sophistication about the program setting are present at the beginning of a study.

This discussion stresses the fact that the kind of information gathered determines the use possible, and the possible user. Research inquires into what can be studied in the terms accepted by the scientific profession; as such it reduces the complexities of life to manageable inquiries. Diagnosis seeks knowledge that is needed by practitioners who have partisan program interests. Although generic knowledge may be necessary in illuminating fundamental organizational strains and conditions, it may not be sufficient for considering specific institutional changes. The diagnosis of problems or of institutional conditions must be undertaken with the potentialities for institutional change in mind. The character of values embodied in potential attempts at change give form and meaning to the kind of diagnostic information required in a specific setting.

It should be clear that no meaningful diagnosis can be undertaken without preliminary conceptualization of the goals of change or of the building of new social institutions. Further, shotgun diagnoses that do not screen variables and do not rely on systematic knowledge bases are unordered, ad hoc activities. They may gather documentary or descriptive material but fail to provide material for enlightened diagnostic interpretations. Thus diagnostic research must be systematized, conceptualized, and generalized, but unlike traditional research efforts, the purpose here is to guide better diagnoses, not to develop a set of testable propositions.

Many social scientists systematically overcollect data, seeking ultimate information on all variables. Sanford (1970) refers to this waste as a form of pollution generated by the social science industry.[2] Diagnostic efforts force an economy of data collection and a parsimony of analysis that stresses the most vital issues. Therefore it requires prior conceptualization and informed guesses to limit data collected and to combat the compulsively hoarding instincts of raw empiricism. But this screening is guided by needs to relate more effectively to reality, not to achieve methodological parsimony or theoretical elegance. Overcollection exacts a further toll in terms of exploitation of respondents for the scientists' stylistic purposes, a bias that should be inconceivable for a diagnostician accountable to his respondents and their interests.

The search for truth is simply not the same as the search for ways to be helpful. Scholars seeking these different avenues think and act very differently.

Once the utilization of knowledge commences, so does partisan utilization. Utilization logically requires acts by some one or some institution for some purpose. Purposes involve preferences, values, and conflicts in values among persons who disagree or who have different partisan interests at stake. Most diagnostic research is conducted by and for highly influential members of major social institutions. Typically they are the sponsors of such inquiry; they have funds and find it easy to approach and trust members of the scientific profession. Caro (1971) argues that such sponsorship controls the outcomes as well as the uses of data. Other scholars have argued that they can retain their autonomy and integrity in these circumstances. It is our view that they may retain the integrity of the conduct of their research, although we have already indicated how unlikely this is, but certainly not its utilization.

Both the basic researcher who feels he is neutral and the applied researcher who knowingly serves establishment interests feed these information-hungry elite groups. As Kelman argues, "One can easily fail to notice the role of value preferences when he works within the frame of the status quo, since its value assumptions are so much second nature to members of the society that they perceive them as part of objective reality" (1968, p. 5). We have already noted several ways in which apparently neutral or value-free research may be used to serve the interests of persons in positions of power or managerial control. Data may be used to interpret organizational problems as minor or as less important than system maintenance; thus they may provide justification for suppression of attempts to create change. At the same time, data may provide management with a rhetoric which enables them to cool out protestors and help individuals accommodate to the institution to which they belong. These uses are not accidental: the nature of political and technological power in society, and the structure of the profession's dependence on the good graces of that power, convert "neutral" research into acts of service to prevailing elites. As Etzioni (1971, p. 9) points out, "Those in power usually can gain research inputs more easily than can those out of power."

Similar uses of data may be seen in recent attempts to understand the nature of student protests and disruptions in urban and suburban secondary schools. Variables such as adult permissiveness, parental lack of control, and adolescent exuberance have been used to help explain unrest and to justify schools' enhanced control over young people. Although these data may be accurate or erroneous, narrowly construed or broadly valid, they help school administrators focus away from organizational issues onto characteristics of students. The failure of teachers and administrators to provide good communication and trust with youngsters can then be seen as temporary aberrations in the otherwise effective operations of our educational system. On the other hand, diagnoses that render wholesale visability to the inadequate content and process of education are not usually accepted or used by those who manage our school system. Thus they are seldom studied by managerially oriented researchers.

A common practice in many applied studies of industrial organizations is to provide feedback of diagnostic data to organizational managers. Sometimes this design is consciously limited to reaching managers, as in the filing of specific research reports with local administrators only. At other times, when no specific attempt is made to put data in the hands of persons other than managers, managers are the only ones with access to the data, to personnel journals, to social scientific reporting agencies, and the like. Data provided to managers help accommodate their psychological feeling of being on top of the organization and support their sense of confidence in their ability to intelligently organize institutional affairs. When the researcher shares finding without attending to the issues of power and control in an organization he wittingly or unwittingly aids individuals in managerial roles with even more data and information.

Our national history makes it very clear that data placed in the hands of certain organizational or cultural entities help prepare and maintain various social mythologies convenient for the majority's control of institutional and social life. For instance, white scholars' interpretations of the intelligence test scores and academic performance data of black youngsters have helped maintain the mythology of black inadequacy. While some have argued that such inadequacy is a product of genetic malformation and therefore blacks need to be controlled and dominated, others have argued that this inadequacy is more a function of environment. However, both analyses lead in the same direction, as they perpetuate a myth of blacks' needs for special forms of help and whites' justification for paternalistic benevolence. Either interpretation, as supported by scientific projections of the inadequacies of black students, lends fuel to white liberal and conservative attempts to dominate, manage, and overprotect blacks. Billingsley (1970) argues the inevitability of this state of affairs when white scientists try to study aspects of black social circumstances. The white establishment listens to and uses information about black and white issues selectively—in partisan ways. Even when attempts are made to communicate clearly the oppressive function of white racism, for instance, only certain portions of the population believe the uncomfortable messages of social science (Supplemental report, 1969).[3]

If black scholars or leaders had access to similar data and channels of scientific communication, they could reinterpret earlier reported data on blacks to destroy the stereotype of black inadequacy and press the view of white cultural domination. As long as whites are in control of these data and interpretations it is unlikely that findings other than messages of inadequacy will find substantial support. This is due partly to the whites' ignorance of or blindness to black issues, partly to whites' desires to protect white sovereignty, and partly because whites who work for or write for other whites wish to express ideas congenial to their audience. To the extent that not only whites but adults of any race are in charge of the data interpreting student dissent, it is unlikely that interpretations consistent with youth's needs and demands for alteration and control of the educational apparatus will be made. For sympathetic data and reports to appear in a consistent manner it may be necessary for youth to hire and reward their own researchers.

We have argued before that some partisan biases are created because most social scientists are funded by agents of a class similar to their own, who expect them to provide information to those who manage social institutions. At a time in history when various professional groups may hold the key to survival, success, and institutional order, scientists, as others, are expected to be loyal to professional interests and concerns (Haug and Sussman, 1970). Professionals—scientists included—have become a social category with interests of their own. Public service or truth is often subsumed to intellectual dogma, technological mysticism, and career mobility. Especially tragic is the circumstance where the interests of scholars and system managers are paralleled and reinforce one another. Truth and the poor, black, and young evidently suffer together.

What is crucial in this regard is that researchers and diagnosticians must be more overt about the consumers and clients of their efforts. Just as it is impossible for scholars to be neutral and for their works to be value free, it is also impossible for their works to be utilized in value-free ways. It is not necessarily inappropriate for scholars to serve the interests of system managers; nor is it inappropriate for them to serve advocates for change, although the former is far more common and highly rewarded than the latter. What is both naive and dangerous is the scholars' assumptions that they serve no one but the truth; in effect they have no institutional master but are a law unto themselves and their profession. Berlack (1970) stresses the need for experts to be accountable to the people. And information surely constitutes a basis for expertise.

Rainwater and Yancy (1967) appear to agree with one part of our discussion as they review the need for more careful diagnostic work and attention to policy issues. In their review of the Moynihan controversy they note "the greater need of government for social scientists who are directly concerned with policy related issues rather than with data gathering or other established and routine functions" (p. 300). The diagnostic function of scholars undoubtedly needs greater emphasis, as we argued earlier. But why such services should be concentrated in the partisan hands of governmental agencies is not clear. All interest groups or systems pursuing humanitarian ends need such services. Not only does government lack a monopoly of such concerns, its great commitment to the status quo of power relations and resource allocations places it in the dangerous position for potential misuse.

Utilization Roles for Partisan Diagnosticians

We have indicated our disagreements with those scholars who elect to ignore the ubiquitous character of utilization and partisanship, or who elect not to deal with the implications of their work for these concerns. But where does the partisan fit, what does he look like, what does he do? The social scientist who conducts diagnoses of social intitutional problems may play a variety of roles in attempts to help utilize those diagnoses. But at this time in history there is neither tradition nor professional legitimacy to guide him.

The increasing number of young scholars seeking activist roles holds great promise for a more accountable and relevant social science. But contemporary models of partisan utilization depict a scholar who is "irrelevantly trained, moonlighting in various causes, unable yet to reconcile his professional role with that of his concerned citizen role" (Kutner et al., 1970). As such, he wanders ambivalently among roles, subject to internal ambiguity and anxiety, and beset with varied and unclear client expectations. Moreover, peer and external political pressures mitigate against exploration of these terms. Clarity about role possibilities and about the risks involved in new role behaviors are essential; the following illustrations seem to have some possibility as guides for partisan utilizers of social diagnoses.

First, he may act as *broker* or *gatekeeper of information* per se. He may decide, in other words, whether diagnoses and information will be shared and with whom they may be shared. Of course, this is only possible when the scholar retains control of his own data; "his own" data, however, are the product of the respondents' minds. Whether the scholar can be considered as owner or custodian of these data, and whether he considers the fruits accountable to himself or respondents, has already been discussed.

Partisan scholars may choose to operate as part of the society's elitist structure and to *serve directly the needs and desires of persons and groups in control* or in high-status positions in certain social institutions. It is clear that there is a historic pattern of collaboration and collusion between action-oriented social scientists and managers of social systems. Without conscious efforts to the contrary, we have argued, this is the direction in which most social science research is developed and utilized. In this context, readily utilizable diagnoses are more likely to be positively or negatively useful than is obscure research.

Scholars may operate as *information disseminators,* as when the ideas, findings, and interpretations of applied or basic researchers are communicated and disseminated to the professional or lay public. As we have suggested, the scholar cannot assume automatically that he is acting neutrally in this regard. Unless he provides equal access to the information for a variety of competing client and consumer groups, he ends up sharing potentially vital information primarily with establishment interests. The structure of dissemination opportunities assures that people most like scholars—in class and style—have greatest access to their written or verbal outputs. Since these people most often represent managerial concerns, mere dissemination unconsciously provides service to one type of partisan group. As in project Camelot (Horowitz, 1967), many liberal scientists assume that people in power will do good if shown the truth. The truth—scientific information—is power, and it helps maintain power arrangements. Guaranteeing access is not the same thing as laissez-faire dissemination; only a deliberate policy to guarantee different groups equal access does anything other than retain access in the hands of managerial groups.

The partisan scholar may also act as a *collaborator* or *consultant to various groups* seeking humanitarian social or organizational change. In this context the scholar may help utilize data and diagnoses; he may aid groups in an organization which have different positions understand and interpret the data. Beyond understanding and interpretation, of course, the scientist may also act as a partisan-advisor to certain groups and as a self-conscious political advocate of their interests and policy concerns stemming from the data. But it should be clear that true advocacy is possible only from the inside. Affluent, adult white scholars never truly advocate poor, young, or black people's interests.

To attempt to advocate another group's interests requires that a social scientist understand the strict limitations of his legitimacy; he can collect data and use his social science skills, but only if these data are seen as the group's property and not his; or he can just turn himself over to the group and let them utilize whatever skills they need. Such actions require almost total commitment by the partisan scholar; this kind of *accountability* is difficult but potentially very important. The true "democratization of knowledge" requires that citizens affected by professional advice and/or control have access both to the knowledge professionals have and to the means they have to exercise control. Recent work in the field of advocacy planning indicates the benefits and difficulties of such a role (Guskin and Ross, 1971).

One example of the role of advocate desired by oppressed community groups is the scholar as *technical aid* (Karenga, 1969). Just as one may act as a statistician for the Department of Housing and Urban Development, one may gather knowledge for poor people fighting HUD rulings. In this example, too, the historic autonomy of the social scientist is voluntarily given up in service to certain groups. One of the ways professionals can provide aid without continuing control is to train client groups or program recipients to conduct their own diagnoses and evaluations (Caro, 1971).

A role that cuts across a number of the foregoing categories is that of a *linker* between opposing groups. This type of social scientist would attempt to provide each of the groups with open access to information of direct relevance to them as well as helping each of the groups understand and deal with the information. If one connects to two opposing groups, all the questions of partisan commitment or loyalty must be encountered.

Modifications of such a role occur when members of one group link directly to another group for purposes of collaboration. The collaborative role of any type of linker, social scientist or other professional, is extremely tenuous—questions of legitimacy, intentionality, and a general paranoia are likely occurrences. This would be particularly true for the nonelite partisan groups. For them, any person who carries information from the elites—whether implicitly or explicitly—is suspect. This realistic paranoia is the result of years of experience dealing with liberal "dogooders" who continuously coopted and "cooled out" the poor and other minority groups. The past and present roles of the social scientist have exacerbated the problem: the social science planning for the poverty program placed major emphasis on changing the victim (e.g., the Job Corps and cultural deficit/Head Start programs) and diverting attention from the source of victimization (e.g., the institutional bases of racism and poverty).

The scholarly cloak of neutrality worn to protect one's professional status from democratic public consideration and attack is simply not viable. The nature of personal preferences, scientific methodology, consumer patterns, and the fabric of the society make value neutrality an impossible activity, let alone a viable conception of one's self. The question is, To what extent will scientists be conscious and deliberate about their partisanship, as opposed to being unconscious and therefore irresponsible? Moreover, it is important to discover to what extent and in what capacities scientists are more than translators of data but are actual definers of policy. At this point the scientists cannot hide behind the cloak of scientific immunity but must air their views in the body politic where "professional" interpretations of data are made with certain valued preferences in mind and must be stacked up against persons who may have less knowledge but just as strong value preferences. In such settings various publics do not have to fight hidden technicians but can exercise their democratic right to decision making and to the implementation of scholarly inquiry.

Notes

1. We acknowledge the assistance of our colleagues at the Educational Change Team and the Institute for Social Research in clarifying our views of traditional and innovative patterns of social science research and action.

2. Survey research institutions and offices literally are stuffed with unanalyzed data.

3. Many people evidently did not believe the basic messages of the Kerner Commission Report (National Advisory Commission on Civil Disorders, 1967).

Donald P. Warwick

Department of Sociology and Anthropology
York University

Herbert C. Kelman

Department of Social Relations
Harvard University

ETHICAL ISSUES IN
SOCIAL INTERVENTION

Social intervention is any act, planned or unplanned, that alters the characteristics of another individual or the pattern of relationships between individuals. The range of acts covered in this definition is intentionally broad. It includes such macro phenomena as national planning, military intervention in the affairs of other nations, population policy, and technical assistance. It also applies to psychotherapy, sensitivity training, neighborhood action programs, experimentation with human subjects, and other micro changes. The concept of social intervention seems more helpful in considering the ethics of social change than the concept of "planned change," which tends to exclude from ethical review a host of activities with serious personal, social, and political implications.

The existing literature on planned change (e.g., Lippitt, Watson, and Westley, 1958; Bennis, Benne, and Chin, 1969) confines itself to a relatively narrow range of interventions. The usual paradigm is concerned with micro efforts such as organizational development or community action programs. An organized attempt by a business corporation to improve communication, morale, and productivity in its U.S. plant is considered planned change; a decision by the same company to build a new plant in Guatemala is not. In fact, the greater the scale and impact of social intervention, the less likely it is to be called planned change. One reason is that models of planned change place heavy emphasis on the role

377

of the change agent, often a social science consultant. In many cases of macro change, it is extremely difficult to fit the facts of the situation into a paradigm involving change agents and client systems. The decision by the General Motors Corporation to build an automobile plant in Oshawa, Ontario, was undoubtedly the result of complex deliberations within the corporation and then further negotiations with the Canadian and U.S. governments. No single change agent was involved, and it would be hard to find a "client" for the action. Yet the result was a major intervention with critical effects on the Canadian economy and, some would argue, on Canadian political autonomy (cf. Levitt, 1970).

A second and very different example further illustrates the need for a broader focus in viewing the ethics of social change. It is now clear that psychoanalysis, which began as a theory of personality and a system of psychotherapy, has had a marked impact on morality and self-conception in Western societies (Seeley, 1967; Rieff, 1961, 1966). In many cases guilt about the presence of strong sexual impulses has been replaced by shame about their absence. Repression has become the secular equivalent of sin, mental health the substitute for salvation. Judged by its effects, psychoanalysis would certainly qualify as one of the cardinal social interventions of the century. Yet by the usual standards it would not meet the test of planned change, nor could Freud properly be considered a change agent in producing these larger effects.

A focus on social intervention, more broadly defined, allows for ethical evaluation of institutional structures and practices with critical social effects, as well as of situations with more readily identifiable change agents. We can thus explore the ethical implications of government policies or intellectual traditions, for example, even though these are not explicitly geared toward producing social change and are not associated with a single individual or agency. The major focus of our discussion, however, will be on deliberate interventions. In many cases the difference between deliberate and nondeliberate intervention is itself the central issue in an ethical evaluation. Insofar as an intervention remains nondeliberate, it is relatively easy to ignore its effects. A heightened awareness of the consequences of social intervention is at the heart of ethical responsibility and concern.

The moral questions raised by social intervention are as old as human society: What are the ends of men? Of the various "goods" known to man, which should be pursued above the others? What are the rights of men and societies? What abridgments of human freedom are necessary for the common good? And, most difficult, what criteria should be used to choose among alternative ends and means?

Value Preferences and Value Conflicts

One can distinguish four aspects of any social intervention that raise major ethical issues: (1) the choice of goals to which the change effort is directed; (2) the definition of the target of change; (3) the choice of means used to implement the intervention; and (4) the assessment of the consequences of the intervention. At each of these steps, the ethical issues that arise may involve conflicting values—questions about what values are to be maximized at the expense of what other values. (We define values as individual or shared conceptions of the desirable, that is, "goods" considered worth pursuing.)

Thus values determine the choice of goals to which a change effort is directed. On the one hand, the intervention is designed to maximize a particular set of values. For example, a government may undertake a massive literacy program with the avowed intention of increasing the freedom of its citizens. On the other hand, those setting the goals of an intervention are also concerned with minimizing the loss in certain other values. These imperiled values thus serve as criteria of tolerable and intolerable costs in a given intervention. Under pressures of rapid demographic growth and limited resources, for example, a government might contemplate a set of coercive population control measures, such as involuntary sterilization, to reduce fertility. The benefit to be promoted by this program would be the common welfare or, in extreme cases, even the physical survival of the country. At the same time the policy makers might be concerned about the effects of this program on two other values: freedom and justice. These values would be seen as social goods to be preserved—benefits that should not fall below some minimal threshold. Values may influence the choice of goals not only in such explicit, conscious ways but also in a covert way. This may happen, as we shall see, when a change program departs from a value-based but unquestioned definition of a "problem."

The definition of the target of change is often based on just this kind of implicit, unexamined conception of where the problem lies. For example, a change effort designed to improve the conditions of an economically disadvantaged group—such as the black population in the United States—may be geared primarily toward changing institutional arrangements that have led to the systematic exclusion of this group from the economic life of the country, or toward reducing the educational, environmental, or psychological "deficiencies" of the disadvantaged group itself. The choice between these two primary targets of change may well depend on one's value perspective: a focus on removing systemic barriers is more reflective of the values of the disadvantaged group itself, whereas a focus on removing deficiencies suggests the values of the more established segments of the society.

Third, values play a central role in an ethical evaluation of the means chosen to implement a given intervention. Questions about the morality of coercion, manipulation, deception, persuasion, and other methods of inducing change typically involve a conflict between the values of individual freedom and self-determination, on the one hand, and such values as social welfare, economic progress, or equal opportunity, on the other. For example, to what extent and under what conditions is a government justified in imposing limits on the freedom to procreate for the sake of presumed long-run improvements in the quality of life?

Finally, conflicting values enter into assessment of the consequences of a social intervention. One of the consequences of industrialization, for example, may be a weakening of traditional authority structures or family bonds. To what extent one is willing to risk these consequences depends on his commitment to such traditional values relative to those values that industrialization is designed to enhance. In other words, our assessment of the consequences of an intervention depends on what values we are willing or unwilling to sacrifice in the interest of social change.

Before examining some of the ethical problems that may arise at each of these four points in the change process, and the value conflicts from which they derive, we shall consider some more general procedural issues that must be faced in any effort at applied ethics. These refer to the procedures to be followed in deriving the values that apply in a social intervention, in determining whose values should be given what weight, and in adjudicating value conflicts.

The Derivation and Content of Values. An analysis of the ethics of social intervention presumes some notion of what values should apply and how they are to be derived. The problem is simplified, of course, if the analyst simply accepts the values held out by the initiators of the change. Hence, if a government agency says that it undertook a population program in order to promote the general welfare, and that it also considered the costs of the program for individual freedom, the analyst might confine his attention to the values of freedom and welfare. Few students of ethics, however, would be content to let the individual or group initiating a change be the sole judge of the relevant values at stake. The human bent toward selective perception and self-deception, not to mention the protection of vested political interests, is simply too great to justify this approach. In the example cited, the concerned observer might also wish to examine the effects of the population program on other values, such as justice, dignity, or the self-esteem of minority groups. By leaving the definition of the ethical situation to the sponsor of a program one abdicates his own moral judgment.

Ultimately the choice of values as well as their application depends on one's final court of ethical appeal. The bases for choosing and using values are varied and often incompatible. Gustafson (1970, pp. 169–170) discusses a number of the different bases that may underlie such choices. For some, especially in the Judaic and Christian traditions, an appeal is made to revelation. The salient values are those contained in scripture. Others, especially members of the Catholic Church, have looked to "natural law" as a basis for moral values. Many outside this religious tradition show a similar belief in the capacity of human reason to arrive at self-evident moral truths. Still others hope to derive a framework of values on an inductive basis through an examination of ethnographic reports and other materials from the social sciences. For their part, social scientists often work with value frameworks derived from their theories of man and society. Lasswell and Kaplan (1950), for example, propose a set of eight values thought to cover a wide variety of human situations. At the opposite end of the spectrum are the cultural relativists who hold that value analysis should be founded on an understanding of the rights and obligations prevailing within a single society, rather than on general paradigms.

In practice the situation is not as hopelessly eclectic as this diversity of approaches would suggest. Closer analysis of the *results* of these positions reveals considerable overlap, often obscured by differing terminology. The most salient values suggested by natural law theories are very similar to those derived from revelation. The notions of freedom, justice, love, and the common good are likely to appear in any general ethical theory, and they usually have their counterparts in social scientific theories. Even the cultural relativists often approach value analysis with a set of categories not unlike those of classical ethics. Still, the task of laying out the content and derivation of values remains a fundamental challenge in any discussion of ethics. Let us consider two examples illustrating ways in which this challenge can be met.

The first comes from *The Cruel Choice* by Denis Goulet (1971), a recent work on the ethics of economic and social development. Goulet asks if it is possible to identify "any common values which all societies desire and which development claims to foster" (p. 87). He concludes:

. . . three such values can be recognized as goals sought by all individuals and societies. These are proper universalizable goals inasmuch as their forms and modalities can vary in different times and places. Nevertheless, these goals relate to fundamental human needs capable of finding expression in all cultural matrices at all times (p. 87).

The first of these is *life sustenance*. The nurture of life is everywhere treasured by sane men. . . . All objects that satisfy men's basic requirements for food, shelter, healing, or survival can be called life-sustaining "goods". . . .

A second universal component of the good life is *esteem*—what Everett Hagen calls every man's sense that he is a being of worth, that he is respected, that others are not using him as a tool to attain their purposes without regard for his own purposes. All men and all societies seek esteem, although they may call it identity, dignity, respect, honor, or recognition . . . (p. 89).

A third trans-cultural component of the good life, valued by developed and non-developed societies alike, is *freedom*. Countless meanings attach to this troublesome word. At the very least it signifies an expanded range of choices for societies and their members, together with the minimization of constraints (external, though not necessarily internal) in the pursuit of some perceived good (p. 91).

Though few would contest the ethical desirability of these three values, certain questions could be raised about the process by which they were derived. In the passages cited and elsewhere Goulet indicates that he used two basic criteria: (1) universality—the degree to which a value represents "goals sought by all individuals and societies"; and (2) the frequency with which "development" claims to foster this value. Presumably, a value would qualify for inclusion by the second criterion if it appeared with some regularity in statements of development goals. One might ask, first, why the author accepts the essentially statistical approach implied in this criterion. Furthermore, assuming that the criterion refers to statements in the existing literature, one might ask why he confined his attention to present possibilities. If a broader criterion had been used, additional values might have been included, such as justice, power, beauty, and affection. In short, the nature of the operative values in any change effort depends on the procedures used in deriving these values. Deliberate attention to these procedures therefore is an important step in an ethical evaluation.

A rather different strategy for deriving values was adopted in a study of ethics and population policy by the Population Task Force of the Institute of Society, Ethics, and the Life Sciences (1971).[1] The Task Force tried to set forth the core values in American society that might affect or be affected by population policy. Its central concern was not cultural universals—values present in all known societies—but rather the values and principles undergirding the traditions and institutions of the United

States. The final report identified four values as central to the American tradition, and several others that form an important part of the culture. The four core values were:

1. *Freedom.* The capacity, the opportunity, and the incentive to make reflective choices and to act on these choices.

2. *Justice.* Fairness in the distribution of goods and harms within the society, including fair bases of distribution.

3. *Welfare.* Maintenance and/or improvement of the health, well-being, and similar vital interests of members of the society. This concept embraces those goods and services required to live decently, such as air, water, natural resources, good health, and perhaps beauty, space, privacy, art, and culture.

4. *Security/Survival.* Remaining alive (survival) and enjoying freedom from fear of extinction or reduction to a subhuman condition, physically or psychologically (security). These concepts may be applied to individuals, the human species as a whole, ethnic, religious, racial, or other groups, a culture, or a nation.

The other values identified in the report included truth-telling, duty, political power, cultural styles and traditions (e.g., of immigrant groups), religious values, and kinship (including a special emphasis on children and child-bearing).

This set of values was derived from an analysis of the cultural and legal traditions in the United States. The fundamental criterion of derivation was thus essentially empirical, though it was obviously guided by ethical and political theory. If the focus had been Africa or Latin America, the list of core values would have been somewhat different. Kinship and religious values might have received greater emphasis than freedom. Also, the specific definitions of the values, such as the bases of freedom, welfare, and justice, would probably have been modified. The approach followed by the Task Force could be criticized on the grounds that the criteria used in arriving at core values were established by the research sponsor, the Commission on Population growth and the American Future. Those who lean toward a more "universal" approach might also object to the nation-specific focus of this study.

The critical point is not that one approach is right or wrong in the abstract, but that the initial choice of value categories is one of the most basic decisions in ethical analysis. Goulet's critique of development theories would have been quite different had he chosen the values of private enterprise, political order, and social stability. The Population Task Force might have drawn another set of conclusions if it had focused on the preservation of world resources, international social justice, and the maintenance of large-family traditions. Though we cannot hope to arrive at a set of value categories that would be suitable for all forms of social intervention, at the very least we can reduce the arbitrariness in selecting the ingredients for ethical discussion. An explicit statement of one's own values is a helpful step in this direction, but it is not enough. Since personal and ideological preferences are involved in the choice of such values, it is also important to indicate how they were derived and why a particular set was adopted. Without this second step ethical debate is left in a hopeless quagmire of "I think" statements.

Whose Values Should Be Given What Weight? Another fundamental procedural question concerns the weights assigned to different, and often competing, sets of values. Discussions of national population policy sharply raise the issue of whose values should prevail. The Population Task Force of the Institute of Society, Ethics, and the Life Sciences (1971) addressed this question in its report:

> The American ethical, legal and political tradition is rich in the elaboration of basic values which have been present since the beginning. That is why it is possible to speak of an American tradition, one which also joins the mainstream of the western tradition as a whole. The United States is also constituted of many different racial, ethnic, class, religious and professional groups, each with value perspectives special (if not necessarily unique) to themselves.
>
> The formation of a population policy must take account of these realities, not only because a traditional commitment to pluralism requires it, but also because any population policy formulated in ignorance of these realities will stand in dire political jeopardy (p. 65).

The report goes on to show variations in cultural values and definitions of the "population problem" among blacks, Spanish-speaking Americans, American Indians, feminist groups, the New Left, the major religious groups, economic groups, and population specialists. Blacks, for example, show a fear of physical or cultural genocide, and a positive concern for group survival and power. Spanish-American culture seems to place a stronger emphasis on family ties and children than U.S. society as a whole. The New Left is suspicious that the current emphasis on population and pollution may be an evasion of more basic problems such as poverty and war. Thus even at the national level the decisions about social intervention must weight the claims and concerns of diverse groups within the society.

The problem of "whose values" becomes even more complex in international programs of development or technical assistance. Such programs are often planned and carried out by individuals and agencies external to the society in which changes are introduced. Because of the real possibility that the values of the change agents may deviate from those of the local population, the question of whose values determine the goals, targets, and means of change takes on special importance. The issue is not only whose interests are being served by the program, but whose conceptual framework generates the definition of the problem and the setting of goals. The latter problem persists even when representatives of the local society are fully involved in the planning and execution of the change program, since these representatives—often trained abroad —may themselves have adopted the conceptual framework of the external agency.

Images of the "ideal person" to which change efforts should be directed provide a good illustration of the possible effects of competing values on the way in which development is conceptualized. Western writers have often described the ideal person (from the point of view of development) as one who possesses those personality traits and attitudes conducive to rapid economic growth and/or political effectiveness. For example, Alex Inkeles (1966) includes the following characteristics in his list of attitudes of "modern man": a disposition to accept new ideas and try new methods; a readiness to form and hold opinions over a broad range of problems and issues; a democratic orientation to opinions; a time sense oriented more to the present and future than to the past; and a sense of personal efficacy. He concludes:

> I have pointed to a set of qualities of mind that I call modern, which I believe have much to recommend them. They are not compatible in all respects with qualities that are widespread in traditional cultures, but I believe that they are qualities men can adopt without coming into conflict, in most cases, with what is best in their cultural tradition and spiritual heritage. I believe they represent some of the best things in the modernization process. But whether we view them as positive or negative, we must recognize these as qualities that are fostered by modern institutions, qualities that in many ways are required of the citizens of modern societies (pp. 149–150).

The set of modern attitudes identified by Inkeles derives, at least in part, from an empirical analysis: these are the attitudes found to be held by individuals, in several societies, who have had experience with "modernizing institutions" such as the factory. Nevertheless, Inkeles' statement reflects, to a considerable extent, his personal judgment and is thus undoubtedly influenced by his own values, rooted in his particular cultural experiences. First, the statement makes certain empirical assumptions that are by no means inevitable. There is certainly empirical support for the proposition that the qualities listed are conducive to economic growth and good citizenship, but the support is not overwhelming, and, in any event, it does not demonstrate that these are the only qualities consistent with development. The statement also assumes that these qualities are usually consistent "with what is best" in various cultural traditions— an assumption for which it would be exceedingly difficult to muster empirical support. Even if the empirical assumptions were entirely correct, however, the decision to promote the modern attitudes identified by Inkeles would constitute a value judgment. These attitudes may indeed facilitate economic and political modernization, but, as Inkeles points out, "they are not compatible in all respects with qualities that are widespread in traditional cultures." It is not a forgone conclusion that the requirements of modernization must be given priority over the protection of traditional values and, indeed, it can be argued that any effort to change personality and basic orientations for instrumental reasons is ethically questionable.

To point out that Inkeles' statement is influenced by his personal and cultural values does not constitute a criticism of that statement. Indeed, it is our position that such statements inevitably reflect value judgments and priorities, even when they are partly based on empirical evidence. Recognition of this fact sensitizes us to the need of asking *whose* values are reflected in a given statement and of giving proper weight to competing points of view. Since the writings of social scientists often provide the conceptual frameworks for development programs, it is particularly important to scrutinize them in these terms.

We shall have more to say about the ethical implications of whose values are reflected in a social intervention—or in the conceptual frameworks that underlie it—in later sections, particularly when we discuss the choice of goals for change efforts.

The Resolution of Value Conflicts. Deliberate attention to the content and derivation of values and to the different groups whose values are engaged by a given action often reveals value conflicts. Different values held within the same group and differences in value priorities set by different groups may present incompatible claims. Perhaps the most difficult challenge for ethical analysis is in providing some approximate guidelines for adjudicating such competing claims.

Consider the case of population policy. Advocates of a noninterventionist policy typically base their arguments on the value of freedom. In this view legal or other limits on procreative behavior place unwarranted restrictions on the liberty of couples to determine their own family size. Those who favor strong population control measures, on the other hand, usually depart from the values of welfare and survival. If population is allowed to grow unchecked, they argue, the resulting numbers of people will pollute the environment, consume an unreasonable proportion of the world's natural resources, and possibly even threaten the survival of the human species. The critical question is the optimum balance between freedom and welfare (including survival). *How much* freedom, in other words, ought to be sacrificed in the interests of welfare?

Similar questions arise in debates over the preservation of traditional cultures in programs of national development. On the one side is a body of opinion holding that agents of "modernization" have no right whatsoever to tamper with traditional beliefs and practices. The arguments offered to support this view include the need for cultural diversity, the right of all peoples to determine their own destinies, and the importance of traditional values as a matrix for the development of self-identity and self-esteem. At the opposite extreme are those who feel that traditional values are by definition obstacles to development and must therefore be changed as rapidly and efficiently as possible. Again the question concerns the most desirable trade-offs between conflicting values: How much traditional culture ought to be sacrificed for the sake of modernization?

Though no neat formulas or mechanistic answers are possible, one can try to establish a rough order of ethical priorities. James Gustafson (1970) provides an example of such priority-setting in the field of biomedical research involving possible danger to human subjects:

> Since the realization of any human values for an individual depends upon the safe and sound development of his physical life, it can well be argued that the value of human physical life is a primary one, or that the right to physical life is primary. If this is granted, at least the benefit of the doubt in any case that would seriously harm or take human life is in favor of the proposed victim. This would not entail that no other values or rights might ever override the right to bodily life, but it would suggest that in questions of this sort not all things are absolutely relative to each other and that at least a summary moral rule can be stated, such as, "Human life ought not to be taken or endangered except where there is a clear and persuasive argument that other claims are ethically prior" (p. 172).

In applying such a priority-setting approach to the population field, one might start with the proposition that freedom of procreative behavior should be respected unless there are clearly demonstrated threats to human survival or welfare, and that even then the limitations placed on freedom should be proportional to the danger involved. By this rule it would not be justified to introduce compulsory sterilization or forced abortions because of the mere possibility that human welfare will be endangered by demographic growth within the next century. It might be ethically justified, on the other hand, to remove incentives to large families, such as family allowances, and to provide free family planning assistance. Similarly, modernization efforts might be guided by the proposition that traditional values should be disrupted only if—and only to the extent that—considerations of survival and social welfare necessitate such disruption.

In discussing the procedures to be followed in resolving value conflicts—as well as those in deriving the values to be applied to social intervention and in considering the competing values of different groups —we have provided no answers to the ethical questions that arise in social intervention. We have merely identified some of the analytical steps that an ethical evaluation calls for. These steps do not eliminate the need for value judgments, but they make such judgments more conscious and deliberate. With these procedural issues in mind, we shall now turn to some of the ethical questions raised by each of the four aspects of social intervention that we distinguished earlier: the choice of goals, the definition of the target, the choice of means, and the assessment of consequences.

Choice of Goals

Social scientists and others writing about social change are always making assumptions—explicitly or implicitly—about the nature and the endpoints of the changes that are necessary and desirable. These assumptions are influenced not only by the values that the individual writer brings to his research, but also by the interests and orientations that surround the issue of social change in his own society, whatever its political coloration or level of development may be. Gunnar Myrdal (1968), writing about development, points out:

. . . quite apart from any formal or informal pressures from the authorities or from public opinion, the individual scientist is himself usually deeply engaged in these momentous events. As an American, a European, or a national of one of the underdeveloped countries, he is bound to be anything but indifferent to the theoretical and practical findings of his research. This must have an influence on his inclinations in research and on how he presents his results to the public—unless he exercises the utmost care to avoid a biased view (pp. 10–11).

We would go further to argue that, even with utmost care, a biased view cannot be avoided. It can be counteracted only insofar as it is made explicit and confronted with analyses based on alternative perspectives.

Our own perspective on social change places it in the context of a world-wide revolution of human rights, which has set into motion powerful forces toward political independence, economic development, and social reform, both in the developing world and within industrialized countries. Given this perspective, we would start the process of delineating goals for social intervention by asking how the challenge posed by this revolution can best be met. What can be done to facilitate social change and to increase the likelihood that it will move in constructive directions? What kinds of institutional arrangements would improve the living conditions of the masses of the population, would be consistent with their needs for security and dignity, and would broaden the base of participation in social, political, and economic affairs? What conditions are conducive to a population's sense of political legitimacy, its feeling of national identity, and its readiness for involvement in citizenship responsibilities, economic enterprises, and social planning? What techniques of change would minimize the use of violence, the brutalization of the active and passive participants in the change process, and the predisposition to govern by coercion and repression? How can social intervention be introduced without destroying the existing culture patterns that provide meaning and stability to a people, while at the same time helping to build the new patterns and values that a changing society requires if it is to remain human? (Kelman, 1968, p. 63).

This list of questions—and the goals for social intervention that it implies—is clearly based on certain value assumptions. It presupposes not only the desirability of social change, but also a preference for certain kinds of change over others. Thus, for example, it assumes that social institutions must be judged in terms of their consistency with human needs, and it favors institutional arrangements that encourage participation, legitimacy, nonviolence, and respect for traditional values.

The statement implies a rough ordering of priorities. It suggests that, in choosing goals for intervention, a major criterion be the concrete needs of individuals rather than some abstract notion of what is good for society. It clearly regards changes that involve violence, coercion, or the destruction of traditional values as unacceptable except under the most compelling circumstances. The application of these criteria to a specific situation, however, requires some difficult judgments. How does one determine which of various alternative policies is most consistent with the concrete needs of individuals, or what circumstances are sufficiently compelling to justify changes that involve varying degrees of violence, coercion, or destruction of traditional values? Different analysts agreeing on these priorities may nonetheless disagree in their specific applications of them.

Beyond such differences in the application of these criteria to concrete interventions, it is also unlikely that everyone will agree with the delineation of goals and priorities implied in the foregoing statement. We would like to believe that these goals are consistent with basic and universal human needs and that they are widely shared over different population groupings and cultures. Yet we are also cognizant of the very real possibility that our ordering of priorities reflects, in some important ways, our own cultural and ideological biases and that—even when it deviates from the governing ideology of our society—it is influenced by our own relatively favored positions within the society and our society's favored position within the international system. Thus, before basing the choice of goals for intervention on such a statement, one must recognize that it represents one perspective, which has to be confronted with those derived from other relevant points of view.

Recognizing that the choice of goals for intervention is determined by the value perspective of the chooser—which is not necessarily shared by all interested parties—is the first and a frequently neglected step in an ethical analysis of social intervention. The goals to be pursued in social change are by no means self-evident. They depend very much on what one considers a desirable outcome and what costs in terms of other values he is prepared to bear for the achievement of this outcome—a complex judgment about which there may be considerable disagreement.

The role of cultural and ideological biases in the choice of goals is often ignored because the change effort may have a hierarchy of values built into its very definition. These values may simply be taken for granted without questioning their source and their possibly controversial nature. A clear example of such covert ideological influence is seen in definitions of national development and modernization. The word *development,* whether used in botany, psychology, or economics, implies an unfolding toward some terminal state. Typically this state, whether it be adulthood, maturity, or an ideal economic system, is also considered desirable. By implication, a "more developed" nation is seen as better in some sense than a "less developed" nation. In the 1950s the dominant models of national development took as their implicit endpoints the economic and political systems of the Western industrial nations. Within this teleological framework primary emphasis was given to economic values. Works such as *The Stages of Economic Growth* (Rostow, 1960) argued, in effect, that the ultimate measure of political and social institutions was their contribution as "preconditions" for economic growth. From an ethical standpoint the most serious problem with these models was that value judgments were slipped into seemingly value-free definitions of historical processes. Statements about goals for change deemed desirable from a particular value perspective were often presented as empirical statements about the conditions for a universal process of development.

The same problem arises with the more recent concept of *modernization*. At first glance this too seems like an ideologically neutral term solidly anchored in scientific theory and data. Closer analysis reveals a definite but elusive set of value assumptions. Specifically, this concept contains value-based notions of what *will* happen and what *should* happen in social change, with substantial overlap between the two. At the level of what will happen, the concept of modernization often includes two types of predictive assumptions: those implying the historical inevitability of certain trends, such as secularization; and those specifying given conditions, including a particular set of societal values, as necessary prerequisites for "modernity." Not surprisingly, the conditions portrayed as necessary or inevitable have strong ideological overtones and often resemble the idealized social system in the writer's own society. Such predictions can become self-fulfilling prophecies when they are treated as fact by some political leaders and translated into policy.

Similarly, the concept of modernization contains explicit or implicit notions of what *should* happen in social change. Most definitions do not include everything modern (in the dictionary sense of contemporary or up-to-date) as part of the end-state of modernity. Air pollution, biological warfare, and other products of a technological civilization are generally omitted (cf. Smith, 1965). In practice the choice of contents for modernity is influenced by what a writer considers ethically desirable. Such latent choices of goals are especially troublesome because they are masked by connotations of scientific rigor and historical inevitability. In other words, when terms like modernization or development are used as if they represented empirical descriptions of generic, natural processes, it is too easy to ignore the particular historical experiences and ideological preferences that enter into one's formulation of these processes.

In recognizing the role of his own value preferences, the change agent (or the social scientist who conceptualizes the process of social change) does not abandon his values or attempt to neutralize them. It is neither possible nor desirable to do so. Rather, awareness of his own value perspective allows him to bring other perspectives to bear on the choice of goals and to reduce the likelihood of imposing his own values on the population in whose lives he is intervening. This process of relating one's own values to those of others in the choice of goals for intervention—without either abandoning or imposing his own values—can often be aided by a distinction between general goals and specific institutional arrangements designed to give expression to these goals. It may be possible to identify certain broad, basic endpoints that are widely shared across different cultures and ideological systems—at least among groups and individuals operating within a broadly humanistic framework. These groups or individuals may at the same time disagree about the specific political, social, and economic institutions that they regard as most conducive to the realization of these ends. Thus one may be able to define the goals for intervention in more or less universal terms, while recognizing that these goals may be achieved through a variety of specific arrangements and that different cultures and ideologies may differ sharply in their preferences for these arrangements.

Taking international programs of development as a case in point, we would identify, at the most general level, three broad goal areas: economic growth, political effectiveness, and individual welfare. It is our impression that there is fairly wide agreement about these general goals, although it may turn out that our statement of these goals may itself be biased by our particular cultural and ideological perspectives. Clearly there is need for discussion here, guided by multiple perspectives. Our purpose for the moment, however, is not to come up with a final list of widely shared goals but to illustrate the potential usefulness of the distinction between broad goal areas and their specific institutional expressions.

The goal area that probably shows the highest degree of cross-national agreement is economic growth. As a minimum, most nations are committed to achieving sufficient economic productivity to eliminate hunger and to provide adequate clothing and shelter for their citizens. There is considerable disagreement, however, on how far and in what direction this process should be carried. For example, Rostow (1960) maintains that the highest stage of economic growth involves high mass consumption, including a widespread use of durable consumer goods, such as the automobile, and a rise in leisure time. His critics have countered that this view is ethnocentric: the process of economic growth need not end in mass consumption, while increased leisure may be an ethically dubious goal in the face of pressing social needs. There is also disagreement, of course, on the most desirable institutional arrangements —in terms of systems of production as well as distribution—for promoting economic growth.

There is probably even greater disagreement in the area of political institutions. It would thus be unreasonable to equate political development with a given set of political forms, such as those found in the Western industrial democracies. On the other hand, it should be possible to specify broad areas of common concern for divergent political systems in terms of a model of political effectiveness. According to this model, the goal for change in the political arena would be to increase the capacity, adaptability, and output of the political system—its ability to initiate action, meet challenges, and win the support of its members. In operational terms a government demonstrates effectiveness by dealing successfully with the six historical crises suggested by LaPalombara (1966): it must establish the *legitimacy* of its actions and decisions, promote the *integration* of diverse elements of its population, meet the *identity* needs of individual citizens, assume its *penetration* into the outlying areas of the nation, provide opportunities for *participation* by new groups in the population, and meet demands for changes in the *distribution* of goods and services. The specific routes leading to political effectiveness, just as those leading to economic growth, may vary widely. Each nation has to handle its crises and to work out its political future according to the demands placed upon it, the resources available to it, and the values and aims shared within its population.

Finally, in the area of individual welfare, there is probably little disagreement about the value of eliminating disease, teaching literacy, and protecting men against such natural disasters as earthquakes and floods. There is greater disagreement about the society's obligation to meet the welfare needs of its individual citizens, particularly about the institutional arrangements best suited to accomplish this end.

There is probably even less consensus on what constitutes personal well-being and individual freedom—on the definition of the "ideal man" to which social change ought to be directed. The choice of goals in this area depends on one's view of what is good for man, of what is happiness, and of how individuals should relate to the state and the surrounding society. We have already mentioned that the instrumental view, which describes the ideal man as one whose personality characteristics and attitudes are most conducive to rapid economic and political development (perhaps of a particular variety) is open to challenge on ethical grounds. Economic and political processes should be designed to serve individuals rather than to be served by them. Moreover, when an outside change agent propounds such a view, he may be imposing his own values on others, in that the personality traits and attitudes that he regards as conducive to economic growth and political effectiveness may be those fostered by the particular economic and political institutions that characterize his own society. We would therefore prefer to define the psychological goals of development in terms of a broader conception of man's needs as he interacts with his physical, interpersonal, and social environment. Thus we would emphasize such personality characteristics as personal efficacy, self-utilization, and self-development in our formulation of broad goals for social change. The specific meaning of these characteristics no doubt varies across different cultures and ideologies. It remains to be seen whether there is cross-cultural agreement about these general characteristics themselves and about the broader conception of human needs to which they are linked.

Ethical issues in the choice of goals for intervention revolve around the question of what values are to be served by the intervention and whether these are the "right" values for the target population. Since answers to these questions are likely to differ for different individuals—and to differ systematically for groups with different cultural backgrounds and positions in society—the question of *what* values inevitably brings up the question of *whose* values are to be served by the intervention. This issue has run through our entire discussion in this section, particularly as we pointed to the danger of imposing foreign values on the selection of goals for social change. The issue is so central to an ethical analysis that it deserves further highlighting.

Any society in which a change program is introduced contains different segments, with differing needs and interests that may be affected by the intervention. Thus a key issue concerns the extent to which the values of these different population segments are reflected in the goals that govern the intervention and the extent to which they participate in the goal-setting process. The question of who decides on the goals often has implications for who ultimately benefits from the outcome of the intervention. Since the interests and values of different groups may, to varying degrees, be incompatible, the change program usually involves some compromise between competing preferences. Representation and participation in goal-setting may thus have an important bearing on how the values of a given group are weighted in the final outcome.

The problem of competing interests and values in the goal-setting process is complicated by the fact that the change agents and those to whom the change effort is directed usually represent different segments of the population. In national programs, the government officials and social engineers who initiate and carry out the intervention and the policy-makers and social scientists who provide the conceptual frameworks on which it is based usually come from the more established, affluent, and highly educated segments of the society; the target population usually consists of poorer and less educated segments, minority groups, or groups that are for various reasons (e.g., age, health, addiction, or criminality) in a dependent status. In international programs, the leadership and conceptual framework (whether Western or Marxist) usually come from the more powerful, industrialized nations, whereas the change is directed at developing countries. Thus, in both cases, the change agent is in some sense an "outsider" to the target population—in terms of social class, or na-

tional affiliation, or both. Moreover, he is usually not a disinterested outsider: social change programs may have important implications for the
wealth, power, and status of his own group. The problem is further exacerbated by the fact that the agents and the targets of change usually
represent groups that are not only different, but different along a power
dimension. The change agents come from the more powerful classes and
nations, the targets from the less powerful ones.

The change agents are in a strong position to influence the choice of
goals for the intervention. Those who formulate and run the program
clearly play a direct role in goal-setting; those who provide the conceptual frameworks may have a more subtle yet highly pervasive impact in
that they establish the perspective from which the goal-setting proceeds
and thus the way in which the problem is defined and the range of
choices seen as available. There is more than a real possibility that the
change agents will view the problem from the perspective of their own
group and set goals that will—often unintentionally—accrue to the benefit of their group at the expense of the target population. Given the
power differential, their intervention may in fact strengthen the status
quo and increase the impotence of those who are already disadvantaged.
It is not surprising therefore that population control or educational programs sponsored by white middle-class agencies in black ghettoes, or by
American agencies in developing countries, are sometimes greeted with
suspicion by the target populations. Whatever the merits of the specific
case may be, there are sound structural bases for fearing that such programs may end up serving the purposes of the advantaged group at the
expense of the disadvantaged.

The ethical problems created by the value and power differentials
between change agents and target groups are not easily resolved. Clearly,
the more the target group participates in the process of goal-setting, the
greater the likelihood that the change program will indeed reflect its values. But bringing in representatives of the target group or turning the
program over to "indigenous" agents may not go very far in correcting
for power imbalances. We have already mentioned that representatives of
developing societies who are brought in by outside agencies may themselves be Westernized, for example, and operating in terms of the
perspectives of these agencies. Similarly, representatives of minority
groups, particularly if they have professional training, do not necessarily
share the perspective of lower-class, less educated members of their own
groups. "Turning over" a project may create its own ethical ambiguities
if, in the process, the outsider arrogates to himself the decision of who is
the proper spokesman for the target population—if he takes on the role
of kingmaker. This may be true whether he turns over the project to the

established government (which may not be "representative") or an opposition group; in either case, he is deciding which side to strengthen in what may be an internal conflict within the target population and thus indirectly imposing goals of his own choice.

Despite the ambiguities that often remain when an outside, more powerful change agent involves representatives of the less powerful target population in the change effort, such involvement constitutes the best protection against the imposition of foreign values. Thus in an ethical evaluation of a social intervention, one would want to consider such criteria as these: To what extent do those who are affected by the intervention participate in the choice of goals? What efforts are being made to have their interests represented in the setting of priorities, and to bring their perspectives to bear on the definition of the problem and the range of choices entertained? To what extent does the process enhance the power of the target population and provide them with countervailing mechanisms of protection against arbitrary and self-serving uses of power by the change agents?

Definition of Target

Social intervention usually begins as an effort to solve a problem. A decision to undertake a program of organizational development, for example, may spring from a concern about poor communication, intraorganizational conflicts, or underutilization of employee abilities. The adoption of population controls may be an effort to deal with the problem of scarce resources or that of preserving the quality of life. In every case, identification of "the problem" represents, in large part, a value judgment. What we consider to be problematic—to fall short of some ideal state and to require action—depends very much on our particular view of the ideal state. Moreover, it depends on the perspective from which we make this evaluation. For example, in the face of demonstrations, riots, or other forms of social unrest, different groups are likely to cite different problems as requiring social intervention: those who identify with the status quo are likely to see the problem as a breakdown of social order, whereas those who identify with the protesters are more likely to see the problem as a breakdown of social justice.

Identification of the problem has important ethical implications because it determines selection of the target to which change efforts are directed. *Where* one intervenes depends on where he—given his value preferences and perspectives—perceives the problem to lie. Thus in the example of reactions to protest, those who see the problem as a breakdown of social order are likely to define the protesters as the proper targets of change. They may use a variety of means, ranging from more stringent social controls, through persuasion and education, to efforts at placating the protesters and giving them a stake in the system. Whatever the means, however, this is the wrong target from the point of view of those who see the problem as failure in social justice and who want to direct change efforts to the existing institutions and policies. In their view, interventions designed to reduce the protesters' ability or motivation to protest merely perpetuate injustices and serve the interests of the advantaged segments of the population at the expense of the disadvantaged. In short, who and what is being targeted for change may have important consequences for the competing interests of different groups and for the fate of such core values as justice and freedom.

Definition of the target is at the center of one of the unending debates in economic planning. Many economists, especially those on the political left, hold that the most effective avenue to economic growth lies in massive changes of unjust or archaic social structures, such as land tenure systems. David McClelland and his associates, on the other hand, lean more toward changing individuals and their motives. Specifically, McClelland has launched a series of programs designed to increase achievement motivation (McClelland and Winter, 1969).

The decision to move to one side or another in this debate rests partly on theoretical convictions about economic development, partly on related value-judgments about appropriate strategies of change. The preference for working with individuals typically grows out of a conviction that economic growth is best achieved through private initiative or entrepreneurship. The major barrier to entrepreneurship is seen as an inadequate supply of individuals who are willing to innovate and take financial risks. The solution is to change the motivational structure of relevant members of society, such as businessmen, to provide the missing ingredient.

Without challenging the empirical evidence supporting the individual approach, one could question the value premises on which it rests. Clearly McClelland regards the basic "problem" as the individual. A Marxist critic might argue that this assumption represents an affirmation of the capitalist structures surrounding the individual. A decision to train the individual to perform better within the system implies an ethical acceptance of that system. Moreover, the critic might continue, by tracing the problem of poverty to individual motivation, McClelland is, at least by implication, exonerating society as a whole from blame for misery and injustice. The ethical critique could, of course, be turned around and applied to the Marxist position; critics might, for example, consider the premises on which that position rests to be inconsistent with the freedom and self-development of the individual. In either event, assumptions about "the problem" of development and the varying definitions of the target of change that these generate flow from value judgments and in turn have important value implications.

Similar elements are intermixed in discussions of the "population problem." The specific crises that constitute this problem may be defined as (1) famine or impediments to economic development, (2) pollution or other ecological damage threatening the possibility and quality of life, (3) exhaustion of physical resources or strains upon the carrying capacity of the earth, or (4) revolution or social disorder resulting from population pressures joined with high levels of aspiration. The scientific evidence on the probability of these crises is highly ambiguous. Thus there is ample room for personal values to enter into the definition of the problem.

The definition of the problem again determines the selection of targets for change. Those who see the problem in terms of the danger of famine and economic stagnation may direct change efforts at increasing economic productivity, including food production. Those who are primarily concerned with pollution and ecological damage may favor interventions directed at reducing the rate of industrialization or at strengthening governmental controls over waste products and other sources of environmental pollution. On the other hand, those concerned with exhaustion of physical resources or with the revolutionary potential of population pressures may prefer interventions aimed at reducing or reversing the rate of population growth. How one defines the problem, and thus whether he then takes national economic policy or the child-rearing family as his target of change, depends on his value preferences and perspectives. For example, groups placing a high value on the preservation of the existing political order are likely to be disturbed by rising population pressures and thus to favor population control. On the other hand, those who advocate revolutionary change may actually favor rapid population growth combined with urbanization as important contributors to political mobilization. These two views, of course, do not exhaust the possible positions on population control, but they again illustrate the point that definition of the target of change has important consequences for the competing interests of different groups within a society.

Social scientists play a major role in identifying, or at least articulating, the problems to which change efforts are to be directed and thus in defining the targets for social intervention. A good example is provided by research on various forms of social deviance. Much of this research has focused on "the deviant behaviour itself and on the characteristics of the individuals and groups that manifest it and the families and neighbourhoods in which it is prevalent, rather than on the systemic processes out of which it emerges" (Kelman, 1970, p. 82). Many reasons for this emphasis can be cited. In part it grows out of the "social problems" tradition, which has fostered among social scientists a commitment to helping troubled individuals and groups. In part it is due to the fact that research on social deviance is often sponsored by agencies whose mission includes the control of deviant behavior and reflects the sponsors' problem-definition. Research on the characteristics of deviant populations is perfectly legitimate in and of itself, but it raises ethical questions insofar as it provides the dominant framework for conceptualizing deviance as a social phenomenon and thus for setting social policy.

By focusing on the carriers of deviant behaviour, social research has reinforced the widespread tendency to explain such behaviour more often in terms of the pathology of the deviant individuals, families, and communities, than in terms of such properties of the larger social system as the distribution of power, resources, and opportunities. The policy implications that such research yields are more likely to serve the interests of the status quo than those of social change. The research points more readily to ways of controlling or at best preventing deviant behaviour than it does to ways of restructuring the social realities that are indexed by this behaviour. The control and certainly the prevention of many kinds of social deviance are worthy social goals, yet they are more reflective of the concerns of those segments of the society that have a vested interest in maintaining the established order than of the poor, the disadvantaged, and the minority groups from whose ranks the deviants are most often drawn (Kelman, 1970, p. 83).

In short, research on social deviance has often derived from and contributed to a definition of the problem in terms of the characteristics of the deviant. In keeping with this problem-definition, the deviant individuals and communities, rather than the institutional arrangements and policies conducive to social deviance, have commonly been singled out as the targets for intervention. This particular way of identifying the problem and defining the target for change tends to reflect the concerns of the more established segments of the population and has potential consequences for the competing interests of different groups within the society.

This example illustrates some of the ethical implications of social science research. Far from being ethically neutral, the models with which social scientists work may play a major role in determining the problems and targets for social intervention. In defining their research problems, choosing their models, and communicating their findings, therefore, social scientists have a responsibility to consider the consequences for the populations affected. More broadly, they have the responsibility to assure that all segments of the population have the opportunity to participate in the research enterprise, which influences the definition of the problems for intervention, and have access to the research findings, which influence the setting of policy.

Choice of Means

The most difficult ethical choices in deliberate social intervention usually concern the selection of means. Is it ever morally justified, for instance, to force individuals to accept a program under the threat of death, physical harm, or other severe deprivation? What ethical problems are posed by manipulating the environment so that people are more likely to choose one alternative than others? Should a change program make full use of group pressures for conformity, or attempt to tamper with basic attitudes and motives? These are real questions in most change programs, and there are no easy answers.

It is possible, however, to clarify some of the issues at stake by relating the various means to the value of freedom. Warwick (1971a, pp. 14–15), has defined freedom as the capacity, the opportunity, and the incentive to make reflective choices and to act on these choices. An individual is thus free when:

1. The structure of the environment provides him with options for choice.

2. He is not coerced by others or forced by circumstances to elect only certain possibilities among those of which he is aware.

3. He is, in fact, aware of the options in the environment and possesses knowledge about the characteristics and consequences of each. Though such knowledge may be less than complete, there must be enough to permit rational deliberation.

4. He is psychologically able to weigh the alternatives and their consequences. In practice this means not only the possession of information but the ability to use it in coming to a decision.

5. Having weighed the relative merits of the alternatives, he can choose among them. Rollo May (1969) has argued that one of the pathologies of modern existence is an inability to choose—a deficiency of will. A person who cannot pass from deliberation to choice must be considered less than free.

6. Having chosen an alternative, he is able to act on it. Among the conditions which may prevent him from doing so is a lack of knowledge about how to implement his choice, anxiety about acting at all, or a low level of confidence in his abilities, even when he has sufficient knowledge to act.

This discussion of freedom suggests a typology of means used in implementing social interventions. At the "least free" end is coercion, a situation in which a person is forced to do something that he does not want to do, or to avoid doing something that he does want to do. Next comes manipulation, then persuasion, and finally, at the "most free" end, facilitation.

Coercion. In simple terms, coercion takes place when one person or group forces another person or group to act or refrain from acting under the threat of severe deprivation. Philosophers have added many qualifications to this definition, but basically coercion arises in two situations: (1) an actor *wants* to perform a certain action or in the normal course of events *would* perform this action, but he is constrained from doing so by physical means or the threat of severe deprivation; and (2) an actor desires *not* to perform a certain action or normally *would not* carry out this action, but he actually does so because of physical compulsion or threats by another party. It is difficult to arrive at a precise definition of "threat" or "deprivation," but basically they refer to the loss of highly valued goods, such as one's life, means of livelihood, or the well-being of relatives. Coercion should be distinguished from compliance occurring within the framework of legitimate authority. In a certain sense tax laws may be coercive in that they cause people to behave in a way that they would prefer not to behave and do so under the threat of penalties. However, to the degree that such individuals comply with the law out of a belief that it is right to do so, in that the law is rooted in consensual processes, their behavior would not be coerced.

Coercion forms an integral part of many programs of social intervention. Some clear examples are the nationalization of a foreign-owned petroleum refinery or the outright confiscation of land in agrarian reform programs. In both cases the government's action is immediately backed by the use of physical force—those who do not comply may be evicted or jailed. The acceptance of the government's legitimate right to carry out such interventions is usually minimal. Other examples hover at the borders of coercion, manipulation, and persuasion. It has been proposed, for instance, that governments try to limit population by levying higher taxes against families with more than two or three children, or by depriving them of social benefits such as free education, welfare, or medical coverage. Such programs could be considered coercive if the threatened deprivation involved highly valued goods or the threat of great hardship, and if those affected would not accept the legal or moral legitimacy of the interventions. If the rewards and punishments at stake were relatively moderate, on the other hand, the means of intervention could be considered either manipulative or persuasive, according to the circumstances.

Is coercion ever ethically justified in social intervention and, if so, under what conditions? Though it is beyond the scope of this chapter to attempt an answer to this tangled question, we can point out two broad conditions commonly invoked to defend coercive methods. The first is a grave threat to basic societal values. Thus highly coercive population control programs are frequently recommended on the grounds that excessive fertility jeopardizes the continued survival of the human race or the material welfare of a nation's citizens. The second justification is the need for prompt and positive action to accomplish the goals of a change program, even when there is no threat to such values as physical survival. This argument is typical of revolutionary governments bent upon executing major reforms in a short period of time. The two arguments are related in the sense that a failure to show swift results might create a drastic loss in basic values such as the legitimacy or credibility of the government.

In the first case an ethical justification of coercion requires the change agent to demonstrate, rather than assume, the threat to basic values. The population field is punctuated with dire predictions of disaster offered to the public with little supporting evidence. The legal concept of "clear and present danger" would seem to be an appropriate test of any proposal for coercion. Even then, however, it may not be justified. In the second case the defense of coercion usually rests on personal evaluations of the system in question. In gross terms, those who favor a given regime will generally support its use of coercion to promote rapid change; those who oppose it will reject its coercive methods. For example, much of Denis Goulet's book on the ethics of development is a plea for voluntarism, participation, and respect for individual dignity and esteem. Yet he writes:

> . . . China's campaign to make intellectuals work in factories and fields is no arbitrary manipulation of a class. On the contrary, it is an effort to instil in professional men populist values which they might otherwise disdain: respect for manual labor, direct contact with primary materials, symbiosis with physical tools. Such mobilization builds up inter-class solidarity and thereby constitutes a profoundly ethical strategy of human resource development (1971, p. 116).

Quite clearly Goulet is selective in his endorsement of coercion. For unexplained reasons these methods are "profoundly ethical" in China but immoral in other settings.

Since the justification of coercive tactics often rests on the legitimacy of those who use them, determinations of legitimacy become an important part of ethical analysis. The legitimacy of a regime, in Western democratic tradition, is evidenced by the fact that its major officials have been duly elected, but there are other ways of establishing that a regime is representative of the population and governs with its consent. Even if the regime is seen as generally legitimate, however, some of its specific policies and programs may be considered illegitimate by various segments of the population, because they exceed the regime's range of legitimate authority, or because they are discriminatory, or because they violate certain basic values. Ethical evaluations become even more difficult when coercive interventions are introduced by revolutionary movements whose claim to legitimacy has not yet been established. In such a case, an observer would be more inclined to justify coercive tactics to the extent that he sees the movement as representative of wide segments of the population and feels that their tactics are directed at power-wielders who themselves are illegitimate and oppressive.

Environmental Manipulation. Individual freedom has two core components: the availability of options in the environment, and the person's capacity to know, weigh, choose, and act on these alternatives. Manipulation is a deliberate act of changing either the structure of the alternatives in the environment (environmental manipulation) or personal qualities affecting choice without the knowledge of the person involved (psychic manipulation). The cardinal feature of this process is that it maintains the semblance of freedom while modifying the framework within which choices are made. No physical compulsion or threats of deprivation are applied, and the individual may be no more than dimly aware that he or the environment has been changed. Somewhat different ethical considerations are raised by environmental and psychic manipulation.

The term "environmental manipulation," though it carries sinister overtones, applies to a broad range of activities generally regarded as necessary and desirable. These include city planning; governmental intervention in the economy through means such as taxation and control of interest rates; the construction of roads, dams, or railroads; and the addition of new consumer goods to the market. In each case a deliberate attempt is made to alter the structure of opportunities available through addition, subtraction, or other modification. And yet few challenge the ethics of these changes, though they may question their wisdom.

Other forms of environmental control arouse greater moral concern. Limitations on the freedom of the news media are widely attacked as abhorrent to a democracy. Job discrimination, ethnic quotas in universities, and other restrictions on the equality of opportunity are similarly condemned. Thus even the public at large draws a distinction between justifiable and unjustifiable control of opportunities.

But what are the limits of justifiable manipulation? And what ethical calculus should be used to establish these limits? Is it morally justified for one group of men to attempt to shape an entire cultural environment in the interest of promoting happiness and survival? In *Beyond Freedom and Dignity* B.F. Skinner (1971) makes precisely such a proposal:

> Physical and biological technologies have alleviated pestilence and famine and many painful, dangerous, and exhausting features of daily life, and behavioral technology can begin to alleviate other kinds of ills. In the analysis of human behavior it is just possible that we are slightly beyond Newton's position in the analysis of light, for we are beginning to make technological applications. There are wonderful possibilities—and all the more wonderful because traditional approaches have been so ineffective (pp. 213–214).

The responsibility for implementing control of the entire population "must be delegated to specialists—to police, priests, owners, teachers, therapists, and so on, with their specialized reinforcers and their codified contingencies" (p. 155). In Skinner's world view there is no place for freedom and dignity. These are outmoded concepts standing in the way of progress and survival, the supreme values. His only concession to freedom is that the controller should be a member of the culture that is to be controlled. The ultimate aim, however, is to get the culture to control itself (p. 172).

Skinner's proposals raise many more questions about manipulation than can be handled in this chapter. For example, a fundamental issue —with serious ethical implications—concerns the scientific foundation on which Skinner builds his elaborate scheme (cf. Chomsky, 1971). Perhaps the key question is who decides what controls are to be instituted. Even Skinner, with all of his confidence in the morality (or at least amorality) of behavior technology, admits that decisions about the precise shape of the new environment are not self-evident. "Who is to construct the controlling environment, and to what end? Autonomous man presumably controls himself in accordance with a built-in set of values; he works for what he finds good. But what will the putative controller find good and will it be good for those he controls? Answers to questions of this sort are said, of course, to call for value-judgments" (p. 22). Indeed they do, but Skinner does not tell us, except by implication, what these value judgments are. Above all else he favors the "survival of a culture," but he provides few clues about what this culture should contain. At root Skinner's book is an apologia for a disembodied technology of behavior change which could be used equally well to design an efficient concentration

camp or a utopian commune built on love. As he puts it: "Such a technology is ethically neutral. It can be used by a villain or saint. There is
nothing in a methodology which determines the values governing its use"
(p. 150). This statement is true only if one accepts the premise that man
is an organism whose behavior is governed by environmental "reinforcers," and rejects any notion of inherent rights to human freedom and
dignity. This seems to be Skinner's basic ethical stance.

Related ethical issues are seen in behavior (or action) therapies. Unlike "insight" therapies, which concentrate on changing motives, perceptions, and other psychic qualities, behavior therapy aims at treating
symptoms. If a patient has a phobia the therapist uses desensitization
methods to reduce his anxiety. The techniques involved are identical to
those suggested by Skinner for the design of cultures. They are based on
the principle of selective reinforcement, through which desired behaviors
are rewarded and undesired behaviors are punished, and they emphasize
specific acts rather than global personality characteristics. Environmental
manipulation is thus a key to the success of these therapies.

Skill at manipulation, anathema to insight therapy, is the moral prize beyond
purchase of the actionists, whose title to exercise control is as certain to them as
their responsibility for healing is clear. To them, successful manipulation is not
merely a useful tactic but a moral imperative which they must satisfy to have
the right to offer help at all. Therapeutic intervention in the patient's life is
the goal and *raison d'être* for their activity (London, 1969, pp. 64–65).

From an ethical standpoint the principal difference between Skinner's macro-manipulation and behavior therapy lies in the degree to
which the individuals affected may control the process. Though there are
vague murmurings in Skinner's book about "participation by those affected," his basic model is one of total control by an elite of culture de-
signers. By contrast, in behavior therapy the patient seeks help with a
problem and is free to terminate the relationship at any time. In other
words, though the therapy process involves careful manipulation of his
behavior, he usually knows what is happening and can exercise a fair degree of control over the process. Further questions could be raised about
the efficacy and the ethics of behavior therapy, but on the scale of freedom used here it comes out relatively well.

Other proposals for environmental control fall somewhere between
these poles. It has been suggested, for instance, that governments try to
limit fertility by manipulating conditions known to have indirect effects
on family size, such as education, job opportunities for women, and income. Specifically, Judith Blake (1969) recommends that women be given
more "competitive roles," such as improved job opportunities, as a means

of reducing fertility. Daniel Callahan (1971) raises several questions about this form of environmental manipulation. On the one hand, he observes, an increase in the number of opportunities outside the family would seen consistent with the value of freedom since it would increase the options for choice. At the same time questions could be raised about a strategy involving the staging of alternatives for choice to accomplish a social goal. Though this strategy underlies many forms of social policy and legislation, Callahan points to the ironic possibility that people can be manipulated by increasing their freedom.

Similar questions arise in any strategy for social change that relies on creating new realities that make it more necessary—or at least more possible—for people to change their behavior. In the field of race relations, for example, observers have noted that an effective way of changing individual attitudes and practices is to introduce a *fait accompli:* if an antidiscrimination law or policy is established without too much ado, people will be confronted with a new social reality which—for both practical and normative reasons—they are more likely to adjust to than to resist. This type of environmental manipulation characterizes the various techniques for overcoming resistance to change, discussed in our earlier chapter, that rely on somehow reducing the salience of the source of resistance. Such environmental manipulation can be justified more readily if it is part of a larger social policy process that itself has been carried on through legitimate channels and exposed to public debate. It is also more justifiable from an ethical point of view if its effect is to expand rather than restrict the range of opportunities.

In sum, the ethical issues involved in any attempt at environmental intervention are usually complex. If human freedom and dignity are taken as critical values, there is reason for concern with deliberate attempts to manipulate one person's environment to serve the needs of another. The value of freedom requires not only the availability of options for choice at a given point in time, but an awareness of major changes in the structure of these alternatives. Complete awareness of these changes and their causes, however, is obviously impossible. There is also the danger of a strong conservative bias in defending the environment of choice within which we happen to find ourselves. Most of us, after all, are not aware of the origins of our present options for choice. Why, then, should we have a right to know when it is being changed? In other words, *how much* awareness of the structure of our present environment and of modifications in this environment is necessary for human freedom and dignity? And, assuming that this awareness will always be less than complete, who should have the right to tamper with the environment without our knowledge and what conditions should govern such intervention? Some thought has been given to criteria for an ethical evaluation of environmental manipulation. For example, manipulation would seem more acceptable to the extent that the people affected participate in the process, their entry and exit remain voluntary, and their range of choices is broadened rather than narrowed; and to the extent that the manipulators are not also the primary beneficiaries of the manipulation, are reciprocally vulnerable in the situation, and are accountable to public agencies. On the whole, however, ethical thought on all of these questions remains very limited.

Psychic Manipulation. Even with a constant environment of choice, freedom can be affected through the manipulation of its psychological components: knowledge of the alternatives and their consequences; motives; and the ability to reason, choose, and implement one's choices. Recent decades have seen dramatic developments in the techniques of psychic manipulation. These include "insight" therapies; the modification of brain functioning through surgery, chemicals, or electrical stimulation; hypnosis; sensitivity training; and programs of attitude change (cf. London, 1969). The emergence of behavior control technology raises fundamental questions about the nature of man and the baseline assumptions about man for ethical analysis.

The ethical questions raised by psychic manipulation are similar to those presented by environmental control, and the same criteria for ethical evaluation are applicable. In many interventions of this type, however, particular attention must be paid to moral problems of deception and incomplete knowledge of effects.

The success of many programs of psychic change rests heavily on the skillful use of deception. For example, in an attitude change experiment the research subject usually enters the situation knowing that something will happen to him. However, knowledge of the precise nature of the experimental manipulation might destroy the phenomenon that the experiment is designed to observe, and might create expectancy effects (Rosenthal, 1966). Hence a prime challenge for the experimenter is to entice the person into the experiment without revealing critical features of its design. The moral problems posed by deceptive methods have received increasing attention in recent years, as they apply to both laboratory experiments (cf. Kelman, 1968; in press) and other research situations (cf. Warwick, 1971b). The constituencies affected include not only the researcher and the research subject, but others in the social science professions and often the public at large. Kelman (in press) has written:

Deception presents special problems when it is used in an experiment that is stressful, unpleasant, or potentially harmful to the subject, in the sense that it may create self-doubts, lower his self-esteem, reveal some of his weaknesses, or create temporary conflict, frustration, or anxiety. By deceiving the subject about the nature of the experiment, the experimenter deprives him of the freedom to decide whether or not he wants to be exposed to these potentially disturbing experiences. . . . The use of deception presents ethical problems even when the experiment does not entail potential harm or discomfort for the subject. Deception violates the respect to which all fellow humans are entitled and the trust that is basic to all interpersonal relationships. Such violations are doubly disturbing since they contribute, in this age of mass society, to the already powerful tendencies to manufacture realities and manipulate populations. Furthermore, by undermining the basis of trust in the relationship between investigator and subject, deception makes it increasingly difficult for social scientists to carry out their work in the future (pp. 22–23).

Similar issues arise in all efforts at psychic manipulation.

In other situations the most serious ethical problem is not outright deception but the participant's incomplete or distorted knowledge of the effects of an intervention. Many individuals enter sensitivity training sessions (T-groups), for example, to learn more about their impact on others in a group. Though such learning may well take place, much more *may* happen. The unsuspecting participant sometimes finds that the group process releases violent impulses or even pathological reactions in himself and others. He may be subjected to harsh personal attacks for his feelings and idiosyncrasies, or engage in such attacks on others. Moreover,

The T-group may foster a concept that anything goes regardless of consequences. Instead of creating interpersonal awareness it may foster personal narcissism. If an individual says anything he wishes, then he may come to assume that just because he feels like expressing himself is justification enough to do so. This may preclude effective communication, for he then ignores whether the other person is receptive to his message, and he ignores the effect of his message on the other person. Communication may not be seen as an interpersonal event but merely as the opportunity to express oneself (Gottschalk and Pattison, 1969, p. 835).

Effects of this sort are scarcely evident in such phrases as "learning about group processes." Of course, properly structured and well-supervised sensitivity training may also bring unexpected benefits. The basic ethical question, however, concerns the right of the participant to be informed of potential dangers in a group experience. The same observation would apply to other forms of psychic manipulation, including brain stimulation or drug experiments. It is all too easy for the experimenter or change agent to present only the probable benefits without mentioning harmful side-effects.

Often the change agent is himself unaware of the fact that he is engaged in manipulative efforts or at least of the ethical implications of these efforts. He may be convinced that all he is doing is conveying information or providing a setting in which self-generated change processes are allowed to emerge, failing to recognize the situational and structural factors that enhance his power over the client and the subtle ways in which he communicates his expectations of him. Even if he is aware of his manipulative efforts, he may be so convinced that what he is doing is good for the client that he fails to recognize the ethical ambiguity of the control he exercises (cf. Kelman, 1968, Chapter 1). Such dangerous blind spots among change agents, which preclude their even raising the ethical questions, are particularly likely to arise in psychic manipulation with its often subtle effects.

Persuasion. The technique of persuasion is a form of interpersonal influence in which one person tries to change the attitudes or behavior of another by means of argument, reasoning, or, in certain cases, structured listening. In the laboratory, as well as in the mass media, persuasion is usually a one-way process. In interpersonal relations in natural settings it is generally a mutual process, with the various participants trying to persuade one another. Persuasion is frequently used as a means of social intervention in the mass media and, at the one-to-one level, in insight therapies. Persuasion initially may seem highly consistent with the value of freedom—almost its exemplification. The communication process appears to be carried out in the open, all parties are free to consider the arguments and then to reject or accept them, and no coercion is practiced. Quite clearly, when compared with outright coercion or the more gross forms of manipulation, persuasion emerges as a relatively free method of intervention. But at the same time its seeming openness may sometimes mask covert and far-reaching efforts at personality change.

Insight therapies such as psychoanalysis would generally be regarded as persuasive means of attitude and behavior change. Through such therapy the individual is led to a better understanding of the source of his complaints—why he thinks, acts, and feels the way he does. The guiding assumption is that self-knowledge will take him a long way toward dealing with the problems. The techniques used to promote understanding are generally nondirective, and the client is urged to assume major responsibility for talking during the therapy sessions.

In principle, at least, insight therapy shows a high degree of respect for the patient's freedom. He does most of the talking, the therapist does not impose his values, and the process can be ended at any time. However, closer analysis reveals numerous opportunities for covert influence. Many patients, for example, report feelings of guilt over violations of sexual standards. Following the moral traditions of psychoanalysis, most forms of insight therapy view the guilt feelings, rather than the sexual behavior, as the problem to be solved. Under the guise of moral neutrality the therapist encourages the patient to understand why he feels guilty, and to see that such feelings are irrational (and therefore unjustified). Similarly, by deftly steering the conversation in certain directions through probes and nods of assent, the therapist can lead the patient toward "desirable" attitudes on moral or other matters. And, as Perry London (1964) observes, even the attitude of moral neutrality in psychotherapy is an ethical stance:

> It is, from the therapist's side, a libertarian position, regardless of how the client sees it (indeed, in some ways he may justly see it as insidious). Expressed in a variety of ways, this position is currently in vogue among psychotherapists of quite dissimilar orientations. Some of the concepts that serve to legitimize and popularize moral neutrality are "democracy," "self-realization" or "-actualization," and "existence." All these concepts are oriented towards people's freedom to do as they please (pp. 13–14).

It is hard to escape the conclusion that the therapist, like the confessor, is an active agent of moral suasion. The ethical problem posed by psychotherapy, however, is that the values guiding the influence process are hidden behind global notions such as "mental health," "self-actualization," and "normality." The problem is mitigated to the extent that the therapist recognizes that he is bringing his own values into the relationship and labels those values properly for the patient. "Among other things, such a recognition would allow the patient, to a limited extent, to 'talk back' to the therapist, to argue about the appropriateness of the values that the therapist is introducing" (Kelman, 1968, pp. 25–26).

When we move from persuasion in the one-to-one context to efforts at mass persuasion, the question of who has the opportunity and the capacity to mount a persuasion campaign takes on central importance. Since such opportunities and capacities are not equally distributed in any society, this question is fraught with ethical implications. It arises, for example, in the debate over the impact of modernization on traditional values, to which we alluded earlier. In this connection, after defending the need for cultural diversity, Denis Goulet (1971) writes:

> Development economists often ask what they should do about local customs which get in development's way. No sensitive change agent is blind to the trau-

matic effects of the "bull-in-the-china-closet" approach to local customs. Nevertheless, persuasive campaigns are sometimes necessary, even if they are unpopular (p. 270).

The question is, Who should be responsible for deciding *when* and *where* persuasive campaigns are necessary? Should the interested parties from a community be involved in the decision about *whether* a campaign should be launched, and not only in the later stages of the intervention? Furthermore, how can illiterate villagers argue on an equal plane with sophisticated national planners armed with charts, statistics, debating skills, and prestige? Those in power usually are in a much better position to launch a persuasion campaign and to carry it out effectively. Thus, even though persuasion itself may be more consistent than other means of intervention with the principles of democratic dialogue and popular participation, it often occurs in a context where some are more equal than others.

Facilitation. Some strategies of intervention may simply be designed to make it easier for an individual to implement his own choices or satisfy his own desires. An underlying assumption in these strategies is that the person has some sense of what he wants to do and lacks only the means to do it. Though facilitation, like persuasion, seems highly consistent with freedom, it too can move close to the borders of manipulation.

Consider an example from the field of family planning—a common form of social intervention. At some level, vague or specific, a woman is concerned about the size of her family. A local family planning service becomes aware of her concern, and tries to devise a strategy of assistance. The following would be among the possibilities of facilitation, running from the least to the most manipulative:

1. The woman is highly informed about the possibilities of contraception, and strongly motivated to limit her family size. Moreover, she has a specific form of contraception in mind (the pill) and is lacking only the means to obtain it. A change program which provided a regular supply of contraceptive pills would be an example of almost pure facilitation.

2. The woman is generally aware of the possibilities of contraception, and strongly motivated to limit her family size, but cannot decide which contraceptive method would be best in her case. A change program is set up to (a) provide counseling on the advantages and disadvantages of various methods of family planning; (b) assist the woman in coming to a decision about the means most appropriate in her case; and (c)

provide the materials or services necessary to implement her choice. In this case facilitation would be mixed with some degree of manipulation or persuasion.

3. The woman is strongly motivated to limit her family size but is totally uninformed about the possibilities of contraception. The clinic recommends a single method—the intrauterine device—without explaining its relative merits in comparison with other methods. This strategy would also involve facilitation, but with even stronger elements of manipulation and persuasion than in the previous case.

4. The woman vaguely feels that she has too many children, but she is not strongly motivated to reduce her family size and possesses no information on contraception. The clinic arranges for visits to her home with the purpose of increasing her level of motivation. Once the vague concern is translated into a concrete intention to practice contraception, the woman is provided free transportation to a local family planning clinic. For purposes of this example we will leave open what happens there. Though facilitation is clearly involved in the later stages of this program, in its origins it is basically a form of either manipulation or persuasion. That is, it requires that motivation be channeled before actual facilitation can take place.

The ethical problems of intervention increase as one moves from more or less "pure" facilitation to cases in which facilitation occurs as the last stage of a manipulative or persuasive strategy. But ethical questions can be raised even about seemingly pure facilitation. The most vexing problem is that the selective reinforcement of an individual's desires, even when these are sharply focused and based on adequate information, can be carried out for someone else's purposes. Here we face a critical question about the ethics of planned change: is it right for party A to assist party B to attain B's own desires when the reason for this assistance is that B's actions will serve A's interests? In other words, does any kind of facilitation also involve elements of environmental manipulation through the principle of selective reinforcement? For example, survey data suggest that many poor blacks and Mexican-Americans in the United States are desirous of family planning services. But racist groups would also like to see these minorities reduce their fertility. If the government decides to provide voluntary family planning services to these and other poor families, is it serving the interests of racism or the freedom of the families in question? Although it is sometimes possible to determine that a given intervention leans more one way than the other, it is often impossible to say whose interests are served most by a change program.

Some have tried to handle the charge of manipulation through facilitation by being "completely honest and open." Consider the case of a church-related action group which approaches a neighborhood organization with an offer of assistance. The group's director could argue that manipulation can be avoided by open dialogue about why each party might be interested in the other, joint setting of goals, and complete liberty on both sides to terminate the relationship. Although such honesty and openness are ethically laudable policies, they do not remove the possibility of manipulation. The fact remains that the church group is making its resources available to one group rather than another. It thereby facilitates the attainment of the goals associated with that group and may weaken the influence and bargaining position of a competing group. In cases where there are numerous groups claiming to represent essentially the same constituency, as among Puerto Ricans in the United States, the receipt of outside aid may give one power contender considerable advantage over the others. Moreover, since the church group retains ultimate control of the resources provided, it can exercise great leverage in setting goals by the implicit threat of withdrawing its support. It is thus essential to distinguish between honesty in the process by which an intervention is carried out and the underlying power relationships operating in the situation.

Assessment of Consequences

A final set of ethical concerns arises from the consequences of a change program—both its products and its by-products. The following are among the questions that might be raised in a specific case: Who benefits from the change, both in the short and the long run? Who suffers? How does the change affect the distribution of power in the society, say between elites and masses or between competing social groups? What is its impact on the physical environment? What social values does it enhance and which does it weaken? Does the program create a lasting dependency on the change agent or on some other sponsor? What will be its short-term and long-term effect on the personalities of those involved? Many of these questions can be grouped under the headings of *direct* and *indirect* consequences.

Direct Consequences. Certain effects flow immediately from the substance or contents of the change. The direct effect of an abortion is to terminate the life of a fetus. A direct effect of the agrarian reform program introduced by Peru in 1969 was to place a certain amount of land in the hands of a certain number of small farmers. An ethical analysis of these effects would relate them to the set of basic values used as criteria for assessing the intervention. This general procedure was followed by the Population Task Force of the Institute for Society, Ethics, and the Life Sciences (1971) in its examination of specific proposals for population policy. The core values used in its report, as noted earlier, were freedom, justice, security/survival, and welfare. Among the specific proposals examined in the light of these values were voluntarist policies, such as providing free birth control information and materials, and penalty programs, including those that would limit social benefits (education, welfare, maternity care) to families with less than N children.

In brief, the Task Force concluded that voluntarist policies had the great advantage of either enhancing or at least maintaining freedom, and in certain cases of promoting the general welfare. At the same time there was some concern that, under conditions of rapid population growth and preferences for large families, voluntarist policies alone might jeopardize the general welfare and possibly survival. Also, questions of justice could be raised if one group in the society was growing at a much faster rate than others. The major ethical drawback of penalty programs, on the other hand, was their possible injustice to those affected. The primary impact of measures such as the withdrawal of educational benefits would be precisely on those who needed them most—the poor. Considerations of justice would also arise if, as is likely, society or the family turned its wrath on the poor creature whose birth order happened to be $N+1$.

Indirect Consequences. Almost any change program will have an impact on areas of society and personality beyond its immediate intentions or scope of influence. These indirect effects must form part of any serious ethical evaluation. To carry out such an evaluation one must have a guiding theory of change—how one part of a system affects another. To put the point another way, it is a form of ethical irresponsibility to tamper with individual personality or social relationships without knowing or at least considering the by-products and side-effects of the change. Unfortunately, many efforts at social intervention completely ignore these "systems effects," or discover them only too late. Among the most common unanticipated effects are the destruction or weakening of integrative values in the society; change in the balance between aspirations and achievement; and strengthening the power of one group at the expense of another.

One of the latent consequences of many programs of modernization is to undercut or challenge existing values and norms, particularly in rural areas. The introduction of a new road, building of an industrial plant, teaching literacy, or even selling transistor radios may expose the isolated villager to a variety of new stimuli that challenge his traditional world-view. Though the direct effects of such programs often serve the values of welfare, justice, and freedom, the indirect effects may generate abundant confusion and a search for new alternatives. Similarly, quasi-coercive population policies can affect societal values in subtle ways.

A careful analysis of proposals for population control must also pay heed to their unanticipated consequences in areas of life seemingly remote from population. It is quite possible, for example, that one of the side effects of a semi-coercive penalty program administered by the federal government would be an increase in political corruption. Some may find it more palatable to bribe local enforcement officials than to limit their procreative behavior. Similarly, in cases where the moral or even political legitimacy of a program was seriously questioned by large segments of the population, a by-product of its implementation might be increased cynicism about government in general. . . . One could also question the advisability of incentive programs which, in effect, bribe people not to have children. Though this practice may successfully reduce family size, its long-term effect may be the encouragement of the same commercial mentality in other spheres of life. . . . Before experimenting with financial incentive programs, therefore, it would be prudent to ask if there are certain goods which we would rather not have bought and sold on the open market, such as one's body, one's vote, and one's personal liberty (Warwick, 1971a, pp. 20–21).

Another common side-effect of change involves a shift in the balance between individual aspirations and the opportunities for achieving them. The delicate ethical question in this case concerns the degree to which a change agent is justified in tampering with aspirations. The dilemma is often severe. On the one hand, to do nothing implies an endorsement of the status quo. On the other hand, in raising aspirations to stir up motivation for change, a program may overshoot its mark. The unintended result may be a rise in frustration.

Questions of this type could be raised about the innovative method of literacy instruction developed by Paulo Freire (1971). His approach, which he calls *conscientização*, attempts to develop not only an ability to read but also a heightened consciousness of one's position in society and the forces shaping his destiny. Freire's method makes use of words that are relevant to personal and local concerns and that are charged with political meaning. The apparent success of this approach in Northeast Brazil and elsewhere raises an interesting ethical problem. To the degree that an individual not only learns to read, but develops a critical consciousness of his position in the social structure, one could argue that his freedom has been enhanced. But a change in critical consciousness and political aspirations without a corresponding modification of the social environment may also be a source of profound frustration. Where collective action to change the system is impossible, because of either strong political repression or other barriers to organization, the net effect may be short-term enthusiasm followed by long-term depression. In fact, the experience of having been stimulated and then frustrated may lead to a lower probability of future action than existed before the intervention. One must thus ask if it is morally justifiable to raise political aspirations without at the same time ensuring that there are opportunities for implementing these aspirations.

A program of social intervention may also have the unintended effect of strengthening the bargaining position of one group vis-à-vis another. This problem was well illustrated in a debate at Harvard University in 1969. The focus of the debate was the Cambridge Project, an interuniversity program aimed at developing and testing computer systems for use in the behavioral sciences. The major point of contention was its sponsorship by the U.S. Department of Defense. Though the project was not designed to carry out military research or provide other direct services to the sponsor, it aroused considerable concern in the Harvard community. The strongest objection was that acceptance of funds from the Defense Department might increase its involvement in university affairs and broaden its constituency among social scientists. In this way, some felt, the project would reinforce the dominant role of the military in U.S. society and simultaneously weaken the university's capacity for critical analysis of that role. In other words, by accepting a major grant from the Defense Department, Harvard would be lending its institutional prestige to the sponsor, legitimizing the Defense Department's involvement in nonmilitary activities, and perhaps creating pressures within the university to refrain from political dissent. The opponents also argued that a heavy infusion of funds into the area of computer applications would change the "ecological balance" of social science research within the university. According to this line of reasoning students and faculty would be drawn to computer-oriented research and away from areas lacking comparable support.

Summary and Conclusions

Social intervention may impinge on human rights and values in many ways—through the ends served by the change, the targets at which it is directed, the means chosen to implement it, and its direct or indirect consequences. At its core, ethical responsibility requires a full consideration of the process and probable consequences of intervention in the light of a set of guiding values. This essay suggests that it is not an easy matter to exercise such responsibility, partly because of ambiguity about which values should apply, partly because of difficulties in assessing the impact of an intervention on the values chosen. The discussion also underscores the intimate connection between ethics and an empirical understanding of social influence. Often moral judgment rests heavily on a prediction about how a specific intervention will affect individuals and groups. Although our knowledge of the processes and effects of social change is still at a rudimentary level, existing theory and research can be of considerable help in arriving at informed decisions. In the end, the search for an ethics of social intervention recalls Plato's comment that "in the world of knowledge the idea of good appears last of all, and is seen only with an effort."

Acknowledgment

The authors are grateful to the Center for the Study of Development and Social Change, Cambridge, Massachusetts, for organizing a discussion of an earlier draft of this chapter. We wish to thank especially James Lamb, Director, Denis Goulet, William Frain, and David Robinson for their helpful criticisms.

Note

1. Donald Warwick was a member of the Task Force and a co-author of its final report.

REFERENCES

Aberle, D. F. (1962). "A Note on Relative Deprivation Theory as Applied to Millenarian and other Cult Movements." In S. Thrupp (ed.), *Millennial Dreams in Action: Essays in Comparative Studies,* pp. 209–214. Comparative Studies in Society and History. The Hague: Mouton and Co.

Adams, J. S. (1965). "Inequity in Social Exchange." In L. Berkowitz (ed.), *Advances in Experimental Social Psychology,* pp. 267–299. New York: Academic Press.

Adelman, I. and Morris, C. (1967). *Society, Politics and Economic Development.* Baltimore: The Johns Hopkins Press.

Adorno, T. W., Frenkel-Brunswik, E., Levinson, D. J., and Sanford, N. (1950). *The Authoritarian Personality.* New York: Harper.

Agency for International Development (1970). Spring Review of Population Programs. Washington, D.C.: mimeo.

Agency for International Development (1971). Population Program Assistance. Washington, D.C.

Agger, R. (1964). "Political Research as Political Action." In R. Cahill and S. Hencley (eds.), *The Politics of Education,* pp. 207–232. Danville, Ill.: Interstate Printers & Publishers.

Ahmad, W. (1971). "Field Structures in Family Planning," *Studies in Family Planning,* 2(1):6–18.

Allport, F. H. (1955). *Theories of Perception and the Concept of Structure.* New York: John Wiley & Sons, pp. 467–530.

Allport, G. W. (1937). *Personality: A Psychological Interpretation.* New York: Holt, Rinehart and Winston.

Allport, G. W., and Postman, L. J (1945). "The Basic Psychology of Rumor," *Transactions of New York Academy of Science,* Series II, 8:61–81.

Allvine, F. (1968). "Diffusion of a Competitive Innovation." In R. King (ed.), *Proceedings of the American Marketing Association,* pp. 341–351.

Anderson, B., Berger, J., Zelditch, M., and Cohen, B. P. (1969). "Reactions to Inequity," *Acta Sociologica,* 12(1):1–12.

Appelbaum, R. P. (1970). *Theories of Social Change.* Chicago: Markham Publishing Co.

Arensberg, C. M., and Niehoff, A. (1971). *Introducing Social Change: A Manual for Community Development.* Chicago: Aldine-Atherton.

419

Argyris, C. (1952). *Journal of Social Issues.* Ann Arbor, Mich.: Society for the Psychological Study of Social Issues.

Argyris, C. (1962). *Interpersonal Competence or Organizational Effectiveness.* Homewood, Ill.: Richard D. Irwin.

Argyris, C. (1970). *Intervention Theory and Methods.* Reading, Mass., Addison-Wesley.

Aronson, E., and Carlsmith J. M (1968). "Experimentation in Social Psychology." In G. Lindzey and E. Aronson (eds.), *Handbook of Social Psychology,* Vol. II. Reading, Mass.: Addison-Wesley, pp. 1–79.

Ball, S., and Bogatz, G. A. (1970). A Summary of the Major Findings in "The First Year of Sesame Street: An Evaluation." Educational Testing Service.

Baratz, S., and Baratz, J. (1970). "Early Childhood Intervention: The Social Science Base of Institutional Racism," *Harvard Educational Review, 40*:29–50.

Barnett, H. G. (1953). *Innovation: The Basis of Culture Change.* New York: McGraw-Hill.

Barringer, H. R., Blanksten, G. I., and Mack, R. (eds.) (1965). *Social Change in Developing Areas: A Reinterpretation of Evolutionary Theory.* Cambridge, Mass.: Schenkman Publishing Co.

Bass, F. M., Pessemier, E. A., and Tigert, D. J. (1969). "A Taxonomy of Magazine Readership Applied to Problems in Marketing Strategy and Media Selection," *Journal of Business, 42*:337–363.

Bauer, P. T. (1966). "Foreign Aid: An Instrument for Progress?" In B. Ward and P. T. Bauer (eds.), *Two Views on Aid to Developing Countries.* London: Institute of Economic Affairs.

Bauer, R. A. (1969). *Second Order Consequences: A Methodological Essay on the Impact of Technology.* Cambridge, Mass.: The M.I.T. Press.

Bawden, D. L. (1970). "Income Maintenance and the Rural Poor: An Experimental Approach," *American Journal of Agricultural Economics, 52*:438–441.

Becker, M. H. (1970). "Sociometric Location and Innovativeness: Reformulation and Extension of the Diffusion Model," *American Sociological Review, 35*(April):267–282.

Bell, W. (1963). "Consumer Innovators: A Unique Market for Newness," *Proceedings of the American Marketing Association,* 85–95.

Bennett, C. (1969). "Diffusion within Dynamic Populations," *Human Organization, 28*(Fall):243–247.

Bennett, E. (1955). "Discussion, Decision, Commitment and Consensus in Group Decision," *Human Relations, 8*:251–273.

Bennis, W. G., Benne, K. D., and Chin, R. (eds.) (1969). *The Planning of Change,* (2nd ed.) New York: Holt, Rinehart and Winston.

Bennis, W. G., Schein, E. H., Berlew, D. E., and Steele, F. I. (1964). *Inter-Personal Dynamics: Essays and Readings on Human Interaction.* Homewood, Ill.: Dorsey.

Berelson, B. (1948). "Communication and Public Opinion." In W. Schramm (ed.), *Communications in Modern Society*. Urbana: University of Illinois Press.

Berelson, B. (1967). "On Family Planning Communication." In D. J. Bogue (ed.), *Mass Communication and Motivation for Birth Control*. Community and Family Study Center, The University of Chicago, pp. 842–857.

Berelson, B. (1969). "Beyond Family Planning," *Studies in Family Planning, 56*.

Berelson, B. (1969). "National Family Planning Programs: Where We Stand." In S. J. Behrman, L. Corsa, and R. Freedman (eds.), *Fertility and Family Planning*. Ann Arbor: University of Michigan Press.

Berelson, B. (1969). "Where We Stand." In S. J. Behrman et al. (eds.), *Fertility and Family Planning*. Ann Arbor: University of Michigan Press.

Berelson, B. (1970). "The Present State of Family Planning Programs," *Studies in Family Planning, 57*.

Berelson, B. R., Lazarsfeld, P. F., and McPhee, W. N. (1954). *Voting*. Chicago: University of Chicago Press.

Berelson, B., and Salter, P. (1946). "Majority-Minority Americans: An Analysis of Magazine Fiction," *Public Opinion Quarterly, 10*(Summer):168–190.

Berlak, H. (1970). "Values, Goals, Public Policy and Educational Evaluation," *Review of Educational Research, 40*:261–278.

Berle, D. K. (1960). *The Process of Human Communication*. New York: Holt, Rinehart and Winston.

Bernard, J. (1967). "Conflict as Research and Research as Conflict." In I. Horowitz (ed.), *The Rise and Fall of Project Camelot*. Cambridge, Mass.: M.I.T. Press, pp. 128–152.

von Bertalanffy, L. (1960). *Problems of Life—An Evaluation of Modern Biological and Scientific Thought*. New York: Harper & Brothers.

Billingsley, A. (1970). "Black Families and White Social Science," *Journal of Social Issues, 26*:127–142.

Black, M. (1972). "Beyond Freedom and Dignity: A Disservice to All," *The Center Magazine*, March/April.

Blake, J. (1969). "Population Policy for Americans: Is the Government Being Misled?" *Science, 164*:522–529.

Blalock, H. M., Jr. (1967). *Causal Inferences in Nonexperimental Research*. Chapel Hill: University of North Carolina Press.

Blau, P. M. (1964). *Exchange and Power in Social Life*. New York: John Wiley and Sons.

Blumer, H. (1946). "The Crowd, the Public, and the Mass." In A. M. Lee (ed.), *New Outline of the Principles of Sociology*. New York: Barnes and Noble.

Bogue, D. J. (ed.) (1967). *Mass Communication and Motivation for Birth Control*. Community and Family Study Center, The University of Chicago.

Boulding, K. E. (1956). *The Image*. Ann Arbor: University of Michigan Press.

Boulding, K. E. (1970). "The Economics of the Coming Spaceship Earth." In G. De Bell (ed.), *The Environmental Handbook*. New York: Ballantine Books, pp. 96–101.

Brandner, L., and Keal, B. (1964). "Evaluation for Congruence as a Factor in the Adoption Rate of Innovations," *Rural Sociology, 29:*288–303.

Brandner, L., and Sistrunk, J. (1966). "The Newspaper: Molder or Mirror of Community Values?" *Journalism Quarterly, 43*(Winter):497–504.

Brehm, J. W. (1966). *A Theory of Psychological Reactance.* New York: Academic Press.

Brehm, J. W., and Cohen, A. R. (1962). *Explorations in Cognitive Dissonance.* New York: John Wiley and Sons.

Bright, J. R. (1964). *Technological Innovation.* Homewood, Ill.: Richard D. Irwin.

Bronfenbrenner, U. (1962). "Soviet Methods of Character Education: Some Implications for Research," *Religious Education, 17:*550–564.

Browning, H. L. (1971). "Migrant Selectivity and the Growth of Cities in Developing Societies." In National Academy of Sciences, *Rapid Population Growth*, Vol. II. Baltimore: The Johns Hopkins Press.

Buckley, W. (1968). "Society as a Complex Adaptive System." In W. Buckley, (ed.), *Modern Systems Research for Behavioral Scientists*. Chicago: Aldine.

Budd, R. W., MacLean, M. S., Jr., and Barnes, A. M. (1966). "Regularities in the Diffusion of Two Major News Events," *Journalism Quarterly 43*(Summer):221–230.

Callahan, D. (1971). "Population Limitation and Manipulation of Familial Roles," unpublished essay, Institute of Society, Ethics, and the Life Sciences, Hastings-on-Hudson, N.Y.

Cameron, W. B. (1966). *Modern Social Movements.* New York: Random House, pp. 27–28.

Campbell, A., and Converse, P. E. (1972). *The Human Meaning of Social Change.* New York: The Russell Sage Foundation.

Campbell, A., Gurin, G., and Miller, W. E. (1954). *The Voter Decides.* Evanston, Ill.: Row, Peterson and Co.

Campbell, D. (1970). "Considering the Case Against Experimental Evaluations of Social Innovations," *Administrative Science Quarterly, 15:*110–113.

Campbell, D. T. (1957). "Factors Relevant to the Validity of Experiments in Social Settings, *Psychological Bulletin, 54:*297–312.

Campbell, D. T. (1968). "Quasi-Experimental Design." In David Sills (ed.), *International Encyclopedia of the Social Sciences*. New York: Macmillan and Free Press.

Campbell, D. T. (1969). "Reforms as Experiments," *American Psychologist,* (April):409–422.

Campbell, D. T., and Erlebacher, A. (1970). "How Regression Artifacts in Quasi-

Experimental Evaluations Can Mistakenly Make Compensatory Education Look Harmful." In J. Hellmuth (ed.), *Compensatory Education: A National Debate*, Vol. 3, *Disadvantaged Child*. New York: Brunner/Mazel, pp. 185–210.

Campbell, D. T., and Stanley, J. C. (1966). *Experimental and Quasi-Experimental Designs for Research*. Chicago: Rand-McNally.

Cancian, F. (1960). "Functional Analysis of Change," *American Sociological Review, 25*:818–826.

Cannell, C. F., Wale, F. G., and Withey, S. B. (eds.) (1953). "Community Change: An Action Program in Puerto Rico," *Journal of Social Issues, 9*:2.

Cannon, W. B. (1932). *Wisdom of the Body*. New York: W. W. Norton and Co.

Carlson, R. O. (1965). *Adoption of Educational Innovations*. Eugene, Ore.: The Center for the Advanced Study of Education Administration.

Carlson, R. O. (1965). *Change Processes in the Public Schools*. Eugene, Ore.: Center for the Advanced Study of Education Administration.

Carlson, R. O. (1968). "Summary and Critique of Educational Diffusion Research," *Research Implications for Educational Diffusion*. Michigan Department of Education.

Caro, F. G. (1969). "Approaches to Evaluative Research: A Review," *Human Organization, 28*:87–99.

Caro, F. G. (1971). "Issues in the Evaluation of Social Programs," *Review of Educational Research, 41*:87–114.

Caro, F. G. (1971). *Readings in Evaluative Research*. New York: Russell Sage Foundation.

Carrole, J. (1967). "A Note on Departmental Autonomy and Innovation in Medical Schools," *Journal of Business, 40*:531–534.

Carter, L. G. (1968). "Population Control: U.S. Aid Program Leaps Forward," *Science, 159*:611.

Carter, R. E., Jr., and Sepulveda, O. (1964). "Some Patterns of Mass Media Use in Stantiago de Chile," *Journalism Quarterly, 41*(Spring):216–24.

Cartwright, D. (1949). "Some Principles of Mass Persuasion," *Human Relations, 2*:253–67.

Cartwright, D. (1954). "Achieving Change in People: Some Applications of Group Dynamics Theory," *Human Relations, 4*:381–392.

Centro de Investigaciones Sociales por Muestro (1966). *Caracteristicas Socio-Economicas de la Ciudad de Arequipa*. Lima: Servicio del Empleo y Recursos Humanos.

Chandrasehar, M. (1960). "A Comment on Dr. Enke's Article," *Population Review, 4*:52–54.

Chesler, M., and Flanders, M. (1967). "Resistance to Research and Research Utilization, *Journal of Applied Behavioral Sciences, 3*:469–489.

Chin, R. (1963). "Models and Ideas About Changing." In W. C. Meierhenry (ed.), *Identifying Techniques and Principles for Gaining Acceptance of Research Results*. Lincoln: University of Nebraska Press.

Chomsky, N. (1971). "The Case Against B. F. Skinner," *New York Review of Books,* December 30, pp. 18–24.

Cicirelli, V. G. (1969). "Project Head Start, A National Evluation: Summary of the Study." In D. G. Hays (ed.), *Britannica Review of American Education,* Vol. 1. Chicago: Encyclopedia Britannica.

Coale, A. J. (1964). "How a Population Ages or Grows Younger." In R. Freedman (ed.), *Population: The Vital Revolution.* New York: Anchor Books.

Coch, L., and French, J. R. P., Jr. (1948). "Overcoming Resistance to Change," *Human Relations, 1*(4):512–532.

Cole, S., and Cole, J. R. (1967). "Scientific Output and Recognition: A Study of the Reward System in Science," *American Sociological Review, 32* (June):377–390.

Coleman, J. S. (1971). *Resources for Social Change: Race in the United States.* New York: John Wiley and Sons.

Commission on Population Growth and the American Future, 1972. Washington, D.C.

Commons, J. R. (1924). *Legal Foundations of Capitalism.* New York: Macmillan.

Cooley, C. H. (1902). *Human Nature and the Social Order.* New York: Charles Scribner's Sons.

Cooley, C. H. (1909). *Social Organization.* New York: Charles Scribner's Sons.

Cooper, C. L. (1969). "The Influence of the Trainer on Participant Change in T-Groups," *Human Relations, 22*:515–530.

Copp, J. H. (1970). "Poverty and our Social Order: Implications and Reservations," *American Journal of Agricultural Economics, 52:* 736–744.

Cottrell, L. S., and Everhart, S. (1948). *American Opinion in World Affairs.* Princeton: Princeton University Press.

Crain, R. (1966). "Fluoridation: The Diffusion of an Innovation Among Cities," *Social Forces, 44*(June):467–476.

Cremin, L. A. (1961). *The Transformation of the School.* New York: Alfred A. Knopf.

Cronbach, L. F., and Furby, L. (1970). "How We Should Measure 'Change'—or Should We?" *Psychological Bulletin, 74*:68–80.

Davies, J. C. (1969). "The J-Curve of Rising and Declining Satisfactions as a Cause of Some Great Revolutions and a Contained Rebellion." In H. D. Graham and T. R. Gurr (eds.), *Violence in America.* New York: Bantam Books, pp. 690–730.

Davis, B. E. (1968). "System Variables and Agricultural Innovations in Eastern Nigeria." Ph.D. dissertation, Michigan State University.

Davis, K. (1967). "Population Policy: Will Current Programs Succeed?" *Science, 158*:730–739.

Davis, R. C. (1949). *The Public Impact of Science in the Mass Media.* Ann Arbor: Survey Research Center, University of Michigan.

Day, G. S. (1971). "Theories of Attitude Structure and Change." A Draft of a paper to appear in S. Ward and T. Robertson (eds.), *Consumer Behavior: Theoretical Sources.* Englewood Cliffs, N.J.: Prentice-Hall.

De Fleur, M. L (1970). *Theories of Mass Communication,* 2nd ed. New York: David McKay.

Demeny, P. (1961). "The Economics of Government Payments to Limit Population: A Comment," *Economic Development and Cultural Change,* 9:641–644.

Densen, P. M. (1965). "The Health of the Population." In P. E. Sartwell (ed.), *Preventive Medicine and Public Health,* 9th ed. New York: Appleton-Century-Crofts.

Department of Health, Education and Welfare (1969). *Toward a Social Report.* Washington, D.C.: Government Printing Office.

Dervin, B. (1971). "Communication Behaviors as Related to Information Control Behaviors of Black Low-Income Adults." Ph.D. thesis, Michigan State University.

Desmond, A. (1966). "How Many People Have Lived on Earth?" In L. K. Ng and S. Mudd (eds.), *The Population Crisis.* Bloomington: Indiana University Press.

Deutsch, K. W. (1961). "Social Mobilization and Political Development," *American Political Science Review,* 55:493–514.

Deutsch, M., and Collins, M.E. (1965). "The Effect of Public Policy in Housing Projects Upon Interracial Attitudes." In H. Proshansky and B. Seidenberg (eds.), *Basic Studies in Social Psychology.* New York: Holt, Rinehart and Winston, pp. 646–657.

Deutschmann, P. J. (1957). "The Sign-Situation Classification of Human Communication," *Journal of Communication,* 7(2):63–73.

Deutschmann, P. J. (1963). "The Mass Media in an Underdeveloped Village," *Journalism Quarterly,* 40(Winter):27–35.

Deutschmann, P. J., McNelly, J. T., and Ellingsworth, H. (1961). "Mass Media Use of Sub-Elites in Latin American Countries," *Journalism Quarterly,* 38(Autumn):460–472.

Dewey, J. (1922). *Human Nature and Conduct.* New York: Holt, Rinehart and Winston.

Dickson, P. (1971). *Think Tanks.* New York: Atheneum.

Dimock, H. S., and Sorenson, R. (1955). *Designing Education in Values: A Case Study in Institution Change.* New York: Association Press.

D'Onofrio, C. N. (n.d.). *Reaching Our "Hard to Reach"—the Unvaccinated.* State of California: Department of Public Health.

Donohew, L. (1967). "Newspaper Gatekeepers and Forces in the News Channel," *Public Opinion Quarterly,* 31:61–68.

Doob, L. W. (1950). "Goebbels' Principles of Propaganda," *Public Opinion Quarterly, 14:*419–42.

Douglas, D. F., Westley, B. H., and Chaffee, S. H (1970). "An Information Campaign That Changed Community Attitudes," *Journalism Quarterly, 47*(Autumn):479–487, 492.

Dubos, R. (1970). *Reason Awake.* New York: Columbia University Press, pp. 206–208.

Dye, T. R. (1966). *Politics, Economics and the Public.* Chicago: Rand-McNally.

Dykens, J. W., Hyde, R. W., Orzack, L. H., and York, R. H. (1964). *Strategies of Mental Hospital Change.* Boston: Commonwealth of Massachusetts Department of Mental Health.

Eapen, K. E. (1967). "Daily Newspapers in India: Their Status and Their Problems," *Journalism Quarterly,* 44:520–532.

Edwards, L. P. (1927). *The Natural History of Revolution.* Chicago: University of Chicago Press.

Enke, S. (1960a). "The Gains to India From Population Control: Some Money Measures and Incentive Schemes," *Review of Economics and Statistics, 42:*175–181.

Enke, S. (1960b). "The Economics of Government Payments to Limit Population," *Economic Development and Cultural Change, 8:*339–348.

Enke, S. (1961a). "Some Reactions to Bonuses for Family Limitation," *Population Review, 5:*33–39.

Enke, S. (1961b). "A Rejoinder to Comments on the Superior Effectiveness of Vasectomy-Bonus Schemes," *Economic Development and Cultural Change, 9:*645–647.

Enke, S. (1962). "Some Misconceptions of Krueger and Sjaastad Regarding the Vasectomy-Bonus Plan to Reduce Births in Overpopulated and Poor Countries," *Economic Development and Cultural Change, 10:*427–431.

Erickson, E. H. (1969). *Gandhi's Truth: On the Origins of Militant Nonviolence.* New York: W. W. Norton.

Evans, F. B. (1963). "Selling as a Dyadic Relationship—A New Approach," *The American Behavioral Scientist, 6*(May):76–79.

Evans, J. W. (1969). "Evaluating Social Action Programs," *Social Science Quarterly, 50.*

Evans, J. W., and Schiller, J. (1970). "How Preoccupation with Possible Regression Artifacts Can Lead to a Faulty Strategy for the Evaluation of Social Action Programs: A Reply to Campbell." In J. Hellmuth (ed.), *Compensatory Education: A National Debate,* Vol. 3, *Disadvantaged Child.* New York: Brunner/Mazel, pp. 216–220.

Evans, R. I. (1970). *Resistance to Innovation in Higher Education.* San Francisco: Jossey-Bass Publishers.

Etzioni, A. (1969). "Toward a Theory of Guided Societal Change," *Social Science Quarterly, 50*(December):749–754.

Etzioni, A. (1971). "Policy Research," *The American Sociologist: Supplementary Issue on Sociological Research and Public Policy, 6*:8–12.

Fairweather, G. W. (1967). *Methods for Experimental Social Innovation.* New York: John Wiley and Sons.

Family Planning Division, Government of Pakistan (1969). *Family Planning Scheme for Pakistan during the Fourth Five Year Plan Period, 1970–1975.* Islamabad, Pakistan, Report.

Federal Trade Commission (1967). "Permissible Period of Time During Which New Products May Be Described as 'New,' " *Advisory Opinion Digest, 120* (April 15).

Feierabend, I. K., and Feierabend, R. L. (1966). "Aggressive Behavior Within Politics, 1948–1962: A Cross-National Study," *Journal of Conflict Resolution, 10*:249–271.

Feierabend, I. K., Feierabend, R. L., and Nesvold, B. A. (1969). "Social Change and Political Violence: Cross National Patterns." In H. D. Graham and T. R. Gurr (eds.), *Violence in America.* New York: Bantam Books, pp. 632–687.

Feldman, J. J. (1966). *The Dissemination of Health Innovation.* Chicago: Aldine.

Festinger, L. (1957). *A Theory of Cognitive Dissonance.* New York: Harper and Row.

Festinger, L. (1964). *Conflict, Decision and Dissonance.* Stanford: Stanford University Press.

Festinger, L., and Katz, D. (eds.) (1953). *Research Methods in the Behavioral Sciences.* New York: Holt, Rinehart and Winston.

Festinger, L., and Thibaut, J. (1951). "Interpersonal Communication in Small Groups," *Journal of Abnormal and Social Psychology, 46*(January):92–99. Washington, D.C.: American Psychological Association.

Finnigan, O. D. (1972). "Planning, Starting, and Operating an Educational Inceptives Project," *Studies in Family Planning, 3.*

Fisk, G. (1959). "Media Influence Reconsidered," *Public Opinon Quarterly, 23*(Spring):83–91.

Fliegel, F. C., and Kivlin, J. E. (1966a). "Farmers' Perceptions of Farm Practice Attributes," *Rural Sociology, 31*(June):197–206.

Fliegel, F. C., and Kivlin J. E. (1966b). "Attributes of Innovations as Factors in Diffusion," *American Journal of Sociology, 72*(November):235–248.

Fliegel, F. C., Kivlin, J. E., and Sekhon, G. S. (1968). "A Cross-Cultural Comparison of Farmers' Perceptions of Innovations as Related to Adoption Behavior," *Rural Sociology, 33*(December):437–449.

Form, W., and Geschwender, J. A. (1962). "Social Reference Basis of Job Satisfaction," *American Sociological Review, 27*(2)(April):228–237.

Forrester, J. W. (1971). "Counterintuitive Behavior of Social Systems," *Technology Review, 43* (January):53–68.

Freedman, R. (1969). *Comments on Evaluation of the West Bengal Family Planning Program.* New Delhi: Ford Foundation, Discussion Paper.

Freedman, R. (1970). "Social Research and Programs for Reducing Birth Rates." Paper prepared for Rockefeller Foundation Conference, Villa Servelloni, Bellagio, Italy.

Freedman, R., and Frazer, R. (1968). "Compliance Without Pressure: The Foot in the Door Technique," *Journal of Personality and Social Psychology.*

Freire, P. (1971). *Pedagogy of the Oppressed.* New York: Herder and Herder.

Freud, S. (1922). *Beyond the Pleasure Principle.* London: Hogarth Press.

Frey, F. W. (1966). "Communication with the Peasant Audience." Unpublished paper prepared for the AID—MSU Seminar on Communication and Change. East Lansing, April 4–7.

Fuchs, L. H. (1967) "The Role and Communications Task of the Change Agent —Experiences of the Peace Corps Volunteers in the Philippines," in D. Lerner and W. Schramm (eds.), *Communication and Change in the Developing Countries,* Honolulu: East-West Center Press.

Gallaher, A., Jr. (ed.) (1968). *Perspectives in Developmental Change.* Lexington: University of Kentucky Press.

Galtung, J. (1967). "After Camelot." In I. Horowitz (ed.), *The Rise and Fall of Project Camelot.* Cambridge, Mass.: M.I.T. Press, pp. 281–312.

Gamson, W. A. (1969). *SIMSOC: Simulated Society. Participants' Manual with Selected Readings.* New York: Free Press.

Gans, H. (1962). *The Urban Villagers.* New York: Free Press.

Gardner, J. W. (1963). *Self-Renewal: The Individual and the Organization in an Innovative Society.* New York: Harper and Row.

Garvey, W. D., Lin, N., Nelson, C. E., and Tomita, K. (1970). "The Role of the National Meeting in Scientific and Technical Communication." Center for Research in Scientific Communication, The Johns Hopkins University (June).

Geschwender, J. A. (1968). "Explorations in the Theory of Social Movements and Revolutions," *Social Forces, 47*(2)(December):127–135.

Glaser, E., and Taylor, S. (1969). *Factors Influencing the Success of Applied Research.* Contract 43-67-1365. Washington, D.C.: National Institute of Mental Health, Dept. H.E.W.

Goering, J. M., and Cummins, M. (1970). "Intervention Research and the Survey Process," *Journal of Social Issues, 25*:49–55.

Goffman, E. (1961). *Asylums: Essays on the Social Situation of Mental Patients and Other Inmates.* New York: Doubleday.

Goodlad, J. I. (1970). "Lay on Making Ideas Work," *The New York Times,* (January), p. 67.

Gottschalk, L. A., and Pattison, E. M. (1970). "Psychiatric Perspectives on T-groups and the Laboratory Movement: An Overview," *American Journal of Psychiatry, 126:*823–840.

Goulet, D. (1971). *The Cruel Choice.* New York: Atheneum.

Government of India Mass Mailing Unit (1972). "Family Planning Programme in India," Ministry of Health and Family Planning, New Delhi.

Graham, S. (1954). "Class and Conservatism in the Adoption of Innovations," *Human Relations, 9:*91–100.

Grambois, D. H. (1964). "The Role of Communication in the Family Decision-Making Process," Proceedings of the American Marketing Association Educators Conference.

Green, P., and Carmone, F. (1970). *Multidimensional Scaling and Related Techniques.* Boston: Allyn and Bacon.

Green, P., and Rao, V. (1972). *Applied Multidimensional Scaling: A Comparison of Approaches and Algorithms.* New York: Holt, Rinehart and Winston.

Greenberg, B. S. (1964a). "Person-to-Person Communication in the Diffusion of News Events," *Journalism Quarterly, 41*(Autumn):489–494.

Greenberg, B. S. (1964b). "On Relating Attitude Change and Information Gain," *Journal of Communication, 14*(June):157–171.

Greenberg, B. S., and Parker, E. B. (1965). *The Kennedy Assassination and the American Public.* Stanford: Stanford University Press.

Greenberg, M. (1969). "Some Applications of Nonmetric Multidimensional Scaling." Paper presented at the 129th Annual Meeting of The American Statistical Association, New York, August.

Greiner, L. E. (1970). "Patterns of Organization Change," *Harvard Business Review, 45.*

Grindstaff, C. F. (1968). "The Negro, Urbanization, and Relative Deprivation in the Deep South," *Social Problems, 15*(3)(Winter):342–352.

Gross, B. M. (1966). "Social Systems Accounting." In R. A. Bauer (ed.), *Social Indicators.* Cambridge, Mass.: The M.I.T. Press.

Guetzkow, H., Alger, C. F., Brody, R. A., Noel, R. C., and Snyder, R. C. (1963). *Simulation in International Relations.* Englewood Cliffs, N. J.: Prentice-Hall.

Guhl, A. M. (1956). "The Social Order of Chickens," *Scientific American, 194*(February):42–47.

Gurr, T. R. (1971). *Why Men Rebel.* Princeton, N.J.: Princeton University Press.

Guskin, A., and Ross, R. (1971). "Advocacy and Democracy: The Long View," *American Journal of Orthopsychiatry, 41:*43–57.

Gustafson, J. M. (1970). "Basic Ethical Issues in the Bio-Medical Fields," *Soundings, 53*(2):151–180.

Guttentag, M., and Strunening, E. L. (eds.) (in preparation). *Handbook of Evaluation Research*.

Hagen, E. E. (1961). "Psychology's Role in Economic Development," *Science*, *134*:1608–1609.

Hagen, E. E. (1962). *On the Theory of Social Change*. Homewood, Ill.: Dorsey Press.

Haire, M. (1956). *Psychology in Management*. New York: McGraw-Hill.

Hardin, G. (1970). "The Tragedy of the Commons." In G. De Bell, (ed.), *The Environmental Handbook*. New York: Ballantine Books, pp. 31–50.

Harris, C. W. (1963). *Problems in Measuring Change*. Madison: University of Wisconsin Press.

Haskins, J. B. (1966). "Factual Recall as a Measure of Advertising Effectiveness," *Journal of Advertising Research, 6*:2–3.

Haug, M., and Sussman, M. (1969). "Professional Autonomy and the Revolt of the Client," *Social Problems, 17*:153–160.

Hauser, P. M. (1971). "World Population: Retrospect and Prospect." In National Academy of Sciences, *Rapid Population Growth*, Vol. II. Baltimore: The Johns Hopkins Press.

Havelock, R. (1969). *Planning for Innovation Through Dissemination and Utilization of Knowledge*. Ann Arbor: Center for Research on Utilization of Knowledge, Institute for Social Research, University of Michigan (July).

Havelock, R. (1971). *Planning for Innovation*. Ann Arbor: Institute for Social Research, University of Michigan.

Hazard, W. R. (1971). *Education and Law*. New York: The Free Press.

Hebb, D. O. (1958). *A Textbook of Psychology*. Philadelphia: W. B. Saunders Co.

Heine, P. J. (1971). *Personality in Social Theory*. Chicago: Aldine-Atherton.

Hero, A. O. (1959a). *Mass Media and World Affairs*. Boston: World Peace Foundation.

Hero, A. O. (1959b). *Americans in World Affairs*. Boston: World Peace Foundation.

Herzog, E. (1970). "Social Stereotypes and Social Research," *Journal of Social Issues, 26*:109–126.

Hickey, J. R. (1968). "The Effects of Information Control on Perceptions of Centrality," *Journalism Quarterly, 45*(Spring):49–54.

Hieder, F. (1946). "Attitudes and Cognitive Organization," *Journal of Psychology, 21*:107–112.

Hill, R. J., and Bonjean, C. M. (1964). "News Diffusion: A Test of the Regularity Hypothesis," *Journalism Quarterly, 41* (Summer):336–342.

Hochbaum, G. (1958). *Public Participation in Medical Screening Programs: A Socio-Psychological Study*. Washington, D.C.: Public Health Service Publication 572.

Hoffer, E. (1951). *The True Believer: Thoughts on the Nature of Mass Movements.* New York: Harper and Brothers.

Hollingshead, A. (1949). *Elmtown's Youth.* New York: John Wiley and Sons.

Homans, G. C. (1961). *Social Behavior: Its Elementary Forms.* New York: Harcourt, Brace and World.

Homans, G. C. (1964). "Contemporary Theory in Sociology." In R. E. L. Faris (ed.), *Handbook of Modern Sociology.* Chicago: Rand-McNally, pp. 951–977.

Hornstein, H. A., et al. (eds.) (1971). *Social Intervention: A Behavioral Science Approach.* New York: Free Press.

Horowitz, I. (1967). *The Rise and Fall of Project Camelot.* Cambridge, Mass.: The M.I.T. Press.

Hovland, C. I. (1959). "Reconciling Conflicting Results Derived From Experimental and Survey Studies of Attitude Change," *American Psychologist, 14*(January):8–17.

Hovland, C. I., Janis, I. L., and Kelley, H. H. (1953). *Communication and Persuasion.* New Haven: Yale University Press.

Hovland, C. I., Lumsdaine, A. A., and Sheffield, F. D. (1949). *Experiments in Mass Communication.* Princeton, N.J.: Princeton University Press.

Hovland, C. I., Mandell, W., Campbell, E. H., Brock, T., Luchins, A. S., Cohen, A. R., McGuire, W. J., Janis, I. L., Feierabend, R. L., and Anderson, N. H. (1957). *The Order of Presentation in Persuasion.* New Haven: Yale University Press.

Hovland, C. I., and Pritzker, H. A. (1957). "Extent of Opinion Change as a Function of Amount of Change Advocated," *Journal of Abnormal and Social Psychology, 54*:257–261.

Howard, L. (1971). "Health Sector Strategy." Washington, D.C.: Office of Health, Technical Assistance Bureau, Agency for International Development.

Huntington, S. P. (1968). *Political Order in Changing Societies.* New Haven: Yale University Press.

Huxley, A. (1965). *Brave New World Revisited.* New York: Harper and Row, Perennial Library Edition.

Hyman, H. H., Levine, G. N., and Wright, C. R. (1967). *Inducing Social Change in Developing Communities.* New York: United Nations.

Hyman, H. H., and Sheatsley, P. J. (1947). "Some Reasons Why Information Campaigns Fail," *Public Opinon Quarterly, 11*(Fall):412–423.

Hyman, H. H., Wright, C. R. (1967). "Evaluating Social Action Programs." In P. F. Lazarsfeld, W. H. Sewell, and H. Z. Wilensky (eds.), *The Uses of Sociology.* New York: Basic Books.

Iacono, G. (1968). "An Affiliative Society Facing Innovations," *Journal of Social Issues, 24*(2):125–130.

Illich, I. (1969). "Outwitting the 'Developed Countries,' " *New York Review of Books,* November 6.

Inkeles, A. (1950). *Public Opinion in Soviet Russia.* Cambridge, Mass.: Harvard University Press.

Inkeles, A. (1955). "Social Change and Social Character: The Role of Parental Mediation," *Journal of Social Issues, 11*(2):12–23.

Inkeles, A. (1966). "The Modernization of Man." In M. Weiner (ed.), *Modernization: The Dynamics of Growth.* New York: Basic Books, pp. 138–150.

Inkeles, A., and Smith, D. H. (1968). "The Fate of Personal Adjustment in the Process of Modernization." Paper prepared for the Tokyo-Kyoto Meetings of the International Anthropological Association: mimeo.

International Bank for Reconstruction and Development (1969). "An Evaluation of the Family Planning Programme of the Government of India," Document No. IAD 69–20.

Internation Planned Parenthood Federation (1971). "Brazil," *Situation Report.*

International Planned Parenthood Federation (1972). "Mexico Adopts National Family Planning Programs," *Planned Parenthood Report, 3:3.*

International Planned Parenthood Federation (n.d.). "Incentive Payments in Family Planning Programmes," London, IPPF, Working Paper 4.

Jackson, B., and Marsden, D. (1962). *Education and the Working Class.* New York: Monthly Review Press.

Jacoby, N. H. (1971). "What is a Social Problem?" *The Center Magazine* (July/August).

James, W. (1948). *Essays in Pragmatism.* A. Castell (ed.). New York: Hafner Publishing Co., pp. 159–176.

Janowitz, M. (1952). *The Community Press in An Urban Setting.* Glencoe, Ill.: Free Press.

Janis, I. L. (1967). "Effects of Fear Arousal on Attitude Change: Recent Developments in Theory and Experimental Research." In L. Berkowitz (ed.), *Advances in Experimental Social Psychology,* Vol. 3. New York: Academic Press, pp. 166–224.

Janis, I. L., Hovland, C. I., Field, P. B., Linton, H., Graham, E., Cohen, A. R., Rife, D., Abelson, R. P., Lesser, G. S., and King, B. T. (1959). *Personality and Persuasability.* New Haven: Yale University Press.

Janis, I. L., and Smith, B. B. (1965). "Effects of Education and Persuasion on National and International Images." In H. C. Kelman (ed.), *International Behavior: A Social-Psychological Analysis.* New York: Holt, Rinehart and Winston, pp. 190–235.

Johns-Heine, P., and Gerth, H. H. (1949). "Values in Mass Periodical Fiction, 1921–1940," *Public Opinion Quarterly, 13*(1):105–113.

Jones, G. N. (1969). *Planned Organizational Change.* New York: Praeger.

Jones, G. W. (1971). "Effect of Population Change on the Attainment of Educational Goals in the Developing Countries." In National Academy of Sciences, *Rapid Population Growth*, Vol. II. Baltimore: Johns Hopkins Press.

Kangas, L. W. (1970). "Integrated Incentives for Fertility Control," *Science, 169*:1278–1283.

Kapoor, S. D., and Chandhoke, A. S. (1968). *Behavioral Characteristics of Camp and Non-Camp Vasectomized Clients: A Comparative Study*. New Delhi: National Institute of Family Planning Mimeo Report.

Karenga, M. R. (1969). "The Black Community and the University: A Community Organizer's Perspective." In A. Robinson, C. Foster, and D. Ogilvie (eds.), *Black Studies in the University*. New York: Bantam Books.

Karlins, M., and Abelson, H. I. (1970). *Persuasion*. New York: Springer Publishing Co.

Katz, D. (1960). "The Functional Approach to the Study of Attitudes," *Public Opinion Quarterly, 24*:163–204.

Katz, D., and Kahn, R. (1966). *The Social Psychology of Organizations*. New York: John Wiley and Sons.

Katz, E. (1960). "Communication Research and the Image of Society: Convergence of Two Traditions," *American Journal of Sociology, 65*:435–504.

Katz, E., and Foulkes, D. (1962). "On the Use of Mass Media as 'Escape': Clarification of a Concept," *Public Opinion Quarterly, 26*(Fall):377–388.

Katz, I., Robinson, J., Epps, E., and Walz, P. (1964). "The Influence of Race of the Experimenter and Instructions on the Expression of Hostility by Negro Boys," *Journal of Social Issues, 20*:54–59.

Kelman, H. C. (1958). "Compliance, Identification, and Internalization: Three Processes of Attitude Change," *Journal of Conflict Resolution, 2*:51–60.

Kelman, H. C. (1961). "Processes of Opinion Change," *Public Opinion Quarterly, 25*:57–78.

Kelman, H. C. (1962). "Changing Attitudes Through International Activities," *Journal of Social Issues, 18*(1):68–87.

Kelman, H. C. (1962). "The Induction of Action and Attitude Change." In S. Coopersmith (ed.), *Personality Research*. Copenhagen: Munksgaard, pp. 81–110.

Kelman, H. C. (1963). "The Role of the Group in the Induction of Therapeutic Change," *International Journal of Group Psychotherapy, 13*:399–432.

Kelman, H. (1968). *A Time to Speak: On Human Values and Social Research*. San Francisco: Jossey-Bass.

Kelman, H. C. (1969). "Patterns of Personal Involvement in the National System: A Social-Psychological Analysis of Political Legitimacy." In J. Rosenau (ed.), *International Politics and Foreign Policy*, 2nd ed. New York: Free Press, pp. 276–288.

Kelman, H. C. (1970). "The Relevance of Social Research to Social Issues: Promises and Pitfalls." In P. Halmos (ed.), *The Sociology of Sociology (The*

Sociological Review: Monograph No. 16), Keele, England: University of Keele, pp. 77–99.

Kelman, H. C. (1971). "Language as an Aid and Barrier to Involvement in National System." In J. Rubin and B. H. Jernudd (eds.), *Can Language Be Planned?* Honolulu: University Press of Hawaii, pp. 21–51.

Kelman, H. C. (1972). "The Problem-Solving Workshop in Conflict Resolution." In R. L. Merritt (ed.), *Communication in International Politics.* Urbana: University of Illinois Press, pp. 168–204.

Kelman, H. C., (in press). "The Rights of the Subject in Social Research: An Analysis in Terms of Relative Power and Legitimacy," *American Psychologist.*

Kelman, H. C., and Baron, R. M. (1968). "Determinants of Modes of Resolving Inconsistency Dilemmas: A Functional Analysis." In R. P. Abelson, E. Aronson, W. J. McGuire, T. M. Newcomb, M. J. Rosenberg, and P. H. Tannenbaum (eds.), *Theories of Cognitive Consistency: A Sourcebook.* Chicago: Rand-McNally, pp. 670–683.

Kelman, H. C., and Baron, R. M. (1968). "Inconsistency as a Psychological Signal." In R. P. Abelson, E. Aronson, W. J. McGuire, T. M. Newcomb, M. J. Rosenberg, and P. H. Tannenbaum (eds.), *Theories of Cognitive Consistency: A Sourcebook.* Chicago: Rand-McNally, pp. 331–336.

Kelman, H. C., and Ezekiel, R. S. (with the collaboration of R. B. Kelman) (1970). *Cross-National Encounters: The Personal Impact of an Exchange Program for Broadcasters.* San Francisco: Jossey-Bass.

Kelman, H. C., and Warwick, D. P. (1973). "Bridging Micro and Macro Approaches to Social Change: A Social Psychological Perspective," in this book.

Killian, L. (1964). "Social Movements." In R. E. L. Faris (ed.), *Handbook of Modern Sociology.* Chicago: Rand-McNally.

King, B. T., and McGinnies, E. (eds.) (1972). *Attitudes, Conflict, and Social Change.* New York: Academic Press.

Kirk, D. (1971). "A New Demographic Transition?" In National Academy of Sciences, *Rapid Population Growth,* Vol. II. Baltimore: Johns Hopkins Press.

Kivlin, J. E., and Fliegel, F. C. (1967). "Differential Perceptions of Innovations and Rate of Adoption," *Rural Sociology, 32*(March):78–91.

Klapper, J. T. (1957–1958). "What We Know About Mass Communication: The Brink of Hope," *Public Opinion Quarterly, 21*(Winter):454–474.

Klapper, J. T. (1960). *The Effects of Mass Communication.* New York: Free Press.

Klapper, J. T. (1963). "The Social Effects of Mass Communication." In W. Schramm (ed.), *The Science of Human Communication.* New York: Basic Books.

Klein, D. (1967). "Some Notes in the Dynamics of Resistance to Change: The Defender Role." In G. Watson (ed.), *Concepts for Social Change.* Washington, D.C.: N.T.L. Institute, N.E.A.

Klonglan, G. E., and Coward, W. E., Jr. (1970). "The Concept of Symbolic Adoption: A Suggested Interpretation," *Rural Sociology, 35*(March):77–83.

Knight, K. (1967). "A Descriptive Model of the Intra-Firm Innovation Process." *Journal of Business, 40*(October):478–496.

Koestler, A. (1964). *The Act of Creation.* New York: Macmillan.

Kohler, W. (1922). "Zur Psychologic des Shimpanzen," *Psychologische Forschung, 1:*1–45. (Berlin: Zeitschrift fur Allgemeine Pschologie, Ethologic und Medizinische Psychologie.)

Kotler, P. (1967). *Marketing Management: Analysis, Planning and Control.* Englewood Cliffs, N.J.: Prentice-Hall.

Kotler, P. (1972). "Elements of Social Action." In G. Zaltman, P. Kotler, and I. Kaufman (eds.), *Creating Social Change.* New York: Holt, Rinehart and Winston.

Krishnakumar, S. (1971). "A Report on the Massive Family Welfare Festival, Ernakulam District, 1 July to 31 July, 1971," Report published by the District Collector, Cochin, Kerala, India.

Krueger, A. O., and Sjaastad, L. A. (1962). "Some Limitations of Enke's Economics of Population," *Economic Development and Cultural Change, 10:*423–426.

Krugman, H. E. (1966). "The Impact of Television Advertising: Learning Without Involvement," *Public Opinion Quarterly, 30:*583–596.

Kuhn, T. S. (1962). *The Structure of Scientific Revolutions.* Chicago: University of Chicago Press.

Kutner, B., Jerome, S., and Buckhaut, R. (1970). "Education for the Professional Social Activist: Activist Corner," *Journal of Social Issues, 26:*155–161.

Ladejinsky, W. (1970). "Ironics of India's Green Revolution," *Foreign Affairs, 48:*758–768.

Lambert, R. D., and Bressler, M. (1956). *Indian Students on an American Campus.* Minneapolis: University of Minnesota Press.

LaPalombara, J. (1966). "Public Administration and Political Change: A Theoretical Overview." In C. Press and A. Arian, *Empathy and Ideology: Aspects of Administrative Innovation.* Chicago: Rand-McNally, pp. 72–107.

Lasswell, H. D. (1948). "The Structure and Function of Communication in Society." In L. Bryson (ed.), *The Communication of Ideas.* New York: Harper, pp. 37–51.

Lasswell, H. D., and Kaplan, A. (1950). *Power and Society.* New Haven: Yale University Press.

Lauer, R. L. (1971). "The Scientific Legitimation of Fallacy: Neutralizing Social Change Theory," *American Sociological Review, 36:*831–889.

Lazarsfeld, P. F., Berelson, B. R., and Gaudet, H. (1944). *The People's Choice.* New York: Columbia University Press.

Ledvinka, J. (1969). "Race of Employment Interviewer and the Language Elaboration of Black Job Seekers." University of Michigan, unpublished Ph.D. dissertation.

Lerner, D. (1958). *The Passing of Traditional Society*. New York: Free Press.

Lerner, D. (1970). Book Review, *Public Opinion Quarterly, 34*(Summer):310–314.

Lerner, D. (1971). "Is International Persuasion Sociologically Feasible?" *The Annals, 398*(November):44–49.

Levine, J. M., and Murphy, G. (1943). "The Learning and Forgetting of Controversial Material," *Journal of Abnormal and Social Psychology, 38*:507–17. (October, Washington, D.C.: American Psychological Association.)

LeVine, R. A. (1966). *Dreams and Deeds: Achievement Motivation in Nigeria*. Chicago: University of Chicago Press.

Levitt, K. (1970). *Silent Surrender: The Multinational Corporation in Canada*. Toronto: Macmillan of Canada.

Lewin, K. (1951). *Field Theory in Social Science*. New York: Harper and Brothers.

Lewin, K., Lippitt, R., and White, R. K. (1939). "Patterns of Aggression Behavior in Experimentally Created 'Social Climates,'" *Journal of Social Psychology*, 271–299.

Lieberman, S. (1956). "The Effects of Changes in Roles on the Attitudes of Role Occupants," *Human Relations, 9*:385–402.

Likert, R. (1961). *New Patterns in Management*. New York: McGraw-Hill.

Lilly, J. C. (1956). "Mental Effects of Reduction of Ordinary Levels of Physical Stimuli on Intact, Healthy Persons," Symposium on Research Techniques in Schizophrenia, *Psychiatric Research Reports No. 5*:1–9. (June, Washington, D.C.: American Psychiatric Association.)

Lin, N., Rogers, E. M., Leu, D., and Schwartz, D. (1966). "The Diffusion of an Innovation in Three Michigan High Schools," East Lansing: Institute for International Studies in Education and Department of Communication, Michigan State University.

Linton, R. (1936). *The Study of Man*. New York: Appleton-Century-Crofts.

Linton, R. (1945). *The Cultural Background of Personality*. New York: Appleton-Century-Crofts.

Lionberger, H. F. (1960). *Adoption of New Ideas and Practices*. Ames: Iowa State University Press.

Lippitt, R. (1965). "Roles and Processes in Curriculum Development and Change." In *Strategy for Curriculum Change*. Washington, D.C.: Association for Supervision and Curriculum Development.

Lippitt, R., Watson, J., and Westley, B. (1958). *The Dynamics of Planned Change*. New York: Harcourt, Brace.

Lipset, S. M., Trow, M. A., and Coleman, J. S. (1956). *Union Democracy*. Glencoe: Free Press.

Liu, A. P. L. (1966). "Movies and Modernization in Communist China," *Journalism Quarterly, 43*(Summer):319–324.

London, P. (1964). *The Modes and Morals of Psychotherapy*. New York: Holt, Rinehart and Winston.

London, P. (1969). *Behavioral Control*. New York: Harper and Row.

Lord, F. M. (1960). "Large-Scale Covariance Analysis When the Control Variable is Fallible," *Journal of the American Statistical Association, 55*:307–321.

Lord, F. M. (1963). "Elementary Models for Measuring Change." In C. W. Harris (ed.), *Problems in Measuring Change*. Madison: University of Wisconsin Press.

Lowenthal, L. (1943). "Biographies in Popular Magazines." In P. Lazarsfeld and F. Stanton (eds.), *Radio Research 1942–43*. New York: Harper.

Lyons, T. C. (1971). "Social/Political/Cultural Considerations in the Population Policy Process." Paper delivered at African Population Conference, Accra, Ghana.

MacKenzie, G. N. (1962). "The Social Context of Curricular Change," *Theory Into Practice, 1*(October):185–190.

Majumdan, M., Mullick, B. C., et al. (1971). "The Use of Oral Contraceptives Through Clinics in Different Settings," Howrah, India, The Humanities Association.

Maloney, J. C. (1961). "Marketing Decisions and Attitude Research." In G. L. Baker (ed.), *Effective Marketing Coordination*. Chicago: American Marketing Association, pp. 595–618.

Maloney, J. C. (1962). "Curiosity vs. Disbelief in Advertising," *Journal of Advertising Research, 2*:2–3.

Maloney, J. C. (1963). "Is Advertising Believability Really Important?" *Journal of Marketing, 27*(4):1–8.

Maloney, J. C. (1966). "Attitude Measurement and Formation." Paper presented at the Test Market Design and Measurement Workshop, Chicago: American Marketing Association, April 21.

Maloney, J. C. (1971). "The Mass Media and Political Violence." Paper presented for the National Programmatic Institute on the Response to Political Violence Through Democratic Means, cosponsored by the Catholic University Law School and the American Jewish Committee, October 21–23, proceedings in press.

Maloney, J. C., and Slovonsky, L. (1971). "The Pollution Issue: A Survey of Editorial Judgments." In L. L. Roos, Jr. (ed.), *The Politics of Ecosuicide*. New York: Holt, Rinehart and Winston, pp. 67–73.

Mann, F. C., and Neff, F. W. (1961). *Managing Major Change in Organizations*. Ann Arbor, Mich.: Foundation for Research on Human Behavior.

Mansfield, E. (1963). "Intrafirm Rates of Diffusion of an Innovation," *Review of Economics and Statistics, 45*:348–359.

March, J., and Simon, H. (1958). *Organizations*, New York: John Wiley and Sons.

Martel, M. V., and McCall, G. J. (1964). "Reality Orientation and the Pleasure Principle: A Study of American Mass Periodical Fiction (1890–1955)." In

L. A. Dexter and D. M. White (eds.), *People, Society and Mass Communications*. New York: Free Press of Glencoe.

Mason, K. O., David, A. S., et al. (1971). *Social and Economic Correlates of Family Planning Fertility: A Survey of the Evidence*. Project SU-518, Research Triangle Institute, North Carolina.

May, R. (1969). *Love and Will*. New York: Norton.

McClelland, D. C. (1961). *The Achieving Society*. Princeton, N.J.: Van Nostrand.

McClelland, D. C., and Winter, D. (1971). *Motivating Economic Achievement*. New York: Free Press.

McClelland, W. A. (1968). *The Process of Effecting Change*. Washington: American Psychology Association (September).

McCombs, M. E. (in press). "Mass Media in the Marketplace," *Journalism Monographs*.

McDill, E. L., McDill, M. S., and Sprehe, J. T. (1969). *Strategies for Success in Compensatory Education: An Apprcisal of Evaluation Research*. Baltimore: The Johns Hopkins Press.

McGregor, D. (1960). *The Human Side of Enterprise*. New York: McGraw-Hill.

McLeod, J., Ward, S., and Tancil, K. (1965–1966). "Alienation and Uses of the Mass Media," *Public Opinion Quarterly, 29*(Winter):583–594.

McNelly, J. T. (1966). "Mass Communication and the Climate for Modernization in Latin America," *Journal of Inter-American Studies, 8*(July):345–357.

McNelly, J. T., and Deutschmann, P. J. (1963). "Media Use and Socioeconomic Status in a Latin American Capital," *Gazette, 9:*15.

McNelly, J. T., and Fonseca, E. (1964). "Media Use and Political Interest at the University of Costa Rica," *Journalism Quarterly, 41*(Spring): 225–231.

McQueen, A. J. (1968). "Education and Marginality of African Youth," *Journal of Social Issues, 24*(2):179–194.

Mead, G. H. (1934). *Mind, Self and Society*. Chicago: University of Chicago Press.

Mendelsohn, H. (1964). "Broadcast vs. Personal Sources of Information in Emergent Public Crises: The Presidential Assassination," *Journal of Broadcasting, 8*(Spring):147–156.

Menzel, H. (1960). "Innovation, Integration, and Marginality: A Survey of Physicians," *American Sociological Review, 25.*

Menzel, H., and Katz, E. (1955–1956). "Social Relations and Innovations in the Medical Profession: The Epidemiology of a New Drug," *Public Opinion Quarterly, 19*(Winter):337–352.

Merei, F. (1949). "Group Leadership and Institutionalization," *Human Relations, 2:*23–39. (London: Tavistock Publications.)

Merton, R. K. (1957). *Social Theory and Social Structure.* New York: Free Press.

Methvin, E. H. (1969). "Changing News Values in the Megamind Era," *Vital Speeches of the Day,* May 14, p. 463.

Michael, D. N. (1968). "On Coping with Complexity: Planning and Politics," *Daedalus, 97*(4)(Fall):1182.

Michelson, S. (1970). "Discussion: Distribution Issues; Trends and Policies," *American Economic Review, 60*:283–285.

Miles, M. B. (ed.) (1964). *Innovation in Education.* New York: Bureau of Publications, Teachers College, Columbia University.

Mills, C. W. (1959). *The Power Elite.* New York: Oxford University Press.

Milsum, J. H. (1969). "Technosphere, Biosphere and Sociosphere," *General Systems,* 14:38–49.

Mishra, V. M. (1970). "Mass Media Use and Modernization in Greater Delhi Basties," *Journalism Quarterly, 47*(Summer):331–339.

Moore, W. E., and Sheldon, E. B. (1968). *Indications of Social Change.* New York: Russell Sage Foundation.

Morgan, J. N., and Sonquist, J. A. (1963). "Problems in the Analysis of Survey Data and A Proposal," *Journal of American Statistical Association, 58*(June):415–435.

Morris, R. (1960). *The Two Way Mirror.* Minneapolis: University of Minnesota Press.

Morrison, D. E. (1973). "Some Notes Toward Theory on Relative Deprivation, Social Movements and Social Change," in this book.

Morrison, D. E., and Steeves, A. (1967). "Deprivation, Discontent, and Social Movement Participation: Evidence on a Contemporary Farmer's Movement, the NFO," *Rural Sociology, 32,*4(December):414–434.

Mort, P. R., and Cornell, F. G. (1941). *American Schools in Transition.* New York: Bureau of Publications, Teachers College, Columbia University.

Moynihan, D. P. (1969). *Maximum Feasible Misunderstanding,* New York: Macmillan.

Myers, S., and Marquis, D. G. (1969). *Successful Industrial Innovations.* National Science Foundation: NSF 69-17.

Myrdal, G. (1968). *Asian Drama,* Vol. 3. New York: Pantheon.

Nafziger, R. O., Engstrom, W., and MacLean, M. S., Jr. (1951). "The Mass Media and an Informed Public," *Public Opinion Quarterly, 15*(Summer):105–114.

National Academy of Sciences (1971). *Rapid Population Growth,* Vol. I Baltimore: The Johns Hopkins Press.

Newcomb, T. M. (1943). *Personality and Social Change.* New York: Dryden.

Newcomb, T. M. (1947). "Autistic Hostility and Social Reality," *Human Relations, 1*:69–86.

Newcomb, T. M. (1953). "An Approach to the Study of Communicative Acts," *Psychological Review, 60:*393–404.

Newcomb, T. M., Koenig, K. E., Flacks, R., and Warwick, D. P. (1967). *Persistence and Change: Bennington College and Its Students After Twenty-Five Years.* New York: John Wiley and Sons.

Nie, N., et al. (1969a). "Social Structure and Political Participation: Developmental Relationships, Part I," *American Political Science Review, 63:*361–378.

Nie, N. (1969b). "Social Structure and Political Participation: Developmental Relationships, Part II," *American Political Science Review, 63:*808–832.

Noonan, J. T. (1965). *Contraception: A History of its Treatment by Catholic Theologians and Canonists.* Cambridge, Mass.: Harvard University Press.

Nortman, D. (1970). "Population and Family Planning Programs: A Factbook," *Reports on Population / Family Planning, 2.*

Nwankwo, R. L. N. (1971). "Communication in a Campus Crisis: A Symbolic Interaction Approach," *Journalism Quarterly, 48*(Autumn):438–446.

Nyerere, J. (1968). "Education for Self-Reliance," *Cross Currents, 17:*415–434.

Ogden, J., and Ogden, J. (1946). *Small Communities in Action.* New York: Harper.

Olson, M. (1971). "Preliminary Thoughts About the Causes of Harmony and Conflict." Unpublished paper, University of Maryland.

Opler, M. E. (1968). "Developmental Change and the Nature of Man." In A. Gallaher, Jr. (ed.), *Perspectives in Developmental Change.* Lexington: University of Kentucky Press.

Orcutt, G. H., and Orcutt, A. G. (1968). "Incentive Experimentation for Income Maintenance Policy Purposes," *American Economic Review, 58:*754–772.

Osgood, C. E., Suci, G. J., and Tannenbaum, H. (1957). *Measurement of Meaning.* Urbana: University of Illinois Press.

Osgood, C. E., and Tannenbaum, P. H. (1955). "The Principle of Congruity in the Prediction of Attitude Change," *Psychological Review, 47:*419–427.

Ostlund, L. (1969). "The Role of Product Perceptions in Innovative Behavior." In P. R. McDonald (ed.), *Fall Conference of the American Marketing Association.* Chicago.

Papanek, G. (1967). *Pakistan's Development: Social Goals and Private Incentives.* Cambridge, Mass.: Harvard University Press.

Papanek, H. (1970). "Pakistan's New Industrialists and Businessmen: Focus on the Memons." Paper prepared for the Conference on Occupational Cultures in Changing South Asia (May), University of Chicago.

Pareek, U. (1968). "A Motivational Paradigm of Development," *Journal of Social Issues, 24*(2):115–122.

Patchen, M. (1964). *The American Public's View of U. S. Policy Toward China,* New York: Council of Foreign Relations.

Perkin, G. W. (1970). "Non-Monetary Commodity Incentives in Family Planning Program: A Preliminary Trial," *Studies in Family Planning, 57:*12–15.

Pohlman, E. (1971). *Incentives and Compensations in Birth Planning.* Chapel Hill: University of North Carolina, Carolina Population Center, Monograph 11.

Piore, M. (1970). "Discussion: Dynamics of Income Distribution, Poverty and Progress," *American Economic Review, 60:*298–299.

Platt, J. (1972). "Beyond Freedom and Dignity: A Revolutionary Manifesto," *The Center Magazine,* March/April.

Polanyi, M. (1968). "Life's Irreducible Structure," *Science,* June 21, pp. 1308–1312.

Pool. I. de S. (1963). "The Mass Media and Politics in the Modernization Process." In L. W. Pye (ed.), *Communications and Political Development.* Princeton, N.J.: Princeton University Press.

Pool, I. de S. (1967). "The Public and the Polity." In I. de S. Pool (ed.), *Contemporary Political Science.* New York: McGraw-Hill.

Pool, I. de S., and Abelson, R. (1961). "The Simulmatics Project," *Public Opinion Quarterly, 25*(Summer):167–183.

Population Council (1968). "Declaration on Population: The World Leader Statement," *Studies in Family Planning, 26.*

Population Council (1967). "Declaration on Population," *Studies in Family Planning, 16.*

Population Task Force of the Institute of Society, Ethics, and the Life Sciences, *Ethics, Population, and the American Tradition.* A study prepared for the Commission on Population Growth and the American Future by the Institute of Society, Ethics, and the Life Sciences, Hastings-on-Hudson, N.Y.

Porter, A. C. (1967). "The Effects of Using Fallible Variables in the Analysis of Covariance." Ph.D. dissertation, University of Wisconsin.

Poston, R. W. (1950). *Small Town Renaissance.* New York: Harper.

Potts, D. M. (1970). "Post Conceptive Control of Fertility," *International Journal of Gynecology and Obstetrics, 8:*57.

Powelson, J. (1969). *The Institutions of Economic Growth.* Boulder: University of Colorado (mimeo).

Presser, H. B. (1970). "Voluntary Sterilization: A World View," *Reports on Population/Family Planning.*

Pye, L. W. (1962). *Politics, Personality, and Nation-Building: Burma's Search for Identity.* New Haven: Yale University Press.

Pye, L. W. (1963). *Communications and Political Development.* Princeton, N.J.: Princeton University Press.

Qadir, A. S. (1966). "Adoption of Technological Change in the Rural Philippines: An Analysis of Compositional Effects." Ph.D. dissertation, Cornell University.

Rainwater, L., and Yancey, W. (1967). *The Moynihan Report and the Politics of Controversy*. Cambridge, Mass.: M.I.T. Press.

Rao, V. V. L. (1967). *Communication and Development*. Minneapolis: University of Minnesota Press.

Raup, R. B. (1925). *Complacency: The Foundation of Human Behavior*. New York: Macmillan.

Ravenholt, R. T. (1969). "A.I.D.'s Family Planning Strategy," *Science, 163:*124.

Ravenholt, R. T. (1971). "Age-Parity Analysis of World Fertility." Paper presented to the American Public Health Association, Minneapolis.

Ravenholt, R. T. (1972). Personal communication.

Ravenholt, R. T., Brackett, J. W., and Chao, J. (1972). "World Fertility Trends During the 1960's." Paper presented at Population Association of America, Toronto, Canada.

Ravenholt, R. T., Piotrow, P. T., and Speidel, J. J. (1970). "Use of Oral Contraceptives: A Decade of Controversy," *International Journal of Obstetrics and Gynecology, 8:*941–956.

Ravenholt, R. T., and Speidel, J. J. (1971). "Prostaglandins in Family Planning Strategy." In P. Ramwell and J. Shaw (eds.), *Prostaglandins: Annals of the New York Academy of Sciences, 180:*537–553.

Repetto, R. (1968). "Temporal Aspects of Indian Development." Ph.D. thesis, Cambridge, Mass.: Harvard University.

Repetto, R. (1969). "India: A Case Study of the Madras Vasectomy Program," *Studies in Family Planning, 1*(31):8–16.

Research and Marketing Services (1970). *A Study on the Evaluation of the Effectiveness of the Tata Incentive Programme for Sterilization*. Bombay: unpublished report.

Reston, J. (1966). *The Artillery of the Press*. New York: Harper and Row, pp. 101–103.

Richard, H. C. (ed.) (1971). *Behavioral Intervention in Human Problems*. New York: Pergamon Press.

Richland, M. (1965). *Traveling Seminar and Conference for the Implementation of Educational Innovations*. Santa Monica, Calif.: Systems Development Corporation, Technical Memo. 2691.

Ridker, D. G. (1969). "Synopsis of a Proposal for a Family Planning Bond," *Studies in Family Planning, 1*(43):11–16.

Ridker, D. G. (1971). "Savings Accounts for Family Planning: An Illustration from the Tea Estates of India," *Studies in Family Planning, 2*(7):150–152.

Rieff, P. (1961). *Freud: The Mind of the Moralist*. Garden City, N.Y.: Doubleday (Anchor Books).

Rieff, P. (1966). *The Triumph of the Therapeutic*. New York: Harper and Row.

Rivlin, A. (1971). *Systematic Thinking for Social Action*. Washington, D.C.: The Brookings Institute.

Robertson, T. (1971). *Innovation and the Consumer*. New York: Holt, Rinehart and Winston.

Robertson, T. (1971). *Innovative Behavior and Communication*. New York: Holt, Rinehart and Winston.

Robinson, J. P. (1967). "World Affairs Information and Mass Media Exposure," *Journalism Quarterly, 44*(Spring):23–31.

Robinson, L. (1971). *Public Awareness of, Attitudes Toward, and Sources of Information Concerning Environmental Pollution*. Unpublished report to the Ford Foundation, which supported the study.

Robinson, W. (1971). "Cost Effectiveness Analysis as an Evaluation Technique in Family Planning Programs: Report on Phase III of the Penn. State/USAID Population Research Project," State College, Pa., mimeo.

Rogers, E. M. (1962). *Diffusion of Innovations*. New York: The Free Press.

Rogers, E. M. (1965–1966). "Mass Media Exposure and Modernization Among Colombian Peasants," *Public Opinion Quarterly, 29*(Winter):583–594.

Rogers, E. M. (1969). *Modernization Among Peasants: The Impact of Communication*. New York: Holt, Rinehart and Winston.

Rogers, E. M. (1971). "Social Structure and Social Change," *American Behavioral Scientist, 767–782.*

Rogers, E. M. (1971a). "Incentives in the Diffusion of Family Planning Innovations," *Studies in Family Planning, 2*(12):241–248.

Rogers, E. M. (1972). *A Proposed Design for a Multi-National Comparative Field Experiment on Family Planning*. New York: Population Council, mimeo report.

Rogers, E. M. (1972a). "The Ernakulam Vasectomy Campaigns." Michigan State University, mimeo.

Rogers, E. M. (1972b). "Field Experiments in Family Planning Incentives." East Lansing: Michigan State University Department of Communications.

Rogers, E. M., and Bhomik, D. K. (1971). "Homophily-Heterophily: Relational Concepts for Communication Research," *Public Opinion Quarterly, 34*:523–538.

Rogers, E. M., and Shoemaker, F. F. (1971). *Communication of Innovations: A Cross-Cultural Approach*. New York: The Free Press.

Rogers, E. M., and others (1970). *Diffusion of Innovations in Brazil, Nigeria, and India*. Lansing: Michigan State University, Department of Communication, Diffusion of Innovations Research Report 24.

Rosenstock, I. (1966). "Why People Use Health Services," *Milbank Memorial Fund Quarterly, 44*:94–127.

Rosenthal, R. (1966). *Experimenter Effects in Behavioral Research*. New York: Appleton-Century-Crofts.

Rossi, P., and Williams, W. (1972). *Evaluating Social Programs*. New York: Seminar Press.

Rostow, W. W. (1960). *The Stages of Economic Growth*. New York: Cambridge University Press.

Royko, M. (1970). "The Fox Fouls Corporate Nest," *Chicago Sun-Times*, December, p. 3.

Rokeach, M. (1960). *The Open and Closed Mind*. New York: Basic Books.

Rokeach, M. (1968). *Beliefs, Attitudes and Values*. San Francisco: Jossey-Bass.

Roszak, T. (1969). *The Making of a Counter Culture*. New York: Doubleday-Anchor.

Sanders, T. G. (1972). "Brazil." In H. Brown and A. Sweezy (eds.), *Population: Perspective, 1971*. San Francisco: Freeman Cooper and Co.

Sanford, N. (1970). SPSSI Presidential Address, "Whatever Happened to Action Research?" *Journal of Social Issues, 26*:2–23.

Sapolsky, H. M. (1967). "Organizational Structure and Innovation," *Journal of Business, 40*:598–610.

Saunders, L. (1970). "Beyond Family Planning." Paper presented at the 2nd National Seminar on General Consequences of Population Growth, Kuala Lumpur, Malaysia.

Saxena, A. P. (1968). "System Effects on Innovativeness Among Indian Farmers." Ph.D. thesis, Michigan State University.

Schein, E. H. (1964). "Brainwashing." In W. G. Bennis, E. H. Schein, D. E. Berlew, and F. I. Steele (eds.), *Interpersonal Dynamics: Essays and Readings on Human Interaction*. Homewood, Ill.: Dorsey, pp. 454–474.

Schein, E. H. (1969). "The Mechanisms of Change." In W. G. Bennis, K. D. Benne, and R. Chin (eds.), *The Planning of Change*, 2nd ed. New York: Holt, Rinehart and Winston.

Schein, E. H., and Bennis, W. G. (1965). *Personal and Organizational Change Through Group Methods*. New York: John Wiley and Sons.

Schramm, W. (1964). *Mass Media and National Development*. Stanford: Stanford University Press.

Schramm, W., and Carter, R. F. (1959). "Effectiveness of a Political Telethon," *Public Opinion Quarterly, 23*(Spring):121–126.

Schroder, H. M., Driver, M. J., and Streufert, S. (1967). *Human Information Processing*. New York: Holt, Rinehart and Winston.

Scott, J. P., and Scott, S. F. (eds.) (1971). *Social Control and Social Change*. Chicago: University of Chicago Press.

Scriven, M. (1967). "The Methodology of Evaluation." In R. W. Taylor, R. M. Gagne, and M. Scriven (eds.), *Perspectives of Curriculum Evaluation*. Chicago: Rand-McNally.

Seeley, J. (1967). *The Americanization of the Unconscious*. New York: Science House.

Selznick, P. (1949). *TVA and the Grassroots*. Berkeley: University of California Press.

Shaver, P., and Staines, G. (1972). "Problems Facing Campbell's 'Experimenting Society,' " *American Psychologist, 27*(2)(February), 161–163.

Sheatsley, P. J., and Feldman, J. J. (1964). "The Assassination of President Kennedy: A Preliminary Report on Public Reaction and Behavior," *Public Opinion Quarterly, 28*(Summer):189–215.

Sherak, B. (1969). "Consumer Segmentation and Brand Mapping: A Methodological Study." Paper presented at the International Conference on Market Segmentation (March). New York: Market Facts, Inc.

Sherif, M., and Cantril, H. (1947). *The Psychology of Ego-Involvement*. New York: John Wiley and Sons.

Shimberg, B. (1949). "Information and Attitudes Toward World Affairs," *Journal of Educational Psychology, 48*:206–222.

Silberman, C. E. (1970). *Crisis in the Classroom*. New York: Random House.

Simon, J. L. (1968). "The Role of Bonuses and Persuasive Propaganda in the Reduction of Birth Rates," *Economic Development and Cultural Change, 16*:404–411.

Simon, J. L. (1969). "The Value of Avoided Births to Underdeveloped Countries," *Population Studies, 23*:61–68.

Singer, B. D. (1970). "Mass Media and Communication Processes in the Detroit Riot of 1967," *Public Opinion Quarterly, 34* (Summer):236–245.

Skinner, B. F. (1971). *Beyond Freedom and Dignity*. New York: Knopf.

Skinner, B. F. (1972). "I Have Been Misunderstood," *The Center Magazine* (March/April).

Smelser, N. J. (1968). *Essays in Sociological Explanation*. Englewood Cliffs, N.J.: Prentice-Hall.

Smigel, E. O. (ed.) (1971). *Handbook on the Study of Social Problems*. Chicago: Rand-McNally.

Smith, M. B. (1968). "Competence and Socialization." In J. Clausen (ed.), *Socialization and Society*. Boston: Little, Brown, pp. 270–320.

Smith, M. B., Bruner, J. S., and White, R. W. (1956). *Opinions and Personality*. New York: John Wiley and Sons.

Smith, W. C. (1965). *Modernization in a Traditional Society*. New York: Asia Publishing House.

Sollins, A. D., and Belsky, R. L. (1970). "Commercial Production and Distribution of Contraceptives," *Reports on Population/Family Planning*.

Spector, P. (1963). *Motivation in Community Development: An Experiment*. Washington, D.C.: Institute for International Services.

Speidel, J. J. (1971). Personal communication.

Speidel, J. J. (1972). "The Role of Female Sterilization in Family Planning Programs." In G. Duncan, R. Falb, and J. Speidel (eds.), *Female Sterilization: Prognosis for Simplified Procedures.* New York: Academic Press.

Speidel, J. J., Brackett, J. W., and Jamison, E. (1971). "Limitations of Foresight Means of Fertility Control." Paper presented to the Population Association of America, Washington, D.C.

Speidel, J. J., and Sprehe, J. T. (1972). "Irreversible Means of Fertility Control: A Neglected Family Planning Strategy." Paper presented to the Population Association of America, Toronto, Canada.

Speidel, J. J., Sprehe, J. T., and Ravenholt, R. T. (1971). "Agency for International Development: Population Research Program." In *Report of the Secretary of Health, Education and Welfare to the Ninety-Second Congress* concerning the Five Year Plan for Family Planning Services and Population Research Programs, Washington, D.C.

Spengler, J. (1969). "Population Problem: In Search of a Solution," *Science, 166:*1234–1238.

Spicer, E. H. (ed.) (1952). *Human Problems in Technological Change.* New York: Russell Sage Foundation.

Spitzer, S. P., and Spitzer, N. S. (1964–1965). "Mass Media and Personal Sources of Information About the Presidential Assassination: A Comparison of Six Investigations," *Journal of Broadcasting, 9*(Winter):45–50.

Spitzer, S. P., and Spitzer, N. S. (1965). "Diffusion of News of Kennedy and Oswald Deaths." In B. S. Greenberg and E. B. Parker, *The Kennedy Assassination and the American Public,* Stanford: Stanford University Press, pp. 99–111.

Sprehe, J. T. (1971). "Incentives in Family Planning Programs: Time for a New Look." In O. D. Finigan (ed.), *Incentive Approaches in Population Planning Programs.* Manila, Philippines.

Srinivasan, K., and Kachirayan, M. (1968). "Vasectomy Follow-up Study: Findings and Implications," *Bulletin of the Gandhigram Institute of Rural Health and Family Planning, 3:*12–32.

Star, S. A., and Hughes, H. M. (1950). "A Report on an Educational Campaign: The Cincinnati Plan for the United Nations," *American Journal of Sociology, 55:*389–400.

Stephens, J. M. (1965). *The Psychology of Classroom Learning.* New York: Holt, Rinehart and Winston.

Study of Parent's Reaction to Educational Innovations (1966). Gallup International, Inc., May, p. 25.

Stycos, J. M. (1955). "Birth Control Clinics in Crowded Puerto Rico." In B. Paul (ed.), *Health, Culture and Community.* New York: Russell Sage Foundation.

Suchman, E. (1967). *Evaluative Research.* New York: Russell Sage Foundation.

Supplemental Report of National Advisory Commission on Civil Disorders (1969). Government Printing Office.

Swanson, C. E. (1967). "The Frequency Structure of Television and Magazines," *Journal of Advertising Research, 7*(June)8–14.

Swanson, G. E., Newcomb, T. M., and Hartley, E. L. (eds.) (1952). "Group Decision and Social Change," *Readings in Social Psychology*. New York: Holt, Rinehart and Winston, pp. 463–73.

Taylor, C. E. (1968). "Five Stages in a Practical Population Policy," *International Development Review* (December):2–7.

Taylor, J. (1970). "Introducing Social Innovation," *Journal of Applied Behavioral Science, 6:*69–77.

Thio, A. O. (1971). "A Reconsideration of the Concept of Adopter Innovation Compatibility in Diffusion Research," *The Sociological Quarterly, 12*(Winter):56–68.

Thomas, W. I., and Znaniecki, F. (1918–1920). *The Polish Peasant in Europe and America: Monograph of an Immigrant Group.* Five volumes. Chicago: University of Chicago Press.

Tichenor, P. J., Donohue, G. A., and Olien, C. N. (1970). "Mass Media Flow and Differential Growth in Knowledge," *Public Opinion Quarterly, 34*(Summer):159–170.

Troldahl, V. C. (1965). "Studies of Consumption of Mass Media Content," *Journalism Quarterly, 24*(Autumn):596–606.

Troldahl, V. C., and Van Dam, R. (1965–1966). "Face-to-Face Communication about Topics in the News," *Public Opinion Quarterly, 29*(Winter):626–634.

Toynbee, A. (1972). "Beyond Freedom and Dignity: An Uneasy Feeling of Unreality," *The Center Magazine* (March/April).

United Nations (1972). "Measures, Policies and Programmes Affecting Fertility, with Particular Reference to National Family Planning Programmes," *UN Document No. ST/SOA/Series A/51.*

UN Economic Commission for Africa (1970). "Report of the Working Group on Fertility Studies and Evaluation of Population Programmes," *UN Document No. E/CN.14/POP/18.*

UNESCO (1968). *An African Experiment in Radio Forums for Rural Development: Ghana, 1964–1965.* New York: UNESCO Publication Center.

U.S. Information Service (1961). *The General Pattern of Exposure to Mass Media in Seven Latin American Countries.* Washington, D.C. (November).

Van Den Ban, A. W. (1960). "Locality Group Differences in the Adoption of New Farm Practices," *Rural Sociology, 25:*308–320.

Van Den Ban, A. W. (1965). "The Communication of New Farm Practices in the Netherlands," *Sociologia Neerlandica, 2*(2):1–18.

Von Frisch, K. (1962). "Dialectics of the Language of Bees," *Scientific American, 207*(August):78–87.

Walker, J. L. (1969). "The Diffusion of Innovations Among the American States," *American Political Science Review, 63.*

Warwick, D. P. (1971a). "Freedom and Population Policy." In Population Task Force, *Ethics, Population and the American Tradition.* Hastings-on-Hudson, N.Y.: Institute of Society, Ethics, and the Life Sciences.

Warwick, D. P. (1971b). "Tearoom Trade: A Case Study of Ends and Means in Social Research." Unpublished paper, York University, Toronto.

Watson, G. (1946). *A Comparison of "Adaptable" vs. "Laggard" YMCA's.* New York: Association Press.

Watson, G. (1966). *Social Psychology Issues and Insights.* Philadelphia: J. B. Lippincott.

Watson, W. S., and Hartmann, G. W. (1939). "The Rigidity of a Basic Attitudinal Frame," *Journal of Abnormal and Social Psychology, 34*(July):314–35.

Watson, W. S., and Hartmann, G. W. (1941). "What Makes Radicals?" *Common Sense, 10:*7–9.

Watts, H. W. (1969). "Graduated Work Incentives: An Experiment in Negative Taxation," *American Economic Review, 59:*463–472.

Weber, M. (1948). *The Protestant Ethic and the Spirit of Capitalism.* New York: Scribner (first published in 1904–1905).

Weiss, C. H. (1970). "The Politicization of Evaluation Research," *Journal of Social Issues, 26:*57–68.

Weiss, R. S., and Rein, M. (1970). "The Evaluation of Broad-Aim Programs: Experimental Design, Its Difficulties, and an Alternative," *Administrative Science Quarterly, 15:*97–109.

Weiss, W. (1957). "Opinion Congruence with a Negative Source on one Issue as a Factor Influencing Agreement on Another Issue," *Journal of Abnormal and Social Psychology, 54:*180–186.

Weiss, W. (1971). "Mass Communication," *Annual Review of Psychology, 22:*309–336.

Weiss, W., and Steenbock, S. (1965). "The Influence on Communication Effectiveness of Explicitly Urging Action and Policy Consequences," *Journal of Experimental Social Psychology, 1:*396–406.

Westley, B. H. (1966). "The Functions of Public Communications in the Process of Social Change." Unpublished paper prepared for the AID-MSU Seminar on Communication and Change, East Lansing, April 4–7.

Westley, B. H. (1970). "Communication Theory and General Systems Theory: Implications for Planned Change," *Public Opinion Quarterly, 34*(Fall):446 (abstract).

Westley, B. H., and Severin, W. J. (1964). "A Profile of the Daily Newspaper Non-Reader," *Journalism Quarterly, 41*(Winter):45–50.

Whiteside, T. (1970). "Annals of Advertising: Cutting Down," *New Yorker* (December 19):42 ff.

Whyte, W. F., and Williams, L. K. (1968). *Toward an Integrated Theory of Development.* Ithaca, N.Y.: New York State School of Labor and Industrial Relations.

Whyte, W. H., Jr. (1956). *The Organization Man.* New York: Simon and Schuster.

Wicker, A. W. (1969). "Attitudes versus Actions: The Relationship of Verbal and Overt Behavioral Responses to Attitude Objects," *Journal of Social Issues, 25*(4):41–78.

Wiebe, G. D. (1951–1952). "Merchandising Commodities and Citizenship on Television," *Public Opinion Quarterly, 15*(Winter):679–691.

Wiener, N. (1954). *The Human Use of Human Beings,* 2nd ed. Garden City, N.Y.: Doubleday.

Wildavsky, A. (1969). "Wildavsky's Prescription for Violence." In D. P. Moynihan (ed.), *Maximum Feasible Misunderstanding: Community Action the War on Poverty.* New York: The Free Press.

Williams, L. K., Whyte, W. F., and Green, C. S. (1966). "Do Cultural Differences Affect Worker Attitudes?" *Industrial Relations, 6:*105–117.

Winham, G. R. (1970). "Political Development and Lerner's Theory," *American Political Science Review, 64*(3)(September):810–818.

Wirth, L. (1948). "Consensus and Mass Communication," *American Sociological Review, 13*(1):1–15.

Witt, W. (1972). "Multivariate Analysis of News Flow in a Conservation Issue," *Journalism Quarterly, 49*(Spring):91–97.

Wood, M. M. (1934). *The Stranger: A Study in Social Relationships.* New York: Columbia University Press.

Woodring, P. (1970). *Investment in Innovation: An Historical Appraisal of the Fund for the Advancement of Education.* Boston, Mass.: Little, Brown and Co.

Wray, J. D. (1971). "Population Pressure on Families: Family Size and Child Spacing." In National Academy of Sciences, *Rapid Population Growth,* Vol. II. Baltimore: Johns Hopkins Press.

Yeracaris, C. A. (1961). "Social Factors Associated with the Acceptance of Medical Innovations: A Pilot Study," *Journal of Health and Social Behavior, 3:*193–198.

Young, J. Z. (1951). *Doubt and Certainty in Science: A Biologist's Reflections on the Brain.* London: Oxford University Press.

Zaltman, G., Kotler, P., and Kaufman, I. (eds.) (1972). *Creating Social Change,* New York: Holt, Rinehart and Winston.

Zaltman, G., and Vertinsky, I. (1971). "Health Services Marketing: A Suggested Model," *Journal of Marketing, 35* (July):19–27.

Zielske, H. (1959). "The Remembering and Forgetting of Advertising," *Journal of Marketing, 23*(3)(January):239–243.

Zollschan, G. K., and Hirsch, W. (eds.) (1964). *Explorations in Social Change.* Boston: Houghton Mifflin Co.

Zurcher, L. A., and Bonjean, C. M. (eds.) (1970). *Planned Social Intervention.* Scranton, Pa.: Chandler Publishing Co.

AUTHOR INDEX

SUBJECT INDEX